Praise for *The New Deal's War on the Bill of Rights*

"This book is not mere history; it is an exposé. You won't know which is more shocking: the lengths to which FDR and New Dealers like Senators (and future Supreme Court justices) Hugo Black and Sherman Minton went to suppress freedom of speech, privacy, and civil rights; or the degree to which these efforts have been concealed by pro-FDR and New Deal propagandists. While the repressive measures taken by FDR and his New Dealers against their political opponents resemble tactics favored by progressives today, Beito shows that the 'good old days' were in some respects even worse. But he also usefully reminds us that resistance to these measures was bipartisan. This is a story that all Americans should know—especially anyone who is headed to college or law school. I will be strongly recommending it to the students in my class on constitutional rights and liberties."

> —**Randy E. Barnett**, Patrick Hotung Professor of Constitutional Law, Georgetown University Law Center; faculty director, Georgetown Center for the Constitution

"All historians who have written about Franklin Roosevelt need to read David Beito's book and, in almost all cases, revise what they said. *The New Deal's War on the Bill of Rights* illuminates Roosevelt's desire for power and his efforts to punish those who tried to thwart him."

> —**Burt Folsom**, professor of history emeritus, Hillsdale College; author of *New Deal or Raw Deal?*

"For all his accomplishments, Franklin Delano Roosevelt had little tolerance for critics and not much respect for the Bill of Rights. David Beito's useful survey of the partially unknown dark side of the New Deal reveals the surprising variety of repressive measures that FDR and his supporters employed—not always successfully—to quash those who opposed his administration. It's a sobering story that reminds us of how precarious our civil liberties have always been."

> —**Ellen Schrecker**, professor emerita, Yeshiva University; author of *Many Are the Crimes: McCarthyism in America*

"This book is exhaustively researched and often insightful, and it has some timeless historical lessons for Americans who value civil liberties and privacy. Beito reveals a dark side of the FDR administration that historians have generally ignored."

> —**David Boaz**, distinguished senior fellow, Cato Institute; author of *The Libertarian Mind*

"In this important book, David Beito shines new light on the civil liberties record of President Franklin D. Roosevelt. Beyond the internment of Japanese Americans,

Beito skillfully documents how FDR undermined free speech through extensive state censorship and surveillance. This well-written book not only clarifies the historical record, but also offers crucial insights into the foundations of contemporary government activities which continue to threaten the civil liberties of Americans. Anyone interested in civil liberties and government overreach should read this book!"

—**Christopher Coyne**, professor of economics, George Mason University

"Long a critic of FDR, I was nonetheless stunned and riveted by what David Beito reveals in this book. That an American president would so callously shred the Bill of Rights is a damning indictment—not just of FDR, but of his enablers in the media and academia who covered it all up for decades. Hereafter, no assessment of the 32nd president can be honest or thorough without factoring in Beito's indispensable contribution to the history of the office."

—**Lawrence W. Reed**, president emeritus, Foundation for Economic Education

"In an age when Americans are critically re-examining our history, New Deal abuses of power and authority are still downplayed and ignored by historians enamored with FDR and the rise of an activist federal government. David Beito's well-written, well-documented book brings those abuses to light, showing that the rise of federal power in the 1930s was accompanied by massive violations of Americans' civil liberties."

—**David E. Bernstein**, University Professor, Antonin Scalia Law School, George Mason University

"This is a *tour de force* capturing the all-encompassing threat Franklin Roosevelt and the New Deal posed to American freedoms. Beito opens our eyes to the wiretapping of political enemies, seizure of private telegrams, violation of tax return privacy, congressional witch hunts, a purge of conservative radio spokesmen, the internment of Japanese Americans, and much more. In eerie parallels to the Left's current obsession with banishing 'disinformation,' New Dealers also sought to criminalize 'false news.' You will not view FDR and the New Deal in the same way after finishing this important work."

—**Jonathan Bean**, professor of history, Southern Illinois University; author of *Race and Liberty in America: The Essential Reader*

"You wouldn't guess it from the soaring rhetoric of his Four Freedoms speech, but Franklin Roosevelt has a rotten record on civil liberties. David Beito's illuminating book explores the censorship, the spying, and the internment camps of the FDR years, as well as the uncomfortable intersection between the New Deal and Jim Crow."

—**Jesse Walker**, books editor, *Reason*; author of *Rebels on the Air: An Alternative History of Radio in America* and *The United States of Paranoia: A Conspiracy Theory*

The New Deal's War
on the Bill of Rights

INDEPENDENT
INSTITUTE

INDEPENDENT INSTITUTE is a nonprofit, nonpartisan public-policy research and educational organization that shapes ideas into profound and lasting impact. The mission of Independent is to boldly advance peaceful, prosperous, and free societies grounded in a commitment to human worth and dignity. Applying independent thinking to issues that matter, we create transformational ideas for today's most pressing social and economic challenges. The results of this work are published in books; in our quarterly journal, *The Independent Review*; and in other publications and form the basis for numerous conference and media programs. By connecting these ideas with organizations and networks, we seek to inspire action that can unleash an era of unparalleled human flourishing at home and around the globe.

100 Swan Way, Oakland, California 94621-1428, U.S.A.
Telephone: 510-632-1366 • Facsimile: 510-568-6040 • Email: info@independent.org • www.independent.org

The New Deal's War on the Bill of Rights

The Untold Story of FDR's Concentration Camps,
Censorship, and Mass Surveillance

By David T. Beito

INDEPENDENT
INSTITUTE

Independent Institute
100 Swan Way, Oakland, CA 94621-1428
Telephone: 510-632-1366
Fax: 510-568-6040
Email: info@independent.org
Website: www.independent.org

Cover Design: Denise Tsui
Cover Image: "President Franklin Roosevelt." Underwood Archives via Getty Images.
Cover Image: "Japanese-Americans interned at Santa Anita." Library of Congress via Getty Images.

Library of Congress Cataloging-in-Publication Data:

Names: Beito, David T., 1956- author.
Title: The New Deal's war on the Bill of Rights : the untold story of FDR's concentration camps, censorship, and mass surveillance / by David Beito.
Description: Oakland, CA : Independent Institute, [2023] | Includes bibliographical references and index.
Identifiers: LCCN 2023015423 (print) | LCCN 2023015424 (ebook) | ISBN 9781598133561 (cloth) | ISBN 9781598133578 (paperback) | ISBN 9781598133585 (ebook)
Subjects: LCSH: New Deal, 1933-1939. | Roosevelt, Franklin D. (Franklin Delano), 1882-1945. | Civil rights--United States--History--20th century. | United States--Politics and government--1933-1945.
Classification: LCC E806 .B4425 2023 (print) | LCC E806 (ebook) | DDC 973.917--dc23/eng/20230418
LC record available at https://lccn.loc.gov/2023015423
LC ebook record available at https://lccn.loc.gov/2023015424

Contents

Acknowledgments

THIS BOOK IS the culmination of more than a decade of research and along the way has taken numerous detours. Early inspirations included the pioneering work of Leo Ribuffo and Brian Doherty (who clued me into the importance of the Buchanan Committee). My interest in the Committee led to an article in *The Independent Review* under the able editorships respectively of Robert Higgs and Robert Whaples. As a result, the project moved back in time to consider the preceding "inquisitorial" lobbying investigations of the 1930s and 1940s. The period of preparation for an article on the Black Committee in the *Journal of Policy History* (then edited by Donald Critchlow) led to enriching dialogue with Mike Czaplicki. The scholarship and good counsel of Burton W. Folsom Jr. were instrumental in helping me to better appreciate the interconnections between New Deal surveillance, tax probes, and limitations on free speech.

As the amount of needed primary and secondary document research seemed to grow almost exponentially, I considered abandoning the book project. At one crucial turning point, Professor Jonathan Bean encouraged me to continue. During another period of frustration, my wife Linda Royster Beito, urged me in no uncertain terms to keep moving forward. Maria Rogacheva of the Institute for Humane Studies arranged a workshop with historians Richard Bell and Anthony Gregory who gave most useful critiques of an early draft.

My departmental chair at the University of Alabama, Joshua Rothman, always helped speed the way when I sought support for opportunities for time off for research and writing. Especially helpful in this regard was a visiting research scholar position at the Eudaimonia Institute at Wake Forest University headed by James Otteson.

Special thanks are due to Preston Lauterbach who revealed to me a gold mine of documents on the J. B. Martin case. The part of the book which discussed that case owed much to the careful research of Walter Sturgeon, who had worked under me as a graduate student.

The late David Theroux of the Independent Institute never lagged in his support. To my unending thanks, he also insisted that I add a chapter on Japanese internment. Our many wide-ranging conversations about the project were always enjoyable.

I've lost count of people who kindly read drafts, but my colleague in the department of history at University of Alabama, Kari A. Frederickson, stands out. She took much time from her busy schedule to share freely suggestions on style as well as substance. Another colleague, Lawrence Cappello, a leading specialist the history of privacy, consistently offered encouragement and insightful commentary.

Throughout the entire process, Jesse Walker could always be counted on to be a close and constructive reader. Others who gave valuable feedback at various points included Irv Gellman, Thomas Hazlett, Randy Barnett, Phil Magness, Roy Carlisle, and Rob Couteau. Anne Lippincott and Christopher Briggs of the Independent Institute were always patient during the final stages of the editorial and production process. Both showed themselves to be consummate perfectionists. If, by chance, I omitted someone, please accept my heartfelt apology. Any errors in the book, of course, are my own responsibility.

Introduction

FEW PRESIDENTS HAVE ranked higher in the estimation of scholars than Franklin D. Roosevelt. In the twenty-four most respected polls of scholars since 1948, he has consistently found a place in the top three of the "greatest" presidents. An obvious factor in this high ranking, of course, is that left-of-center historians and political scientists have long dominated discourse on the New Deal period. They may have an understandable tendency to take for granted that the rise of the welfare-regulatory state was overdue and that Franklin D. Roosevelt deserves plaudits for making it possible. No president, other than perhaps Lincoln, is more favorably cited as a model for leaders to emulate in a national crisis.[1]

Even Roosevelt's most ardent defenders among historians agree, however, that the internment of Japanese Americans represented a major black mark on his record. At the same time, they have often subtly mitigated blame for that decision, both in their phrasing and presentation of facts. A common pattern in ten major US history survey texts is to depict his executive order as a reaction to outside pressures or as a "glaring" or "painful" exception to an otherwise good civil liberties record. Discussion of the topic rarely touches on Roosevelt's motivations or his actions but instead focuses on such factors as the precipitating role played by General John L. DeWitt, the xenophobia unleashed by Pearl Harbor, or pervasive anti-Japanese feeling on the West Coast. The overall impression is that of an otherwise great president regrettably carried away, like so many other Americans, by the hysteria of the moment. Too often missing is a depiction of Roosevelt as a determinative historical actor who shaped or created events that might not have otherwise occurred.[2]

It makes more sense to examine Roosevelt's civil liberties record in a broader context over time, including his early direct and indirect political influences. When Roosevelt was born in Hyde Park, New York, in 1882, progressive ideas were just beginning to make inroads among elites. Several trends came together to make this possible. One was the increased popularity of German universities for American students. That country, then dominated by the policies of Otto von Bismarck, offered affordable and extensive opportunities in both undergraduate and graduate education. The professors, influenced by the doctrines of the German Historical School of political economy, rejected the classical liberal traditions of limited government that still had great sway in the United States. To varying degrees, their American students came to embrace such German-inspired policies as compulsory insurance, public housing, and zoning.[3]

Concurrent in time, advocates of the social gospel in the United States, such as Washington Gladden and Walter Rauschenbush, were promoting similar ideas among Protestant elites, including many academics. Their hope was that governmental uplift, if carried to its full potential, would usher in a postmillennial kingdom of heaven on earth. In many cases, proponents of the social gospel had also studied in Germany. A prominent example was Richard Ely, who, in 1885, was instrumental in founding the American Economic Association. The new organization represented an impressive gathering of progressive academics. The founding document, drafted by Ely, offered this statement of purpose: "We regard the state as an educational and ethical agency whose positive aid is an indispensable condition of human progress. While we recognize the necessity of individual initiative in industrial life, we hold that the doctrine of laissez-faire is unsafe in politics and unsound in morals; and that it suggests an inadequate explanation of the relations between the state and the citizens." Ely came to have great influence over future progressive politicians. He was one of Woodrow Wilson's seminar professors at Johns Hopkins University and was instrumental in shaping the "Wisconsin Idea" of administrative efficiency and expertise (as embodied by appointed regulatory commissions) under Governor Robert M. La Follette. For his part, Theodore Roosevelt declared, "I know Dr. Ely. He first introduced me to radicalism in economics and then made me sane in my radicalism."[4]

Although Franklin D. Roosevelt was not a deep intellectual thinker, these increasingly popular progressive ideas helped to determine his worldview, albeit in a more watered down and nuts-and-bolts way. The most direct, and most formidable, influence, of course, was his illustrious distant cousin Theodore, who came from the Oyster Bay branch of the family. Franklin was so smitten by the policies and persona of "Uncle Ted" that he broke from the Democratic family tradition and campaigned for the McKinley-Roosevelt ticket in 1900. To top it off, he joined the Republican Club while at Harvard and, in 1904, cast his first presidential vote for Uncle Ted. The relationship between the younger and older Roosevelts also had a personal dimension. In 1905, for example, the president gave away the bride when his niece Eleanor Roosevelt married Franklin. Uncle Ted also gave encouragement when Franklin successfully ran for the New York State Senate in 1910. The younger Roosevelt's choice of party (Democratic) was more by happenstance than planned. He might just as well have run as a Republican if that party had tried to recruit him, but 1910 was a Democratic year, and the local party presented an opportunity.[5]

Meanwhile, Woodrow Wilson, most recently president of Princeton University, won the governorship of New Jersey. Even as Franklin continued to have close and friendly political ties with Uncle Ted, Wilson was becoming his second most important political role model. "Those tracing the origins of New Deal ideas," writes Frank Freidel, "go back to two main fountainheads—Wilson's New Freedom and Theodore Roosevelt's New Nationalism. The ideology and techniques of both men left a deep impress upon Franklin D. Roosevelt."[6]

In 1911, Franklin D. Roosevelt attained the rare status of becoming an "original Wilson man" when he went on record for Wilson's presidential aspirations. After working diligently in the campaign, he sought, and secured, the position of assistant secretary of the navy, thus self-consciously emulating the educational and career trajectory of Uncle Ted, who had held that office after also both attending Harvard and serving in the New York legislature. After taking up residence in Washington, DC, Roosevelt came into ever-closer contact with such progressive notables as Louis Brandeis, Oliver Wendell Holmes Jr., and Felix Frankfurter. While Roosevelt later boasted that he was a Wilsonian "liberal," that term never entailed an affinity for civil liberties.

Throughout his life, he repeatedly operated under the assumption that the desired end was far more important than the means used to achieve it. In his view, the protections of the Bill of Rights, while laudable in theory, took second place when they conflicted with policy goals considered more vital.[7]

Illustrative of this mindset was an unquestioning support for Woodrow Wilson's crackdown on free speech during World War I, including his enforcement of the Sedition and Espionage acts. As Kenneth S. Davis points out, Roosevelt during this period "went along with prevailing trends in the realm of the national spirit, uninhibited by any strong ideological commitment to the Bill of Rights." After the publishers of an antiwar socialist pamphlet were found guilty of violating the Espionage Act, Roosevelt sent a letter of congratulation to the federal prosecutor. In another case, when the perceived offense involved a personal slight, he outdid the government in supporting repressive measures. After an anarchist journal published a satirical article stating that Roosevelt's support for compulsory military service illustrated hypocrisy because he was not in uniform, he urged on the Department of Justice to initiate a prosecution that might "send the writer and his whole plant to [the federal penitentiary in] Atlanta for the rest of their natural lives." Assistant Attorney General Charles Warren replied that the department had no basis for taking legal action.[8]

In the Newport sex scandal, however, Roosevelt moved from the status of bystander or cheerleader of governmental repression to direct instigator. The controversy began in 1919 when Roosevelt, with the encouragement of Secretary of the Navy Josephus Daniels, created Section A of the Office of the Assistant Secretary of the Navy to investigate homosexual activity at the US naval base in Newport, Rhode Island. Roosevelt's "Newport Sex Squad" had forty-one operatives that used methods of entrapment and intimidation. As a result, some twenty defendants languished behind bars for several months without charges. They and others were ultimately convicted for "scandalous conduct" on the testimony of witnesses who did not even attend the court-martial hearings. The matter did not end there, however. Historian Irwin F. Gellman concludes, "To Roosevelt, homosexuality was immoral and he would expend every effort to ferret out offenders." Criticism of his methods, however, became so heated that both a naval board of inquiry and the US Senate Committee on Naval Affairs opened investigations.[9]

Roosevelt tried to fend off his accusers by denying any knowledge of the "Sex Squad's" unsavory activities. Few believed him. Earlier he had vigorously defended the conduct of the investigation in a letter to Daniels. His rationalization fit a pattern repeated often in later years. If the motivations, and the final goals, were proper, so too were the methods. The "only clear distinction in law relates to the question of intent," he wrote to his boss. "In other words, if the intent of those authorized to investigate crime is honestly to obtain evidence without active solicitation, then the basic law declares that no crime has been committed." Citing a highly dubious analogy, Roosevelt compared his investigators to a police officer who justifiably breaks into a home because he has foreknowledge of a possible robbery on the next day.[10]

While Roosevelt's motivations in this specific case were also opportunistic, his emphasis that certain ends took priority over procedure and other rules characterized many progressives. The best-known example was Herbert Croly, who, in *The Promise of American Life*, published in 1909, praised Theodore Roosevelt (though he too eventually made a transition to Wilsonianism) for focusing on the ultimate goal of achieving a "genuine democratic community" rather than worrying too much about rigid and formulaic constitutional procedures. Croly had a conflicted and ambiguous attitude toward the protections of the Bill of Rights. "The time may come," he warned, "when the fulfillment of a justifiable democratic purpose may demand the limitation of certain rights, to which the Constitution affords such absolute guarantees." Croly praised Alexander Hamilton for realizing that "genuine liberty was not merely a matter of a constitutional declaration of rights."[11]

In 1921, the final report of the Senate Committee on Naval Affairs dealt Roosevelt a stunning rebuke for his role in the Newport sex scandal. His office, it declared, had violated "the moral code of the American citizen, and the rights of every American boy who enlisted in the Navy to fight for his country." As to Roosevelt himself, it judged his "direct supervision" to be "morally responsible" for the use of entrapment and other "immoral acts." More devastating, the committee suggested that Roosevelt was unfit to hold any public office. The front-page headline of the *New York Times* on July 23, 1921, was clear in assigning blame: "Lay Navy Scandal to F. D. Roosevelt — Details Are Unprintable." Roosevelt's legendary luck prevailed in the end. He was able to survive relatively unscathed and eventually, after his bout with polio, which occurred soon thereafter, stage a political comeback.[12]

A similar insensitivity toward constitutional protections would characterize Roosevelt's tenure as president. During the 1930s, he gave aid and comfort to several highly inquisitorial congressional investigations of political adversaries that often trampled on privacy and free speech. The most far-reaching of these probes was the US Senate's Special Committee to Investigate Lobbying Activities, more widely known as the Black Committee, named for its chair, Senator Hugo L. Black (D–AL), a zealous and efficient New Deal loyalist. Black was recruited at Roosevelt's behest, and the administration gave crucial help to the investigation, often behind the scenes. The Department of the Treasury granted Black access to tax returns dating back to 1925 of such critics as David Lawrence of the *U.S. News*. The Federal Communications Commission (FCC), in turn, authorized the Black Committee to search through copies of millions of private telegrams sent by, and to, New Deal opponents. The courts eventually ordered a stop to this practice but only after it was pretty much completed.

Roosevelt also did not hesitate to use, or otherwise support, questionable methods to manipulate radio, a medium that had become his most potent means to shape public opinion. Throughout his administration, the Federal Communications Commission relied on early precursors of the fairness doctrine to chill dissenting voices. The courts, falling back on a scarcity argument, generally stepped aside. By the end of the decade, anti-Roosevelt commentators had largely vanished from network radio. By contrast, the print press was one of the few havens for the president's critics, but even that could not be taken for granted. In 1938, Senator Sherman Minton (D-IN), an enthusiastic administration loyalist, both led an intrusive lobbying investigation of anti–New Deal newspapers and proposed a bill to make it a crime to print any article "known to be false." Many suspected that the administration had secretly put him up to it. He too received support from the president in securing the tax returns of witnesses who came before the committee. Minton, however, had overestimated the willingness of Americans to support these measures and had to scuttle his bill. By the end of the 1930s, polls showed that an overwhelming majority of the public favored a free press, including in radio.

Roosevelt's readiness to put the New Deal regulatory and welfare state apparatus at the service of big city bosses represents perhaps the least examined aspect of his civil liberties dark side. During the 1930s, the president did nothing when his close Democratic Party ally, Mayor Frank Hague of Jersey City, New Jersey, routinely used fire codes and other regulations to deny meeting halls to opponents. Hague also ordered deportations of American citizens from the city on such pretexts as disturbing the peace. Roosevelt showed even fewer qualms during the early 1940s when another ally, Edward H. "Boss" Crump, used similar tactics to quash the free speech and assembly rights of black Republican leaders in Memphis, including forced expulsion from the city. The president took no action against these abuses, despite the willingness of prosecutors in the Department of Justice to move forward, in great part because Crump, like Hague, was a reliable friend who swung votes Roosevelt's way both at conventions and at election time.

The stubborn reality is that the Roosevelt who authorized concentration camps for Japanese Americans was the same Roosevelt who endorsed World War I repression, supervised the Newport Sex Squad, cheered on the Black and Minton committees, ordered wiretaps and tax audits of political adversaries, and tolerated civil liberty abuses by allied big city bosses. He knew what he was about. Attorney General Francis Biddle's assessment of the president's attitudes toward internment, with a tweak here and there to fit diverse contexts, reveals a single defining thread: "I do not think he was much concerned with the gravity or implications of this step. ... Nor do I think that the constitutional difficulty plagued him ... he was never theoretical about things." The recollections of Robert H. Jackson, Biddle's predecessor as attorney general, were consistent with this assessment: "Because he thought that his motives were always good for the things he wanted to do, he found difficulty in thinking there could be legal limitations on them. The president was not a legalistic-minded person."[13]

Many examples of Roosevelt's willingness to cast aside constitutional and other rules still remain hidden from history. These often have to be pieced together from other sources, such as the memoirs of eyewitnesses. Ever aware of the necessity to have deniability, Roosevelt rarely committed to print any blunt statement about possible retaliation against adversaries. He was much more candid with people he trusted. A few such examples were captured by a recording system he had ordered installed from equipment provided by David Sarnoff, the head of RCA/NBC. The president's main goal was to get an exact transcript of his "off the record" press conferences so as to counter possible misquotation. Inadvertently, the device also picked up several private conversations, including one from around August 1940 between Roosevelt and Lowell Mellett, a staffer. One of the topics covered was an ongoing affair between Republican presidential candidate Wendell Willkie and Irita Van Doren, the books editor of the *New York Herald Tribune*. Roosevelt told Mellett to "[s]pread it [the dirt about Willkie's affair] as a word of mouth thing, or by some people way down the line. We can't have any of our principal speakers refer to it, but the people down the line can get it out. I mean the Congress speakers, and state speakers, and so forth. They can use the raw material. Now, now if they want to play dirty politics, we've got our own people." While Roosevelt later told Secretary of Labor Frances Perkins that he had since decided not to use this information against Willkie because it might "boomerang" against the Democrats, the recording provides a relatively rare first-person glimpse into the thought process of the unfiltered Roosevelt.[14]

Whether it was ordering internment, supporting surveillance by lobbying committees, or wiretapping and snooping into tax returns, Roosevelt never let up on his pursuit of the desired end. In the 1930s, that desired end was to defend the New Deal agenda, while in World War II, it was not only to beat the Axis but to solidify wartime unity behind him. The protections of the Bill of Rights were secondary, and often dispensable, if they seemed to conflict with those ends. While it can be daunting to identify whether the president first suggested a particular tactic to skirt normal constitutional procedures, or if it was from the initiative of zealous subordinates or New Deal supporters, Roosevelt himself was crucial in setting the overall standard.

In 1941, Roosevelt famously proclaimed freedom of speech as the first of his "Four Freedoms," but his behavior throughout his twelve years in office often belied the flowery prose. In times of peace as well as war, he never hesitated to exploit opportunities to restrict the individual rights of dissenters. Adding to this several-fold in magnitude was his decision to put 120,000 people of Japanese ancestry in concentration camps, two-thirds of them US citizens. Obstacles frustrating the president's agenda, however, appeared repeatedly in the actions and statements of journalists, military leaders, judges, and individuals in the federal bureaucracy. Fueling this resistance by Americans were vivid memories of federal civil liberties abuses so many of them had observed during World War I and its immediate aftermath.

I

New Deal Mass Surveillance: The "Black Inquisition Committee"

ALMOST NO PRESIDENT in American history had greater discretion than that enjoyed by the newly inaugurated Franklin D. Roosevelt in March 1933. Because of a sense of national emergency, implementation of his initial New Deal proposals was never in doubt. Roosevelt's mastery of both the press and Congress was formidable. As journalist Frank Kent puts it, "Every department, board, bureau and commission has its quota of paid press agents, and these keep flowing a steady stream of stimulating stuff, designed to convince the country that everything is lovely and the goose hanging high."[1]

By 1934, however, Roosevelt faced stiffer winds as media and congressional critics became more confident and assertive. Elisha Hanson, counsel for the American Newspaper Publishers Association, observed in mid-1935 that "whereas in 1933 practically all the columns read like pro-Administration propaganda, today the reverse is substantially true." Beginning in February 1934, according to an analysis of the Democratic Party's leading internal pollster, Emil Hurja, Roosevelt's popular approval had eroded at a steady 1 percent each month from a high of 69 percent, bottoming out at 50 percent in September 1935.[2]

As New Dealers became more insecure, however, they showed greater inclination to turn to heavy-handed strategies against opponents. The establishment of the US Senate Special Committee to Investigate Lobbying Activities in 1935, also known as the Black Committee for its chair, Senator Hugo L. Black (D-AL), was a key indicator of this trend.

The committee monitored private communications on a scale previously unrivaled in US history, at least in peacetime. Working in tandem with the

Federal Communications Commission and the Roosevelt administration, it examined literally millions of private telegrams with virtually no supervision or constraint. Those singled out for this surveillance were anti–New Deal critics, including activists, journalists, and lawyers.

Only a handful of historians have dealt with the Black Committee in the context of surveillance. Some of the best discussions in recent years are by Frederick S. Lane (on implications for the right of privacy) and Laura Weinrib (on the relationship to free speech in the 1930s). Michael Stephen Czaplicki has an especially thorough treatment. He puts the Black Committee in the context of the period's anticorruption investigations and uses it as a means to explore the tension between privacy rights and demands for transparency. For the most part, however, historians, including specialists on such topics as governmental eavesdropping, congressional investigations, free speech, and privacy, have not discussed the Black Committee as an instrument of political surveillance. Indeed, they have rarely applied the term "mass surveillance" to the United States during the New Deal era. In part, this lack of attention is a by-product of a longtime tendency to focus on the role of the FBI. J. Edgar Hoover's haphazard and sporadic eavesdropping on "subversives" (usually no more than a few hundred on any given day) was indeed a world apart from the National Security Agency's systematic data mining.[3]

The immediate impetus for the creation of the Black Committee was a rapid succession of setbacks to the New Deal in the spring and summer of 1935. The most significant of these was the US Supreme Court's ruling on May 27 in *A.L.A. Schechter Poultry Corp. v. United States*, striking down the National Industrial Recovery Act as unconstitutional. A little over a month later, the House rejected the so-called death sentence of the Wheeler-Rayburn Bill. This provision authorized the Securities and Exchange Commission to abolish utilities unable to prove they were part of a "geographically or economically integrated system." In arguing for the death sentence, Roosevelt characterized the utilities as "the most powerful, dangerous lobby ... that has ever been created by any organization in this country." The unexpected resistance to the death sentence threw New Dealers off balance. By the end of June 1935, more than 800,000 letters and telegrams had poured into congressional offices condemning the bill as an assault on free enterprise and constitutional rights.[4]

Still smarting from defeat, and hoping to revive the bill, Roosevelt sent his personal emissary, Thomas "Tommy the Cork" Corcoran, to Senator Burton K. Wheeler (D-MT), one of the authors of the death sentence. Corcoran asked him to chair a probe into the opposition campaign. Wheeler begged off, fearing that he would be perceived "as a prosecutor and not an investigator," but recommended Senator Black, who proved eager to take the job. It made sense for both Black and Roosevelt. Widely dubbed "Chief Ferret" and "Chief Inquisitor," Black had a reputation for both ruthlessness and tenacity. He was second to none in loyalty to Roosevelt and had already made a splash for the New Deal as chair of a headline-generating committee probing the Hoover administration's awarding of airmail contracts. A foe of big business, Black regarded the utility companies as particularly dangerous. He did not want to regulate them but rather to "destroy them as holding companies with their network of chicanery, deceit, fraud, graft and racketeering." Another of Black's (and Roosevelt's) goals in following this approach was to promote governmentally controlled alternatives to the power companies, most notably the Tennessee Valley Authority.[5]

With Black lined up, the Senate sped through a resolution creating a committee of five "to make a full and complete investigation of all lobbying activities and all efforts to influence, encourage, promote or retard legislation, directly or indirectly, in connection with the so-called 'holding company bill,' or any other matter or proposal affecting legislation." Black recruited two of the other members, Sherman Minton (D-IN) and Lewis B. Schwellenbach (D-WA), both in their first terms. He had reason to count on them. Along with the freshman Harry S. Truman (D-MO), they had secure reputations as the "Young Turks" of the New Deal. The other committee members, Lynn Frazier (R-ND) and Ernest W. Gibson (R-VT), were progressive Republicans who generally sat silently on the sidelines.[6]

While Roosevelt supported giving Black all the powers he asked for, no direct evidence has surfaced of ongoing coordination of effort. The two did not really have to work closely in tandem, however. Black and Roosevelt were of common mind in their zeal to protect the New Deal from its enemies. As Czaplicki puts it, "Roosevelt gave critical support to Black, but it was a relationship of affiliation and shared ideology rather than of CEO to subordinate." Roosevelt knew that Black could be trusted to do the right thing, from the president's perspective. Later, he told his son James that if "you want something done in the Senate, give it to Black. He'll do it ... Father said that the New Deal would have not been the same without Black."[7]

Emboldened by a sweeping Senate authorization, Black moved with great haste. Much as he had as chair of the Senate Special Committee to Investigate Air Mail and Ocean Mail Contracts, he leaned heavily on blanket *duces tecum* subpoenas ("under penalty bring with you"). Also known as dragnet subpoenas, they required the witness to bring to the hearing room all relevant (sometimes defined in sweeping terms) papers, including correspondence and financial information. To make these subpoenas stick, Black made highly elastic use of the contempt power. This allowed the affected chamber of Congress to cite recalcitrant witnesses and turn them over to prosecution in a federal court for potential jail time (a maximum of one year). Black set new records in applying this sanction, at least for the twentieth century up to that time. The two committees he chaired (Air Mail and Lobbying) generated every one of the six contempt citations by the Senate in the 1930s. While his counterparts in the equally high-profile US Senate Committee on Banking and Currency (Pecora Committee) investigation of Wall Street (1932–33) and the Senate Special Committee on Investigation of the Munitions Industry (Nye Committee) (1934–36) also issued subpoenas *duces tecum*, they had not recommended contempt citations.[8]

Black's potent combination of these subpoenas and the contempt power was, as Czaplicki notes, "designed to eliminate his target's capacity for choice and discussion through his presentation of constraining binaries: provide the information/go to Washington; swear under oath/go to Washington." Philip H. Gadsden, the chair of the Committee of Public Utility Executives, was the first to feel the full force of the dragnet subpoena. Black brought him in to testify only a day after the Senate had authorized creation of the committee. Staffers presented the understandably bewildered Gadsden with a subpoena in his hotel room and whisked him off to the hearing room. As he testified, others gathered up evidence, which they ferried over in boxes.[9]

While under questioning, Gadsden pushed back by castigating the political nature of the investigation. He identified two kinds of lobbies: "One is a group that comes down here trying to get some selfish advantage out of the Government in preference to other taxpayers. I think the other group is a group like myself that come down here to do what they can to resist the effort of their Government to destroy their property." Black [interposing]: "They all claim that." Speaking later to reporters, Gadsden declared that "this isn't Russia" and complained that the committee had rifled through all his papers, including his personal checkbook. Although the members had the advantage of surprise, they had no luck extracting damaging testimony.[10]

But four days later, on July 16, they struck pay dirt, which transformed the investigation in Black's favor. After Representative Denis J. Driscoll (D-PA) reported that a suspiciously high number of telegrams against the death sentence had poured in from the small town of Warren, Pennsylvania (many with last names starting with "B"), another witness identified a utility lobbyist who had copied names from the city directory as the source. The revelations uncovering thousands of "fake telegrams" from Warren and other locations injected into the investigation tremendous momentum. Although as utility company executive, and future GOP presidential candidate, Wendell Willkie noted, these were "an infinitesimal percentage of the total protests of utility stockholders," the sheer volume was enough to put future witnesses on the defensive for quite some time.[11]

The fake telegrams gave Black his opening wedge for a widened investigation. A few days later, he asked the US Bureau of Internal Revenue to issue a "general blanket order" for access to the tax returns of possible witnesses. The bureau (quite likely with Roosevelt's approval) gave Black everything he wanted. While making the arrangements, Secretary of the Treasury Henry Morgenthau Jr. privately observed that the senator was "in an awful hurry about it." Black had long dismissed philosophical or constitutional concerns about the privacy of tax returns as a false front for vested interests. Citing powers previously granted in the airmail investigation, the bureau authorized the release of any return that "may properly be made subject of inspection." This permissive wording left the choice of names entirely up to the committee.[12]

Context is important here. Although privacy was the general rule for income tax information after 1870, Congress had passed a law in 1934 requiring all payers of income tax to submit a separate form for public disclosure. Printed on pink paper, it included their names, addresses, gross income, taxable income, and deductions. Black had backed this so-called pink-slip provision as a beneficial reform to end "the secrecy with reference to the

Income Tax return" so as to shame the wealthy to pay more rather than seek loopholes. In April 1935, however, a well-organized campaign forced repeal of the law. Repeal attracted wide support (though only the well-off were liable for income taxes) because many viewed the "pink slip" as a threat to privacy. Although Roosevelt ultimately signed the repeal, this was perhaps the first important setback for the progressive wing of the New Deal, including for Black. In asking the Bureau of Internal Revenue to selectively disclose returns only months after this vote, Black seemed oblivious to the political risks of revisiting this hot-button issue.[13]

The tax return request also illustrated Black's sweeping approach to obtaining evidence even when it seemed to compromise privacy. Most of the individuals on his list had no conceivable role in fake telegrams. Also, Black asked for returns from as early as 1925, predating the death sentence by a decade. The names included David Lawrence, anti–New Deal columnist for the *U.S. News*, and those of two leading congressional opponents of the death sentence, US Representatives James W. Wadsworth Jr. (R-NY) and George Huddleston (D-AL).[14]

Although Black's approach as chair was more draconian than most, precedent was still on his side. In the preceding decades, the courts had regularly deferred to Congress's resort to subpoenas *duces tecum* backed up by contempt citations. In *McGrain v. Daugherty* (1927) and *Sinclair v. United States* (1929), the Supreme Court reaffirmed the right of a Senate committee investigating the Teapot Dome and related scandals to issue broad subpoenas and compel witnesses to testify. In *McGrain v. Daugherty*, it held that a "legislative body cannot legislate wisely or effectively in the absence of information respecting the conditions which the legislation is intended to affect" and that "some means of compulsion are essential to obtain what is needed." The Supreme Court's ruling in *Jurney v. MacCracken* (1935), which involved a contempt case from Black's airmail investigation, further bolstered the powers of Congress.[15]

Spurred by these court rulings as well as a perception that the lobbyists were on the ropes, the committee under Black's leadership greatly widened the focus of the investigation. Making use of a federal requirement that telegraph companies keep copies of the originals, it told Western Union that it wanted carte blanche to search all incoming and outgoing telegrams sent through Washington, DC, from February 1 to September 1, 1935. This went too far for company executives. They refused to comply, fearing that customers would see compliance as an invasion of privacy. In taking this stand, Western Union was following a decades-long general policy of resisting even more limited subpoenas of this type. Again, Black turned to the Roosevelt administration for help. He asked for, and secured, FCC authorization to require the telegraph companies to comply with this demand. The FCC also provided staffers to aid the committee on the official basis that it too was investigating fake or destroyed telegrams. This wasn't just a dragnet subpoena. It was in a whole new category.[16]

In early October, staffers from both the Black Committee and the FCC began poring over thousands of copies of incoming and outgoing telegrams. There were virtually no restrictions. As one staffer happily informed Black on October 5, "We have at last worked out arrangements by which we can review all the telegrams in the offices of the telegraph companies." Paul C. Yates, the secretary of the lobbying committee and a former speechwriter for FDR, made the ultimate decisions on procedure. Investigators scanned all telegrams sent to, and from, people on their lists. While Yates urged them to avert their gazes from content of a personal nature, he gave few other restrictions. He instructed that all telegrams be pulled for further examination and potential duplication if "in any way connected with lobbying activities." The committee's definition of lobbying encompassed just about any political references. In December, the search was extended to the offices of the Radio Corporation of America (RCA) and the Postal Telegraph Company.[17]

Because the Committee had directed the subpoena to these companies and did not give notice to the senders or receivers, most of the targets found out, if they did at all, when a senator confronted them during a hearing. Black viewed this procedure as entirely consistent with the powers of the Senate. "Repeatedly," he proclaimed, "it has been held that the Senate can call for what it pleases."[18]

While the extent of the Black Committee's surveillance did not quite rival the modern national security state, it was remarkable by 1935 standards. Over nearly a three-month period, staffers dug through great stacks of telegrams sent through Washington, DC, between February 1 and September 1, 1935, by sundry company employees, lobbyists, newspaper publishers, and political activists as well as every member of Congress. Finally finishing on January 3,

1936, they had worked on an almost daily basis. Writing to Black, one investigator stated that they had gone through "from 35,000 to 50,000 per day"
during this period. Later estimates that they had examined some five million
telegrams during the investigation seem entirely plausible. In 2023, this would
be somewhat akin to staffers from a congressional committee and the FCC
teaming up at the headquarters of Google and Microsoft and then spending
months secretly searching all emails for specific names or organizations based
on any political references.[19]

Either because of a desire to keep potential targets in the dark or out of fear
of questionable legality, Black stressed to subordinates the need to maintain
secrecy. Writing to H. A. Blomquist, the committee's chief investigator, Yates
stated that it was "Black's wish that we do everything possible to uncover
all the facts. ... It would, of course not be wise to mention the source of our
information."[20]

Even as his staffers culled through these telegrams, the Black Com-
mittee was using what it had found as a basis for more specific subpoenas.
An early target was a leading anti–New Deal voice in the Northwest, the
W. H. Cowles Publishing Company of Spokane, Washington, publisher of the
Spokesman-Review of Spokane, the *Spokane Chronicle*, the *Oregon Farmer*, and
the *Washington Farmer*. On November 12, 1935, the committee subpoenaed
Western Union and other telegraph companies for all incoming and outgoing
telegrams in the United States.[21]

Troubling electoral signs for Democrats continued to give urgency to
Black's pursuit of the probe. While the slide in Roosevelt's approval in the
polls had abated, his party lost two open House seats in 1935, including one
in a traditionally Democratic district in Rhode Island. In November 1935,
the Republicans captured the New York Assembly (FDR's home state), scored
legislative gains in New Jersey, and won mayoral contests in Cleveland and
Philadelphia. The new year brought more discouraging news for the Democrats. On January 6, the US Supreme Court demolished a keystone of the
First New Deal by striking down the Agricultural Adjustment Act as unconstitutional. Meanwhile, secret White House internal polls concluded that the
president was likely to lose New York and Illinois and faced a close race in
Iowa, Indiana, and Minnesota. As historian William E. Leuchtenburg frames
it, Roosevelt's reelection as of January 1936 seemed "very much in doubt."[22]

With one eye on the presidential campaign, Black mounted a more frontal assault on the New Deal's enemies. On January 25, as former Democratic standard-bearer Al Smith was speaking at a highly publicized American Liberty League dinner, the committee was mailing out questionnaires to hundreds of individuals. These asked under oath for itemized answers for any contributions over the previous two years to the American Liberty League as well as to the following other anti–New Deal groups: the Crusaders, the New York State Economic Council, the American Taxpayers League, and the Sentinels of the Republic. The mailings warned recipients to be prepared to testify. Not without reason, many critics suggested that a key goal of the probe was to help Roosevelt's campaign by scaring away potential donors fearful of being hauled before a congressional committee or subjected to tax audits. In a predictable response, the American Liberty League said it was being singled out for advocating "constitutional principles" and did not intend to comply because it was not a lobby.[23]

None of these attacks fazed Black in the least. At the beginning of 1936, he was at the height of his power in the Senate. Few senators past or future were his equal, not excepting the blustering and sloppy Senator Joseph McCarthy, in putting witnesses through the wringer. In February 1936, political reporter Arthur Sears Henning elaborated on Black's technique: "When he takes a witness in hand before his dreaded tribunal he is all purr. He smiles, he ingratiates, he leads his victim from one commitment to another, and he seeks to tangle the witness in his own testimony. Then when he thinks he has the subject in his toils he pounces. … Fortunate is the man able to bear up under the ordeal. The experience is one that most men dread." Black's first inclination was to publicly dismiss resistance from these anti–New Deal organizations as predictable subterfuge from conspirators against the public good. Expressing feigned surprise, he wondered why the American Liberty League was so suspicious "lest somebody answer questions." In an article for *Harper's Magazine*, he characterized these complaints as typical of the "perennial objections to this congressional right to summon and to inspect papers" dating to the founding of the Republic. Black repeatedly denied that he was doing anything out of the ordinary. "Whenever a congressional committee inspects the so-called private papers of a corporation official," he declared matter-of-factly, "the cry goes up that this is an outrageous invasion of the rights of private citizens."[24]

Meanwhile, Black, acting without the knowledge of the public or potential witnesses, was pulling the noose tighter via more dragnet subpoenas on Western Union, although this time without the FCC's direct help. The committee was also expanding the probe of anti–New Deal organizations to include allied newspapers and law firms. On February 8, for example, it subpoenaed all messages of the Times Publishing Company of Wichita Falls, Texas, which published the *Times* and *The Record-News*. By the beginning of March, the committee had served more than one thousand separate subpoenas. Missing from this list were some of the most powerful anti–New Deal voices, including the *Chicago Daily Tribune* and the Associated Press. It is not clear why. The committee might not have subpoenaed them because it already had information from the earlier catch-all search at Western Union. Just as likely, it feared the political repercussions of targeting too many powerful critics, though it had included the *Tribune*'s publisher, Robert R. McCormick, in the January questionnaire.[25]

The broad reach of the subpoenas alarmed Western Union's executives, who feared driving away privacy-conscious customers. In early February, the company implemented a policy of automatically informing all individuals receiving new subpoenas that the Black Committee had searched their telegrams. Before this time, the committee was able to do its work in secret, and most targets had no clue about what was happening. The change virtually guaranteed a lawsuit.[26]

The first legal action, brought on March 2 by Silas Hardy Strawn on behalf his law firm Winston, Strawn, and Shaw, dramatically shifted the course of the investigation. He sued to prohibit Western Union from handing over copies of the telegrams generated by the firm after finding out that the committee had subpoenaed all telegrams, including those of its "known officers, employees, and agents." Strawn's prominence made big headlines almost inevitable. He was not only a partner in a prestigious Chicago law firm but also a past president of the American Bar Association and the US Chamber of Commerce, as well as the former national finance chair of the Republican Party. Strawn's lawyer, Frank J. Hogan, alleged that the committee had launched an inquisition that was exposing client information "of a private nature and which should not be subjected to public scrutiny."[27]

Strawn's suit shifted the balance of power against Black, at least for the time being. No longer was it possible to depict the investigation as a limited probe of fake telegrams or even an exposé of utility legislation lobbying. It was relatively easy to brush off the complaints of particular individuals about dragnet subpoenas or rifled files. It was more difficult to ignore evidence that investigators had scanned millions of private telegrams, copied thousands of them, and took notes at their own discretion.

Of the many Americans who found out that the Black Committee had looked through their messages, few responses matched the red-hot anger of Newton D. Baker. Baker had served as Woodrow Wilson's secretary of war and was a cautious critic of the New Deal. After Western Union informed him that the committee had examined his telegrams for an entire year, he wrote, "Man of peace as I am, I am quite sure I could not keep my hand off the rope if I accidentally happened to stumble upon a party bent on hanging him [Black]." The new Western Union policy considerably weakened Black's once formidable element of surprise. It did not destroy it, however, since the committee still had no obligation to share the actual contents of telegrams with witnesses.[28]

More than ever, top newspapers vigorously condemned the committee's methods. As expected, the anti–New Deal *Chicago Daily Tribune* labeled the inquiry as "terroristic," but more establishment voices also joined in. The *Washington Post* detected a threat to representative government "when private messages are indiscriminately exposed to official scrutiny without the consent of the sender," while the *Baltimore Sun* observed that "resistance to New Deal policies" appeared to be the only criteria for investigation. Mark Sullivan, a popular syndicated columnist, charged that any misdeeds by utilities did not justify targeting anti–New Deal organizations as a whole. Washington, DC, United Press bureau chief Raymond Clapper, who was generally sympathetic to Roosevelt's policies, asked a question on many minds: "Why doesn't the Black Committee seize the telegrams of prominent Democrats who have been selling their influence with the Administration for fat legal fees?" while Arthur Krock of the *New York Times* blasted the "snooping of Congressional bodies more interested in getting political ammunition against the enemies of the party in power than in contributing to the orderly consideration of legislation."[29]

Signs of discontent were also more apparent in Congress. Representatives Wadsworth, John J. Cochran (D-MO), and Andrew J. May (D-KY) put the

FCC's enabling role on center stage. Wadsworth was upset that the committee had seized "tens of thousands of telegrams," including many "confidential or private in character … some of them passing between husband and wife." In the US House, a rare voice who spoke up for Black was Representative John E. Rankin (D-MS), who brushed aside the objections as just so much "power propaganda." The ultrasegregationist Rankin was, like Black, very much a New Dealer and shared his disdain for the holding companies. Throughout, he was a fast friend of the committee.[30]

Black continued to pooh-pooh the critics. His actions were not extraordinary, he proclaimed, and he did not ask for or care whether witnesses backed "one administration or another administration." Somewhat in contradiction to this assurance, he stated that his mission was to expose the "lobbyists, propagandists, and so-called patriotic societies supported by tax dodgers and racketeers." Instead of undermining the First Amendment, he was upholding it because the true threat to free speech came from that small minority "who have grown rich out of the Public Treasury" by failing to pay taxes. To top it off, Black denied that the courts had jurisdiction over the committee's actions, pointedly warning that "if any judge ever issued an injunction to prevent the delivery of papers that were sought by this body through subpoena, the Congress should immediately enact legislation taking away that jurisdiction from the courts."[31]

Despite this outward self-confidence, Black had cause for concern. Most worrisome, he was getting flak from unexpected quarters, including a leading spokesman of liberal reform: syndicated columnist Walter Lippmann. Lippmann had joined the fight only five days after Strawn filed his suit. His prose was as strident as any from conservatives. The committee was "becoming an engine of tyranny in which men are denied the elementary legal protection that a confirmed criminal caught red-handed in the act can still count upon." Lippmann, who had impeccable civil liberties credentials (including defenses of Sacco and Vanzetti and John T. Scopes), saw similarities between Black's investigation and those of right-wing red-hunters who "cared nothing [about] whom they slandered." Lippmann unsparingly challenged Black's motivations and abilities: the "Senator is an enthusiast for investigations but in the realm of justice he is an obvious illiterate." He closed by calling for an investigation of the investigators.[32]

The following day it looked as if Lippmann might get his wish. William E. Borah (R-ID), who was also the dean of the Senate, proposed a bill requiring the FCC to explain its role in any inspection of telegrams. Leading off the spirited debate on the bill, Senator Frederick Steiwer (R-OR) compared the committee to the OGPU (Soviet secret police). Black retorted that it was "absurd" to allege that he had any partisan interest in private telegrams, adding that this "loud clamor" was just obfuscation by the "mouthpieces of greed and grab." Black's colleagues seemed less inclined than ever to listen to him. By a voice vote, the Senate approved Borah's resolution.[33]

On March 11, Chief Justice Alfred A. Wheat of the Supreme Court of the District of Columbia (later renamed the District Court of D.C.) dealt another setback to Black by granting an injunction prohibiting the committee from examining and seizing more telegrams from Winston, Strawn, and Shaw. Contra Black, Wheat asserted that he had jurisdiction to protect Strawn's Fourth Amendment rights against unreasonable search and seizure from Congress: "This subpoena goes way beyond any legitimate exercise of the right of subpoena duces tecum." Wheat did not object to a more limited subpoena directed to specific telegrams or individuals but rather to a catch-all approach. Though Strawn had sued Western Union, not the Black Committee, the company preferred that the plaintiff prevail. The ruling, as Roger K. Newman observes, "was one of the few times in American history that a court had restrained a congressional investigating committee." Black responded that he was pondering a bill stripping the courts of the power to issue injunctions in such cases.[34]

While the energized congressional opposition quickly dashed any hope of that happening, Black showed no signs of relenting as he steered into a new controversy. At the center was the most famous newspaper publisher in American history: William Randolph Hearst. An exuberant nationalist and law-and-order advocate, Hearst was instrumental in securing Roosevelt's nomination in 1932 but had since turned against his old ally. Roosevelt reciprocated this animus by instructing the Department of the Treasury to closely monitor Hearst's taxes. On February 8, the Black Committee served a direct subpoena on Hearst for a specific telegram he had sent on April 5, 1935, to James T. Williams Jr., editorial writer for the Hearst papers. In that communication (marked "Confidential"), Hearst had instructed Williams to write editorials calling for the impeachment of Representative John J. McSwain (D-SC), the chair of the House Committee on Military Affairs: "He is the enemy within the gates of Congress. … He is a Communist in spirit and a traitor in effect. He would leave the United States naked to its foreign and domestic enemies." It is rather odd that Black publicly subpoenaed the original from Hearst given that he already had a complete copy of it from the earlier search of the Western Union office. Perhaps he was skittish about raising potentially embarrassing questions about the secretive nature and methods used in that search.[35]

On March 13, Hearst petitioned the Supreme Court of the District of Columbia to enjoin Western Union from handing over the telegram. Hearst's lawyer, Elisha Hanson, who was also general counsel of the American Newspaper Publishers Association, charged that the committee had violated the First, Fourth, and Fifth Amendments. He stressed the illegality of the act, adding that the telegram had no reference to lobbying.[36]

Black's first instinct was to counterattack, but this time he did so in an uncharacteristically clumsy way. On March 18, he sent, on the committee's behalf, a copy of the Hearst telegram to both the press and McSwain. Black apparently hoped that his colleagues would be so offended by Hearst's inflammatory prose that they would rally to the committee. In a coup de grâce, Black minimized any potential legal damage by also withdrawing the subpoena. He claimed that since the committee already had a copy, no "good purpose can be served by a one-sided court battle in the nature of a mock trial of an injunction proceeding affecting the basic constitutional powers of the Congress of the United States."[37]

At the same time, Black unleashed his anger at Western Union for its uncooperative attitude toward the committee. In a public letter to the head of the company's Washington, DC, office, he implied that the owners were putting the needs of one particularly high-volume customer, William Randolph Hearst, ahead of the public good: "The Western Union Telegraph Co. would naturally not desire to bring out the fact that an effort had been made by its patron to intimidate and coerce in the performance of his legislative duty a Member of Congress [McSwain], whose reputation for loyalty and patriotic service is above criticism."[38]

Black's colleagues on the committee, Minton and Schwellenbach, used the occasion to mount a well-coordinated attack on Hearst and all he represented.

They revisited Hearst's misdeeds dating back to the Spanish-American War to expose the publisher's hypocrisy and double standards on issues such as free speech. Hearst, Minton proclaimed, "would not know the Goddess of Liberty if she came down off her pedestal in New York Harbor and bowed to him. He would probably try to get her telephone number." Like Black, Minton depicted Hearst and other anti–New Dealers as the real enemies of free speech for spreading fascist propaganda and stealthily promoting a financial dictatorship.[39]

Buried in the rhetoric of Black Committee members, however, were statements about the nature of the investigation that were false or misleading. Most stunningly, Schwellenbach flatly declared that "no telegram sent into or out of Washington by any person, association, or corporation not engaged in lobbying activity was at any time examined by the committee or any member of the committee or any of its agents or employees." He also denied, without qualification, that the committee had ever used "the Federal Communications Commission in an effort to secure information."[40]

This was demonstrably untrue. Earlier that month, Black had received a confidential and detailed update on how committee and FCC staffers had examined the telegrams in Western Union's Washington office in the fall and winter. Minton and Black were somewhat more circumspect in their wording. They skirted over accusations that staffers had examined millions of telegrams by focusing on the relatively small number (about 13,000) actually copied. When Minton and Black used the term "seized," they meant it only in that narrow sense. An example was Minton's carefully parsed challenge to detractors "to name some of the private citizens whose unrelated telegrams have been seized."[41]

The release of the Hearst telegram backfired for Black in a major way. As many pointed out, it directly contradicted the committee's pledge on March 8 to reveal only telegrams found to be relevant. The release of the telegram showed, the *Washington Post* editorialized, that the Black Committee had become "rather too smart for success." Instead of discrediting Hearst, the action had instead "sharply underlined the indefensible nature of its own dragnet tactics," which had revealed "a private wire from a citizen who has filed a charge of conspiracy against the committee." *Editor and Publisher* wondered "if anything is safe" when a congressional committee and the FCC were able to fish a "private message out of the Western Union office for political reasons solely." Arthur Krock dubbed the release a misguided ploy to "gain public approval of Snoopnocracy" that had no justification even if Hearst was as terrible as his detractors charged.[42]

Caught flatfooted, Black's defenders repeated that they were following precedent set by congressional investigations, most notably *McGrain v. Daugherty* and *Sinclair v. United States*. But those earlier, more limited subpoenas, which had named specific individuals, had not even approached the open-ended demands for telegrams by the Black Committee. The search at Western Union, more than any of the others, was a true mass "fishing expedition" under which investigators scanned millions of telegrams exchanged between thousands of often unspecified individuals. Black did not help his cause by a continuing tone-deafness toward privacy concerns. An example was his claim after the Strawn decision that the "law doesn't recognize that a telegram is a man's" but "is the telegram company's and is retained for subpoena purposes."[43]

Resumed testimony by witnesses from mid-March to April increasingly vied for media attention with the Hearst telegram imbroglio. In those new hearings, Black left nothing to chance, or so he thought. Instead of calling well-known figures in the American Liberty League, such as Al Smith, John J. Raskob, or Pierre S. du Pont, he focused on the officers of smaller, and more vulnerable, allied organizations, such as the American Taxpayers League, the Crusaders, and the Farmers' Independence Council. By weaponizing the telegrams, Black still had a crucial advantage achieved through the use of what privacy scholars refer to as "asymmetrical knowledge." Because he had their private telegrams, and they usually did not, he could throw them off balance by asking about actions or statements described in these documents that had occurred months earlier.[44]

Committee members drew blood in the questioning of the most combative Vance Muse of the Southern Committee to Uphold the Constitution. Muse made several embarrassing admissions about his role in a "grass roots convention" in Macon, Georgia, in January 1936 to launch Democratic governor Eugene Talmadge's campaign against Roosevelt for the presidential nomination. Muse related that three leading donors to the American Liberty League—Pierre S. du Pont, Alfred P. Sloan of General Motors, and John J.

Raskob (also of the DuPont company)—had helped defray the costs of the event. Muse admitted that he had distributed copies of a picture at the rally of Eleanor Roosevelt being escorted by two black men during an appearance at Howard University in a ploy to inflame racial passions.[45]

Muse said that these donors did not have prior knowledge of this action, though Talmadge's racism in a general sense, of course, was no secret. Also troublesome to Black's critics, though somewhat less so, was information that Alexander Lincoln, president of the Sentinels of the Republic, had made anti-Semitic comments. Roosevelt had also privately expressed anti-Semitic and racist views and forged his own unsavory alliances with segregationists such as Senator Theodore G. Bilbo (D-MS), Senate Majority Leader Joe T. Robinson (D-AR), and Representative Rankin. Even so, the revelations unearthed by Black proved extremely damaging.[46]

The testimony of Kurt Grunwald of the Farmers' Independence Council, which received considerable publicity, was not as helpful to the committee. Black's goal was to spread the perception that outsiders funded the council and that it was not a genuine farmers' group. The main story of the day, however, was Grunwald's vigorous resistance. When Black asked him to name people who had aided his fight against the Agricultural Adjustment Act, Grunwald refused, saying he did not want to "get anybody into trouble." Black pressed further: Did he really believe that? Grunwald retorted, "You bet your boots. I'd get them in trouble under this New Deal." Senator Minton had no better luck with the witness. When he asked Grunwald about his citizenship status, Grunwald countered that he "expected that because we men of foreign birth have to go through hell sometimes with 100 percent Americans."[47]

Black made more progress with other witnesses representing the Farmers' Independence Council. He was able to highlight that some key donors to the group also had ties to the American Liberty League and that many nonfarmers were in the leadership. While an officer of the council later boasted to members that it had successfully shielded membership lists from the scrutiny of the "Black Inquisitorial Committee," he also lamented worsening "hand to mouth" finances. Echoing the concerns of the council's president, rancher Dan D. Casement stated that he feared that Black was making headway in branding the group as a "smoke screen" for big business.[48]

If Black scored some propaganda points, however, he also lost the aid of a crucial ally. To fend off a possible injunction against it, the FCC announced that any telegrams it had seized were now "in the possession of the Special Committee of the United States Senate." Moreover, it did not intend any "further investigation or examination" of telegrams at Western Union. An editorial in the *Washington Post* attributed the FCC's decision to "public outcry against the OGPU methods followed by Senator Black's investigators." Short of funds, and under fire, Black had no other choice but to announce that the committee had completed its "field investigations."[49]

The FCC's decision forced the Black Committee to retreat on future searches but also shielded it from direct legal sanctions. Chief Justice Wheat made this clear, conceding his helplessness to intervene because the seizures had stopped and Black had withdrawn the Hearst telegram subpoena, which had led to the suit in the first place. At the same time, the committee had already acquired a vast store of material from a year of investigation. This led columnist and Republican pundit Alice Roosevelt Longworth (the daughter of Theodore Roosevelt) to quip that Black's "snoopers up to their eyebrows in their booty" had to be satisfied with "the millions of trophies of their acquisitiveness; engaged in the congenial occupation of ferreting out other people's business."[50]

Undeterred, Hearst not only appealed the FCC's decision in the courts but demanded the return of all other seized telegrams. His newspapers continued to be as strident as ever. Not even the *Chicago Daily Tribune* (which represented the gold standard in anti–New Deal journalism) rivaled them in intensity and volume. A representative editorial charged that Black had become the "symbol of the modern American Inquisition." One of several cartoons showed a giant black keyhole captioned "Will the People allow the Light of Liberty to be swallowed up by Black?" Hearst's newspapers did not limit their salvos to editorials or cartoons. Resident poet Berton Braley also took part. On April 11, he wrote:

You may have thoughts

But you must not speak
Or you'll be summoned
By a New

Deal
Sneak![51]

On May 2, he returned to this theme:

> This is a country where speech is free
> And thoughts have absolute liberty
> Subject, of course, to the third degree
> By Senator Black's committee.[52]

Also writing in the Hearst press, Arthur "Bugs" Baer, one of the nation's best-known humorists, quipped: "If you see members of the Black Committee on the roof with bird dogs and scatter guns you will know Western Union and Postal Telegraphy are training carrier pigeons to take the place of messenger boys."[53]

A most unfamiliar bedfellow for Hearst in the fight against the Black Committee was the American Civil Liberties Union (ACLU). As early as March, it had released an open letter calling for the committee to return "improperly seized" telegrams. As he had with Lippmann, Black found it perplexing that he had to worry about his left flank. Replying to the head of the Kansas state chapter, he wondered why a group claiming "to protect the masses of the people from loss of their economic and political liberty" had aligned itself with those who valued "property" over "human" rights. The ACLU renewed its campaign against the committee after news reports that the National Woman's Party, led by equal rights crusader Alice Paul, was on the target list. ACLU executive director Roger N. Baldwin queried Black as to why he was probing an organization that had nothing to do with utility legislation. Black evaded an answer, pleading that it was improper to give details in a case where subpoenas were pending. After emphasizing that the committee's procedure did not depart from time-worn American traditions, Black added, somewhat ominously, that he was "sure that upon mature consideration, you will wish to withdraw your request for information."[54]

The conflict culminated in a fiery exchange in letters between Senator Minton and New York ACLU attorney Dudley Field Malone. Minton demanded, "Who are you to lecture me on my duties? When we reach the point in this country where there is nobody left but you and William Randolph

Hearst to defend our liberties, we had better give the country back to the Indians." Uncowed, Malone promised that millions of Americans would fight against "you and the Black committee's effort to invade the private affairs of citizens."[55]

The combined impact of the Strawn decision, the Hearst telegram, and the FCC's withdrawal of support even prompted some longtime New Dealers, notably US Representatives Emanuel Celler (D-NY) and John McCormack (D-MA), to break ranks with Black. A lightning rod was a vote to pay for counsel to defend the committee against Hearst's appeal. No less controversial was the fact that the counsel in question was Black's former law partner, Crampton Harris of Birmingham, Alabama. Celler was relentless: "Commandeering private papers by the ton cannot be excused by the assertion that private wires are no longer private if they refer to public matters." To Celler, Black's release of the telegram to McSwain showed that wholesale subpoenas "can be made an instrument of oppression." The names or reputations of those targeted were beside the point, Celler argued. He did not care whether it was a Strawn or Hearst; the committee had no right to examine five million telegrams. Celler went so far as to compare Black to Benito Mussolini and King George III in his use of espionage. If the Senate was not going to sanction Black, he asserted, it was up to the House to give him "a rap across the knuckles."[56]

In more restrained rhetoric, McCormack faulted the committee's disrespect for rights and smearing of "the character and reputation of others, whether Members of this House or humblest citizens of the United States." Nevertheless, McCormack supported paying Harris, but only to get clarification from the courts on Congress's power to examine "papers and effects" in investigations. Yet again, one of the few members to rise in Black's defense was Representative Rankin, who lauded the committee for doing "more for the American people than any other investigating committee I have ever known."[57]

In the Senate, it was pretty much left to members of the Black Committee to carry the water for the proposal. As usual, Minton went on the attack, saying that denial of the funds was tantamount to giving aid and comfort to the American Liberty League, "whose pockets are lined with the blood money of the munitions manufacturers." He elaborated that the framers of the First Amendment never intended to protect communications between a newspaper owner and subordinates. The investigation was a legitimate means, according to Minton, to find out if Strawn had tried to influence the Reconstruction Finance Corporation during the Hoover administration to get a loan for the Dawes Bank of Chicago. No such evidence of any influence was uncovered. The final US House vote on the bill to deny the funds for paying Crampton (153 to 137) was a stunning rebuke to the Black Committee. The *Chicago Daily News* celebrated that the House had stymied Black's attempt to "secure a fat fee for his former law partner" and added that the senator's record of defending individual rights was "as dark as his surname."[58]

Following on the heels of the vote, the American Newspaper Publishers Association's committee on free speech excoriated the Black Committee for waging "a campaign of persecution and harassment against individuals, organizations and newspapers which have in any manner criticized or opposed the policies of the present national administration." Despite the Black Committee's claims of objective truth-seeking, the real purpose was to "punish any who presume to exercise their rights of citizenship." Continuing his line of attack from the Strawn case, Lippmann castigated the initial seizure of the Hearst telegram as a "plain outrage," not just against the "freedom of the press but against the freedom of all individuals."[59]

A few voices linked their critique of Black's methods to his alleged ties to the Ku Klux Klan. After he was on the Supreme Court, Black admitted past membership, but at this point his involvement was just the stuff of rumors. The *Chicago Daily Tribune* was the most prominent in bringing it up. In February 1936, Arthur Sears Henning reported that "[s]ome said" that Black had belonged to "that secret organization of persecution," which was as dreaded as "the Black committee today." Regarding the questionnaires sent out in January, an editorial speculated that Black had not quizzed about the KKK "because it elected him in Alabama and he knows too much about it." Even more pointedly, the front page that day featured a cartoon showing a group of hooded night riders. In the lead was "Senator Black of Alabama," carrying a banner titled "Black Inquisition."[60]

By this time, Black's main defenders came from the most reliably progressive wing of the New Deal coalition. Referring to the Strawn injunction, Paul W. Ward of the *Nation* predicted that if "this thing keeps up, it will not be necessary for Congress to have these privateers-men [sic] thrown out of the court; they'll be laughed out." These arguments were most persuasive, albeit in a purely negative way, when they underlined the hypocrisy on the other side. Hence, the *Progressive* editorialized that those "forever defending 'constitutional liberties' for the fat boys" did not care about the violations of free speech under criminal syndicalism laws and other restrictions on the poor and vulnerable. Typically, these voices characterized the American Newspaper Publishers Association's crusade for free speech as a ploy by big metropolitan dailies to mask "greed and selfish aims."[61]

The committee's most powerful champion was Roosevelt himself, although he carefully avoided tipping his hand in public. On April 14, Black's name figured prominently in a private discussion with Secretary of the Interior Harold Ickes about possible picks to chair a new Special Senate Committee to Investigate Campaign Expenditures of Presidential, Vice Presidential, and Senatorial Candidates. According to Ickes, Roosevelt laid out two options. The first was to "name a perfectly respectable Senator as chairman, one who stood pretty well in public opinion," and the second was to choose Black backed by "a vigorous, aggressive chief investigator." Senate leaders apparently did not agree, and Augustine Lonergan (D-CT), a conservative freshman who had voted against the death sentence, got the nod.[62]

Roosevelt referred more specifically to the Black Committee at a meeting on May 3 as recorded by former "Brain Truster" Raymond Moley. In the midst of a "nightmarish conversation [that] went on and on in circles for some two hours," Moley opined that he preferred letting the guilty "go free than to establish the principle of dragnet investigations." He bluntly asked Roosevelt a question: where was the president's "moral indignation" when Black's Committee had "ruthlessly invaded the privacy of citizens?" Roosevelt responded with "a long discourse of how Black's invasion of privacy had ample precedent." The inference drawn by Moley was that for Roosevelt "the end justified the means." The conversation left Moley "with the harrowing intimation that Roosevelt was looking forward to nothing more than having the opposition of his 'enemies'—the newspapers, the bankers, the businessmen—reelect him."[63]

Although Minton and others talked periodically in the next few months about resuming the deliberations, the committee never met again under Black's chairmanship. In June 1936, the Senate bypassed the House by voting to pay Harris's fee from its own funds but showed no appetite for more investigations. Black's methods, while sometimes digging up dirt on anti–New Dealers, had proved too toxic. Moreover, even if the committee had tried to continue, and had the funds, Justice Wheat's ruling in the Strawn case (made permanent on June 25) had removed its main leverage over witnesses. The Black Committee was not completely forgotten in the final months before the election, however. In an obvious reference, the Republican Party National Platform charged that New Dealers had bullied "witnesses and interfered with the right of petition" through "investigations to harass and intimidate American citizens." But, in the end, Republicans rarely returned to the issue in the campaign. Black himself had moved on to other concerns as one of the leaders of an effort to rally progressive voters for Roosevelt.[64]

Although as late as July, two Gallup polls showed Alf Landon winning, electoral trends were very much in Roosevelt's favor. Signs of economic improvement, Landon's lackluster campaign, and adept funneling of patronage and funds to doubtful states bolstered the confidence of Roosevelt's advisers. Few of them took seriously the *Literary Digest*'s now infamous poll showing a Landon victory, and all three major preelection commercial polls predicted otherwise. On November 4, Roosevelt's historic landslide victory, carrying every state but Maine and Vermont, brought with it an even more lopsided Democratic congressional majority.[65]

The absence of public opinion polling on the Black Committee makes it hard to gauge its impact, if any, on the campaign. To be sure, the committee's methods produced some headaches for the administration in Congress and trouble with civil libertarians. On the positive side of the ledger for Roosevelt, it had successfully spread the view that the main anti–New Deal organizations represented a small cabal of big business interests. The committee, by calling into question the reputations of those targeted for investigation, had a chilling effect on criticism. An illustrative case was the Farmers' Independence Council, which never overcame the stigma that it was just a front for big business. As the election approached, the same Kurt Grunwald, who had a few months earlier dramatically refused to name names, reported that the Republican Party wanted to distance itself because of the council's growing reputation as a cat's-paw of the American Liberty League. Meanwhile, the league's own executive committee was so fearful of harming the GOP that it suspended formal operations for the last five weeks of the campaign.[66]

The post-election decision of the United States Court of Appeals of the District of Columbia in the Hearst case on November 9 gave only mixed solace, at least in the short term, to Black Committee foes. The court blasted the FCC for sanctioning a "wholesale" examination of telegrams and then turning these over to the Black Committee "without authority of law and contrary to the very terms of the act under which the Commission was constituted." It declared that "telegraph messages do not lose their privacy and become public property when the sender communicates them confidentially to the telegraph company," elaborating that in many states it was a "penal offense" to violate this privacy. The court also affirmed that it had jurisdiction over the FCC's actions. The final decision, however, was essentially the same as the one by the lower court in holding that there was no constitutional basis to assert jurisdiction over a congressional committee despite the "unlawful nature of the search." But Minton's proclamation that there was "nothing in the decree to keep us from subpoenaing all the telegrams we want" also missed the mark. Both the Strawn and Hearst rulings stood as important precedents against any future mass seizure of private telegrams by a congressional committee.[67]

Press reaction to the ruling was sparse, no doubt because it did not impose sanctions for past actions and because Roosevelt's landslide dominated the news. Nevertheless, a few prominent media voices spoke up. An editorial in the *Washington Post*, for example, praised the court's repudiation of the Black Committee's "wholesale seizure of private telegrams … one of the blackest chapters in the history of legislative fishing expeditions." The release of Hearst's telegram to Williams, the *Post* charged, had represented "the tactics of fascism" and was "utterly at variance with the American principle of freedom from promiscuous governmental snooping." It accurately predicted that the court had effectively killed off any resumption of the hearings, at least in their current form.[68]

The Court of Appeal's prohibition of wholesale examination of telegrams put new roadblocks in the way of any future investigations. It meant that hostile witnesses were much better able to shield private information from congressional committees, though, in some cases, the price might be a few months of jail time. The practice of "ambushing" witnesses with their own private comments also became more difficult. The record of later high-profile investigations illustrates the contrast.[69]

Few works have examined, at least in any detailed way, the Black Committee as an engine of surveillance. Historians of the New Deal era, when they mention it at all, have also shied away from analogies to the red-hunting investigations that came after it. In his multivolume work on the period, for example, Arthur M. Schlesinger Jr. contends that while Black's questioning was often "harsh," he never tried to "slander reputations, drag in innocent persons, or indulge in promiscuous character assassination" or inquire into opinions. Schlesinger agrees with US Supreme Court Chief Justice Earl Warren that after World War II "there appeared a new kind of congressional inquiry unknown in prior periods of American history." Putting the committee in an even more positive light, legal scholars William A. Gregory and Rennard Strickland assert that "only bitter partisans could accuse Black of a witch hunt."[70]

Several prominent historians, however, have dissented from this view. William E. Leuchtenburg favorably quotes political scientist Earl Latham's observation that "Senator Black in 1936 was the kind of legislator that Justice Black had no use for twenty years later." Roger K. Newman, one of Black's biographers, concludes that a hatred of big business "caused him to trample over witness's rights protected by the Fourth Amendment. He used to the fullest the investigatory powers of Congress ... but directed them only toward hard-core conservatives. If they had been aimed at the other end of the spectrum, he would have been the first to howl at the infringement of constitutional rights." Despite the many differences between Black and Senator Joseph McCarthy, Michael Czaplicki aptly observes that "they were linked by a faith in the unchecked power of congressional investigating committees." Czaplicki emphasizes the clash between Black's goal of transparency in the service of the New Deal agenda and constitutional protections of privacy: Black's "desire to eliminate mediators between state and citizen threatened to allow no concept of a private sphere free from the state ... [and] could easily infringe on individual rights."[71]

In subsequent years, Supreme Court Justice Black himself came to have second thoughts about his Senate investigative record. His judicial opinions in the 1950s and 1960s, backing the rights of witnesses to withhold private information, such as donor and membership lists, and for limiting the contempt power, were directly at odds with his record as a senator. He even expressed regret for initially brushing aside Walter Lippmann's critique, which, in retrospect, struck him as "wholly reasonable." Even so, Black continued to defend his lobbying investigation as essentially valid.[72]

By some measures, the Black Committee posed a greater threat to individual rights than the "witch hunts" of the 1940s or 1950s because it enjoyed comparatively vast powers of mass surveillance. Ironically, one of the reasons why the Black Committee did not leave a deeper impression in history was that the courts precluded successor committees from using the FCC to examine private telegrams in a similarly wholesale way. This precedent, however, was not the only factor keeping Congress from revisiting anything akin to blanket telecommunications surveillance. As Frederick S. Lane comments, the Black Committee's "excesses [had] made people more sensitive, at least temporarily, to the potential abuses of legislative committees."[73]

Indicative of this new sensitivity, though Congress was not involved, were two key Supreme Court rulings limiting surveillance over telephone communication. In *Nardone v. U.S.* (1937), followed up by *Nardone v. U.S.* (1939), it ruled that wiretaps were inadmissible as evidence in the federal courts. The decisions rested on Section 605 of the Federal Communications Act of 1934, which stated that "no person" could "intercept and divulge" a "communication by wire or radio" without authorization of the "sender." The court's application of the law's "plain words" (words, incidentally, that did not explicitly mention telephone communication) probably went beyond anything that Congress had intended when drafting this provision. While *Hearst v. Black* had also quoted Section 605, which did, after all, specify "wire or radio," the rationales for the decision centered on more generic questions of trespass.[74]

Later court rulings, and more importantly presidential directives, loosened the standards for national security cases, but *Nardone v. U.S.* continued to be the guiding precedent. Although telegram use was already on the wane (declining from about 50 percent of long-distance communication in 1931 to only 23 percent to 1940), wiretapping never approximated in extent the surveillance used by the Black Committee. In testimony to Congress in the 1940s and 1950s, J. Edgar Hoover stated that at any particular time, the FBI had between 50 and 200 telephone taps (all for national security cases) and a smaller number of microphone bugs. He did not, of course, report that the FBI was also carrying out an undetermined number of illegal eavesdrops through "black bag" operations. Understandably, neither Hoover nor his superiors had any interest in sharing the fruits of their surveillance, authorized or not, with congressional committees.[75]

On a wide range of issues, including privacy, surveillance, and the rights of congressional witnesses, the Black Committee represented an important turning point in the history of congressional investigations. While Black never suffered anything approaching a "have you no shame" Joseph Welch moment, he had unintentionally established a legal standard that constrained his successors. Later congressional committees did not possess this kind of surveillance power, whether of telegrams or other forms of private communication. The course of history might have been quite different if the anti-Communist committees of later decades had enjoyed similarly broad search and seizure authority.

Comparisons between the Black and McCarthy committees, however, fall short in one major respect: the contrast in the origin story and demise of each. The Black Committee was first and foremost a creature of Roosevelt's wish to establish a congressional committee to discredit opponents. After the president had made that decision, he sought out Black, a loyal political foot soldier, to take charge. McCarthy, by contrast, was the quintessential independent actor who was both oblivious to, and contemptuous of, the priorities of presidents or congressional leaders. Without his notorious, and entirely self-generated, speech in Wheeling, West Virginia, he would have continued as an obscure junior senator.

Black's investigation ended because the president no longer needed it, while McCarthy's ended because, in great part, President Eisenhower intervened in a hostile way. Shorn of power, McCarthy moved on to obscurity, while Black's patron rewarded him with a seat on the US Supreme Court. When political events once again conspired against Roosevelt in late 1937, however, the president was instrumental in establishing, and then actively aiding, a second investigation, this time led by a protégé of Black.

2

The Minton Committee: An Anti–Free Speech Bridge Too Far

FEW PERIODS BROUGHT a more rapid shift in American free-speech history than the two years following Roosevelt's reelection, though he did not intend that result. His main influence in making this possible was his response to a series of unpredictable events. The president's second term began with three months of uninterrupted triumph followed by interludes of confusion, embattlement, false starts, several high-profile setbacks, an economic dip, and finally a determination to retaliate. The Special Committee to Investigate Lobbying Activities, this time under Black's successor, Senator Sherman Minton (D-IN), was a leading component in this strategy of retaliation. The goal of the new chairman was to strike hard against Roosevelt's enemies, most notably officers of the National Committee to Uphold Constitutional Government (NCUCG). The Minton Committee's heavy-handed methods, however, produced widespread anger, thanks, in part, to the machinations of an all-too-obviously partisan chair. Rather than protecting and advancing the New Deal as intended, its actions had the opposite effect.

At the beginning of 1937, FDR had no reason to anticipate these unhappy events. His resounding landslide in 1936 brought lopsided congressional majorities in both Houses. He appeared to have the broadest of mandates. Roosevelt said as much in a post-election article he dictated for *Collier's* under the byline of presidential adviser George Creel: "It was the nation that spoke through the voice of an overwhelming majority and [Roosevelt] holds that what this voice declared and imposed was the national will."[1]

On the surface, Roosevelt enjoyed even more freedom of action than in the emergency period of the first 100 days. Naysayers appeared helpless to prevent a Third New Deal if Roosevelt wanted one, and want one he apparently did. One clue that this was true was his election-eve proclamation at Madison Square Garden: "I should like to have it said of my first Administration that in it the forces of selfishness and of lust for power met their match. I should like to have it said of my second Administration that in it these forces met their master." Roosevelt had foreshadowed this attitude, however, months earlier when he confided to Secretary of the Treasury Henry Morgenthau Jr.: "Wait until next year, Henry, I am really going to be really radical. ... I am going to recommend a lot of radical legislation."[2]

The origins of the Minton Committee stemmed directly from several administration setbacks for this "radical" strategy. The most important of these was the Senate's rejection of FDR's plan to boost the size of the Supreme Court and thus install a pro-administration majority. The president had long regarded the court as the main obstacle to his agenda of protecting and expanding the New Deal. In his second term, it threatened to make the passage of a wages and hours bill and other initiatives exercises in futility. To neutralize this threat, the president asked the Senate to give him the power to appoint up to six new justices for each one over age seventy, thus boosting the court's size from nine to as high as fifteen.[3]

In the vanguard of the opposition to Roosevelt's scheme was the National Committee to Uphold Constitutional Government (NCUCG). Created in February 1937 just days after the unveiling of the court-packing proposal, it had a large war chest and some powerful sponsors. The founders were publisher Frank Gannett, who paid the bills, Amos Pinchot, a well-known civil libertarian and anti-war activist, and Edward A. Rumely. Rumely was a publisher, a former Bull Mooser, and the head of a company that manufactured tractors and other farm equipment. Among the politically diverse members were journalist Dorothy Thompson, civil-libertarian John Haynes Holmes, Pulitzer Prize–winning novelist Booth Tarkington, publisher S. S. McClure, and historian James Truslow Adams. The energetic Rumely ran day-to-day operations. The mailing list of the NCUCG, specifically conceived as a leadership-centered organization, included 161,000 lawyers, 137,000 ministers, 23,000 farmers, and 121,000 doctors.[4]

A cornerstone of the NCUCG's strategy against court packing was to urge members to deluge doubtful senators with telegrams and phone calls. Before the controversy was over, the group had sent out over ten million mailings charging that court packing gave Roosevelt, or a successor, unbridled power that verged on dictatorship. As daily headlines blared the intrigues of real-life dictators, such as Hitler and Mussolini, this resonated even with many normally supportive of the administration. In making its case, the NCUCG tailored its message to appeal across political, racial, occupational, and class lines. For example, Gannett related a conversation with his barber, who said, "I am a Jew, and therefore one of a minority. I realize that if it were not for the Supreme Court, I might be treated here as they treat the Jews in Germany!" Gannett concluded: "Members of the colored race must feel the same, for the Supreme Court, again and again has protected the rights of colored people." When the Senate effectively killed court packing on July 31, 1937, Gannett and Rumely justly claimed much of the credit.[5]

The NCUCG was on a roll. Only a few weeks after the defeat of court packing, it was instrumental in torpedoing the Black-Connery bill to restore some of the wages and hours provisions of the National Industrial Recovery Act. In a targeted effort to sway key Republicans in Congress, Gannett reported that he had "sent long telegrams to every state [Republican] committeeman and every national committeeman and did a lot of telephoning." Had FDR pushed Black-Connery in February, he would have probably prevailed, but the successful mobilization against court packing had emboldened his critics. The defeat of the bill in July gave FDR no respite. Even the appointment of Hugo L. Black (the coauthor of Black-Connery) to the US Supreme Court soon became tainted after confirmation of allegations that he had belonged to the Klan.[6]

As his defeats began to pile up, Roosevelt's relations with the press worsened even more. Newspaper scrutiny of the administration, observes historian Gary Dean Best, had "lifted the 'curtain' and exposed Roosevelt's hidden intentions through thousands of words in editorials and columns." According to Richard W. Steele, Roosevelt's "once 'private' quarrel [with the press] now took on the aspect of a publicity campaign aimed at discrediting the press. His message seemed to be—recognize newspaper owners as your enemies and do not trust what you read in your papers." Negative press commentary on Roosevelt's program became more pronounced than ever. Walter Lippmann, a prominent civil libertarian, who had often championed New Deal reform measures, accused Roosevelt of plotting to "muzzle the press as he would like to pack the court. In the quest for power one thing leads to another and the incredible soon comes to be regarded as necessary and then accepted as inevitable."[7]

These political setbacks put Roosevelt increasingly in a mood for reprisals. Shortly after the defeat of Black-Connery, a supportive article in the *Nation* warned that "when Mr. Roosevelt hates, he hates deeply and vengefully. The President never forgets an affront or injury." His contempt for the newspapers came more out into the open. At a press conference in August 1937, the president testily lectured the reporters: "I understand. You fellows are placed in such a position very often. … We can talk about it in the family and off the record. I can appreciate what you are told to write … it does not take away, in any way, from my affection for the group of you."[8]

In August 1937, the Minton Committee came to life in this toxic political environment with a private meeting in the chair's office. The original members carried over from the long-moribund Black Committee with one new addition: Senator Theodore F. Green (D-RI), who fortified Minton and Senator Schwellenbach in the zealously pro–New Deal majority. The committee's equally ideological chief investigator, H. A. Blomquist, confided to Minton that his overriding goal was to further "the advancement of the New Deal's objectives."[9]

New Dealers seemed to have found an ideal champion in Sherman Minton. As a biographer later put it, his loyalty to the president and his agenda, "uncommon even among fellow true-believers," included a "strong strain of populism, and belief that government must be powerful." Though still a freshman, Minton was moving up fast, so much so that Senate Democratic Leader Joe T. Robinson (D-AR) made him assistant majority whip. In effect, he became Robinson's right-hand man to take the slack from the rather desultory Majority Whip, J. Hamilton Lewis. At age 46, Minton brought dynamism and determination to a Democratic congressional leadership that had an average age of 66. A profile in *Nation's Business* stressed his eagerness "to take on some of the harder and meaner chores of the Administration forces which the elder senators wanted to shun." Nobody in Congress more energetically pushed court packing than Minton. It was he, not Robinson, who was the de facto leader of that fight. A grateful Roosevelt asked him to fill the first available Supreme Court slot. Minton demurred because he wanted to stay in the Senate, and the job went to Black.[10]

At first, the Minton Committee flew under the radar, generating only scant press coverage. A rare mention came in a column by the pro–New Deal duo, Drew Pearson and Robert S. Allen. They touted the committee as "the toughest aggregation on Capitol Hill," led by the president's "no. 1 senatorial shock trooper." Pearson and Allen reported that "administration master minds" were cheering on Minton's hunt for the "Big Game," which had played a major "behind-the-scenes role in defeating the President's Supreme Court bill and stymying the wage-hour measure." These same insiders anticipated "sensational disclosures," courtesy of the committee's corps of "sleuths," likely to "boomerang" against enemies of the New Deal. Committee staffers gathered up every scrap of paper they could find concerning groups opposed to such administration proposals as court packing and Black-Connery. The main unanswered question was the identity of those to be targeted in hearings for the spring.[11]

In December 1937, Roosevelt affirmed his confidence in the Minton Committee by inviting all three Democratic members to an eight-man "council of war" to plot strategy for 1938. The apparent prerequisite for inclusion was down-the-line loyalty to the president, especially on such hot button issues as court packing and Black-Connery. Minton articulated the group's consensus by recommending a fighting stance. "The opposition isn't satisfied with a conciliatory attitude," he declared. "The only thing they understand is a swift kick where it hurts." He urged a "crack down" on the taxes of the rich and resubmission of the wages and hours bill. Roosevelt was more than receptive, chiming in, "We have just begun to fight."[12]

Meanwhile, the administration was shifting its priorities from old fights to the reorganization bill. The Minton Committee followed suit. Like court packing, Roosevelt's original plan for reorganizing the federal government was sweeping and ambitious. Prepared primarily by progressive reformers Louis Brownlow, Luther Gulick, and Charles Merriam, the goal was, in the words of historian Charles Schilke, to implement "continuous central planning and program coordination." A friendly observer from the *New Republic* went so far as to conclude that reorganization would empower the president to "do almost anything that came into his head." Unfortunately for the proponents of the plan, daily reminders of Hitler's and Stalin's stepped-up persecution of dissenters stoked up fears about giving Roosevelt more power. When the original plan was presented to a select group of senators, their response was so hostile that the administration clumsily put it under wraps. A significantly watered-down reorganization bill came too late to appease the skeptics.[13]

A major blow to the bill's prospects was the economic plunge, sometimes called Depression II or the Roosevelt Recession. In ten months, beginning in the fall of 1937, industrial production fell over 30 percent and stock prices by 50 percent. The GDP shrank precipitously as joblessness spiked to over four million. The economy continued to sputter for over a year. Letters to Roosevelt from Americans repeatedly complained about his preoccupation with reorganization during economic hard times. "I cannot pay my bills," one said. "We had confidence in you but that confidence is fading."[14]

After some hesitation, the NCUCG, fresh off its victories over court packing and Black-Connery, launched a campaign against the reorganization bill. Its strategy was to target members of Congress in marginal districts with a barrage of telegrams and letters. NCUCG leaders cleverly ignored the revised plan and concentrated fire on the original version. In an open letter to Roosevelt, Amos Pinchot of the NCUCG dismissed "the various reorganization bills" then under consideration as not indicative of the administration's true intent. "I am discussing only your bill," Pinchot declared, "written for you by Messrs. Brownlow, Gulick and Merriam ... providing for unparalleled changes in a nation's government." To Pinchot, Roosevelt's past support for the old wording ruled out any reason to trust him.[15]

An informal lobby centered on the Forest Service was mobilizing against the bill for reasons of its own. The main motivation was to oppose the transfer of that agency from the Department of Agriculture to the Department of the Interior. The ranks of the Forest Service lobby included lumber interests, individual foresters, and conservationist organizations, such as the Izaak Walton League. They had a mutual distrust of Ickes because of his administrative style, lack of knowledge of Western problems as an urban Midwesterner, and tendency to seek after bureaucratic empires. Unlike that of the NCUCG, which relied on swaying diverse opinion leaders, the Forest Service lobby's method was to mobilize organizations at the local and state levels. It did not have a distinct ideological basis and included more than a few who otherwise backed the New Deal. Illustrating this ideological diversity was the leadership role in it of Gifford Pinchot, progressive Republican governor of Pennsylvania and famous Bull Moose advocate of conservation. In fighting reorganization, he cooperated closely with his brother, Amos Pinchot of the NCUCG.[16]

The self-described "spark plug" of the Forest Service lobby was Charles G. Dunwoody, "a hearty, affable, go-getter." A cousin of Theodore Roosevelt, Dunwoody had repeatedly proven his organizational and improvisational mettle by such actions as putting together a successful private brigade to fight forest fires. He came to Washington in 1937 to lobby on behalf of the California Chamber of Commerce and quickly jumped into the reorganization fight. He was battling the bill even before the NCUCG had taken a position and had deployed the Chamber's "Reorganization Fund" of $11,000 to lobby on Capitol Hill. Working closely with Gifford Pinchot, Dunwoody used his charms on members of Congress, many of whom knew him well and respected his knowledge of forest issues. Pinchot wrote in November 1937 that "pretty much all the Senators from the Western states, which have National Forests, are against Huffy Harold [Ickes] and his buccaneering plans." Pinchot considered the prospects for derailing the bill to be "excellent, thanks to Dunwoody."[17]

In setting out to bag "big game," Minton had a fast friend in journalist Paul Y. Anderson. A Pulitzer Prize winner (for investigative stories on Teapot Dome), he had a well-established reputation for intrepid reporting and memorable prose. Although H. L. Mencken often differed with Anderson politically, he praised him as "one of the finest journalists in the country." Anderson kept alive the muckraking tradition through his work for Joseph Pulitzer II's *St. Louis Post-Dispatch* as well as the *Nation*. Before 1938, Anderson had shown himself to be an ideological soulmate for Minton, ready to be of service to the New Deal agenda. In 1935 and 1936, for example, Anderson had provided active aid to the New Deal majority, including Minton, on the Black Committee. At the time, *Editor and Publisher* had reported that during the hearings of that committee, Anderson had passed helpful notes to members or gave pointers "in a half-whisper easily heard by investigators." When Black took his seat on the Supreme Court, once of his first acts was to invite Anderson to lunch in his chambers. During the same period, Roosevelt regarded Anderson as an "old friend" and a "grand fellow." In February 1938, however, Anderson lost his job with the *Post-Dispatch* because of a chronic drinking problem and absenteeism. Quickly hired by the *St. Louis Star-Times*, he showed a new burst of energy in early March by digging up information to help the Minton Committee investigation.[18]

Dunwoody was the focal point of Anderson's first articles for the *Star-Times*. He even called him the "generalissimo of the elements opposing the bill," but this was an exaggeration. Although Dunwoody was a key player in the Forest Service lobby, his influence did not extend much beyond that realm. Perhaps unintentionally, he may have conveyed a different impression to Anderson by boasting that he was coordinating the efforts of 251 "key men" in organizations and agencies. Anderson (who smelled a major scoop) was more than ready to amplify this depiction and become fixated on Dunwoody's role.[19]

The powers that be at the *St. Louis Star-Times* exuberantly featured Anderson's revelations under front-page banner headlines. "The disclosure by the Star-Times today," Anderson informed the paper's readers, "is likely to result in a congressional investigation. If that happens, some of the highest hats on Capitol Hill may be blown off in the resulting gale." The next day he reiterated that "the bitter fight against the President's government reorganization bill is being directed from behind the scenes here by Charles G. Dunwoody, high-pressure lobbyist from California."[20]

Soon thereafter, Minton (and Anderson) closed in for the kill (or so they thought). As Dunwoody exited the office of Senator Key Pittman (D-NV), Anderson pointed him out to Committee Chief Inspector Blomquist, who served a subpoena that commanded him to appear in the morning and to "produce all records, papers, letters, memoranda, books, accounting records and documents in your possession which relate in any way to efforts to influence, suppress, or foment public opinion, or to influence or defeat federal legislation, or to influence public contracts, activities or concessions." A committee staffer escorted Dunwoody to his hotel room to search for any records. Anderson quoted a committee investigator that the result had netted evidence that "fully substantiated" accounts of Dunwoody's activities "as described in the Star-Times."[21]

Despite this dramatic prelude, Minton called off Dunwoody's testimony only hours before his scheduled appearance. Minton said nothing about why this happened, aside from a curt announcement that the committee had determined that Dunwoody's activities were "not important." This was not persuasive. While Anderson had overplayed Dunwoody's grand ringmaster status, he was undeniably significant. Minton's own staff had admitted as much only a day before disinviting him.[22]

Many years later, Dunwoody gave his own, quite fascinating, version of what had occurred between his subpoena and scheduled appearance. In an interview with historian Amelia R. Fry in 1966, he recalled that after getting served by Blomquist, he had headed over to the offices of Senator Pittman, a political ally, and Secretary of Agriculture Henry A. Wallace. Wallace had initially opposed reorganization for understandable bureaucratic reasons. Dunwoody flatly told both that he was going to appear before the committee in the morning to "tell the truth, and somebody was going to get hurt." He promised to reveal how members of Congress had offered him "all sorts of special attention if I'd get certain of their people a job in this, that, or the other thing, asking for a bribe almost" and that he had the documentary evidence to prove it.[23]

According to Dunwoody's account, Pittman carried this news back to Minton, appending his own prediction that the testimony in the morning would "blow the lid off the Capitol." This new development prompted Minton to make a midnight phone call to Dunwoody to tell him that he no longer had to appear. Sensing that the committee was on the defensive, Dunwoody demanded that his testimony go forward as originally scheduled and vowed to tell the whole truth. Soon after the call ended, a messenger arrived with a $1,500 check to fight the reorganization bill made out to Dunwoody from the "American Nazi Party." Suspecting a frame-up to smear him as subversive, Dunwoody strolled into Minton's office that morning, put the check on the table, and said he wanted credit for turning it in. He then asked, "Senator, when does the hearing start?" Minton repeated that the committee had canceled the hearing and that, apparently, was the end of that.[24]

In his interview with Fry, Dunwoody also alleged that Ickes (working with Minton) had sent detectives to tail him. He tried to throw his pursuers off balance by asking them to share his cab to save money. He added, "They searched my wastebaskets, broke in at night and searched my files." Dunwoody also claimed that someone from the Department of the Interior sent a woman to his hotel room to try to put him in a compromising situation. Dunwoody's charges are almost impossible to verify. Minton's papers do not survive from the period, and the records of the Department of the Interior, as well as Harold Ickes's diary, have nothing to say about such machinations, though Ickes's disdain for Dunwoody was well known. Dunwoody mentioned to Fry that he would discuss all of this in his "memoirs," but no copy of that manuscript has surfaced. Nevertheless, something of substance must have happened to prompt Minton to drop such a promising lead.[25]

One day after Minton's forced retreat on Dunwoody, the committee had almost entirely shifted its priorities to the NCUCG. It seemed to have had a trump card: Rumely had served time in a federal prison on charges of aiding Germany during World War I. These legal troubles had arisen from his decision in 1915 to borrow funds from an American citizen then living in Germany to purchase the *New York Evening Mail* as an intended voice for the Bull Moose (Progressive) movement. Rumely later claimed that he did not know that all such loans had to be funneled through the German government. Nor, he emphasized, was the United States in the war at the time. After the declaration of war, the federal government prosecuted Rumely under the Trading with the Enemy Act for taking money from the German government. Rumely was convicted and, after several appeals, went to prison in 1923. In 1924, the Coolidge administration commuted the sentence after most of the jurors and the prosecutor recommended leniency.[26]

Blomquist and Minton did not concern themselves with such nuances. "We have a convicted felon, aiding and abetting the enemy in time of war," Blomquist exulted to Minton, "now masquerading as an 'Upholder of Constitutional Government.' A public airing of … this … would unquestionably result in a different interpretation of the aims and purposes of this honorable Committee to Uphold Constitutional Government."[27]

The next morning Blomquist and an assistant arrived at the NCUCG's New York offices with a sweeping subpoena *duces tecum*. It commanded Rumely not only to appear before the committee in the morning but to produce "all records, papers, letters, memoranda, books, accounting records, and documents in your possession, or under your control, which in any way relate to efforts to influence or suppress or foment public sentiment, or to influence the passage or defeat of Federal legislation, or to influence public contracts, activities, or concessions." Acting under this broad mandate, Blomquist and his staff proceeded to go through file drawers and copy any document considered to be useful. A perturbed Rumely rushed to his office to call his lawyer, Elisha Hanson, a veteran of many battles of this type. Hanson had represented William Randolph Hearst in the telegram case in 1936 and was counsel to the American Newspaper Association. When Rumely returned, he told the searchers that on advice of his lawyer, he was ordering them out. The search had lasted less than an hour.[28]

When Rumely appeared before the committee in the morning, Minton, as expected, asked for the subpoenaed documents. Rumely, as also expected, refused, blasting the probe as an unconstitutional "fishing expedition" and said it was his "understanding that you must be specific and not just walk into an office to get everything in a man's place." After pressing perfunctorily a bit more, Minton's main allies, Green and Schwellenbach, lowered the boom: "[B]ecause of your unpatriotic activities weren't you indicted and convicted?" Not satisfied with Rumely's answer that he was innocent of the charge, which he attributed to "war feeling," Schwellenbach piled on. Minton finally moved in to finish the job by quoting the legal charges from the court record that Rumely had conspired to defraud the government by preventing it "from seizing and administering a certain indebtedness of the defendant Rumely to the German imperial government." After Rumely quipped that he was "standing on a fundamental American right," Minton retorted, "O, yes? I used to hear lawyers plead the same grounds in defense of bootleggers."[29]

If Minton had prepared carefully, so too had Rumely, who went all out to turn the tables. "Gesturing broadly," wrote Anderson, "half-rising from the witness stand, and frequently addressing himself direct to the press table, the 'Doctor' continued to spout." From a different perspective, Amos Pinchot said that Rumely had "kept his head, was good natured, and by his personality … put the OGPU on the defensive." With his lawyer Elisha Hanson at his side, Rumely pointed out that Coolidge had commuted his sentence. He also stressed that his *New York Evening Mail* had defended neutral rights against both sides equally and stressed his cordial relationship with Theodore Roosevelt at the time. Rumely added that "[a] great many things happen in this country … whenever a crowd gets dominant and tries to beat down the opposition." He dared the members to go over to the Library of Congress and find anything unpatriotic in the editorials in the *Evening Mail* from the period. After more verbal fencing, Minton asked the question again but, as before, Rumely changed the subject. "Do not give me that," Minton answered. "I do not want that kind of an answer. Will you produce it [the subpoenaed papers] or won't you?"[30]

Score one for Rumely. In the aftermath of this confrontation, momentum in the press and the Congress was beginning to shift against the Minton Committee. On the same day Rumely testified, Senator Burton K. Wheeler complained that the committee was attempting to "browbeat" the witness in a one-sided "kangaroo court." He privately confided to Pinchot that Minton was likely to lose a contempt vote in the full Senate. Pinchot added that the committee "and the President, who stands behind it, stubbed their toes when they put on their show on Friday." Minton tried to regain the initiative by countercharging that Wheeler was cooperating behind the scenes in a "social lobby" led by Alice Roosevelt Longworth, the stridently anti–New Deal daughter of the former president. But it had little effect. When Senator Rush Holt (D-WV) took Wheeler's side during this exchange, Minton walked off in a huff. [31]

Perhaps sensing that the committee had overreached, Minton, as he prepared to call back Rumely to testify, relied on a more narrowed subpoena instead of a *duces tecum*. The result, however, rather than undermining the NCUCG's will to resist or forcing it on the defensive, was to give it a new issue to rally around: the requirement that Rumely produce the names of all those who had donated over $1,000 to the organization. Minton's goal in this new demand was to expose "any motive other than appears on the surface," but for the NCUCG it was a brazen attempt to intimidate donors and invade personal privacy. Minton struggled to regain the high ground. In a radio debate with a critic of the committee, he charged that Gannett was directing his "propaganda machine from his sunny villa in Florida" and that "98 per cent of all the metropolitan newspapers" were trying to smear the committee. When Rumely had his next faceoff before the committee, it lasted only thirty minutes. Yet again Rumely refused to produce the records. In comments to reporters, Minton dismissed this defiance as a minor obstacle and part of the "old dodge of delay through legal process" and doomed to "collapse in the end."[32]

Minton's allies expressed confidence that the NCUCG would soon be exposed and brought to account. Paul Y. Anderson considered it "obvious that the basis for a contempt citation against Rumely had been adequately laid." Reporter Kenneth Crawford of the *New York Post*, an outlet for pro–New Deal publisher J. David Stern, took a similar line. He considered a contempt prosecution likely and predicted many "sensations" yet to come. The *Post* ran a front-page editorial accusing Gannett of hypocritically raising "a bogeyman cry about invasion of the home." After crediting Anderson, then a frequent contributor, for prompting the investigation, the *Nation* opined that "a government that does not have this power [to subpoena the NCUCG's records] will be crippled in its attempts to deal with paid pressure groups."[33]

These were exceptions, however, and press commentary overwhelmingly condemned the Minton Committee. The *Chicago Daily Tribune* characterized it as "the GPU of this administration," while the *New York Herald Tribune* considered it guilty of "terrorism" and of "harrying citizens and prying into private affairs that are of no public concern." In a long opinion piece, Frederic Nelson, an editorial writer for the *Baltimore Sun* and a well-regarded civil libertarian, recoiled at efforts to disparage members of the NCUCG as comparable to "the frequenters of a gambling house" and to suppress contributions to intimidate "the people on the list so that they decide it might be a good idea to lay off the reorganization fight."[34]

Some of the most persistent criticism of the Minton Committee came from a former ally of FDR, Hugh S. Johnson, who had headed the defunct National Recovery Administration. In an open "Dear Sherman" letter to Minton, he announced that he had dedicated himself to defeating the reorganization bill and looked forward to the possibility that he might be hauled up before "your Black OGPU committee." Johnson warned that his testimony "would be a lot of fun—but not for you. If you have a nice hoosegow or inquisitorial chamber, I am a candidate for them too."[35]

Meanwhile, the NCUCG's campaign against the reorganization bill chugged ahead at full throttle. By late March, it had disseminated over 350,000 mailings, a quantity equaling that of the Supreme Court fight. For a while, however, it looked like it was all for naught, as the administration seemed to regain its footing. When the Senate passed the reorganization bill on March 29 by a comfortable margin, the *St. Louis Star-Times* asserted that the NCUCG was "weakening as a propaganda force over Congress."[36]

Even as the prospects for final passage of the reorganization bill seemed to improve, Minton started to quietly back off from pursuing contempt charges, pointing to the short time left in the current session. Another possible factor, as reported by *Newsweek*, was that looming victory for reorganization might render it a moot issue. Yet another reason, left largely unspoken, was the strong possibility of stiff opposition against a resolution from prominent Democrats. But Minton did not completely give up yet on possible sanctions for Rumely. He asked the Department of Justice to consider a prosecution on its own.[37]

Perhaps ironically, or perhaps not, a person who was instrumental in closing off that avenue of attack was John J. Abt. At the time, Abt was not only special assistant to the attorney general but also a secret Communist. Twenty-five years later, Lee Harvey Oswald sought out Abt (then official legal counsel for the Communist Party USA) to represent him. In a long internal memo on March 26, 1938, Abt urged the Department of Justice not to take up the Rumely case. He did not mince words. He pointed to the "extremely doubtful validity" of the Rumely subpoena, stating that it did "not sufficiently describe the nature of the documents to inform the witness of what he is expected to produce." Securing a conviction was improbable because "the ordinary jury does not consider failure to produce documents in response to a Senate subpoena a very serious offense." Such a prosecution, he predicted, was more likely to discredit contempt citations for any future Senate investigation.[38]

Abt feared that Rumely's lawyer would successfully "convert the trial of his client into a trial of the Senate Committee, and this subpoena will prove a very effective weapon for that purpose." As evidence, he cited his own failure to secure contempt convictions while legal counsel to another committee. Many of Abt's fellow Communists did not share his measured tone. Only two weeks after his memorandum, the *Daily Worker* blasted Rumely as a wartime shill for Germany and for his "treasonous-subversive plotting for American reaction in the reorganization debate."[39]

Although he must have known that any legal punishment for Rumely was no longer on the table, Minton continued to give the possibility lip service. Speaking on the radio two days after Abt's memo, he stated that no decision had been made on whether to bring charges. More than a little dubiously, he cited *Hearst v. United States* as a favorable precedent for possible action. Minton asked, "If they [the NCUCG] are so pure, why not let in the light of day on their efforts to influence legislation? Honest men have no fear of the processes of senate committees." Paul Y. Anderson, perhaps looking through the lens of the young journalist who had exposed Teapot Dome crimes, was one of the last to hold out the possibility of a contempt citation. A later NCUCG publication summed up the reality by recalling that everyone had "anticipated that something terrible would happen to Dr. Rumely—and to other officers of the Committee. But no retribution fell. When the dragon was defied, it evaporated."[40]

Roosevelt and his inner circle publicly kept quiet about the Rumely controversy, but privately they were paying attention. A case in point was the administration's response to a letter from Sherman Steele, dean of the law school at Loyola University in Chicago, to Roosevelt's secretary, Marvin H. McIntyre. Steele suggested that the Department of Justice investigate Rumely for "disloyal activities," pointing to his World War I–era conviction. He quoted Representative Lindsay Warren (D-NC), who had identified Rumely as "a sweet-scented rosebud of unsavory reputation" directing the "propaganda" against the reorganization bill who had "gone to every length and every extreme … to annihilate and destroy our President." In response, Roosevelt had Attorney General Homer Cummings look into the matter; Cummings, in turn, tasked J. Edgar Hoover to prepare a special report on Rumely's background. Hoover reported "numerous allegations in the files that Rumely was a member of the German spy ring in the United States during the World War." Beyond that, the Department of Justice appears to have taken no further action.[41]

The month of April 1938 was, as described by Richard Polenberg, "a low point in his [Roosevelt's] Presidential career." As the economic downturn finally hit rock bottom, the reorganization bill collapsed in defeat in the House on April 8. In public, Roosevelt took the high road. He promised that "the legislative developments of yesterday offer no occasion for personal recrimination, and there should be none." But retaliation was still very much an administrative priority. One day after his conciliatory statement, he had approved Minton's request (later codified in an executive order) for full access to the tax returns of twelve individuals associated with the magazine *Rural*

Progress. The president's order cited as a legal basis the same 1935 law that had authorized the Black Committee to inspect tax returns "in connection with the so-called 'holding company bill,' or any other matter or proposal affecting legislation."[42]

Armed with sweeping new tax power from Roosevelt, Minton moved quickly to schedule hearings for May 2, centering on the magazine *Rural Progress.* This must have seemed like an ideal opening to discredit both Rumely, who was one of the stockholders, and the publisher, Glenn Frank, who was both the former president of the University of Wisconsin and the current finance chair of the Republican National Committee. A frequent critic of the New Deal, Frank was already getting mentioned as a possible GOP presidential candidate for 1940. Minton also hoped that probing the magazine's bottom line might dig up some dirt. In its three years of existence, *Rural Progress* had consistently lost money.[43]

Minton's renewed effort to go on the attack using tax information led to another backlash. Harsh commentary in the press dominated in the weeks before the hearings were to begin. The *Philadelphia Inquirer* depicted Minton as "a promoter of political fishing expeditions" working in tandem with the pro–New Deal lobbyists Tommy Corcoran and Benjamin Cohen, who were willing to sacrifice "the rights of innocent bystanders." More biting still was an editorial in the *Los Angeles Times* that highlighted the Black Committee connection: "When Hugo L. Black discarded the white bed sheet for the ebon silk robe, his mantle fell upon worthy shoulders." Minton's goal, it summarized, was "to intimidate organized opposition to the New Deal."[44]

The tax controversy heated up even more after a full-bore attack on the Minton Committee by Walter Lippmann, who had two years earlier expressed similar concerns about Black. Lippmann condemned the Minton Committee as another effort by New Dealers "to embarrass, worry, terrorize and destroy." He asked, "If this is not to be described as arbitrary government and capricious tyranny, what is the accurate way to describe it?" Lippmann closed by urging the American Civil Liberties Union to lead "the fight against the lawlessness of men like Black and Minton."[45]

Among those favorably impressed by Lippmann's column was Grenville Clark, a leading Wall Street lawyer, who passed it on to his old Harvard classmate Roger N. Baldwin of the ACLU. Clark's views carried some weight in both civil libertarian and New Deal circles. He had clerked in the same law firm as Roosevelt, whom he counted as a longtime friend. As a cofounder of the National Economy League, Clark was instrumental in writing the president's Economy Act of 1933. Although he had voted for Roosevelt in 1936, he broke away from the president in 1937 by assuming a prominent role in the fight against court packing.[46]

Clark had personal reasons to be encouraged by Lippmann's condemnation of the administration's tax retaliation. Shortly before the final vote on court packing, the Bureau of Internal Revenue had singled him out along with six other "men of wealth" as tax evaders who were accused of nefariously establishing trusts to reduce their tax obligation. The result of this campaign to demonize Clark, however, was to blow up in the face of the administration. Both the chief and assistant chief counsel of the Bureau of Internal Revenue resigned in protest rather than participate. Leading press outlets accused the administration of violating the rule protecting the confidentiality of tax information and of engaging in political retaliation. Roosevelt suffered further embarrassment when news came to light that Eleanor Roosevelt had benefited from the exact same, perfectly legal, tax rule. The president quietly dropped the matter, but the experience left a lasting impression on Clark and others.[47]

The most prominent of those who stepped forward to defend the administration's release of tax returns to the Minton Committee were the left-of-center magazines, the *New Republic*, the *Nation*, the *New Leader*, and the *Progressive*. The *Progressive* opined that this order was the only way to expose hidden money supporting the NCUCG. It observed approvingly that the American Liberty League had "withered and died" once required to reveal its funding sources and wanted the same thing to happen to the NCUCG. The *Progressive* predicted the demise of "Gannett's organization with the highfalutin' name if the contributors to this $400,000 assault on the Roosevelt administration are made public." The NCUCG made precisely the same argument, emphasizing that a key consequence of governmental attempts to forcibly reveal the names of financial contributors was to scare away potential donors and members.[48]

Initially, one of the most influential defenders of the Minton Committee, including its controversial release of tax returns, was the newspaper chain owned by J. David Stern, a New Deal enthusiast and Roosevelt confidant.

On April 20, his *New York Post* endorsed a law "compelling every pressure organization, every lobby group [including Gannett's "ruthless" committee] ... to reveal periodically the source of all its funds and nationalities of its members." This was, it underlined, more a matter of "publicity" than "suppression." The *Post* reiterated its support for such a law in a follow-up editorial that proclaimed, "Never before was the work of the Minton lobby committee so necessary to provide this information."[49]

Two days after the first of these editorials, Stern met with James A. Farley, perhaps FDR's closest adviser, and urged him to recommend to the president the appointment of a committee to counter the NCUCG's continuing anti-administration "propaganda." Although Farley promised to raise the matter with the president, Stern need not have worried. On the previous day, Roosevelt had delegated the long-inactive National Emergency Council to lead such a campaign. His choice to head it up, journalist Lowell Mellett, had caught the president's eye in 1937 after resigning from the Scripps Howard News Service in protest of his employer's opposition to court packing. Roosevelt found out almost right away and contacted him about a possible job.[50]

News of Mellett's hire gave Ickes hope that the "President has at last agreed to set up a propaganda unit" and, indeed, the NCUCG was not far from Roosevelt's mind. After an interview with the president, Paul Y. Anderson reported that Roosevelt had "reached the conclusion that systematic propaganda, such as was disseminated by Frank E. Gannett's organization, is a positive threat to representative government." Roosevelt no longer wanted to entrust columnists and radio commentators to "interpret" his words, Anderson elaborated, but was looking for ways to communicate directly to the people.[51]

Roosevelt's war with the press intensified on April 21 at a private conference of newspaper editors. He complained that anti-administration editors had routinely forced reporters to slant their coverage and boasted that he was "more closely in touch with public opinion ... than any individual in this room." Like many pro-administration observers, the *Nation* took heart that the president had become "more rigid in his resistance to his enemies." Nobody cheered on Roosevelt's new fighting mood more than Minton, who saw his committee as providing needed aid for the administration's campaign against a hostile press.[52]

If Minton and Roosevelt felt enveloped by enemies, Grenville Clark's lead address at the annual meeting of the American Newspaper Publishers Association (ANPA) in late April gave them even more to worry about. Drawing inspiration from Lippmann's column, Clark mounted an all-out defense of free speech. He blasted the Minton Committee's "arrogant" and "unconstitutional" effort to inspect tax returns and "to seize the private papers of an association of citizens opposed to the Reorganization Bill." It was "perfectly plain that those tactics are designed to intimidate persons who dare, in a country supposed to be free, to oppose legislation desired by the administration in power."[53]

It was not Clark's speech, however, but a seemingly unrelated ANPA report that most drew Minton's ire. It questioned the current federal policy of granting six-month short-term licenses to radio stations. The report concluded that this regulatory practice made "broadcasters unduly sensitive …, if not subservient, to the administration in power." In addition, it speculated on whether Roosevelt's frequent fireside chats on four hundred out of the seven hundred stations in the US were a precedent for a future "dictatorship," noting that the other regimes had used radio "to destroy liberty."[54]

Minton gave a speech the following day that seized on the ANPA's report to hit back against the anti–New Deal press. Minton had done this before, but this time he added something new. In his conclusion, he proposed a bill to impose criminal penalties for newspapers that published "false" news. In doing so, he set off an unpredictable chain of events that helped to reshape the national discourse on free speech in ways that neither he nor the president had ever intended.

3

Senator Minton and Mayor Hague: The Dawn of a Left–Right Bill of Rights Coalition

WHEN SENATOR MINTON made his proposal on April 28, 1938, to criminalize "false" news, he must have expected headlines. If so, he was right. His bill led to far more media coverage than anything else he did in his Senate career. It failed spectacularly, however, to aid his investigation or to put his foes off balance. Of even greater import, the reaction to his proposal unwittingly gave new energy to an incipient pro–free speech coalition spanning elements on both the left and right.

Minton's bill was short and unambiguous. It made it a felony for newspapers or other periodicals to publish as "fact anything known to the publisher, or his, or its, responsible agents, to be false," punishable by up to a two-year prison sentence or a $10,000 fine. Rather than interpreting the report of the American Newspaper Publishers Association (ANPA) as a caution against censorship of radio, as most did, Minton saw it as a newspaper plot to "strangle" the medium. The report's reference to fireside chats, in his view, was a sly attempt by the "so-called free press" to "deny the President the right to sit-down before a microphone in his own home and speak to the people of the country about their Government." Through his bill, Minton hoped to force the "Tory" newspapers (90 percent of which by his estimate opposed the president) to curb their "false propaganda." His list of prime offenders included such anti–Roosevelt voices as the *Philadelphia Inquirer*, the *Washington Post*, the *New York Herald Tribune*, and "the unspeakable" *Chicago Daily Tribune.*[1]

With good reason, media pundits considered it likely that Minton was acting at the behest of someone else. As a longtime administration loyalist, entrusted to the position of assistant majority whip in his freshman term, he fit the profile of a disciplined team player rather than a person to go off half-cocked. Soon after the introduction of the bill, *Newsweek* said as much. "Those who know Senator Minton," it suggested, "say he must have had Roosevelt's tacit approval before introducing a bill to make news distortion a felony." Paul Y. Anderson did not quite attribute the bill to Roosevelt's instigation but came close. He found it "significant" that "such a proposal came from an administration senator of Minton's understanding." To Anderson, the bill represented a "true measure of the deep resentment" toward the press "which pervades the administration from top to bottom." An editorial in the generally pro–New Deal *Christian Science Monitor* was more explicit, finding "little doubt" that Minton's proposal "reflected the views of Mr. Roosevelt."[2]

There were other indications that Minton had encouragement from above. An unidentified "veteran Capitol Hill reporter," who was close to Minton, told historian David N. Atkinson that "someone in the administration" had put Minton up to introducing the "gag law." If true, this would be consistent with Roosevelt's habit of floating trial balloons. The timing also fits. Roosevelt's regard for the print press was at a low ebb in April 1938, so much so that he gave approval to a "propaganda" unit in the administration to counteract press criticism just days before Minton proposed his bill. Moreover, Roosevelt took such unprecedented actions as barring reporters from the "convoy ship" that accompanied his cruises and making it publicly known that he was compiling a "'box score' of false predictions, contradictory reports, and factual errors made by Washington commentators and columnists."[3]

But if FDR had any responsibility for the bill's origins, he was not about to tip his hand, at least not yet. Asked directly for comment the day after Minton's speech, and just as an adverse reaction was starting to become apparent, he punted. Instead of answering directly, the president jokingly suggested that it might be time to refer the proposal to the Federal Bureau of Prisons but added that it did not have sufficient funds to accommodate all the convicts that might be punished under such a law. Before moving on to the next question, and getting a good laugh, he quipped to the reporters, "You boys asked for it, you know."[4]

If Roosevelt had floated a trial balloon, however, it deflated rapidly. Just about everyone, it seemed, either hated the bill or avoided comment. One of the first to speak out was Senator Edward R. Burke (D-NE), a conservative-leaning Democrat. After holding his peace through Minton's speech, he ex-claimed: "Whenever I find any who berates the press, I can put my finger on some one who, if he had his way, would limit the expression of anyone who takes a different view from his." Minton's pro–New Deal colleagues, normally in his corner, were nowhere to be found. Reporter Robert S. Allen of the Stern-owned *Philadelphia Record* observed that the bill "struck a sour note in an otherwise justifiable condemnation" of the press. "Minton's liberal associates" had privately confided to Allen that they opposed his proposal. Probably the two most receptive voices on the Senate floor (though neither took a stand for the bill) were Senator George Norris (Independent-NE), a well-known progressive, who used the occasion to call for banning ownership of radio stations by newspapers, and Senator Schwellenbach, who made sure to provide a reminder that Rumely, "Mr. Gannett's Man Friday," had "spread German propaganda" during World War I.[5]

Although pro-Roosevelt partisans generally avoided taking a stand, the rest of the press was not so reticent. The *Washington Post* condemned "Min-ton's ridiculous bill," which it characterized as based "on the Hitler-Mussolini technique." The *Milwaukee Journal* asked, "Who is to say what is true and what is false—some distant bureau in Washington?" Hands down, the most stridently antagonistic was the *Philadelphia Inquirer*. The publisher, Moses "Moe" Annenberg, had backed Roosevelt's reelection but had rebelled after court packing. On a single day, the paper ran both a cartoon of Minton wav-ing a "press gag" flag and a special front-page editorial signed by Annenberg that blamed Roosevelt for pushing the bill as a means to "punish, muzzle and coerce the press" and referred to Minton as "a perfect servant of an august master." The German government's official news service did Minton's cause no favors by volunteering that every "decent person will approve [his bill] 100 percent."[6]

The bill's odds for success were poor under the best of circumstances, but seemingly unrelated events in Jersey City, New Jersey, conspired to make them even less likely. Just as Minton was trying to restrict First Amendment rights in one realm, Mayor Frank Hague was doing it in another. Beginning in 1937, Hague began a sustained effort to drive out from the city organizers from the Congress of Industrial Organizations (CIO), which he regarded as a Communist tool and a disrupter of business conditions. Backing the rival American Federation of Labor (AFL) instead, he arranged for the city to deny speaking and meeting permits to the CIO and allied groups, such as the American Civil Liberties Union (ACLU). His other methods were to selectively enforce building codes, impose discriminatory tax assessments, use intimidation to close off private meeting halls, and take steps to muzzle the dissident press. Although the CIO bore the brunt of Hague's repression, more conservative speakers, such as future Republican New York governor Thomas E. Dewey, also suffered.

While the names of Minton and Hague came in 1938 to widely symbolize a common threat to free speech, the two men as individuals provided many contrasts. The relatively young Minton was charming, polished, idealistic, well-educated and fairly handsome, while the much older Hague was balding, unschooled, crude, and personally corrupt. The two generally moved in different circles, and it is probable that they either had never met or only knew each other casually. Yet, by the late 1930s, both had gained considerable influence in national Democratic politics albeit following different paths, Minton as assistant majority whip and Hague as vice chairman of the Democratic National Committee (DNC). Their most important similarity as political figures was a close reciprocal relationship with the president. Roosevelt needed both men almost as much as each of them needed him. Minton was an essential New Deal point man in the Senate, while Hague's main value was as a reliable generator of votes in a crucial swing state.[7]

In contrast to Minton, Hague's relationship with Roosevelt began even before there was a New Deal. Although he had backed Al Smith for the 1932 Democratic nomination, the mayor had quickly won Roosevelt's favor by staging one of the largest Democratic campaign rallies in American history. Thereafter, he had dependably put Roosevelt over the top at election time, reaping as a reward a constant flow of federal money. It was Hague, rather than the governor or a senator in New Jersey, who controlled the dispersal of all New Deal funds and had a veto over all of the state's federal judicial and patronage appointments. Because of Hague's close relationship with Harry Hopkins, the administrator of the Civil Works Administration (CWA) and later the Works Progress Administration (WPA), he was able to control nearly 100,000 federally funded jobs in the state. The electoral interests of Hague and Roosevelt had become so close that at least one WPA director in the state habitually answered the phone: "Democratic Headquarters." In addition, jobholders hired through federal funds had to "tithe" three percent of their salaries to the Hague machine. The stench of corruption was palpable, but Roosevelt and Hopkins chose to ignore it.[8]

Hague's antics posed a dilemma for Roosevelt because they served to alien-ate key elements in the New Deal coalition that he needed. Roosevelt's initial strategy to handle the growing pressure was to appear to be above the fray even as he quietly continued to run interference for the mayor. At the height of the CIO organizing drive, Postmaster General James A. Farley found out that a henchman of the mayor was reading the mail of one of Hague's politi-cal enemies. Telling the president that he had hard evidence, Farley proposed prosecuting Hague for both mail tampering and tax evasion. Roosevelt, who had shown no reluctance to pursue similar high-profile cases against the likes of the politically weakened Tom Pendergast (Democratic mayor of Kansas City) and Andrew Mellon (Republican former secretary of the treasury), wanted no part of it. He responded to Farley: "Forget prosecution. You go tell Frank to knock it off. … But keep this quiet. We need Hague's support and we want New Jersey."[9]

The Hague free speech controversy came to a head just two days after Minton's controversial speech. At the center was the perennial, but well re-spected, Socialist Party presidential candidate, Norman Thomas. Thomas was pivotal in transforming just another labor-organizing controversy into a national test case on protections for free speech and assembly. On April 30, Thomas showed up in Jersey City to speak at an open-air rally even though he had been turned down for a permit. Ready to spring, police immediately arrested him when he got out of his car to address a crowd of one thousand who had gathered to hear him. Thomas barely had time to say "So this is Jersey justice" before the officers whisked him way.[10]

By the close of April 1938, a broad cross section of American newspapers began to feature front-page headlines highlighting imminent perils to free speech. The crucial distinction, depending on where the particular paper fell on the political spectrum, was the name of the chief offender. For many on the left, the main threat to free speech came from Hague, but for those on the right, it was usually Minton. While few credible newspapers could completely ignore both Minton and Hague at the same time, the coverage often sharply diverged in emphasis. Anti–New Deal publications, such as the *Chicago Daily Tribune* and *Philadelphia Inquirer,* spared no outrage over the Minton bill but tended to downplay Hague's free speech violations. Following a typical pattern on the left, J. David Stern's *New York Post* responded to the extra-legal expulsion of Thomas from the city with the headline "Fight Against Fuehrer Hague Warming Up on Two Fronts" while skirting entirely the Minton bill.[11]

An increasing number of people on both sides of the ideological divide, however, were beginning to pair Hague and Minton as common dangers to free speech. Perhaps the earliest to do so was Walter Lippmann, who had criticized Minton's use of tax returns even before he had proposed his bill. For Lippmann, exercise of this power involved "as fundamental a question of civil liberty as Mayor Hague's recent performances." The main distinction between the two men, he suggested, "which ought not to be considered a difference at all," was that Minton's victims tended to be "rich men" while Hague's were primarily "members of the C.I.O."[12]

Lippmann soon got reinforcement from a major Republican figure: Alfred M. Landon, the GOP standard-bearer in 1936. When Landon got word about Thomas's "deportation," he fired off a letter of support to his 1936 Socialist opponent blasting Hague's actions as a "gross violation of our sacred rights of free speech." The two men struck up a lifetime friendship. Landon hoped that the incident would "draw together all those who have common ideals of freedom and tolerance" and pledged to stand "shoulder to shoulder with you in this fight for free speech." Landon's comments portrayed the New Deal, Hague, and Minton as closely aligned threats to free speech. Minton's bill represented not only "a dire threat to the press" but also "a New Deal attitude toward the press" that "may reflect the president's attitude." At a minimum, Roosevelt's "views have, no doubt, encouraged Senator Minton and others." More pointedly, Landon accused the president of allowing "this dangerous precedent in Jersey City" even as Senator Minton "Frank Hagues" the American press. To Landon, no other group was more intolerant of differing points of view than "the so-called New Deal liberals."[13]

While Landon served as the most prominent bridge between free speech defenders on the right and left, he was not alone. Another example was Thomas's own lawyer, Arthur T. Vanderbilt, from the prestigious business dynasty of the same name, who two years earlier was a Landon delegate to the Republican national convention. Vanderbilt, who also headed the American Bar Association (ABA), took on the case pro bono. Upholding the First Amendment was not an unfamiliar enterprise to Vanderbilt, who had often represented labor unions and various left-wing groups suffering harassment. For months, he had prodded the ABA to create a committee to defend the Bill of Rights.[14]

Pro–New Deal voices against Hague, such as the *Louisville Courier-Journal*, *New York Post*, and *Philadelphia Record*, praised Landon's letter but (straining credibility) depicted the 1936 Republican presidential nominee as an aberration from the rest of his party. The main priority of these newspapers was to defend Roosevelt and the credibility of his agenda. "The Democratic Party," the *Post* warned, "cannot go into the coming elections as a champion of democracy without inviting public ridicule. Unless it does something about its own Half-Pint Hitler [Hague]." The *Courier-Journal* showed frustration that Roosevelt had evaded taking a stand while the "titular" head of the GOP had spoken out against Hague. Although some pro–New Deal publications, at least mildly, faulted Roosevelt, they were not quite ready yet to completely repudiate Minton. Their usual approach was to evade comment on the press bill even as they egged on the senator's exposés of right-wing lobbyists. An example was the *Courier-Journal,* which, on the one hand, praised the Minton Committee's investigation and, on the other, characterized his proposal as the "most asinine bill introduced in the present Congress."[15]

With the date of the new hearings looming, however, the bad publicity stung enough that Minton let his bill die in the Senate Committee on Interstate Commerce (chaired by one of his leading Democratic adversaries, Burton K. Wheeler). But rather than concede any fault, he boldly proclaimed victory. Minton explained that it was never his intention to get the bill enacted but only to shame newspapers into acknowledging, and covering, his general critique of the press, "[o]therwise the reactionary press would have ignored" him. Minton's insincere regrets helped keep the issue very much alive. In response to news of the bill's withdrawal, the anti–New Deal *Philadelphia Inquirer* ran two cartoons. The first showed Minton in a tar barrel underneath the slogan, "Honest—I Was Only Kidding," while the other, "Franklin Discovers Lightning Again," featured a kite flown from the White House labeled "Sen. Minton's attack on the Free Press." The kite, described as a "White House Feeler," carried a bolt of lightning that hit the executive mansion.[16]

Soon after Minton's partial retreat, albeit with guns blazing, he counterattacked on May 6 when the committee resumed hearings. The target was *Rural Progress*, a magazine catering to farmers. Edward A. Rumely of the NCUCG had loaned start-up money and promoted advertising for the publication. While the Democrats on the committee prepared carefully by scrutinizing the tax returns of those involved in the publication, they uncovered scant evidence that any of them, Rumely excepted, had anything to do with anti–New Deal political activities. The weaknesses in the majority's case became obvious during the appearance of publisher Maurice V. Reynolds, who was the first, and destined to be the only, witness. Seemingly on an entirely different wavelength than his questioners, Reynolds touted *Rural Progress* as a pioneering special-interest magazine (for farmers) paid for entirely by advertisers. "Ours is the first magazine with free circulation," he declared, "to be mailed free to the consumer." The Democratic members, on the other hand, started from the assumption that *Rural Progress* was a stealthy and deceptive scheme to propagate anti–New Deal ideas among farmers. As evidence, they cited several articles over three years that had negative references to federal farm policies, court packing, and wages and hours legislation. The Democrats in their questions emphasized that *Rural Progress* had consistently lost money, prompting Reynolds to respond that this was normal for new publications. When Schwellenbach pressed further about Rumely's past conviction and jail sentence, Reynolds pled ignorance, stating he had no interest at all in politics.[17]

The magazine's content did not bear out the committee's narrative that *Rural Progress* represented a stealthy scheme to spread "subtle propaganda" against the administration. The claim that most of the articles that had political references were critical of the New Deal was mostly true but highly misleading. The focus of the editors and publishers of *Rural Progress* was more on the technical and economic side of farming or topics of general concern such as humor, nonfiction, and features. There is every reason to take the characterization by Reynolds at face value: the main purpose of *Rural Progress* was to reach farmers and make eventual profits through advertising.

Even Rumely's participation in the magazine was generally consistent with this goal. Reynolds explained that he had recruited Rumely upon the recommendation of Eugene F. McDonald, the well-known polar explorer and head of the Zenith Radio Corporation, after a chance meeting. McDonald suggested Rumely for the task because of his talents in providing advertising for Zenith and his long experience in the farm market as a seller of tractors. To be sure, Rumely probably helped to find some of the "political" writers, such as S. S. McClure, a member of the advisory committee of the National Committee to Uphold Constitutional Government (NCUCG), and Senator William Borah (R-ID), but anything they wrote touching on issues of the day was incidental to the magazine's overall character.[18]

Given Rumely's involvement, however, the Democratic majority's decision to target *Rural Progress* was entirely understandable. Their questions centered on the roles played by both Rumely and Glenn Frank, the publisher of *Rural Progress* and a former president of the University of Wisconsin. Although not summoned as a witness, Frank showed up anyway. He was a source of irritation for the majority by repeatedly volunteering information to the committee or giving pointers to Reynolds during his testimony. Thoroughly exasperated, Senator Green admonished Frank "not to attempt such communications with the witness." In a rare sign of pushback from the Republican minority, Senator Gibson asked rhetorically if it was not "quite the practice for a witness on the stand to rely on somebody else for information?" This had no effect on the Democratic members. Senator Schwellenbach, who reflected the consensus of the majority, vowed to prevent Frank from using the hearings as a forum for "his Republican views." During two other testy exchanges, Green demanded that Frank "sit down." Undaunted, Frank asked for "the courtesy of making a statement as a taxpaying citizen." To nobody's surprise, Minton brushed this aside, but Frank was playing mainly to the media anyway. Reynolds's appearance had lasted one day. The committee never held hearings again.[19]

Hostile press coverage had dashed any of Minton's remaining hopes to recoup his political losses by, instead, keeping the focus on Frank's showdown with the committee. Typical headlines were "Frank Suppressed at Lobby Hearing" in the *New York Times* and "Dr. Frank Hushed by Senate Probe" in the *Macon* [GA] *Telegraph*. The *Washington Post* characterized the Democratic majority as "thoroughly discredited" and uninterested in "getting at all the facts." Marginally less antagonistic, the *Baltimore Sun* blamed Minton for creating a "low-down street brawl" by unfairly silencing Frank. Perhaps most critical of all, the *San Francisco Chronicle* accused the committee of suppressing newspapers "from printing things displeasing to the Administration. This is fascism." The *Chronicle* wondered why the committee had shielded the "biggest lobby of all" (the US government), which sent out New Deal government propaganda "free by the carload—franked through the mails."[20]

Senator Green, who had become Minton's most vocal ally, tried futilely to swim against the tide. The investigation had nothing to do with quashing free speech, he proclaimed, but was "merely a purification of the press which the press ought to welcome." To this, Frank retorted that the Democrats were waging "a carefully-laid campaign of terror and intimidation against the newspapers." He pointed out that not even Minton had accused the officers of *Rural Progress* of engaging in lobbying: "His only contention is that it has published articles critical of administration measures." Another ominous sign for the committee was that Minton faced an all-out rebellion from the Republican minority. Gibson announced that the usefulness of the Minton committee had ended and that both he and Senator Lynn Frazier (R-ND) were thinking of resigning. According to Gibson, the breaking point was the majority's unwillingness to let Frank testify.[21]

The decidedly mixed reaction to this controversy from the pro–New Deal press did not give any solace to the committee's Democrats. On the positive side for Minton, the *Louisville Courier-Journal*, which had condemned Minton's press bill, praised the *Rural Progress* investigation for promoting the people's right to know. Freedom of the press, it asserted, "bears a corresponding accountability. … the press is not free if it is secretly dominated by selfish and private interests." Grasping somewhat at straws, Minton appended the editorial to his extended remarks. While such pro–New Deal periodicals as the *Nation* and the *New Republic* were mostly silent, the leftist *New Leader* championed the committee for exposing a "Tory magazine which has lost $951,000" and dismissed any alleged threat to free speech as nonsense.[22]

Even these mostly tepid plaudits were canceled out by unexpected criticism from Stern's newspapers. His *Philadelphia Record* responded to the Frank controversy by featuring both an anti-Minton cartoon and a brass knuckle editorial condemning both his press bill and, in a significant shift, the committee's probe of *Rural Progress*. "The Senate of the United States," it declared, "should sit on Minton: Quick." It warned that Minton's "gag bill" was playing "into the hands of the reactionary newspapers of this country by trying to suppress them." It attacked the committee for exceeding its mandate without evidence that the magazine had engaged in "improper lobbying." *Rural Progress*, the *Record*'s editorial concluded, was "devoted almost exclusively to fiction and articles of technical interest to farmers." If the few political articles in the publication were "subtle propaganda," it asked pointedly, what of it? "How is that Senator Minton's business? Since when has it become a crime in America to be unjustly critical of this Administration?" According to the *Record*, the threat to Roosevelt's agenda from the bad publicity had become so acute that Democrats in the Senate now had a duty to "squelch Minton before Minton Smears the New Deal."[23]

If Minton had alienated Stern, it was time for a full alarm. This was strong stuff, stronger still coming from an outlet owned by a man who was one of Roosevelt's most powerful media allies. Until then, Stern's publications had avoided comment on the bill, lauded the *Rural Progress* investigation, and belittled claims that the committee posed a danger to privacy. The president, an avid newspaper reader, probably knew about the editorial, and, if so, the content would have done nothing to instill more confidence in the Minton Committee's usefulness to the New Deal.

Less directly of concern to the president, perhaps, but still a sign of cracks in the emerging New Deal coalition, was an editorial in the *Chicago Defender,* a leading black newspaper that had supported Roosevelt in the last two elections. The *Defender*'s condemnation of the Minton Committee made those of the *New York Post* and *Philadelphia Record* seem tame by comparison. It drew a contrast between Glenn Frank for his "fair treatment" of African Americans, while president of the University of Wisconsin, and Minton's "pronounced record of prejudice toward our race" while a student at the University of Indiana, where he had allegedly refused to debate a black student. It also zeroed in on Minton's demonstrably close ties to Hugo L. Black, a former Klan member who had filibustered antilynching legislation. "If men of the standing of Dr. Frank are not allowed to speak in defense of themselves," the editorial concluded, "it is time that we, as a race, should become more alarmed at the activities of such advocates of muzzling the press as Senator Minton." The *Defender*'s depiction of Minton was not entirely fair. His closeness to Black was undeniable, but he had consistently voted for antilynching legislation, though it must be said that he was ineffective in fighting Southern filibusters.[24]

Throughout May, headlines about both the Hague and Minton controversies vied for attention. The combined effect was to strengthen sensitivity to civil liberties on both the left and right and, incidentally, to further undermine Minton and Hague. Even as Frank was squaring off with the Democrats at the hearing on May 6, Representatives Jerry O'Connell (D-MT) and John Bernard (Farm-Labor Party-MN) were en route to a pro–free speech rally in Jersey City. Both had secret ties to the Communist Party and, arguably, were the two most left-wing members of Congress. Their plans were to speak in protest against the "deportation" of Norman Thomas a week earlier, even though the city had denied them speaking permits. In response to their imminent visit, Daniel J. Casey, Jersey City's director of public safety, vowed not to permit the two "imported Reds" from infringing "upon the rights of our citizens." The head of the pro-Hague Catholic War Veterans awaited with eight hundred uniformed veterans, many with rubber hoses.[25]

On May 7, a crowd of as many as 65,000 waited in vain for several hours to hear O'Connell and Bernard. At the last minute, the pair had decided not to make the trip at the urging of former Representative Vito Marcantonio of New York, who saw no benefit "to be gained by letting Jersey City policemen slug these congressmen." Hague had won again. Like many on the left, O'Connell, who promised to return in two weeks to speak again, permit or no permit, expressed frustration at Roosevelt's inaction, warning that the president had an obligation "to demand the immediate resignation of Frank Hague from the vice chairmanship of the Democratic National Committee." Agreeing, the pro–New Deal *St. Louis Star-Times* pointed out that as "Landon has damned Boss Hague," the "very tories who share Hague's economic views will cry out against the President's silence as shrilly as the witches in Macbeth."[26]

To be sure, there was some truth in the *New York Post*'s theory that "Republicans won't fight Hague because the reactionary, labor-baiting boss of Jersey City is right up their own reactionary alley." But Hague's ever more obvious abuses, combined with his continuing close association with Roosevelt, pushed conservatives, even if they otherwise appreciated Hague's opposition to the CIO, to give greater credence to the dangers of free speech suppression in Jersey City. By the end of May 1938, it was becoming rare for conservatives in the press and in Congress to defend Hague in any way. Added to this, despite Thomas's socialist views, some on the right were beginning to express grudging respect for his principled stands for civil libertarianism, his opposition to Communism, and his independence from Roosevelt.[27]

One of the first prominent conservative voices who attacked the president's response (or lack thereof) to Hague and Minton was prominent columnist George Sokolsky, who charged that Roosevelt and his New Deal had entered into an unholy alliance with both men. "The so-called liberals and progressives," he declared, were responsible for the Minton Committee and had "supported the court-packing trick, the disorganization of government trick, the Black committee and the Black appointment." He depicted the CIO's coercive strike methods and Hague's assaults on democratic norms as equal threats to free speech.[28]

As more people than ever on both the left and right were linking Hague and Minton as analogous threats to liberty, the ACLU remained conspicuously missing in action. In contrast to its early dogged fight for free speech in Jersey City, it was laggard in taking a stand on either the Minton Committee or Minton's libel bill. Despite urgings from Arthur Garfield Hays and other members, the national board laid on the table a proposal to protest the president's order on tax returns because the matter did not involve "an issue of civil rights." More difficult to fathom was the ACLU's continuing silence on Minton's libel bill even though it was very much in the news. A possible factor in explaining this slowness to react was the increased coziness between several ACLU officials, including Roger N. Baldwin and Morris Ernst, and the New Deal. The closeness went both ways. Several prominent administration officials, notably Ickes, were ACLU members. Despite some internal dissention, the ACLU's board had generally embraced the president's labor policies, rejecting claims that they may have undermined the civil liberties of employers and non-union workers. Making a fuss now about Minton, the majority on the board might have reasoned, would only undermine this budding alliance with the administration.[29]

The president's press conference on May 10 did nothing to reassure pro–New Deal civil libertarians in the press and in the ACLU. When asked about threats to "free speech and assembly in Jersey City," Roosevelt evasively dismissed the controversy as a "local police matter." As to removing Hague as DNC vice chairman, he demurred that the best person to comment was the

Democratic national chairman, James A. Farley. The overall impression conveyed by the president was to further tarnish the New Deal's civil-liberties pretensions and, just as importantly, create an opportunity for conservatives to attack.[30]

One of the first Republicans in Congress to do so was Representative Harold Knutson (R-MN), who did his best to worsen any Democratic discomfort created by Roosevelt's press conference. From the House floor, Knutson charged that Roosevelt had the power to quash Hague and uphold Norman Thomas's rights but had shied away for reasons of political expediency. "[T]he violation of the first amendment of the Constitution of the United States," he asserted, "is not a local matter." As to the failure to remove Hague as DNC vice chairman, "[o]ne word from him [Roosevelt] would be enough." Knutson linked the press bill and Hague's deportations as interrelated ploys to "muzzle" free speech, pointedly observing that Minton was "closer to the President than any other Member of this body." Knutson asked rhetorically "if what Mayor Hague has done up in Jersey City and the introduction of this bill were done with the approval of the President[?]" While Knutson admitted he had no proof that Roosevelt had put Minton up to introducing the bill, he quipped in answer to his question that "[i]t looks suspicious." Roosevelt cared so little for civil liberties that he had promoted Black to the Supreme Court, despite his record of rifling through "private files ... in violation of the fourth amendment." If Roosevelt disapproved of such tactics, Knutson further pressed, why had he appointed Black?[31]

Knutson had struck a nerve, as revealed by the tenor of his exchange with the normally combative Representative Maury Maverick (D-TX), a Roosevelt ally. In taking up the unenviable task of both condemning Hague and (at least partially) defending the president, Maverick unconvincingly declared that "of course" Roosevelt was not culpable in the actions of either Minton (whom he did not explicitly name) or Hague, but these were "not relevant to the case." Other than that, Maverick passed over Knutson's reference to the Black Committee. He expended most of his ammunition in going after Hague himself. At the same time, he graciously thanked Knutson for reminding Democrats of "the faults of the majority party" and for denouncing the "cheap, ignorant, tawdry, villainous little dictator" of Jersey City. In another conciliatory gesture, Maverick agreed that the Constitution protected the free speech not only of Communists and radicals but also of conservatives.[32]

New Dealers expressed mounting dismay that Roosevelt's inaction was playing into the hands of conservatives who wanted to sully the New Deal. These feelings only grew more pronounced when Representative Jerry O'Connell returned to Jersey City on May 27 to speak without a permit at Pershing Field. After a pro-Hague crowd rushed the stage, police pushed O'Connell into a patrol car and sped him to the New York ferry. This time he never returned. In response to these and similar developments, the *New York Post* fretted that Republicans were "catching on" to Landon's efforts to tie together "Hagueism" and New Dealism and thus successfully rebranding the GOP as "the champion of liberty and enemy of repression." If Landon could pull this off, big losses awaited the Democrats in the 1938 elections. But Roosevelt had the power to snatch the issue "away from the Republicans overnight by a forthright denunciation of Hagueism."[33]

Nearly a month after Lippmann's appeal to the ACLU to take action, the persistence of Arthur Garfield Hays and other board members finally bore some fruit. A press release on May 19 blasted Minton's libel bill as "[p]lainly offensive to every conception of liberty of the press." This condemnation was purely symbolic, since the bill had no chance of success and Minton had pretty much abandoned it. More substantial was a very belated criticism of the committee's release of private tax returns. A week after the ACLU had condemned the libel bill, national chairman Harry F. Ward, Arthur Garfield Hays, Roger N. Baldwin, John Haynes Holmes, and Osmond K. Fraenkel sent a joint letter to Minton protesting his use of the tax returns and warning that it might cause "witnesses to hesitate before expressing themselves on pending legislation in the face of their inability to resist improper retaliatory measures."[34]

Although the ACLU had finally taken action, its protest letter had carefully selective wording that kept the focus on Minton and never mentioned Roosevelt or officials in the executive branch. The effect of this approach was to exempt, by implication if nothing else, Roosevelt from any hint of blame, even though the administration had approved the release of the tax returns in the first place. The careful parsing in the wording of its public statements shows an organization that was extremely anxious to avoid jeopardizing its increasingly close ties to the New Deal leadership. For his part, Minton, although undeniably a chief player in this controversy, also served the convenient role of scapegoat.

Minton's response to the ACLU protest letter showed a bemusement akin to that of Senator Hugo L. Black in 1936 when he tried to rebuff similar ACLU criticism of his committee's seizure of telegrams. In his answer, Minton began by saying that he was in "hearty accord" that "all citizens have a right to express themselves freely and fully on pending legislation" but added that this issue had no bearing on what he was trying to do. His only goal was "to enlighten the people … from where the opposition [to the reorganization bill] comes, who directs it, and who pays the bill." But Minton's ham-fistedness and conspiratorial mindset were also in evidence. He reminded the ACLU that two of the individuals listed on its letterhead, John Haynes Holmes, a cosigner of the joint letter, and Amos Pinchot, were also members of the NCUCG. "I am sure your organization," he suggested with mock sincerity, "would not be intimidated by the so-called free press of the country or lend yourself to the avowed purpose of the National Committee to Uphold Constitutional Government to discredit the lobby committee."[35]

Minton's reaction to the ACLU protest, however, was tame compared to that of Paul Y. Anderson, who shot off a telegram blasting the ACLU's protest against the release of tax returns as "not merely contemptible" but "stupid." He exclaimed, "If you don't know what is going on in the world why in the hell don't you ask somebody. You have made yourself an adjunct of Gannett." Few journalists had longer and more visible records than Anderson in defending such ACLU-favored causes as the right of assembly for unions and radicals, but now he was thoroughly alienated from that organization. As to Minton, he was more politically isolated than ever.[36]

Some indication of the extent of that isolation came during a heated Senate debate before the June recess. Minton tried to regain the initiative by changing strategy. He asked for additional funds for the committee to conduct an "objective study" of newspapers, including their sources of "news columns, false statements, colored statements, or representations." Minton promised that this study would not single out any newspaper because of its political stance. Few believed this assurance. Senator Champ Clark (D-MO) compared the proposed study to Nazi censorship, while Senator Edward R. Burke (D-NE) volunteered that the US could "survive" without it. When it became apparent that a filibuster was in the offing, Majority Leader Alben Barkley (D-KY) persuaded Minton to drop the request for new funds, though Minton gamely promised to conduct the investigation at some later time with a smaller staff.[37]

As anger toward the Minton Committee showed new life, so too did outrage against Hague. On June 1, hearings began in the federal district court on an omnibus injunction filed by the CIO and the ACLU to restrain Hague and other city officials from violating rights of free speech and assembly. For the entire month, a parade of witnesses came forward to relate the many ways in which Hague had violated constitutional rights. City officials, including Hague himself, did little to refute the evidence. Instead, they tried to justify their actions as necessary to stem mob violence and an "invasion" by Communists into the ranks of the CIO. Hague's testimony did him no favors: "Whenever I hear a discussion of civil rights and the rights of free speech and the rights of the Constitution, always remember you will find him [the advocate of these rights] with a Russian flag under his coat." The proceedings put even more pressure on Roosevelt to do something about Hague.[38]

In "Conservatism and Civil Liberties," a speech before the Nassau County Bar Association, Grenville Clark again identified Minton and Hague as interconnected threats to civil liberties: "[T]he callous disregard of the Constitution by Mayor Hague is in essence no different than the intimidating tactics of Senator Minton." At the same time, he warned that conservatives, when defending property rights, too often forgot "the great rights guaranteed by the First Amendment, including freedom of speech, of assembly, and of petition." For Clark, conservatives had an obligation to embrace "an attitude of firm and impartial defense of the rights of the citizen under the Bill of Rights in every case where these rights are threatened."[39]

The speech prompted a phone call to Clark from outgoing ABA president Arthur T. Vanderbilt to say that he wanted to implement the proposal. Vanderbilt also contacted incoming ABA president Frank J. Hogan, who had represented Silas H. Strawn in the telegram case two years earlier. Hogan's civil libertarianism owed much to his many legal battles during the Prohibition era against police intrusions into private residences. The Clark, Vanderbilt, and Hogan trio set into motion a chain of events leading to the creation of the ABA's Bill of Rights Committee in July.[40]

As the conservatives increasingly took the initiative, anti-Hague New Dealers gave new vent to their anger about Roosevelt's passivity. In an open letter, Oswald Garrison Villard questioned whether Roosevelt was a "true patriot" because he had not taken the first train to Jersey City, to "stand up in the public square there without asking for any permit." Similarly, the *New Republic* lamented that Hague was basking "in the continuing approval of President Roosevelt," while the *Nation* wanted to cut off Hague's control of state WPA projects that his "machine now uses to tighten its grip on the entire state. Roosevelt must choose between Hague and O'Connell."[41]

Pressed on all sides, as well as by a dismal economy, Roosevelt realized that he had to do something to solidify his base while, at the same time, keeping in line the Democratic machines so essential to turning out the vote. On June 24, he made his move with a fireside chat. He did not specifically mention Hague or Jersey City, but the message between the lines was hard not to miss. Roosevelt expressed concern "about the attitude of a candidate or his sponsors with respect to the rights of American citizens to assemble peaceably and to express publicly their views and opinions on important social and economic issues," adding that the "American people will not be deceived by anyone who attempts to suppress individual liberty under the pretense of patriotism."[42]

These admonishments enabled Roosevelt to protect his left flank when he made his far more controversial statements in the same fireside chat proposing to purge "copperheads" in upcoming Democratic primaries and replace them with more reliable "liberal" allies. "We all know that progress may be blocked by outspoken reactionaries," he asserted, "and also by those who say 'yes' to a progressive objective, but who always find some reason to oppose any specific proposal to gain that objective. I call that type of candidate a 'yes, but' fellow."[43]

If Roosevelt had intended to blunt attacks on him related to the Hague controversy, he more than succeeded. The press devoted far more space to the purge than to the oblique, and comparatively short, passage that referred to Hague's abuses, but what commentary did appear about that passage was overwhelmingly positive. The *New York Times*, for example, concluded that "all thoughtful Americans, 'conservatives' and 'liberals,' supporters and opponents of the Administration," could agree on the president's defense of free speech. The *Baltimore Sun* gave more hedged praise. After thanking the president for speaking out against Hague, it concluded "that it may be more dangerous to offend John L. Lewis [the head of the CIO] than to offend Frank Hague." But Roosevelt had no intention of toppling Hague from his perch. He kept him as vice chairman of the DNC, left his patronage intact, and continued to brush aside recommendations from James A. Farley to move legally against Hague for a myriad of offenses, despite incriminating evidence.[44]

The speech succeeded, at least as indicated by the press reaction, in both ramping up pro-FDR enthusiasm from the New Deal base and quieting their worries about Hague. The *New Republic* exuded that the president had "put many of his bitterest opponents very much in the wrong" but politely called for further efforts by the administration to prune Hague's power. The *Nation* rated the speech as "easily one of his most successful" and added that the "attack on the 'Copperheads'" gave "the progressives a new slogan against the reactionary Democrats." Like the *New Republic*, the *Nation* took much solace in the "guarded allusion" to Hague, though it warned that "the proof of vigorous words must lie in eventual action." Norman Thomas had perhaps the harshest assessment on the left, demanding that Roosevelt pull Hague's patronage and free access to WPA funds, and remove him as vice chair of the DNC. But even he led off by expressing "gratification" for the endorsement of constitutional rights.[45]

While events had forced the president to issue a somewhat vague admonition about threats to free speech, Republicans rallied around a more expansive and forthright agenda that explicitly named Hague, Minton, Roosevelt, and the New Deal as co-offenders. The most prominent voice taking this approach was former president Herbert Hoover. In an interview for *Liberty Magazine*, he charged that Roosevelt's priority was to centralize power rather than to uphold true liberalism. The president had flunked "the first test of liberalism," which was "absolutely [for] free speech, free worship and free assembly." Using this original standard, Hoover asked, "Do you think of Mayor (Frank) Hague of Jersey City as a pillar of liberal administration? Do you think Senator Minton and his allies trying to intimidate the American press are real liberals? Do you think the pressure from the New Deal who muzzle radio commentators are liberal measures?"[46]

As Minton faced increasing resistance, the pro-FDR *New York Daily News*, nicknamed the "New Deal News," threw him a temporary lifeline of sorts. Under its publisher, Joseph Medill "Joe" Patterson, who was the cousin of the very anti–New Deal Robert R. McCormick, it achieved the highest circulation of any daily in the United States and had backed the president almost down the line, including his Supreme Court packing plan. After two months of failing to comment on the Minton controversy, Patterson ran a lengthy editorial on July 1 belatedly praising the senator's fallback proposal to investigate the American press. It even volunteered the *Daily News* to be the first target of the probe. Such an "impartial commission," covering all aspects of newspaper operation, including working conditions and the influence of advertisers, might finally expose how "anti-New Deal newspapers and magazines" had tried to "build up a fanatical hatred of President Roosevelt." Though Patterson's editorial was certainly welcome news for Minton, it did nothing to revive his already moribund proposal.[47]

Indeed, the Minton Committee itself was rapidly fading away. By the end of July, funds had run out. A faint remaining sign of life was a brief tussle over what to do after Rumely sent a bill to Minton for the committee to cover his expenses for coming to testify. Agreeing with Minton, Chief Investigator Blomquist rejected paying a witness who had "knowingly and willfully refused to produce the documents demanded by the Committee ... to Hell with Dr. Rumely." It was a meaningless victory.[48]

The Minton Committee had been long defunct when the American Bar Association launched the Bill of Rights Committee on July 29, 1938, but it would be impossible to tell from ABA Bill of Rights Committee Chairman Grenville Clark's speech on the occasion. Minton's bill was far too useful as an illustration. Carefully striking a cross-ideological tone, Clark called for redirecting the "zeal and power" of the campaign against court packing to repel other ongoing attacks on civil liberties. His three examples were Hague's "suppression of free speech and assembly," Minton's harassment of the people's "right of petition concerning legislation," and, finally, proposals "to establish Governmental radio broadcasting." The ABA's new president, Frank J. Hogan, gave full backing to the new committee. Like Clark, Hogan repeatedly linked Hague and Minton as twin enemies of liberty, declaring that "violations of the Bill of Rights are intolerable" regardless of whether they were from the "Mayor of an American city" or "a committee of the United States Senate."[49]

If the Bill of Rights Committee was putting Minton back in the spotlight in a negative way, his own actions helped keep him there. In a fiery and unrepentant speech, he boasted that he had once introduced "a little bill" to spur newspapers to stop trying to clean up "the house of radio" and instead put their "own house in order." He dismissed claims that his intent or the effect was to threaten the First Amendment. The framers of the US Constitution, he asserted, had wanted to uphold truth, not "protect corporate publishers to make six percent on their investment." Rather than trying to muzzle the press, he elaborated that he had only "wanted to muzzle the liars who knew they were lying." But Minton did not stop there. He charged that newspaper publishers were willing "to throw this country into Fascism rather than surrender their privileges." Columnists and reporters were mere instruments to this end.[50]

Minton's speech generated nearly as much outrage from his detractors as had his libel bill nearly four months earlier. Expressing a common theme, columnist Westbrook Pegler declared that Minton had "a right not only to tell lies on the floor but to publish them in the Congressional Record, a document so mendacious, scurrilous, and slanderous that the press which he attacks for lying long ago learned to quote it only with extreme caution lest culpable libel be done." Echoing this, Walter Winchell, soon to be closely aligned with Roosevelt, praised the view that "had the senator's ill-starred bill became a law, no newspaper would have been able to publish all of Senator Minton's speech." Columnist Jon Byrne compared the senator to Buzz Windrip, the demagogue protagonist in Sinclair Lewis's novel *It Can't Happen Here*.[51]

Through it all, Minton could not resist keeping the pot at a boil. In September, he rehashed the same arguments in dueling radio speeches with both Frank Gannett and Robert R. McCormick. His verbiage was typically over the top: "Not Hitler, but Hearst; not Mussolini, but McCormick; not Stalin, but Gannett tells us what we shall read in America. We have private censorship here, while they have governmental censorship there." Minton gave yet another, though this time more explicit, postmortem defense of his bill, saying that it would be a good thing to make it "an offense to libel, or deliberately lie about, not only an individual but a group, such as labor, religious, political, or other organizations."[52]

Roosevelt kept his silence on the latest Minton outbursts, but much of his verbiage continued to be rather Mintonesque. At his presidential press conference a little over a week after Minton's speech, Roosevelt declared that 85 percent of newspapers were "Tory." When a reporter pointed to a recent poll that three hundred out of eight hundred of them had supported the president's position on Hague, Roosevelt said that he did not believe it. He seemed again to be channeling the senator in November when, in a letter to the *St. Louis Post-Dispatch* on the eve of the 1938 election, he proclaimed that "our newspapers cannot be edited in the interests of the general public, from the counting room." He mused on the possibility of "a national symposium on that question, particularly in relation to the freedom of the press. How many bogies are conjured up by invoking that greatly overworked phrase."[53]

More revealingly, Roosevelt still regarded Minton as enough of an asset to seriously consider him as for an appointment to the Supreme Court after the death of Justice Benjamin M. Cardozo in July 1938. Minton had turned down the previous opportunity for the seat ultimately filled by Black. Apparently, this time Roosevelt did not ask him, and Felix Frankfurter got the nod instead. While the president never said why he chose Frankfurter rather than Minton, it would have been out of character, especially in that environment, for Roosevelt to have stirred up needless controversy. Columnists Joseph Alsop and Robert Kintner had given a preview of the likely political fallout when they characterized the possibility of a Minton appointment as "discreditable."[54]

Similarly, the administration still ran interference for Hague from behind the scenes. An ACLU-organized petition of "60 prominent liberals" urging the Senate Committee on Education and Labor, Subcommittee Investigating Violations of Free Speech and the Rights of Labor (better known as the La Follette Civil Liberties Committee) to investigate continued abuses in Jersey City made no headway. The Senate had established the committee in 1936, headed by Senator Robert M. La Follette (Progressive-WI) to investigate harassment and other pressures against labor organizers by employers. Meanwhile, Department of Justice officials informed the press that Hague had not violated federal law. After some outcry in response to this statement, Attorney General Homer Cummings said that this information was mistaken and that no decision had "been reached on the question of whether there have been violations of Federal criminal statutes" in Jersey City. This did not amount to much, however.[55]

But a few voices kept trying to prod the administration to act. The ever-persistent Norman Thomas charged that Roosevelt represented "the party of Frank Hague," while Albert Jay Nock, an individualist and civil libertarian, blamed what he regarded as Roosevelt's disdain for the Constitution on New Deal policies of centralization. Roosevelt, according to Nock, "advises Congressmen not to be too particular about the constitutionality of a measure which interests him; how long a step from that is it to Governor Murphy's flat nullification of law, or to Mayor Hague's assertion, 'I am the law'? Given a Roosevelt who manipulates or disregards the law as he sees fit, and you immediately spawn a tribe of Murphys, Hagues, Ickeses, Wallaces, Blacks, Mintons, who may freely manipulate or disregard the law as *they* see fit" (emphasis Nock's). The ACLU was less outspoken but, as historian Laura Weinrib observes, the "Roosevelt administration's tepid response to Mayor Hague pushed the ACLU, once more, toward the federal courts."[56]

The failure of the La Follette Committee to address the Hague matter, as well as the continuing prominence of Minton in the news, conspired to enhance the credibility of the ABA's Bill of Rights Committee as it prepared for the long-delayed ruling in *Hague v. Committee for Industrial Organization*. Grenville Clark moved with remarkable and unprecedented speed in assembling an amicus brief. "Such was his prestige he could swing it," Roger N. Baldwin later recalled. "I marveled at it then and told him so." The brief emphasized that "the right to express unpopular opinions" was "the essence of American liberty." Clark received letters of praise from across ideological lines, including one from former Democratic presidential candidate John W. Davis.[57]

Meanwhile, in September 1938, Clark gave a more substantial speech to the American Bar Association outlining the strategy of the Bill of Rights Committee as well as his own philosophy of ecumenical civil liberties. While not mentioning Hague or Minton specifically, Clark again paired governmental abuses in Jersey City with those of congressional investigating committees as "recent breaches of the letter or the spirit in our Bill of Rights." Clark also identified a worrisome portent to the future of liberty that reflected his moderate Republican worldview. Chief among these was "the continuance of deficit financing by the Federal Government to the point where the currency may become radically depreciated … and a tendency to a vastly increased centralization of governmental power." Clark urged everyone across the political spectrum to recognize that "history shows ... the connection between the breakdown of a nation's finances and the impairment of civil liberties" because fiscal crises often empowered authoritarian leaders. In calling for the federal courts to limit Hague, he also praised decentralized units of government as the safest means to protect liberty and constrain power.[58]

While Clark denied that he was singling out anyone, he made a not too thinly veiled reference to Roosevelt when he warned about the "artificial perpetuation in power of a governmental regime for too long a time." Still not naming Roosevelt directly, Clark cited the danger of misusing the WPA and other federal agencies for political purposes through coercion and force, and in the disbursement of funds and patronage. "Nothing of this nature on anything like the same scale," he elaborated, "has ever been experienced in American history." It was only logical, he specified, "for those who owe their appointment to the administration in power to favor the continuance of that administration."[59]

While Clark pointed with concern to the ongoing "tendency of centralized power to feed on itself," he also saw this trend as largely inevitable. Instead of tilting at windmills, it was better to seek realistic "safeguards whereby even a central authority that is much stronger than we have ever known will be compelled to reconcile its powers with the essentials of our civil rights." Such a safeguard, of course, was the Bill of Rights Committee, which sought to bring together people in an ideological coalition, ranging from the ABA to the ACLU. Clark hoped to foster a new "civil libertarian sensibility" that might have the incidental by-product of shielding property rights from attacks by the administrative state. Clark elaborated more explicitly to Douglas Arant, a board member whom he had recruited to the Bill of Rights Committee, that he wanted to establish a "line of thought" of "firm resistance to authoritarian ideas ... whether in suppressing assembly, or censoring the radio or unnecessarily regimenting the children or intimidating employers from speaking their minds or impairing the independence of the courts or in any other way tending towards the undue subordination of the individual to the State."[60]

The ACLU/ABA strategy of relying on the courts bore fruit on October 27 when a federal district court judge issued a sweeping final decree prohibiting any further "deportations" in Jersey City or interference with the right of citizens to picket and exercise free assembly in public parks and other open-air venues. While the ruling did not find sufficient evidence that city officials had tried to intimidate owners of private halls from renting to the members of the aggrieved organizations, the overall result was a stunning victory for the ACLU/ABA free speech agenda. Hague, of course, appealed immediately, and the case rapidly worked its way through the federal courts.[61]

Leading elements on the left and right hailed the role of the ABA's Bill of Rights Committee in making the court ruling possible. On the left, the *Nation* found the victory to be an "encouraging indication of an awakening on the right to the menace that Hagueism represents in American life," while the *Chicago Daily Tribune,* representing a very different ideological perspective, lauded the committee as a "highly necessary" way to defend "citizens who find themselves incapable of self-protection against powerful autocratic interests."[62]

Despite these cross-ideological plaudits, writers on the left still generally depicted conservatives as Johnny-come-latelies on civil liberties. This was not at all true. In 1931, for example, Robert R. McCormick, publisher of the *Chicago Daily Tribune,* had funded the successful appeal of *Near v. Minnesota,* which led the US Supreme Court to strike down prior restraint laws. That same year, John W. Davis, a founder of the American Liberty League, represented Theodore Dreiser, John Dos Passos, and others who fought extradition to Kentucky for their role defending strikers in Harlan County. In 1936, the conservative trio of McCormick, Davis, and Elisha Hanson, the general counsel of the ANPA, had played key roles in *Grosjean v. American Press Co.* In that case, the anti–New Deal Supreme Court cited the due process clause of the Fourteenth Amendment to void a license tax of newspapers in Louisiana as a violation of the First Amendment.[63]

Reflective of this trend, Grenville Clark, in his critique of court packing in 1937, had argued that the court's reliance on the due process clause had simultaneously advanced economic liberty and "free speech and the right of assembly." Lawyers like Clark, Hogan, and Davis seemed to be building a set of precedents to justify more rulings in favor of free speech.[64]

By 1938, however, after the appointment of two New Deal justices, and the switch in voting of another, the court's justices were groping toward other rationalizations to affirm that goal. In April 1938, this took tangible form in the famous Footnote 4 of *United States v. Carolene Products Co.,* which privileged the first ten amendments over the protection of "ordinary commercial regulation." Footnote 4 also led to a split in the court's emerging New Deal majority on the meaning of the due process clause. Some, such as Felix Frankfurter, remained strongly averse to overturning laws enacted through the democratic process. Others, such as Black and William O. Douglas, however, were much more willing to deploy Footnote 4 as a basis to strike down legislation and even, in some cases, tax and regulatory laws, seen to contradict the Bill of Rights.[65]

Elements in the civil liberties wing of the New Deal coalition were getting to be powerful enough that the administration felt more need to accommodate them. Shortly before the Supreme Court ruled in *Hague v. Committee for Industrial Organization*, for example, the Department of Justice established a new Civil Liberties Unit, later renamed the Civil Rights Section. Frank J. Hogan may have exaggerated when he boasted that the ABA's Bill of Rights Committee had inspired its creation, but he was not completely off base either. The Civil Liberties Unit relied on two Reconstruction-era statutes of the Federal Criminal Code that allowed punishment of persons violating the constitutional rights of "any citizen" and subjected the actions of local officials, including police officers, to federal authority if such violations occurred. The Civil Liberties Unit's activities were initially modest symbolism and primarily centered on labor issues rather than those involving African Americans, but, as Kenneth O'Reilly puts it, "[T]he precedent [for federal involvement in these matters] nevertheless, had been set."[66]

Somewhat reluctantly, Roosevelt was beginning to recognize that he was not served well by perceptions that he had a cavalier attitude toward civil liberties protections. His association with Hague and Minton, combined with his much-publicized attempted purge, had further encouraged suspicions among civil libertarians, who otherwise favored his New Deal agenda, that Roosevelt did not share their beliefs in the Bill of Rights. The ultimate costs at the ballot box were all too obvious. Nearly every member of Congress that Roosevelt had targeted in his purge had won. More seriously, the Democrats suffered serious reverses in November, and more conservative elements assumed de facto majority control. The administration suffered further embarrassments after the election when both news reporting and the Special Committee to Investigate Senatorial Campaign Expenditures and Use of Government Funds uncovered compelling evidence that the WPA had selectively been used to favor or punish certain candidates. These revelations were instrumental in bringing about the Hatch Act of 1939, which limited political activities by employees in the executive branch, except for the president and vice president.[67]

The changes in Congress proved crucial in short-circuiting the power of an official "propaganda unit" to fight anti–New Deal groups such as the National Committee to Uphold Constitutional Government. Harold Ickes, of course, had intended the newly revamped National Emergency Council (NEC) to serve as that unit. Senator Burton K. Wheeler, however, characterized the NEC as a budding pro-Roosevelt political machine controlled by Corcoran, Ickes, and Hopkins to "engineer conservative Democrats out of office because they voted their convictions on the Court Bill." In the House, Representative Paul W. Shafer (R-MI) argued that the NEC was "the clearest example of a Government agency devoted primarily to propagandizing as distinguished from publicity." Its method, he charged, was to "coolly inform voters in particular localities of the amount and kind of beneficence the New Deal generally, and Senators and Congressmen particularly, have bestowed."[68]

This criticism had an element of truth, but the NEC never become the all-out propaganda unit that Ickes had wanted. Historical trends in the United States increasingly ran counter to that possibility. By late 1938, the increasingly negative connotations of propaganda led to greater skepticism by many members of Congress about the NEC's funding and activities. Finally, the then head of the unit, Lowell Mellett, realized, by temperament and experience, that heavy-handed propaganda would alienate his journalistic colleagues.[69]

The Supreme Court's ruling in *Hague v. Committee for Industrial Organization* in June 1939 was somewhat muddled, but there was no doubt that Hague had lost. Holding that the "privilege of a citizen of the United States to use the streets and parks for communication of views on national questions … must not, in the guise of regulation, be abridged or denied," the court warned that the seemingly innocuous standard of "comfort and convenience" should never be "made the instrument of arbitrary suppression of free expression." As precedents, it cited two key Supreme Court rulings from prior to the era of full New Deal control: *Near v. Minnesota* and *Grosjean v. American Press Co.*[70]

The court's decision seemed anticlimactic in a time when the level of support for civil liberties had risen to recent highs. According to Weinrib, "[B]y the spring of 1939, civil liberties had a popular salience that would have astounded dissenters during the First World War. Public approval of the outcome in *Hague* was a forgone conclusion. The dominant sentiment in press coverage of the decision was that the Supreme Court had not gone far enough." Hague had long before accommodated this new consensus by making a truce with the CIO to cooperate against the GOP, which both deemed "anti-labor."[71]

A well-timed illustration of the popular spread of pro–First Amendment attitudes was the movie *Mr. Smith Goes to Washington* (1939), which was in development and production during the Minton Committee and Jersey City controversies. The makers of the film represented a fascinating ideological mix. Director Frank Capra, described by some acquaintances as a "bitter Roosevelt hater," had consistently voted Republican in presidential elections, supported the gold standard, and opposed court packing. The two main screenwriters on the film were Sidney Buchman, a secret member of the Communist Party and an organizer for the Screen Writers Guild, and Myles Connolly, a Catholic conservative.[72]

In *Mr. Smith Goes to Washington*, a corrupt governor, who is a lackey of the "Taylor machine," appoints the idealistic Jefferson Smith (played by James Stewart) to fill a vacant US Senate seat. One of the models for that character was Senator Wheeler, who, at some risk to his career, had led a controversial investigation of Harding's attorney general for corruption in the 1920s. In the film, the governor hopes to exploit the honest, but naïve, Smith as an unwitting tool to improve the image of the machine. Soon, however, Smith discovers that buried within a popular deficiency bill is a secret scheme by the Taylor machine to siphon off "graft" from a dam project. Defying the entire Senate, Smith conducts a one-man filibuster against the bill. The Taylor machine strikes back through methods that could have been taken from Hague's playbook, including police brutality toward demonstrators, breaking up opposition newspapers, and closing off free assembly. Bucking tremendous odds, Smith eventually triumphs and wins almost universal acclaim. It is significant that in 1939 such ideological opposites as Capra, Buchman, and Connolly had worked together effectively to create one of the most compelling celebrations of free speech in the history of the American cinema. The narrative they constructed under Capra's supervision also struck a popular chord at the box office, making the film's grosses second only to *Gone with the Wind* in Hollywood's golden year of 1939.[73]

While shifts in American attitudes toward free speech were prompting Roosevelt to start paying more lip service to that issue, he was not about to abandon Hague or Minton. Both men were too valuable. Roosevelt continued to provide Hague with the strings of patronage for New Jersey; Hague reciprocated by helping in a coordinated effort to engineer the president's nomination in 1940 for a third term. Later that year, he was instrumental in delivering the state's vote to the president and did so again in 1944. Hague continued to exercise the main levers of power when he voluntarily retired in 1947 at age 79 as mayor and two years later as vice chairman of the DNC.[74]

Like Hague, Minton, who stayed firmly in place as assistant Democratic whip during the remainder of his time in the Senate, benefited immensely from Roosevelt's continuing support. After Minton lost reelection in 1940, in part because, as one constituent put it, he was "the person who wanted to censor newspapers," Roosevelt came to the rescue with an appointment as a special adviser and then as a judge of the Seventh Circuit Court of Appeals. More astounding, according to journalist Frank Kent, in a letter to DNC chair Robert E. Hannegan in 1944, Roosevelt named Minton, along with four others, as acceptable running mates. In 1949, more than ten years after first being offered the job and turning it down, Minton became a justice on the Supreme Court, courtesy of his old Senate colleague and friend, Harry S. Truman. Justice Minton's record on the court was very much that of a New Dealer, albeit of the Frankfurter tradition of judicial restraint rather than the activism increasingly pushed by Hugo L. Black and William O. Douglas.[75]

By 1939, the United States had reached a turning point in the history of the First Amendment and in American attitudes toward free expression in a broader sense. The reaction to perceived abuses by Hague and Minton conspired to nurture a broad cross-ideological coalition for civil liberties. Roosevelt was more obstructer than enabler to this trend. He actively aided the work of the Minton Committee, and whether or not the Minton press bill reflected his exact views, he did nothing to stand in the way. It was Congress and the press that stopped the bill dead in its tracks. Similarly, Roosevelt's default position on Hague's abuses was to ignore them. Pressure from journalists, government officials, and judges finally forced him to act, and then in a cautious and partial way. Despite the undoing of the efforts of Hague and Minton, the triumph of civil libertarianism was incomplete. While the protections of the First Amendment had expanded for the print press and the right of free assembly, they were shrinking for the leading form of mass communications in the United States.

4

The Necessary First Stage: Radio and the Quashing of a Free Speech Medium

NO PRESIDENT IN American history depended more on radio for the success of his administration than Franklin D. Roosevelt. His fireside chats and other speeches over the airwaves were instrumental in both selling the New Deal and protecting it. Ironically, the actions of Presidents Coolidge and Hoover did more than anything else to facilitate Roosevelt's legendary domination over radio. Their policies of politicization, most notably the quasi-nationalization of the airwaves, enabled Roosevelt to take it to the next level. Because of Republican policies, the de facto free speech protections of radio, which had once approximated those of the print press, were seriously impaired. These policies provided precedents, as well as a firm foundation, for what came later.

In 1920, governmental regulation of content for commercial radio was close to nonexistent. Designed purely for point-to-point communication, the Radio Act of 1912 (especially as interpreted by the courts) hemmed in the discretion of the Department of Commerce to granting licenses. Pretty much the federal government's only role was to assign wavelengths and police against interference. The end result was a de facto property rights regime. By the early 1920s, as Charlotte Twight observes, "[t]he market alternative was well understood: lively markets in which broadcasting licenses were purchased and sold had existed in the years preceding adoption of the 1927 act." The 1927 Act established the Federal Radio Commission, which was the precursor of the modern Federal Communications Commission. In 1928, James Patrick Taugher likened a license under the 1912 Act "to the Homestead Laws under which the government's land (the free element—in radio, the ether) becomes the user's irrevocably in fee simple."[1]

This de facto property rights regime greatly constrained the ability of regulators to restrict content. The regulators knew this only too well. When asked in 1926 to specify what powers the federal government had over radio speech, Stephen B. Davis Jr., the solicitor of the Department of Commerce (a position akin to a general counsel), quipped, "Absolutely nothing." Similarly, in 1925, Harold P. Stokes, a high official in the department, flatly denied the existence of "federal authority of any kind by which the Secretary of Commerce may suppress advertising, or in any way interfere with the character of radio programs. His very limited authority extends only to questions of interference between stations." Practical considerations, in addition to real or perceived legal obstacles, also deterred federal regulators from meddling with content. If such meddling occurred, Secretary of Commerce Herbert Hoover asserted, "the complaints would double and treble and there would be immediate demands for a senatorial investigation." A consequence of this hands-off policy was to give broadcasters a degree of security akin to newspapers and allow breathing space for controversial expression. [2]

The Department of Commerce's unwillingness or inability to censor, however, did not mean the states were free to step into the regulatory breach. Federal authorities had constricted power over the ether, but they jealously guarded what little power they did have from other levels of government. When Edwin J. Coughlin, a member of the New York state assembly, proposed a bill in January 1927 to license and censor "obscene or indecent programs," for example, the Department of Commerce swiftly gave its firm disapproval. New York, Davis warned, lacked jurisdiction because of the interstate nature of radio. Coughlin never made any headway with his bill, which, in retrospect, was chiefly significant for its rarity. [3]

The failed attempt in New York aside, localities and states showed little apparent appetite to censor radio during the 1920s. "The agitation for censorship of the radio," according to an editorial in the *Exhibitors Herald* from 1924, "is now weak in character and very limited in scope." One factor holding back potential state regulations was that the federal government had already staked out an exclusive domain of granting licenses, designating wavelengths, and policing against interference. Still, the relative absence of action by localities and states in this area is somewhat puzzling, given their predilection to restrict such forms of speech as film and theater and the right of public assembly, and even to impose prior restraint on newspapers.[4]

The main forms of content control were variants of "private censorship," somewhat akin to the editorial discretion exercised by newspaper editors. In the heyday of the "radio trust" in 1922 and 1923, this sometimes had a politicized tinge. The trust was directly fostered by the federal government and derived its authority from an exclusive cross-licensing agreement between the American Telephone and Telegraph Company (AT&T), General Electric, the Radio Corporation of America (RCA), and Westinghouse. The consortium had exclusive patents on radio-related products ranging from vacuum tubes to transmitters. The trust tried to dominate the broadcasting industry by requiring all stations to pay license fees as a condition both to purchase the necessary broadcasting apparatus, including transmitters produced by Western Electric, and to receive programming over telephone lines.[5]

In 1922, AT&T, acting as the lynchpin in the trust, launched WEAF in New York City in a long-term scheme to establish a broadcasting network of thirty-eight high-powered stations linked together over its telephone lines. Rather than producing programs, AT&T provided a platform for others to do so upon payment of a fee. It also prohibited stations from selling time for advertising, except for WEAF, or risk a lawsuit for patent infringement. Stations established by trust members, including Westinghouse and General Electric, were governed by similar rules. To beat back potential rivals, members of the trust refused to sell new stations transmitters of more than 500 watts in power. An Illinois broadcaster was typical in fretting that his station might "have to discontinue on account of the large license fee which the AT&T wants us to pay."[6]

Under this system, the radio trust exercised full control over speech on stations in its orbit and did not hesitate to exercise it. Perhaps the most famous example involved future broadcasting legend H. V. Kaltenborn, then a popular columnist for the Brooklyn *Daily Eagle*. In 1923, WEAF persuaded the publishers of that paper to produce a daily program of Kaltenborn's commentary in exchange for a fee paid to AT&T. Several other stations, including WCAP of Washington, DC, picked up the program. Accustomed to the comparative freedom of a newspaper column, Kaltenborn refused to trim his sails despite much pressure to do so. When an AT&T executive cautioned him to moderate his commentary lest it offend a judge in a rate case involving the company, Kaltenborn declared flatly, "You can't expect me to take one attitude as an editor of the Brooklyn *Daily Eagle* and then to ignore that attitude when I am on the air *for* the Brooklyn *Daily Eagle*."[7]

For the time being, Kaltenborn stayed on the radio with his integrity intact. One year later, however, he did not fare so well after he chastised Secretary of State Charles Evans Hughes for his hostility to US recognition of Russia. After Hughes heard the offending broadcast on WCAP, he called AT&T to demand that Kaltenborn be silenced. At the time, the company, which depended for its life blood as a regulated public utility on maintaining political good will, was also under investigation by both the Department of Justice and the US Congress for manipulation of radio patents. Skittish company executives responded to Hughes's complaint by dropping the program on WCAP and revoking the *Daily Eagle*'s contract with WEAF. As justification for these actions, William P. Banning, a public relations executive with AT&T, stated that his company wanted "complete cooperation with every government institution."[8]

But the "radio trust," as most cartels eventually do, was already starting to implode as smaller broadcasters rebelled through both litigation and noncompliance. The resisters won some public support by accusing AT&T of censoring their free speech. More quietly, and more seriously, many stations did not bother to obtain an AT&T license. By the end of the year, the level of noncompliance became so widespread that AT&T dropped its patent litigation and its dream of dominating national broadcasting. The breakdown of this system dealt a severe blow to "private censorship" and allowed an outlet for more ideological diversity. An indicator of the radio trust's vulnerability against those who flouted it was Kaltenborn's quick career rebound after his firing, eventually landing jobs with two stations outside the orbit of the radio trust: WAHG, for a very short time, and then WOR in late 1925. Despite pressure from several powerful, aggrieved parties, including Mayor Jimmy Walker of New York, WOR's management consistently defended Kaltenborn's free speech.[9]

But other developments countered any tendency for the property rights model, which then prevailed in the print press, to make inroads in radio. Secretary of Commerce Hoover, his allies in Congress, and the big commercial stations rejected the possibility out of hand. Beginning in 1921 at a series of radio conferences, Hoover pursued, sometimes in fits and starts, an alternative vision for radio. "We hear a great deal about the freedom of the air," he proclaimed. "But … Freedom cannot mean a license to every person or corporation who wishes to broadcast his name or his wares and thus monopolize the listener's set." Hoover also operated under the premise that radio listeners, unlike newspaper readers, were unable to skip over "obstructive advertising."[10]

While Hoover recognized that current law allowed him no discretion to regulate content, he most certainly wanted that power. Though he shied away from an outright endorsement of censorship, Hoover's tenure combined hostility to extension of First Amendment protections to radio with an equally strident opposition to any hint of property rights taking hold in wavelengths. At the 1922 radio conference and later, he proclaimed the "necessity to establish public right over the ether roads. … There must be no national regret that we have parted with a great national asset." In his memoirs, Hoover recalled his determination to head off unnamed "Radio men" who were planning to preempt "channels through the air as private property." His immediate goals as secretary of commerce were to shrink the numbers of stations, especially in "congested centers," and to prevent existing broadcasters from keeping their "wave-lengths permanently in their favored positions irrespective of their service." Combined with this, Hoover used his authority to consistently favor stations that had generic and broad appeal rather than those catering to particular constituencies or those centered on "naked commercial selfishness."[11]

Hoover had a long wish list, but in 1923, the Supreme Court of the District of Columbia in *Hoover v. Intercity Radio Co.* severely constrained his already limited discretion. The court ordered the Department of Commerce to grant licenses to all applicants who met the minimum qualifications but also affirmed the department's authority to assign specific wavelengths and impose time sharing. Thereafter, the department's main role was to enforce a squatters' rights approach of de facto property rights in frequencies.[12]

A consequence of *Hoover v. Intercity Radio Co.*, in addition to hemming in the authority of regulators, was to nurture a highly diverse broadcasting sector encompassing some six hundred stations. These included roughly one hundred educational stations and about fifty owned by various religious entities, ranging from small churches to the Paulist Fathers, a society of Roman Catholic priests. An assortment of other stations were likewise operated by fraternal societies, unions, and socialist organizations. While private for-profit businesses owned about two-thirds of the stations, these too did not fit into a single pattern. Their ranks included newspapers, utility companies, and automobile dealerships, which, in most cases, primarily sought profits for the core business, rather than from that of the station itself.[13]

In contrast to the standardized commercial sector of later years, this regime gave great leeway to "rogue" broadcasters, or, as one detractor dubbed them, "the smaller and irresponsible stations." Among the owners were such popular firebrands as Jerry Buckley, John R. Brinkley, and Robert P. Shuler. These and other independent broadcasters, as Clifford J. Doerksen observes, "vastly outnumbered high-class corporate stations throughout the 1920s." Often self-financed, they had deep ties to local, small-town, and rural markets, leaving them relatively insulated from elite pressures or standard commercial considerations.[14]

Amid these developments, Hoover tried to reassert his dwindling authority. Beginning in 1922 and 1923, the Department of Commerce began to impose a division of radio stations into lower power and higher power categories. In a few cases, the imprimatur of the department permitted the higher power (Class B) stations to be heard over several states. The lowest rung on the ladder were Class C stations. The department consigned those to the most crowded part of the spectrum and often forced them to share times. They included many educational and religious broadcasters. Under Hoover's regime, the domain of these lower power stations became, as Erik Barnouw notes, "an inferno of the unfavored ... a place of howls and squeals and eternal misery." Sometimes acting on dubious legal authority, he used all possible means to discriminate in favor of those stations that were intended to appeal to a wide listener cross section.[15]

In close cooperation with Congress, Hoover also worked assiduously to prevent any potential property rights model from asserting itself. On March 21, 1924, he praised one of the leading regulatory bills introduced by Representative Wallace H. White Jr. (R-ME) for granting the department wide discretionary power to protect the "public interest." He considered this mandate as necessary to circumvent any encroachment of a "vested right in the use of the ether." Hoover was speaking to the choir. A key indicator that the Republican-controlled Congress was on Hoover's side was the broad support given to a proposed joint House/Senate resolution in 1924 affirming that radio was a "public possession and provided for limited grants for its use."[16]

Despite *Hoover v. Intercity Radio Co.*, the Department of Commerce, citing increased scarcity on the broadcast spectrum, pursued an unofficial policy of turning down license applications beginning in 1925, sometimes in a highly selective and legally dubious way. A case in point was its treatment of Rufus F. Turner, an acclaimed African American inventor and broadcasting pioneer, who set up a station in the St. Augustine Roman Catholic Church in Washington, DC, to broadcast sermons and choir music. When Turner informally inquired about applying for an official wavelength, R. Y. Cadmus, regional "radio inspector" for the Department of Commerce, advised against it, saying no more were available. As Turner soon noticed, however, Cadmus, despite what he had said earlier, found enough room to give licenses to three stations in the city. When Turner responded to this apparent double standard by making a formal application, he was summarily turned down. He then proposed assuming the license of one of several discontinued local stations but was turned down again. "Mr. Cadmus has done all he possibly could to keep us from going on the air," Turner complained.[17]

As all this was happening, Hoover was meeting persistent roadblocks in getting formal action from Congress to give his department more discretion. Quite simply, the public demand was lacking. Most Americans, unlike policymakers, did not seem too inclined to overturn the radio status quo, which functioned, albeit in a haphazard way, to meet their needs. In 1927, legal scholar Frank S. Rowley stated that the "situation was fairly well in hand. There was some interference, due to the surplus of stations over the number of available channels, but in almost every case, station-owners showed a willingness to cooperate in making beneficial adjustments." Despite more than a few individual complaints, neither listeners nor those connected directly with the industry revealed any great sense of urgency for change, much less of crisis.[18]

A crisis did finally come, however, and it was politically engineered. In April 1926, Judge James Herbert Wilkerson handed down *United States v. Zenith Radio Corporation et al.* in the District Court of the United States for the Northern District of Illinois. At the center of the case was a Chicago station owned by Eugene F. McDonald, the head of the Zenith Corporation. The Department of Commerce had restricted the station's broadcasts to only two hours per week over a shared frequency. McDonald made a great show of fighting back by jumping his station to a better wavelength that the department had allotted to Canadian use. When he refused to relent after a warning, the department took him to court. Handing McDonald a resounding victory, Wilkerson ruled that the Department of Commerce was powerless to make such basic regulations as enforcement of wavelengths and time regulations.[19]

Although McDonald resented the department's limits on his station, he was essentially on Hoover's side in seeking enhanced federal control. As a subcommittee member of the Radio Conference in January 1926, he had called for a centralized authority "which must have the right, through issue of licenses, control of power, assignment of wave lengths and other appropriate measures." McDonald showed his admiration in more tangible terms through a Zenith press release with the adulatory headline: "Hoover in Office One Hundred Years." Any challenge he made to Hoover's authority was that of a friend, and more than a little tongue-in-check.[20]

Hoover's next action precipitated even further chaos. He assigned Acting Attorney General William J. Donovan, sometimes described as "Hoover's Merlin," to draft a legal opinion outlining the extent of the department's authority. Donovan, who later gained fame as the head of the Office of Strategic Services (OSS), responded with an unusually narrow reading of the Radio Act of 1912. He interpreted the law as giving him no power to assign or enforce wavelengths or impose time-sharing agreements. Showing himself to be of the same mind as Hoover on the final goal, Donovan called for "new legislation, carefully adapted to meet the needs of both the present and the future."[21]

Hoover v. Zenith, or more accurately Donovan's interpretation of it, conflicted with *Hoover v. Intercity*, which had permitted the department to enforce wavelengths and time sharing. Revealingly, Hoover did not take the customary route of appealing to a higher court to resolve the contradiction, but instead, on July 9, he completely stood down from any regulatory role (aside from as a register of licenses). In doing so, he gave free rein for stations to jump frequencies, boost power, or flout time-sharing agreements. This was, as Thomas Hazlett puts it, the onset of Hoover's "strategic manufacture of airwave chaos" aimed at prodding Congress to enact more restrictive legislation. Hoover's decision, as described by Senator Clarence C. Dill (D-WA), an author of the two leading bills then pending, seemed "almost like an invitation to broadcasters to do their worst." One of the byproducts was to make Americans "completely 'fed up' with uncontrolled radio with its wave piracy, interferences, and blatant noises under the guise of programs" and to demand "that the 'program smearer' be regulated into a semblance of order."[22]

Station owners did not react passively to this manufactured chaos. They moved into the breach to re-create the de facto property rights system destroyed by the *Zenith* decision and Donovan's legal opinion of it. Paul B. Klugh, executive chairman of the National Association of Broadcasters, predicted the onset of lawsuits "to protect stations' [property] rights." He considered it a near certainty "that such cases could be won, and the offending stations would no doubt be enjoined from broadcasting." In October, Klugh's prediction began to come to pass. The *Chicago Daily Tribune*, the owner of radio station WGN ("World's Greatest Newspaper"), sued the Oak Leaves Broadcasting Company, the owner of WGES, after that station intruded into WGN's wavelength shortly after the *Zenith* decision. The *Tribune* mobilized the services of Kirkland, Fleming, Green, Martin, and Ellis, a prestigious law firm cofounded by publisher Robert R. McCormick. In response to WGES's wavelength encroachment, Louis G. Caldwell, the lawyer from the firm assigned to the case, countered that WGN had established a property right because of prior use.[23]

In a long-waited opinion, Judge Francis S. Wilson ruled for the *Tribune*. Although he acknowledged that the nature of the case seemed "novel in its newness," he identified helpful precedents in the common law. Chief among these was case law upholding prior appropriation rights of water users and enjoining interlopers from electronic interference in telephone lines. Using these for guidance, Wilson stated that in "the circumstances of this case priority of time creates a superiority in right." Backing Caldwell's argument, Wilson ordered WGES to cease interfering with WGN's established wavelength.[24]

Despite Wilson's firm anchoring of this ruling in well-established common law traditions, almost all commentary from the press and legal community depicted *Oak Leaves* as a stopgap to inevitable federal legislation, not as a permanent solution. Judge Wilson said as much in his opinion. But speculation also increased that Congress might even use the ruling as a basis for national law. The *Chicago Daily Tribune*, which had already promoted "property rights in the ether," reprinted an editorial from the *Press-Gazette* of Green Bay, Wisconsin, which was hopeful that in the short term "other stations which are having trouble with trespassers will take steps to protect their property rights in the air as the TRIBUNE has done." Similarly, the *Georgetown Law Journal* hailed *Oak Leaves* as a "pioneer application of settled equitable principles to an altogether novel situation." Even before the court's ruling, *Radio Broadcast* urged that first users get "a priority over that wavelength regardless of any number of followers who may later covet it."[25]

If most commentators did not champion the application of the common law as a permanent solution to radio chaos, it was often because they regarded that approach as politically unrealistic rather than impractical on the merits. Many subscribed to the view that a legislative solution by Congress was a fait accompli. But by this time, small but increasing numbers were showing doubts that the inevitable was indeed inevitable. Key policymakers began to express concern that the courts, building on the *Oak Leaves* precedent, might short-circuit the drive for federal regulation. Most notably, Representative Wallace H. White Jr. (R-ME), one of the main architects of potential legislation, feared that the failure of Congress to act made it "inevitable" that the courts would eventually apportion property rights and close the door to federal regulation. The other main architect, Senator Dill, agreed.[26]

Some influential players in broadcasting were even starting to take steps to promote or at least accommodate themselves to a permanent system based on common law property rights. Most notably, the Committee on Air Law of the American Bar Association charged that the much-touted White bill conflicted with the "sound law" of *Oak Leaves* because it failed to "create any rights" to wavelengths and deprived "the citizens of property rights under the pending legislation." The committee also went on record against the establishment of a federal radio commission to administer any new law, referring to "a constant tendency on the part of Commissions to enlarge their own powers."[27]

Ultimately, the momentum in favor of congressional action to close off the alternative of common law property rights was too great to overcome. In February, President Calvin Coolidge signed the Radio Act of 1927, which combined the ideas of the White and Dill bills. His justification was that "many more stations have been operating than can be accommodated within the limited number of wave lengths available … the whole service of this most important public function has drifted into such chaos as seems likely, if not remedied, to destroy its great value." The stated purpose of the new law was to maintain federal control "over all the channels … and to provide for the use of such channels, but not the ownership thereof, by individuals, firms, or corporations." The act empowered a new five-member Federal Radio Commission (FRC) to approve licenses of up to three years.[28]

Directly at odds with the property rights approach of *Oak Leaves*, the act required licensees to waive any existing claims to wavelengths and mandated that any sales or transfers by existing stations first be approved by the commission. Representative White, the main sponsor in the House, emphasized that one of the goals of legislation was to forever cast aside the "principle" of the 1912 act that "an applicant received his license as a matter of right." The Radio Act of 1927 also opened the first sliver of an entering wedge for what eventually became the fairness doctrine by mandating equal (though not necessarily free) time to "legally qualified candidates."[29]

On the face of it, the act's affirmation of the "right of free speech" in Section 29 was nearly absolute, the only exceptions being "obscene, indecent, or profane language." This anti-censorship guarantee, however, clashed directly with another provision authorizing the commission to reject any license seen to conflict with the "public interest, convenience, or necessity." Nothing like that wording had appeared in the Radio Act of 1912. Although signed by one of the most conservative presidents in American history, the Radio Act of 1927 was a bold leap forward in governmental intervention in economic affairs. Dill, the main Senate sponsor, even went so far as to say that the premise upon which it rested was "the Government's absolute control of the situation." The *Los Angeles Times* did not greatly exaggerate, characterizing the act as "the most sweeping regulation ever imposed by the government upon any private enterprise."[30]

Most broadcasters, including those from the National Broadcasting Company (NBC), the first of the networks founded in 1926, supported the act. Hoover cited radio as one of the rare examples "when the whole industry and country is praying for more regulation." Given the context, this was not surprising. The FRC board members often came from the ranks of the large commercial broadcasters, and Secretary Hoover had emphasized protection of "the American system" of private broadcasting, albeit on "public" and regulated wavelengths. If a case ever can be made for an example of "industry capture," the creation of the FRC stands out as one of the most compelling.[31]

At their first meeting, the new FRC commissioners left no doubt about their intentions. They had before them several feasible proposals to both solve the interference problem and avoid any deletion of existing stations. The first option was to lengthen the top end of the broadcasting band through a technical fix. Although this might have accommodated all the stations then on the air, the commissioners rejected it, arguing that it was unfair to listeners who might have to buy new sets to get reception from all the stations. Contradicting this, but apparently forgotten at the time, however, was the statement of Stephen B. Davis Jr. during the previous year that it was feasible to accommodate "all the radio stations in the world in the one meter wave length" and that "you can shift that band any way that it is desired to." The second proposal under consideration by the commission was to reduce the separation between existing frequencies so as to negate the need to purchase new sets. This was rejected as well. "The commissioners," stated *Radio Broadcast* in June 1927, "were convinced that less stations was [sic] the only answer." As Hazlett concludes, the rejection of these measures "did not protect listeners, but rather deprived them of a wide array of radio programs." Even under the existing regime, *Oak Leaves* or not, radio manufacturers may well have eliminated much of the "chaos" engineered by Hoover via such devices as inexpensive "mufflers" for existing radios. These technological innovations were making it more feasible, as Steven Phipps notes, for ordinary listeners to filter out much, "if not all, of the interference … simply by upgrading to a receiver with higher 'selectivity,'" thus giving listeners "the ability to tune out competing stations."[32]

After an interlude of relative inaction, the FRC began culling the herd with a vengeance in 1928 through General Order 40. Of some 732 stations then in existence, the commission ordered 164 to demonstrate that their continued operation served the "public interest, convenience or necessity." The FRC did not precisely define the phrase, noting with some merit that it resembled a well-established standard for the regulation of other industries and was "no less certain or definite than other phrases which have found their way

into Federal statutes and which have been upheld by the Supreme Court. …
An example is 'unfair methods of competition.'"[33]

While the FRC as a general practice gave priority to the first users of
wavelengths, it carefully denied any intention of granting a property right
or vested interest. Hoover had consistently argued that such an idea had no
place in radio regulation. He recalled that when he had assumed office, he
had set out to "avoid granting any property rights in the ether and … so far
as they exist, [those rights] are vested entirely in the government." This did
not mean full government operation in the European sense, however. The
American approach left "broadcasting in the hands of private enterprise as
nearly as possible free to work out its own salvation." But, as bears repeating,
the "American system" did not constitute laissez-faire in content nor, for that
matter, in keeping "the present users of wave-lengths permanently in their
favored positions irrespective of their service."[34]

From almost the beginning, the commission waged all-out war on alleged
"propaganda stations," a category of rather murky meaning. Singularly unhelpful in arriving at a definition was the FRC's characterization of "propaganda" content as programming intended mainly for "private interests of …
individuals or groups." Given the scarcity of wavelengths, the commission
regarded it as anathema to the public interest to allow "room in the broadcast
band for every school of thought, religious, political, social and economic to
have its own … mouthpiece in the ether." Instead, the FRC held out the ideal
of presenting "balanced" political views to be achieved through "preferential"
treatment to "public service" stations that appealed to a broad cross section
rather than a segmented market. The essential "sameness" of the broadcasting dial of subsequent decades began in earnest with General Order 40. In
Great Lakes Broadcasting Co. v. Federal Radio Commission (1930), the Court of
Appeals for the District of Columbia agreed with the FRC's contention that
advancement of the public service goal took precedence over programming
that was "interesting or valuable to … only a small portion of that public …
the rest of the listeners are being discriminated against."[35]

The FRC hobbled the "propaganda stations" in a multitude of ways. In
1925, for example, the Roman Catholic Paulist order owned one of the high-
est-wattage stations in the US. In its first year, the FRC forced it to share a
wavelength with a commercial station of only 500 watts and limited broad-

casts to no more than two hours a day. The fate of another religious station, WCBD, owned by Wilbur Glenn Voliva, was similar. Founded in 1923, it had become one of the most powerful and well-capitalized voices on the ether, propagating the esoteric theology of Alexander Dowie. Under General Order 40, the FRC consigned it to a wavelength not available on many sets and limited it to daylight hours, when signals did not carry as far.[36]

Of course, not all the "propaganda" stations were religious. WCLF, operated by the Chicago Federation of Labor, was also a victim of General Order 40. The station started in 1926 at 5,000 watts, but in September 1928 the FRC confined it to a less desirable frequency shared with another station and barred it from the more lucrative nighttime hours. Further to the political left, a similar fate befell WEVD (from the initials of the Socialist Party leader Eugene Victor Debs). Although it was able to barely escape unscathed from the first round of deliberations under General Order 40, the FRC admonished it to "operate with due regard for the opinions of others." The reprieve was temporary, however. In 1929, the FRC moved WEVD to a less desirable frequency shared by three other stations, singling it out as one of "the potential purveyors of propaganda."[37]

The treatment of nonprofit stations (many of them pioneers in early broadcasting) repeated the pattern of wattage limitation, forced time sharing, and consignment to the daytime. The latter was especially harmful to the ninety-five college stations because night classes were a key means of earning revenue. These suffered a period of carnage as their numbers plunged by more than 50 percent from 1927 to 1930. The decline in nonprofit broadcasters as a whole was even steeper, falling from 200 stations in 1927 to 65 in 1934. The survivors almost all had lower power and a more constricted listener base. Communications historian Bill Kirkpatrick observes that before 1927, "small stations faced little existential threat from regulators. They might go out of business (and often did), but the Commerce Department lacked the explicit authority to revoke licenses or kick smaller stations off the air."[38]

A most obvious illustration of FRC favoritism toward the emerging networks under General Order 40 was through the bestowal of "clear channel" status. These high wattage channels had a broader geographical reach and crowded out the wavelengths of local stations. "Of the first twenty-five stations set aside for clear channels by the FRC," Robert W. McChesney notes, "twenty-three had been licensed to broadcasters affiliated with NBC." The FRC's reasoning was that clear channel status fostered generic programming over that appealing to discrete local, ethnic, religious, educational, or political groups. For many of the smaller, and older, stations, the result was either oblivion or confinement to a crowded and less desirable frequency, and reduced broadcasting time.[39]

Well after General Order 40, the primary obstacle to the survival of the nonprofits and the smaller commercial independents was that the owners lacked sufficiently deep pockets to defend themselves before regulators. The FRC-required regular updates and record keeping strained limited budgets, as did licensing renewals and appeals, which usually meant expensive trips to Washington, DC, or hiring lawyers. *Variety*, no friend of the small stations, complained of "the FRC's tendency to reduce stations to the role of perpetual supplicant for favors." On top of this pattern of discrimination came General Order 116, which mandated installing costly frequency monitors and other equipment. From the perspective of the FRC, having a more localized focus was apparently not an asset but an obstacle to overcome. FRC general counsel Louis G. Caldwell stressed the "universal agreement" that the airwaves had "far too many broadcasting stations (particularly those of the regional class) in simultaneous operation." The overriding FRC goal was standardization of format. Summarizing the mindset of regulators, Kirkpatrick asserts that the "FRC was not interested in preserving local idiosyncrasies and regional identities."[40]

Leading the legal attack on General Order 40 in the courts was Wilbur Glenn Voliva, who charged that the FRC's seizure of WCBD's original wavelength violated the Fifth Amendment's takings clause. Bereft of allies, his cause had little hope. The American Civil Liberties Union, always leery of property rights in radio and partly because of distrust of potential private monopoly, offered no help. The same was true for the Committee on Air Law of the American Bar Association, which had abandoned its previous support for the property rights model. The final decision in 1930 of the Court of Appeals of Washington, DC, set a pattern for later rulings by flatly rejecting any "property right as against the regulatory power of the United States, to engage in broadcasting."[41]

The dust from General Order 40 had barely settled when the FRC began to resort to more punitive measures. From 1930 to 1931, it conducted, in the words of historian Clifford J. Doerksen, a "systematic crackdown on troublemakers," nearly all of whom had begun broadcasting prior to the Radio Act of 1927. The first on the target list in this FRC "cleanup" period was John Romulus Brinkley, owner of radio station KFKB in Milford, Kansas. Founded in 1923, the station's powerful transmitter reached a large section of the country. It featured a full complement of locally produced programming including crooners, country singers, religious broadcasts, and storytellers. A relatively small part of programming was hosted by Brinkley, who publicized such dubious medical techniques as a "goat-gland" cure and aired his political and social views. It did not take long before Brinkley's medical advertising and on-air advice drew the ire of the American Medical Association.[42]

In 1930, KFKB became the very first station to lose its license specifically because of program content. The FRC rejected license renewal, citing Brinkley's matter-of-fact "health talks" on sex as offensive and thus contrary to the public interest, convenience, interest, or necessity. During a temporary stay, Brinkley ran as a write-in candidate for governor of Kansas. He came in a strong third and might have won but for a last-minute rule throwing out all ballots not specifically and exactly marked "J. R. [both in capital letters] Brinkley." In its final ruling against Brinkley in *KFKB Broadcasting Association v. Federal Radio Commission* (1931), the Court of Appeals (unconvincingly) denied any restraint of free speech: "In considering the question whether the public interest, convenience, or necessity will be served by a renewal of appellant's license, the commission has merely exercised its undoubted right to take note of appellant's past conduct, which is not censorship."[43]

As freedom of speech was narrowing drastically on the radio, it was expanding in the print press. More succinctly, the late 1920s brought the harbingers of what eventually became a free speech revolution. Prime instigators of this revolution included Robert R. McCormick, the conservative Republican publisher of the *Chicago Daily Tribune*, and his law firm, Kirkland, Fleming, Green, Martin, and Ellis. In 1926, the firm, represented by attorney (and future FRC general counsel) Louis G. Caldwell, had won *Oak Leaves*. As already mentioned, however, any possible precedent was rendered moot by the Radio Act of 1927.

Not long after that legislation took effect, McCormick and his associated law firm celebrated a far more publicized legal victory that created a long-lasting precedent for protection of the print press. The events leading up to this victory began in the spring of 1928 when McCormick became head of the American Newspaper Publishers Association's (ANPA) Committee on Freedom of the Press. He immediately began the search for a possible landmark court case for free speech in the print press.[44]

He discovered it in a case centering on the *Saturday Press*, a "scurrilous rag" published by Jay M. Near. At the time, Near was appealing his conviction under Minnesota's Public Nuisance law, or "gag" law. Enacted in 1925, the law imposed prior restraint on any "malicious, scandalous and defamatory newspaper, magazine or other periodical." Near was an unsympathetic figure. He mixed sometimes effective crusades against public corruption with anti-Semitic and racist conspiracy rants. Although the American Civil Liberties Union, like McCormick, held no brief for his screeds, it seized on the case as a precedent to overturn prior restraint laws. In 1928, McCormick deployed Kirkland, Fleming, Green, Martin, and Ellis to assume control of the case. The lead lawyer was Edward G. Caldwell, assisted by his brother Louis, who had resigned as general counsel of the FRC.[45]

In 1929, Near lost the first round when the Minnesota Supreme Court unanimously upheld the gag law as a legitimate exercise of the state's police powers. As Near's lawyers appealed to the US Supreme Court, however, McCormick, joined by the ACLU, worked tirelessly to build a groundswell of press support to overturn the conviction. Although he encountered much apathy and lethargy from his fellow ANPA members in raising money for the legal costs, he eventually persuaded nearly all of them to go on record in favor of overturning Minnesota's law. On June 1, 1931, a narrowly split court did just that and provided a game-changing precedent against prior restraint laws. The left–right coalition for free speech had an early triumph.[46]

In the months immediately after wrapping up *Near*, Kirkland, Fleming, Green, Martin, and Ellis provided defense counsel in another potential landmark free speech case, this time in radio. It involved station KGEF (Keeping God Ever First) in Los Angeles, founded by evangelist and political populist Robert P. Shuler in 1926. The listenership on some days spanned from Mexico to Canada. As minister of the Trinity Methodist Church, Shuler declaimed against municipal corruption, for stronger Prohibition enforcement, and against the doctrines and practices of Sister Aimee Semple McPherson. Ray

Duncan of *Los Angeles Magazine* summed up Shuler's power and appeal: "Politicians feared him, criminals avoided him, police hated him, newspapers deplored him, ministers preached against him, and City Hall trembled before him. Nobody spoke well of him except the public." Shuler's rambunctious style also brought him enemies in the Hoover administration and the FRC.[47]

At the time of the victory for free speech in *Near*, Shuler was facing ever greater pressure from federal radio regulators. But unlike most other rogue or propaganda broadcasters, he had sufficient financial resources to hire competent and experienced counsel. The scheduled license renewal hearing in November 1931 promised to be a battle royale. After failing to persuade Representative James Montgomery Beck (R-PA), a leading conservative Republican in the US House and former solicitor general, to act as counsel, Kirkland, Fleming, Green, Martin, and Ellis agreed to provide the defense. The attorney assigned to the case was Louis G. Caldwell and, exchanging previous roles, his brother Edward C. Caldwell assisted him.[48]

From the beginning, however, the Caldwell brothers were of one mind on their legal strategy. In an article for the *Journal of Radio Law* in October, one month prior to the FRC hearings, Edward C. Caldwell asserted that Shuler's free speech rights were protected by Section 29 of the Radio Act of 1927, which prohibited censorship of political opinion over the airwaves. That section, he asserted, barred the FRC from denying applications or rejecting renewals because "the programs consist of the utterance of serious opinions and sentiments, of propaganda bearing upon the social, political, and economic life of the country, or of the exposure of supposed wrongs suffered by individuals or communities." He conceded that the FRC might have discretion to regulate nonpolitical programing, including sports and entertainment, and to prohibit direct (but not indirect) advertising, but political speech, broadly defined, was in a protected category. Fresh from his triumph in *Near*, Edward C. Caldwell's main conclusion was that the prohibition of prior restraint in the print press should also apply to radio.[49]

At the FRC hearings in November, the radio preacher's enemies showed up in force, including a prosecutor he had once driven from office. In a decision handed down only days after the hearings, the FRC refused to renew KGEF's license, castigating the station as a "forum for outrageous and unfounded attacks on public officials" and as "sensational rather than instructive." As had occurred in the Brinkley case, the decision instantly wiped out thousands of dollars of investment just because of a single program in a full broadcasting day.[50]

At this point, Gordon W. Moss, the ACLU's national secretary, wrote Shuler offering aid if he wanted to appeal. Responding courteously, Shuler admitted that he had come to more greatly appreciate the need to ensure civil liberties for everyone. Although the appeal went forward, there is no evidence that the ACLU participated any further during the full year after Moss's letter. The reason is something of a mystery. Shuler's political views, which included fundamentalist anti-Catholicism and past, largely pragmatic, alliances with the Klan in Los Angeles to enforce Prohibition, probably had something to do with it. Near, of course, had even more extreme views, but he was easy to dismiss as a harmless irritant. Shuler, by contrast, had presided over a radio and religious empire that had swayed major elections.[51]

Nevertheless, ACLU leaders were genuinely conflicted on the issue. Soon after the exchange of letters between Moss and Shuler, Clifton J. Taft, the director of the Southern California branch, wrote "An Open Letter to Bob Shuler," stating that he "would have a lot more heart to go to bat for you" if Shuler had expressed greater concern about the free speech rights of labor unions and others on the left. Whatever the reason for the ACLU's one year of inaction, Kirkland, Fleming, Green, Martin, and Ellis continued to carry the water in the case.[52]

On November 28, 1932, the federal Court of Appeals dashed the hopes of Shuler's lawyers yet again by upholding the FRC's revocation of KGEF's license. Waving aside the contention of the Caldwells, the opinion denied the existence of censorship or prior restraint and argued that Shuler was perfectly free to say whatever he wanted. Using a standard that the courts had almost universally rejected for the print press, it stated that "he may not, as we think, demand, of right, the continued use of an instrumentality of commerce for such purposes, or any other, except in subordination to all reasonable rules and regulations." The revocation of Shuler's license, it explained, did not violate the Fifth Amendment's takings clause because of "a marked difference between the destruction of physical property … and the denial of a permit to use the limited channels of the air." The court concluded that radio, in contrast to the print press, was subject to highly permissive federal regulation because it fell under the category of interstate commerce.[53]

Undaunted, Shuler's lawyers responded by hitting back with a writ of certiorari to get the case considered by the US Supreme Court. They put Section 29 of the Radio Act front and center, hoping as a result to "learn for the first time whether a federal commission has the right of censorship over public opinions expressed on the air. We contend that it has not that right." Those who disparaged extending the First Amendment fully to radio, they continued, confused the means with the ends of free speech. That doctrine, in their view, entailed the equal right "to speak to a present audience" and "to address invisible listeners." Missing from the case constructed by the Caldwells was any explicit reference to property rights in the wavelengths along the lines of *Oak Leaves*. The closest they came was to assert that the FRC had violated the takings clause of the Fifth Amendment by rendering "a large investment in physical capital worthless."[54]

Because the same Court of Appeals had rejected Voliva's assertion of property rights in 1930, the Caldwells may have been wise to skirt the issue. But that choice, while perhaps unavoidable, created a fatal disadvantage. Highlighting Shuler's right to the wavelength because of prior use might have also complemented the analogy to the print press that also rested on a foundation of property rights. On the other side, that approach risked alienating those progressives, such as Oliver Wendell Holmes Jr. and Louis Brandeis, who were the most favorable to applying a "free speech in ideas" to the print press but were reluctant to do so for radio. Of course, since Louis G. Caldwell in his role of FRC general counsel had quite zealously rejected a property rights approach, reversing course so quickly might have been awkward. The end effect, again probably unavoidable, was to cede the high ground to the FRC, which used the scarcity theory to trump arguments for extending the "free trade in ideas" to radio.[55]

When the US Supreme Court denied Shuler's appeal on January 16, 1933, the ACLU, after one year of staying aloof, came to the rescue by offering to submit an amici curiae brief for a rehearing. Whatever the reason for this lifeline, Louis G. Caldwell was overjoyed at the help, opining that "the only chance of securing a rehearing is through intervention by an organization such as yours." Though Holmes had retired since he had cast the decisive vote in *Near*, it was still a worthwhile gamble that an ACLU endorsement might carry weight with several pro–free speech justices, most notably Brandeis.[56]

The ACLU's amici curiae brief mostly took the same approach as Shuler's lawyers, though it jettisoned entirely the already threadbare appeal to the Fifth Amendment. Stressing that the radio and the print press were essentially the same, the brief asserted that the First Amendment "applies to the microphone no less than it does to the platform." The brief sidestepped somewhat the scarcity argument. It noted, however, that though "the channels of the air cannot be made available to all," the same could be said about other forms of free speech, pointing out that all "the citizens of the land could no more mount the rostrum at one time than they could go on the air." Unless the Supreme Court overturned the ruling of the Court of Appeals, a chilling effect would occur under which "no broadcaster will dare turn over his microphone to trenchant controversy. Radio programs will be sapped of the little vitality they have shown." Specifically comparing the facts of the case to those in *Near*, the ACLU warned that "the practice of pre-censorship will become a thousand-fold aggravated."[57]

The Hail Mary pass of Shuler's lawyers proved a failure. The Supreme Court refused a rehearing. If the truth be told, it was not the type of case to appeal to any discernable element on the court. The Brandeis faction had never shown much sympathy for second-guessing federal regulatory commissions armed with powers of interstate commerce, and to the extent it promoted First and Fourteenth Amendment rights, these involved the actions of states and localities, not the federal government. The members of the conservative "four horsemen" faction, by contrast, had already shown their hand by voting to sustain Near's conviction. The likelihood that they would support even stronger action against the FRC was slim. A property rights argument, at least in theory, might have appealed to the conservatives, but Shuler's lawyers never made it.[58]

Although the legal profession's reputation was that of a conservative bulwark, the American Bar Association expressed no sympathy for Shuler's plight. The ABA's Standing Committee on Communications, which had initially advocated a property rights/hands-off approach, hailed Shuler's defeat in the Supreme Court, hoping that it "should and doubtless will act as a deterrent to a type of broadcaster which unfortunately has been altogether too numerous. It clearly establishes that the right to broadcast is a privilege which gives rise to correlative rights and obligations and not an absolute right to be exercised when once obtained in perpetuity and according to the whim and caprice of the individual licensee."[59]

The left–right coalition that had scored such a dramatic victory for free speech in the print press proved unable or unwilling to do the same for radio. Members of that coalition were also generally absent in responding to the extensive, but less obviously apparent, limitations on radio speech imposed by the FRC under General Order 40. While outright license revocation had pretty much ended as an FRC technique by the close of Hoover's term, the informal practice of issuing three-month licenses rather than the maximum of three years allowed under the Radio Act of 1927 kept stations routinely on edge. One former FRC commissioner pointedly observed that "the chief function of capital punishment is not to electrocute murderers, but to restrain people from committing murder by warning them of the results if they get caught at it." He elaborated that "[e]very broadcaster in the country lives in abject fear of what the Commission may do."[60]

As the new president, Franklin D. Roosevelt, took office in March 1933, the basic foundation of radio regulation for later decades was in place. Both Coolidge and Hoover had erected the necessary institutional structure for Roosevelt to expand and to manipulate for his own ends. Most stations, albeit with some variations in format, had become largely interchangeable from location to location. The FRC cleanup campaign, in combination with other measures such as briefer license periods, time sharing, and frequency reassignment, had completed the job begun by General Order 40 of 1928. The Federal Radio Commission had successfully purged or marginalized many diverse voices, including socialist radicals, African Americans, labor organizations, right-wing evangelists, and populist cranks, and in their place had hastened the spread of homogeneity and uniformity in the ether.

5

A New Deal for Radio and a New Uniformity

BY SOME KEY measures, Roosevelt's stance toward radio represented continuity with his two predecessors. As before, federal regulators promoted the model of generic and network-dominated programming that eschewed market segmentation and "controversy." Politically, this made sense, of course, since experience showed that so-called propaganda broadcasters, whether on the left or right, eventually turned their guns against those in power. The new president also continued, and more aggressively deployed, the six-month license period and accelerated the Hoover-era trend of speeding the hegemony of the networks. By 1935, 34.8 percent of commercial broadcasting stations had a network affiliation accounting for 74.5 percent of all business revenue, and more than 90 percent of broadcasting power in the lucrative nighttime hours. Moreover, of the sixty-two stations in the United States with power of 5,000 watts or more in 1935, all but four had a network affiliation.[1]

Hoover was either unwilling or unable to make use of radio as a campaign tool, and his voice and style were ill suited for the medium that, ironically, he had so successfully shaped. He complained, quite revealingly, in 1932 of the difficulty of dealing "with anything over radio except generalities, without embarrassing actual accomplishments which are going forward." By contrast, Roosevelt had a legendary knack for the political weaponization of radio. The new president's warm and finely honed voice, "sincere … and good natured even in attack," gained easy access to millions of living rooms. It was often said that he had the requisite natural talent to thrive as a radio announcer or commentator. Exploiting these advantages to the hilt, Roosevelt not only finished the edifice built by Hoover and Coolidge but also put his own peculiar stamp on it and, in doing so, transformed the relationship between radio and the federal government.[2]

Roosevelt had few, if any, scruples about hatching schemes to covertly sideline, or even quash, dissenting radio voices. He was the master of behind-the-scenes intrigue, usually via private sector or governmental intermediaries. In contrast to his predecessor, he adeptly manipulated the revolving door of regulators and industry executives. In return for getting unhindered federal access from broadcasters to the airwaves, Roosevelt rebuffed proposals for nationalization. Illustrative of the president's power over radio was his relationship with Herbert L. Pettey, his appointee as FRC secretary. Pettey had overseen radio for Roosevelt in the 1932 campaign and continued to work in tandem with the administration after his appointment to the Democratic National Committee (DNC) to handle "radio matters."[3]

It did not take long for broadcasters to align themselves with the new regime. For example, former FRC commissioner, and then current CBS vice president, Henry A. Bellows, a Democrat and Harvard classmate of FDR, promised to reject any broadcast over the network "that in any way was critical of any policy of the Administration." He elaborated that all stations were "at the disposal of President Roosevelt and his administration." Bellows specified that CBS had a duty to support Roosevelt, right or wrong, and privately assured presidential press secretary Stephen Early that "the close contact between you and the broadcasters has tremendous possibilities of value to the administration, and as a life-long Democrat, I want to pledge my best efforts in making this cooperation successful."[4]

The day after Roosevelt took office, the networks and the National Association of Broadcasters (NAB) jointly announced that all broadcasting facilities were on "an instant's notice" at the service of the administration. They adopted a "right of way" policy of requiring affiliates to break into their regular broadcasts for the president's speeches. In the first year alone, the networks carried fifty-one of Roosevelt's speeches, far more than they had for Hoover in a similar period. This permissive access to the airwaves extended to the president's political allies and family members. At NBC's invitation, presidential adviser Louis Howe hosted a weekly series that often floated "useful trial balloons" for the president. At Howe's suggestion, the FRC asked each station to supply copies of "all addresses on public affairs," a practice that allowed administration friends to head off critical commentary by making friendly warnings to the stations.[5]

It was the president's fireside chats, however, that had first priority for the networks. This format was ideal for making a personal pitch to the voters and bypassing the newspapers. According to media historian Betty Houchin Winfield, the fireside chat cast the president simultaneously as "the newsgatherer, the reporter, as well as the editor." When Roosevelt later proposed a weekly newspaper to publisher J. David Stern to refute the "poisonous propaganda of the conservative press," Stern quipped to the president that he did not need "such a vehicle. You did it alone on the radio."[6]

Radio proved indispensable for the promotion of the linchpin of the First New Deal, the National Recovery Administration (NRA). In August 1933, FRC Commissioner Harold A. Lafount warned that stations had a "patriotic, if not the bounden and legal duty," to reject advertisements from those "disposed to defy, ignore or modify the codes established by the N.R.A." Lest the consequences were insufficiently plain, he elaborated that "radio stations, using valuable facilities loaned to them temporarily by the government," must "not unwittingly be placed in an embarrassing position because of greed or lack of patriotism on the part of a few unscrupulous advertisers." In 1937, Ruth Brindze pointed out in *Not to Be Broadcast* that "any similar effort to control the [print] press would have created a sensation. Not so with radio."[7]

Regulators and broadcasters alike continued to do the administration's bidding after the establishment of the Federal Communications Commission (FCC) in 1934. Except for new centralized authority over the telephone and the telegraph, all of the FRC's powers were carried over. In 1936, Roosevelt sent an indirect message (his usual method of communicating on touchy issues like this) urging the FCC chairman to turn down applications from stations viewed as hostile to the administration. CBS, in turn, assured Roosevelt that he had carte blanche access to its studios.[8]

As most of the print press lined up against the president in the 1936 campaign, radio remained securely in his corner. A writer in *Broadcasting* magazine even attributed "the perpetuation of the Roosevelt Administration" to the "friendliness of radio." A key distinction between radio and the newspapers was in the political context. Potential FCC sanctions, including the tense waiting for that six-month license renewal, led broadcasters to not only tread lightly but err on the side of favoring the administration when in doubt. Republicans complained in vain about this cozy relationship.[9]

The 1936 campaign illustrated that keeping the administration happy was never far from the minds of network and station executives. Most notably, the networks carried many of Roosevelt's speeches gratis as news or "civic affairs," thus avoiding the expensive equal time obligations of the Radio Act of 1927. This included highly politicized utterances such as Roosevelt's bare-knuckle State of the Union Address blasting the "economic autocracy" who "steal the livery of great national constitutional ideals to serve discredited special interests" and "engage in vast propaganda to spread fear and discord among the people." When the head of the Republican National Committee, Henry P. Fletcher, tried to counter the speech through a series of anti–New Deal skits, NBC president Lennox Lohr turned him down under the pretext that "such dramatic programs as you have offered would place the discussion of vital political and national issues on the basis of dramatic license rather than upon a basis of responsibly stated fact or opinion." Fletcher also met a rebuff from CBS President William S. Paley, who, overlooking the partisan tenor of some of Roosevelt's own speeches, explained that "appeals to the electorate should be intellectual and not based on emotion, passion or prejudice." A GOP official complained that the networks had "surrendered their independence to and joined the 'dictators of the New Deal.'" In the end, an independent station, WGN (owned by the anti-Roosevelt *Chicago Daily Tribune*), carried the skits.[10]

As the 1936 election kicked into high gear, Roosevelt continued to bend FCC rules to his full advantage. Up to the official launch of the campaign in late September, the networks had carried twenty-two of his speeches for free and, of these, seven were obviously political in nature. All the while, the administration kept an eagle-eyed watch for recalcitrants. When two Los Angeles stations refused to carry a fireside chat in September 1936, Presidential Press Secretary Stephen Early urged the DNC to cease any further purchase of time from them.[11]

The FCC did not have to intervene, or even intend to intervene, to tip the scales for Roosevelt. The mere possibility was usually more than enough. A most revealing incident came in October after Senator Arthur Vandenberg (R-MI) used recordings in a broadcast of Roosevelt to stage a mock debate between himself, defending Landon, and the president. Half of the CBS af-filiates cut it off after confusing messages from the network about whether it violated the rules. After Republicans blamed "intimidation of all broadcasters by the New Deal administration," CBS refunded the money but refused all future ads based on the debate format as improper political dramatization. Over time, the Landon campaign shifted more of its ad-buying budget to the independent stations. Because those stations needed the money, they were more likely to take chances by carrying the ads, though these reached a much smaller audience.[12]

Various "loopholes" in the law and FCC interpretations of the rules, com-bined with the almost habitual network deference to the federal government, gave Roosevelt a tremendous leg up. According to Becky M. Nicolaides, the "networks granted free time to at least 12 New Deal and federal agencies in the pre-convention period." Among these were three dramatic programs provided at taxpayer expense. As governmental agencies, the normal network rule against dramatization in campaign ads did not apply to them.[13]

The value to the administration of these electoral bounties was almost in-calculable. In 1938, for example, some 375 stations carried over eight thousand hours of the transcribed programs of the Federal Housing Authority and the Federal Housing Administration, while the WPA had its own network radio show. When journalist Stanley High asked local station owners why they ran these programs for free, a typical reply was "We know what is expected of us." Bending over backward in this way was also an understandable strategy to win favor at license renewal time. According to High, "[S]tation owners, since they can never be sure that they are more than six months from the noose, are inclined to be on edge even in the best of times."[14]

Although network radio was largely a Rooseveltian domain, and even more so over time, the independent stations and small regional networks were comparatively receptive to anti–New Deal content. As founder of the Crusaders, host Fred G. Clark had focused on Prohibition as an example of bureaucratic overreach, but beginning in 1933 his priorities shifted to attacks on such New Deal initiatives as the National Recovery Administration, the Agricultural Adjustment Act, and the Wagner Act. In 1934, Clark pulled off a rare feat of getting William S. Paley to pick up his new program, *Voice of the Crusaders*, as a form of public service. To pay for additional expenses, seed money came from funds raised by top business executives from DuPont, General Mills, Montgomery Ward, and other leading firms. Always eager to curry Roosevelt's favor and leery of controversial content, however, Paley soon regretted the decision and dropped the show after six months. But it eventually found a home on the new Mutual Broadcasting System, a decentralized cooperative of quasi-independent stations. Because Mutual needed the money, and Clark was a paying customer, it was more willing to risk controversy.[15]

In September, the same month that CBS dropped the show, Hugo L. Black's lobbying committee put the Crusaders into the crosshairs through a "full and exhaustive questionnaire regarding … their structure, purposes and methods." As this was happening, Black and his colleagues were examining copies of incoming and outgoing telegrams of the company's officers sent through Washington, DC, and Chicago. When Clark testified in April, Black, with these telegrams in hand, probed aggressively about financial and other activities including *Voice of the Crusaders*. To counter the intended impression that he was a sinister big business tool, Clark accused Black of leading a runaway investigation that exceeded its original mandate. In raising money for *Voice of the Crusaders*, he pointed out, "[n]ot one word was spoken about public utilities or public utility legislation." Adding a charge of hypocrisy, Clark asked why Black had sent questionnaires to "six patriotic societies" but not to various unions or "Red" and "Pink" organizations. Clark's strategy scored some points with the public, but, on balance, the Black Committee investigation dealt greater damage and *Voice of the Crusaders* soon disappeared.[16]

The American Family Robinson, a clever little fifteen-minute serial, which premiered in 1935, had a similar agenda of imparting pro–free enterprise views, but its method was dramatization and comedy rather than straightforward commentary. The National Association of Manufacturers, a frequent critic of Roosevelt's policies, covered the production costs, while local employers paid for airtime. Sometimes stations gave it away for free. It ran three times per week, and the main characters were Luke and Myra Robinson and their relatives, who lived in the fictional town of Centerville. As editor of the town's paper, Luke good-naturedly explained the importance of thrift, property rights, self-reliance, and limited government. The series combined story situations typical of a soap opera, often with a comedic touch, with plot lines about bureaucratic boondoggles, antibusiness regulation, and confiscatory federal taxes. The writing and direction were generally on a high level, and the actors were experienced professionals. The main networks consistently refused to pick up the program. NBC executives feared that this "decided propaganda," though potentially profitable for the bottom line, might be interpreted as flouting the "'public interest,' convenience and necessity." As with *Voice of the Crusaders*, hundreds of often cash-strapped small and independent broadcasters carried the show. The listenership, while impressive in terms of sheer numbers, paled compared to that reached by the networks.[17]

Father Charles E. Coughlin was no friend of the ideological worldview promoted by either *Voice of the Crusaders* or *The American Family Robinson*. Although he never owned a station, he had much in common stylistically with such rogue broadcasters as Brinkley and Shuler. Patching together dozens of hookups of independent stations to carry his talks, Coughlin eventually reached as many as forty million listeners who tuned in for his populist jeremiads. Because Coughlin's declamations against the "plutocrats" and bankers overlapped with much early pro–New Deal rhetoric, he initially allied himself with the administration, proclaiming "Roosevelt or Ruin." This relationship began to sour by the end of 1934, however, as the radio priest strayed from the president on such issues as proposals to advance the payment of a promised bonus to World War I veterans or whether the United States should join the World Court.[18]

Top administration officials began to ponder strategies to marginalize Coughlin if the need arose. Postmaster General James A. Farley prepared a study for the president of stations carrying his show, including a list of their political connections. The radio priest finally made a full break from the president, now dubbed "Franklin Double-Crossing Roosevelt," in the last months of 1935. Coughlin vowed to retire from politics if his favored candidate for president, Representative William Lemke (R-ND), who, despite his Republican affiliation, was running on the third-party ticket of the Union Party, failed to receive nine million votes. When Lemke fell far short of this goal, Coughlin kept his promise (but only temporarily) to leave the air. He returned two months later, but his influence had considerably diminished.[19]

But Coughlin was not the most listened-to anti-Roosevelt commentator in the late 1930s. That distinction belonged to Boake Carter. Unlike Coughlin,

Voice of the Crusaders, and *The American Family Robinson*, Carter rose to long-term prominence on a major network and sometimes vied with Lowell Thomas in ratings. In 1938, CBS carried his commentaries five days per week, and listeners tuned in for his barbs against sacred cows ranging from admirals to labor union bosses. His ratings were so impressive that sponsors came forward to underwrite him. Before this time, most shows of that type were on a sustaining (broadcaster-subsidized) basis and were commercial free. Carter also had independent success as a columnist, and by 1940 only Walter Winchell and Dorothy Thompson had more readers.[20]

Carter's trademark independence and unpredictability raised alarms with administration insiders. Although FCC chairman Pettey told the president in 1934 that he had information that might force Carter off the air, Roosevelt tried instead to cultivate the popular commentator, who, despite some quibbling with administration policies, was generally an ally. The president had a private meeting with Carter, and top officials, including Farley and the head of the FCC, came on his show as guests. Conciliation appeared to pay off as leading Democratic politicians heaped praise on the radio commentator from the Senate floor. While most newspapers opposed Roosevelt in 1936, Carter made no secret that his vote went to the president.[21]

No federal agency had better relations with Carter than the FBI. Carter repeatedly hailed the efficiency of J. Edgar Hoover and his G-men and demanded that Congress show its gratitude through budget increases. A grateful Hoover reciprocated this support with ever more effusive private praise. In 1937, Hoover wrote to Carter no less than thirteen times, in each case with laudatory comments. In early January 1937, Hoover exuded, "[Y]our friendship has been very helpful and most encouraging." The FBI director also issued a "cordial invitation" to meet with Carter at his convenience, and a few weeks later, Hoover started using "Dear Boake" in all his salutations. Hoover was so elated after Carter received some two hundred fan letters after a single pro-FBI broadcast that he approved an arrangement to have the agency send all the replies to those letters. Carter's relations with Roosevelt were becoming increasingly icy, but those with Hoover were ever more genial. In September 1937, after one broadcast, Hoover waxed uncharacteristically poetic: "[Y]ou can't imagine the feeling of warmth that swept over me as your familiar voice came over the air."[22]

By this time, however, Carter had taken on more trouble than he could handle by opposing the CIO's tactics, especially in reference to the Little Steel Strike of March 1937. The union vigorously retaliated by boycotting Carter's main sponsor, Philco. After Philco's sales took a hit, Carter met with John L. Lewis, the head of the CIO, to smooth things out. An agreement for the commentator to stop talking about the union in return for calling off the boycott fell apart when the CIO rank and file vetoed it. Although revenue losses prompted Philco to drop its sponsorship in February 1938, Carter quickly bounced back by finding a replacement: General Foods. This time he seemed to have some bargaining power. Colby M. Chester, the chairman of the board of General Foods, had a shared antagonism to the New Deal and had belonged to the American Liberty League. Some added protection was that Carter's manager was the brother-in-law of William S. Paley.[23]

Carter's break with Roosevelt, which occurred in roughly the same time frame as his quarrel with the CIO, began after he initiated a multiple-front attack on the administration in 1937, including State Department policy and court packing. Carter even went so far as to imply that the high-pressure situation created by Roosevelt's relentless push for the court bill sent Senate majority leader Joe T. Robinson (D-AR) to an early grave. Both Roosevelt and his backers showed greater urgency in searching for ways to either silence or otherwise tamp down the commentator.[24]

As usual, the public had little inkling of these subterranean machinations. In November 1937, Marvin H. McIntyre, Roosevelt's secretary of appointments, and sometimes described as his "right-hand man," sent a memo to Presidential Press Secretary Early, outlining a strategy to stop Carter. McIntyre suggested an approach to Early's friend, Marjorie Merriweather Post, a director of General Foods. Her husband was Joseph Davies, recently appointed ambassador to the Soviet Union and, like his wife, a veteran of Democratic causes. But despite some warnings, Carter showed no signs of backing down. After the Japanese sank the American river gunboat, the *USS Panay*, in December 1937, he accused Roosevelt of stoking up prowar feeling.[25]

Finally, the pressure on Carter seemed to bring results for the administration. Prodded on by both Post and Davies, the advertising agency for General Foods persuaded Carter to sign an agreement promising to be "constructive" in his political commentary and show "suitable restraint of language and without invective or criticism of the motives, character, and mental or moral attributes of personalities." In a triumphant mood, Davies informed "the Boss" (FDR) about the terms, which, in his view, meant that Carter had pledged to eschew interpretation and "be confined exclusively to reporting the news."[26]

But Carter did not see the agreement the same way as Davies. His next broadcasts were as strident as ever. According to a diary entry of Harold Ickes in February 1938, the "President told [Secretary of Labor] Miss [Frances] Perkins that he would be happy if she could discover that Boake Carter, the columnist and radio commentator, who has been so unfair and pestiferous, was not entitled to be in this country. It appears that an investigation of his record is being made." It was indeed. The Department of the Treasury was scrutinizing Carter's background and his 1936 taxes, while the State Department searched (unsuccessfully) for a pretext to deport him. When a noticeably rattled Carter heard of these efforts, he wrote to the president: "Beware! Libel me at your peril."[27]

To top it off, several highly placed officials in the Department of State, including roving ambassador Norman H. Davis, met in New York City to discuss strategies to muzzle the commentator for his attacks on US foreign policy. Somehow Carter got word about this plot and found a sympathetic ear in long-time Roosevelt critic Representative Martin L. Sweeney (D-OH). On March 14, Sweeney proposed a resolution to investigate whether Davis and his cohorts were interfering "with the constitutional right of any American citizen in the exercise of free speech." Not long after, however, Carter began to tone down his commentary.[28]

Perhaps buoyed by these signs of capitulation, Roosevelt broke his public silence, stating in a letter on April 6 that the "President of the United States cannot engage in a radio debate with the Boake Carters and Father Coughlins of life!" Administration ally Paul Y. Anderson went even further, relating that "this writer happens to know that White House officials recently saved Carter's bacon. But for their intervention he might be off the air now." The historical record contradicts this benign version of the events. The history of White House efforts to defang the commentator through helping to orchestrate the General Foods agreement and Department of Treasury investigations are too well documented to deny. Also revealing is author Jerre Mangione's vivid account of a dinner conversation with the president. A strong FDR partisan at the time, Mangione recalled that as the evening wore on, Roosevelt gleefully volunteered that he was having Carter "thoroughly investigated" and that the results, when revealed, "would put an end to his career." Mangione was crestfallen: "That Roosevelt, the statesman I had admired, should admit to such vindictiveness came as the greatest jolt of all."[29]

Even as Carter's radio commentary turned uncharacteristically placid, he continued to express his feisty side in his newspaper column. He lambasted such initiatives as Minton's press bill, which, in his estimation, betrayed an "arrogant disregard of the spirit of the Bill of Rights." He reminded readers that "it was the same Mr. Minton, who personally requested an Executive order permitting him to inspect and publicize the income-tax returns of any one in the Nation, whenever the spirit so moves him." Not holding back, Carter characterized Minton as "the outstanding rubber stamp of the White House. As goes the White House, so goes Minton." Another column lauded Grenville Clark for speaking out against Hague and Minton and added that "politicians of the Minton stripe rush to the radio—already under the thumb of the Government through the FCC and the necessity of licensing."[30]

While Carter's syndicated column remained popular for quite some time, the reverse was true for the tepid version on the airwaves. "I pulled my punches," he lamented, "and because of this and, contributing reasons, my radio rating, which had been at the top, began to drop." In August, CBS discontinued the program. On his last broadcast, Carter read, without comment, from John Stuart Mill's defense of free speech in *On Liberty*. In a lecture tour later that year, he accused the "Great White Father in Washington" (Roosevelt) of bullying station owners worried about six-month license renewals and of intimidating CBS into firing him. Freedom of speech, to the extent it was genuine, he reported regretfully, applied only to the print press, not radio. "Despite the fact that newspapers also depend on advertising for their buns and coffee," Carter asserted, "newspaper … publishers can write what they want. … The unhampered radio commentator is a thing of the past."[31]

Through it all, however, J. Edgar Hoover stood by Carter as a reliable friend. By this time, Hoover had sufficient clout to plot his own course, at least to some extent. During 1938, Hoover sent five additional fan letters to Carter for various pro-FBI broadcasts. There is no hint in Carter's FBI file during this period that he was under investigation by that agency. Even as the administration was stepping up its siege against Carter, for example, Hoover stressed again in May 1938 how much he appreciated "the support you have given the FBI during the period of our financial crisis" and then followed up in June by calling him a "true and real friend." In February 1939, long after Carter's decline from power as a radio commentator, Hoover volunteered with hope that "we can get together real soon for a long talk" when Carter was next in the vicinity.[32]

Roughly concurrent with Carter's radio demise, much the same thing happened to another commentator, former brigadier general Hugh S. Johnson. Johnson had unlikely credentials for a leading critic of Roosevelt. When he was head of the National Recovery Administration (NRA) from 1933 to 1935, few names were more synonymous with the New Deal than his. His friendly association with the president continued after the NRA closed up shop when Roosevelt named Johnson to head the Works Progress Administration for New York City. Beginning in 1935, he wrote a popular syndicated column and, while not always in lockstep with the New Deal, supported the president's reelection in 1936.[33]

Johnson began regular commentaries five days per week for NBC in August 1937 but only weeks later landed in hot water, after some impromptu commentary after one of Roosevelt's fireside chats. While, according to news reports, his words were rather tame, network executives apparently felt otherwise. Frank Russell, NBC vice president, phoned Stephen Early to apologize and give assurance that he was going to take Johnson off the air. Going even further, he promised not to allow future programs of any kind featuring controversial discussions. "Early, although no doubt pleased," writes Richard W. Steele, "was apparently embarrassed by this acknowledgment of White House–network cooperation and told Russell that the administration had no interest in and would take no cognizance of the action."[34]

After that, Johnson, if anything, became even more of an annoyance to the administration. He also weighed in on other controversies, not directly related to Roosevelt. For example, after the FCC threatened to extend censorship because of Mae West's suggestive Adam and Eve skit on the *Chase and Sanborn Hour*, Johnson condemned the agency for exercising "arbitrary power of economic life or death" and "clearly and improperly against free expression of opinion." Apparently, listeners liked his outspokenness.[35]

But Johnson's days at NBC were numbered. Without ceremony or explanation, his name disappeared from the network lineup in mid-February 1938, only five months after his maiden broadcast. His eventual replacement was John Franklin Carter, using the pseudonym Jay Franklin, "an unblemished New Dealer" with close ties to FDR. He was also, according to the careful research of former CIA officer Gene A. Coyle, a possible Soviet agent. Ironically, in a previous column, Carter had cited Johnson to prove "no cause for alarm" about free speech in the ether: "With commercial sponsors free to use the best stations and hours to hire people like Boake Carter, Dorothy Thompson, and Gen. Hugh Johnson to curse out Roosevelt, the threat to freedom of the microphone is small indeed." Johnson's expulsion from the air, as Robert J. Brown observes, was yet another illustration that "[r]adio commentators who were not well disposed toward the Roosevelt administration enjoyed short careers."[36]

After losing his job as a commentator, Johnson continued to be a successful syndicated columnist and freely expressed himself on matters related to censorship of the radio. In a column written not long after his show ended, he zeroed in on FCC misuse of the standard of "public interest, convenience, or necessity" to restrict free speech: "What more justification is there for the FCC … to control what may be said on the air, than for the War Department, for example, to control what may be said on a street corner?" At the same time, Johnson took some of the wind of his critique by lauding the FCC as an "absolute necessity" for preventing "the air from becoming a pandemonium of bedlam" through the allocation and policing of scarce wavelengths.[37]

While not a commentator in the sense of Carter or Johnson, William J. Cameron, the director of public relations for Ford Motor Company, was a rare surviving anti–New Deal voice on the big networks after 1938. Beginning in 1934, the *Ford Sunday Evening Hour* on CBS featured his regular five- to ten-minute intermission commentaries. His targets included the NRA and the wages and hours bill as well as other New Deal priorities. In July 1938, the Institute for Propaganda Analysis (IPA) singled out Cameron's talks for "stack[ing] the cards in favor of the Ford Motor Company and against writers, government officials, labor leaders, and others who do not approve of Ford policies. This is obviously what he is paid to do. He does it effectively." After the removal of Carter and Johnson, however, Cameron faced increased isolation and pressure. CBS warned him to steer away from "controversial issues," and the CIO, which had already demonstrated its muscle against Carter, was openly hostile. But Cameron was better placed than Carter or Johnson to buck this trend. The network could ill afford to lose Ford's business, because it spent more on radio advertising than General Motors and Chrysler combined.[38]

By 1938, the reach of the Roosevelt administration's manipulation of broadcasting extended more than ever to the smaller stations and regional networks. A prime illustration of this trend was Father Coughlin's final fate in his radio career. At first, his return to the air in January 1937 looked promising. The radio priest successfully repeated the strategy of assembling informal hookups for his talks via independent stations and the Colonial/Yankee regional networks in New England. His listenership fell far short of the old days but still probably numbered in the millions. Moreover, because Coughlin was willing to pay for his time, the stations seemed to be better able resist pressure from the networks, sponsors, or the government. By the end of 1938, however, calls grew louder to force him from the air, especially as explicitly anti-Semitic commentary started to crop up in his shows.[39]

As Coughlin made ever deeper forays into the lunatic fringe, Frank R. McNinch, chairman of the FCC, took vigorous countermeasures. In a speech in November 1938, he pledged the FCC to "employ every resource" to stop radio from becoming "an instrument of racial or religious persecution." McNinch did not mention Coughlin by name as the chief offender, but he did not have to. Broadcasters clearly understood what he meant and responded accordingly. Specifically relying on McNinch's admonitions, Donald Flamm, president of WMCA in New York, reneged on carrying a scheduled transcribed address by Coughlin because it violated "our inescapable responsibility under the terms of our license." He elaborated, "Freedom of speech is a precious privilege. That is why those of us who are entrusted with the instruments of free speech must be so careful not to permit anyone to defile them." For Coughlin, the loss of this large market was devastating. Two other stations, in Gary, Indiana, and Chicago, also pulled the broadcast.[40]

Few in the broadcasting industry had any sympathy for Coughlin's anti-Semitic rants, but they were also uncomfortable with McNinch's apparent endorsement of censorship. The pushback was sufficiently strong that the

FCC chairman rapidly backtracked, or it so it seemed. Only a week after his original statement, McNinch fervently denied that he wanted censorship, labeling it "impracticable and definitely objectionable." He committed himself to fight "any such measure" if brought before Congress but left some ambiguity by stressing that stations had the obligation to provide "complete and rounded discussion" of controversial issues. Mixed messaging of this type prompted a writer in *Broadcasting* to complain that the FCC reliance on the public interest, convenience, or necessity concept was so capricious that it was no "small wonder … that broadcasting shivers in its boots. … Nobody knows much about it; least of all, it sometimes seems, those who administer it."[41]

The perceived futility of trying to read FCC tea leaves prompted the National Association of Broadcasters (NAB) to adopt a landmark "voluntary code" in July 1939. The most obvious goal, as it openly admitted, was to align with the real or perceived FCC goal of forcing Coughlin off the air. But the long-term implications of the code were far more sweeping, including bans on the sale of commercial time for discussing "controversial issues" (except for party electoral broadcasts), editorializing by either newscasters or commentators, and "attacks upon another's race or religion." The Code Compliance Committee expressed well the Janus-like nature of its standards by stating that it had no intention to bar anyone "*from using radio. It simply denies the right to buy time*" (emphasis in the original). Rigid compliance was the safest response for most cautious and practical-minded broadcasters. "By citing its ban on self-sponsorship of controversial views," Richard W. Steele observes, "broadcasters could more comfortably rid themselves of a long-standing nuisance [Coughlin] while demonstrating the industry's oft-expressed commitment to neutral programming."[42]

Newspaper editorials generally lauded the code. Two refrains stood out: first, radio was different from the print press because of scarce wavelengths and, second, that the "public forum" exception gave an adequate outlet for controversial opinions via "a series of fairsided discussions on public issues" under the direct control of the station or network. J. David Stern's *Philadelphia Record*, normally a tiger for an unchained print press, declared that "freedom of speech on the air" was meaningless without "the money to talk back." A writer for the always opportunistic *Daily Worker* praised the code as the "[m]ajor hope in driving Father Coughlin from the air."[43]

The most vigorous opposition to the code came from conservatives and others leery of the New Deal. One of the first to make his voice heard was Hugh S. Johnson in his capacity as a syndicated columnist. After obliquely referring to a "somewhat close acquaintance with the problem," he charged that the code was an instrument of censorship and that the practical prohibition of editorial comment on current news if not stopped "could spell the beginning of an era of aerial goosestepping." While Johnson opposed the ban on the sale of commercial time, he also wanted a "rigid" rule requiring equal time to be sold or "donated," for an alternative point of view.[44]

David Lawrence, the publisher of *U.S. News*, was, by far, the most uncompromising foe of the code. Going even further than Johnson, he rejected the whole premise that radio was in a special category. He flatly depicted radio as a private business, "no more 'affected with the public interest' than is the newspaper business." One by one, Lawrence tackled the arguments put forward by defenders of the code. Regarding claims of scarcity, he observed that the "vast majority" of communities had only one newspaper, and ongoing technical improvements promised a rapid increase in the number of stations that could be accommodated by existing wavelengths. He predicted that the future offered even more potential for competition, including innovations such as "'wired radio' [which] will make possible millions of outlets in the homes of America and an unlimited number of transmitters can be built for this purpose." Alleged scarcity provided no basis for putting radio's "head in the noose of regulation of programs" and served to "surrender at the outset what the press through centuries of legal struggle has managed to preserve."[45]

Quite predictably, the National Committee to Uphold Constitutional Government (NCUCG) was also prominent in fighting the Code. The chairman of the NCUCG, former Representative Samuel Pettengill (D-IN), championed the need to protect "a free microphone," while Frank E. Gannett, the group's main donor, added that recent court rulings for free speech, if applied at all consistently, must cover radio. He cited as justification the US Supreme Court's recent ruling in *Schneider v. New Jersey*, which struck down a local ordinance on handbills on the grounds that free speech took precedence over considerations of public order.[46]

Fresh off its free speech victory against Hague, the ACLU expressed "complete accord" with the code. A joint letter by board members Arthur Garfield

Hays, Morris Ernst, and Quincy Howe hailed it as "wholly in the interest of free speech since it puts everybody on the basis of equality and puts people without money on precisely the same footing as people with it." The letter condemned as "highly improper" the comments of John F. Patt, the vice president of three stations carrying Coughlin's talks, who called the code "a solar plexus blow to freedom in this country" that went "beyond mere self-regulation into the realm of strangulation, stagnation and censorship."[47]

While the ACLU's full-throttled endorsement of the code appeared to contradict its legal defense of Shuler several years earlier, this was not entirely the case. From the beginning, the ACLU's statements on radio free speech were ambiguous and inconsistent. As Robert McChesney points out, the dominant consensus in the organization by the mid-1930s rejected "laissez faire" in radio on the premise that there was "physical scarcity in the number of channels available for use." The ACLU's statements on radio free speech often included imprecise qualifiers that the airwaves were in a special category compared to the print press. Related to this trend was an increasing faith among civil libertarians in the beneficence of federal regulation, a faith rein-forced by mounting distrust of commercial companies as protectors of free speech. Hence, Morris Ernst supported FCC favoritism to nonprofits, while Roger N. Baldwin outlined the potential benefits of extensive governmental ownership of stations. In 1935, ACLU publicity director Clifton Reed matter-of-factly described the "doubtful social validity" of applying free speech to radio, because stations had a "lucrative monopoly" for which they "had paid nothing." Their "single obligation is to present programs in 'the public inter-est, convenience, and necessity.'"[48]

Norman Thomas, who, for many, was the exemplar of absolutist free speech and assembly in Jersey City, seconded the ACLU's endorsement of the code. He considered the limits on wealthy broadcasters as a salutary reform "to prevent the radio from becoming the most powerful propaganda weapon in existence." The danger of federal censorship of radio did not seem to greatly trouble him. He concluded that the freedom of the print press "can be guar-anteed by the intelligent interest of citizens, but the number of channels for radio transmission is narrowly limited."[49]

A more immediate factor in stilling opposition to the code by civil libertar-ians and others was a speech at the annual NAB conference by Presidential

Press Secretary Early. The delegates, who had just adopted that document, took heart from his "reassurance" at the outset that "[w]hen the time comes that this Government dictates what its people shall hear; what they shall read or see, then freedom ends and democracy is no more." Those most inclined to take solace, however, tended to ignore a more ambiguous passage much later in the speech that to "permit the individual or group with the greatest financial resources to utilize radio to peddle their own particular brand of social or economic philosophy would be a grave mistake for radio." Nearly two months later, Early hedged even more when he proclaimed that in the event of war, radio must prove itself a "good child" or the government might have to teach it "manners."[50]

The cumulative impact of Early's alleged "reassurance," and pressure from the code itself, led John Shepard III, the president of Yankee and Colonial networks, and perhaps the leading maverick broadcasting owner in the US, to drop Coughlin's program. Following suit were other stations in leading markets, which were Coughlin's bread and butter. All cited the code as the reason. In September 1940, Coughlin, venting his frustration, left the air. [51]

The adoption of the code had implications that went far beyond the question of Coughlin's free speech, however. A case in point was the NAB's prohibition of stations accepting "free offers" if the purpose was to recruit members for an organization or to foster a point of view. "Unless the station presents the other side of the picture," it warned, "it might be accused of bias." In June 1939, the NAB specified that both the National Association of Manufacturers, which produced *The American Family Robinson*, and the ACLU, which regularly sent out scripts to stations providing commentary from a civil liberties perspective, were on its list of potential offenders. *NAB Reports* urged stations to "write to Headquarters for information about these." In answer to accusations that *The American Family Robinson* was anti–New Deal, the NAM responded somewhat defensively that it was "not 'anti-' anything or anybody." Rather the goal of the program was to "present openly, and as effectively and attractively as radio will permit, the fundamental principle that freedom of speech and of the press, freedom of religion, and freedom of enterprise are inseparable and must continue to be if the system of democratic government under which this country has flourished is to be preserved." [52]

The content of *The American Family Robinson* began to shift markedly after the code started to go into effect in late 1939. The plotlines became ever more innocuous and often indistinguishable from a typical substandard soap opera. The previous eagerness of characters to question, or even discuss, the New Deal welfare and regulatory states gradually faded away. To the extent that the later episodes expressed ideas or broader social goals, they took the form of simplistic bromides on such topics as the importance of marital understanding and the need for concerted cooperation for national defense mobilization. While there were other contributors to this transformation in program content, such as the shift in national priorities on the eve of war, the repeated NAB warnings could only make stations, as well as the show's producers, more skittish about politically charged topics. When the final episode left the air in September 1941, *The American Family Robinson* had long since become only a shell of its former self.[53]

As already noted, the code did not just hamper Roosevelt's critics on the right. Labor unions also suffered because of the rules against selling time to organizations promoting membership or perceived controversial ideas. Beginning in 1938, local stations repeatedly made the code a basis for spurning offers by unions to purchase time. To no avail, the CIO protested "the discriminatory denial of the use of radio facilities to labor unions while corporations are free to make both direct and subtle use of the radio to champion their interest."[54]

The code played an important role in shaping—or more accurately stifling—debate over foreign policy in the period before World War II. During the presidential campaign of 1940, it blocked the purchase of fifteen-minute spot announcements by the antiwar America First Committee (AFC). The denial resulted in enough outcry, however, that the NAB later decided to split the difference and carved out an exception that was also applied to the AFC's nemesis, the pro-intervention Committee to Defend America by Aiding the Allies. This temporary loophole came only a month before the election and was pretty much too late to make a difference.[55]

One year later, AFC officer and 1940 Socialist presidential nominee Norman Thomas—ironically one of the code's most visible earlier enthusiasts—had a similar negative experience. In a letter in November 1941 to his compatriot in the AFC leadership, John T. Flynn, he reported that radio station WQXR in New York had reneged (on advice of the NAB) on a contract for a series of speeches against US intervention. Thomas had raised the money himself to pay for the speeches. (Coughlin had done the same, of course!) Thomas agreed that "the speeches are controversial and do violate a strict interpretation of the Code, but they are neither more nor less in violation of the Code than the continual remarks of Walter Winchell and Eleanor Roosevelt on sponsored programs." The NAB code had hoisted Thomas by his own petard and he probably knew it. He complained to Flynn "that we are dealing with a situation on the radio in which practically all commentators are on one side, in which people who talk on public affairs on sponsored programs are almost, without exception, interventionists."[56]

The NAB's "voluntary" code was voluntary in name only. De facto FCC backing gave it life and force. That backing became even more vigorous under the tenure of James Lawrence Fly, appointed in 1939 as FCC chairman. His policies formalized and extended the rules laid down by the code, which he endorsed as exemplifying "democracy at work." While rhetorically affirming the importance of free speech, Fly appended the usual qualifier, though perhaps with more than the usual gusto, that wavelength scarcity justified broad regulatory discretion over both content and the providers of that content. Endorsing the NAB's prohibition of the sale of commercial time for controversial issues, Fly asked rhetorically, "Shall this mode of expression be sold to the highest bidder?" The government did not license a station, he added, "because it thinks that the owner has any legal right to be heard."[57]

On the surface, the code's heightened restrictions were out of step with a shift in broader public attitudes toward favoring free speech. By several key indicators, popular feeling against censorship, including of radio, had never been stronger. According to a *Fortune* poll in 1939, for example, only 26 percent of respondents supported any governmental supervision of radio production. But, of course, it is possible that this disconnect between public attitudes and practice was not a disconnect at all, but just a matter of a "rose by any other name." While the FCC and allied NAB code enforcers vigorously denied censoring programs, the conclusion is inescapable that they were, in fact, doing precisely that, and at unprecedented levels. This does not mean that the American public saw it as such, however.[58]

The NAB code was the main precursor of the FCC's Mayflower Doctrine of 1941, which was the most tangible expression of FCC content control under Fly. Revealingly, at the center was the often dissident Shepard and his regional Yankee Network. In 1938, a disgruntled employee of the Boston affiliate complained to the FCC about editorials carried on the station from Yankee's news division. The case languished until 1940, when Shepard applied for renewal of the station's license, noting that the editorials had ceased in March 1938 just prior to the complaint. In granting a renewal in January 1941, the FCC also took the opportunity to release a special statement (the famous Mayflower Doctrine) of future policy. Starting from a premise long favored by Fly that "the broadcaster cannot be an advocate," it mandated "full and equal opportunity for the presentation to the public all sides of public issues." Radio, to be truly free, the statement continued, must never "be used to advocate the causes of the licensee. ... The public interest—not the private—is paramount."[59]

In retrospect, the proclamation of the Mayflower Doctrine represented more continuity than a break from the past. The main provisions reflected longstanding FCC practice, later affirmed by the NAB. "[T]he ban on editorializing," Louis G. Caldwell aptly observed, "goes back at least as far as the Shaeffer, Brinkley, Baker, and Shuler cases, decided in 1930 and 1931." The 1931 Court of Appeals ruling of *Great Lakes* had set another, though more indirect, precedent. In that case, the FRC had persuaded the court that if "all the programs transmitted are intended for, and interesting or valuable to, only a small portion of that public, the rest of the listeners are being discriminated against." In essence, the Mayflower Doctrine served to formalize standards that the FCC and allied private entities had long enforced, sometimes in an ad hoc way, and closed some possible loopholes for the remaining malcontents.[60]

The Mayflower Doctrine, as well as earlier variants such as the NBA code, rested on the premise that radio was fundamentally distinct from the print press because of scarce frequencies but, as David Lawrence noted at the time, many communities had more radio stations than daily newspapers. In 1941, there were 912 broadcasting stations compared to 1,998 daily newspapers. By 1949, the number of daily newspapers had fallen by two hundred while broadcast authorizations had climbed to over four thousand, and radio was the primary news source for Americans. Of course, in the 1920s, the FRC itself was a leading author of great scarcity by squeezing down the number of viable stations.[61]

With Fly at the helm, the FCC ratcheted up pressure against William J. Cameron, the sole surviving anti–New Deal commentator on the main networks. CBS sent repeated admonishments, and the Canadian Broadcasting Corporation banned him entirely. In a parallel to the Carter case, the Canadian-born Cameron faced new questions about his citizenship status. In January 1941, Representative Lee E. Geyer (D-CA), an avid New Dealer and CIO ally, proposed that the Committee on Immigration and Naturalization investigate his possible deportation. Making no secret of his motivations, Geyer characterized Cameron as "Henry Ford's mouthpiece" in the propagation of "subversive" ideas. The anti-Cameron campaign in Congress culminated when Representative Samuel Dickstein (D-NY), the chair of the committee, convened a hearing. After Geyer and a journalist who shared his views testified, the next witness, L. B. Schofield, the special assistant to the attorney general, completely derailed the investigation by reporting that he had found no irregularities in Cameron's citizenship.[62]

In January 1942, however, Ford discontinued the program, citing, somewhat mysteriously, the "war emergency." Ford briefly revived it in 1946 but without Cameron or any other intermission commentary. Yet the Cameron radio controversy had a strange, but revealing, afterlife. In September 1943, Fly cited network willingness to tolerate the likes of Cameron while, at the same time, denying CIO purchases of airtime as an unfair double standard under which unions had to settle for "backdoor handouts." But, though few seemed to notice, Fly was combating a straw man, as he must have known. By this time, Cameron's commentaries were long gone from the airwaves.[63]

Throughout these controversies, New Deal reformers, such as Fly and key leaders of the ACLU, vigorously denied any intention of hindering the free expression of ideas. To the contrary, they envisioned a flowering of such formats as roundtable discussions. They had several existing examples to cite. The most prominent was *America's Town Meeting of the Air*, which premiered on the NBC Blue Network in 1935. It featured a weekly discussion with guests spanning the ideological gamut from conservatives, such as Robert A. Taft, to New Dealers, such as Harold Ickes, and socialists such as Norman Thomas. George V. Denny Jr., the director of *America's Town Meeting of the*

Air, "heartily concur[red] with the new Code," which he boasted had given a stamp of approval to his method of presenting "all sides of controversial issues." It was through the roundtable discussion format that Fred G. Clark (formerly of *Voice of the Crusaders*) was able to return to the air and achieve a measure of bipartisan "respectability." In 1939, Clark's American Economic Forum launched *Wake Up, America* over NBC. Bearing no resemblance to the defunct *Voice of the Crusaders*, it had an ideologically diverse lineup of guests.[64]

For the American Civil Liberties Union, the roundtable format was proof that controversy was alive and well and assuaged any private misgivings of its leaders about supporting bans on ideological content in paid time or in the newsroom. Writing in 1941, Arthur Garfield Hays, the ACLU's general counsel, stressed that the networks went "to great lengths to find competent representatives of minorities" in this format and thus showed "a real sense of the importance of free expression, and that they are doing a good practical job in promoting civic discussion over the air." Hays reaffirmed his previous support of the code's content restrictions, asserting, "[T]he necessary limitation due to the number of wave lengths, the radio must necessarily be subject to control." But Hays had oversold his case or, at least, given an incomplete picture. There was more than a germ of truth in Hugh S. Johnson's characterization: "The 'forum' type is not debate. It is only one stuffed shirt reading one canned speech which another stuffed shirt hasn't seen—and then he reads his."[65]

While the roundtable format was an important outlet, it fell far short of furthering ideological diversity. Overall, pro-administration voices still had a substantial advantage in the expression of ideas. By the end of 1938, they had achieved a near monopoly among CBS and NBC (Blue and Red Networks) commentators as well as extensive free, and unchallenged, airtime for Roosevelt and other governmental officials.

As Richard W. Steele explains, many on the left who were normally sympathetic to civil liberties were willing to accept the tradeoff of content restriction for roundtables because they had come to regard the federal government as a free speech ally rather than potential adversary. Along with a tendency to take for granted federal good intentions, they put ever greater trust in the federal courts to counter threats to free speech at the local and state levels. A by-product of this attitude, of course, was to sometimes foster complacency toward presidential and other federal abuses. These abuses included more than a few double standards.[66]

The experience of Walter Winchell, perhaps FDR's leading champion on the ether, exemplified that some commentators were more equal than others in the application of the rules for controversial content. The Winchell/FDR alliance began in December 1939 when, as reported by Assistant Secretary of State Adolf A. Berle, the commentator volunteered "to put his radio time at our disposition ... to develop any angle of foreign affairs the administration might deem worthwhile." Thereafter, Winchell worked in tandem with Ernest Cuneo, counsel to the Democratic National Committee. Cuneo simultaneously was Winchell's ghost writer and his conduit to both the White House and British intelligence services. He also gave Winchell invaluable "leaks," which, in turn, the commentator passed on to both radio listeners and readers of his popular syndicated column.[67]

Unlike Clark, Carter, Johnson, and Cameron, Winchell was able to stand up and win against network interference in a post–Mayflower Doctrine world. A major showdown came in March 1941 when he openly defied the warnings of NBC Director of News and Special Events A. A. Schechter. Schechter had instructed Winchell to excise from his script an "exposé" of an earlier trip to Russia by Senator Burton K. Wheeler (a leading critic of Roosevelt's foreign policy). When Winchell went ahead anyway, Schechter retaliated by cutting off the broadcast mid-transmission for this obvious code violation. "Winchell's material is nothing but blackmail now," Schechter complained, "and he has gotten into a psychotic state where he is defending all of America. ... I think the decision must be made whether Walter Winchell is bigger than the National Broadcasting Company." The decision was made but not in Schechter's favor. Winchell stayed on the air and continued to freely skewer administration enemies.[68]

By 1941, much had changed in free speech policy and attitudes since the *Zenith* decision in 1926. At the beginning of this period, radio was arguably as free as the print press and in some ways more so. In 1926, such varied outlets as nonprofits and rogue commercial broadcasters competed in a rough-and-tumble marketplace of ideas. Libel law did not generally apply to radio, and federal regulators, by their own admission, were almost helpless to control content. In contrast to radio's relative freedom, local and state governments were still able to exercise prior restraint and other controls over newspapers. By the late New Deal period, however, this regime was becoming a distant memory. Even as the courts were striking down political restrictions on the print press and freedom of assembly, they were moving in the opposite direction for radio. Both New Deal reformers and regulators had come to spurn the same laissez-faire model for radio that they were often vigorously upholding for other forms of free expression.

6

"A Most Complete Espionage Service": Boss Crump Cracks Down on Dissent

IT WAS OCTOBER 1940 and the election between Franklin D. Roosevelt and Wendell Willkie was looming. Republicans were making inroads into Memphis's black electorate. In the forefront was John (J. B.) Martin, a prominent black entrepreneur who chaired the Shelby County Republican Party. He predicted a Willkie victory both nationally and statewide and that African Americans might constitute the winning margin. But Edward H. Crump, the formidable boss of the Memphis Democratic machine, had different ideas. When Martin defiantly staged a series of preelection rallies, Crump set out to silence him and, eventually, drive him out of the city.

In some ways, the Memphis free speech controversy resembled those surrounding Hague and Minton. Central to all three were examples of governmental surveillance, harassment, Roosevelt's sometimes duplicitous and abetting role, and the rise of countermovements for free speech on both the left and right. The parallels were particularly close between Edward H. Crump and Frank Hague. Each man was a master of diverse oppressive methods ranging from blunt force to selective manipulation of regulations and welfare spending. But the differences between the two city bosses were significant. Crump's clampdown on free speech, though perhaps unequaled in the United States during this period, did not begin in earnest until *after* the emergence of an American pro–free speech consensus in the late 1930s. Crump, unlike Hague, put heavy reliance on the rhetoric of white supremacy, though primarily to retain and enhance power rather than as an end in itself.

J. B. Martin was a native of Senatobia, Mississippi, arriving in Memphis as a young man. He gradually prospered as the proprietor of one of the largest black-owned drugstores in the South. Along with his three brothers, he opened the Martin Stadium in 1927 and established one of the first black-owned baseball teams. Using this as a springboard, Martin eventually became president of the Negro American [Baseball] League. His businesses were in the legendary Beale Street area (still sometimes called by its original name, Beale Avenue), a hub of black enterprise, entertainment, and social life. Many African American visitors stopped at the US Post Office substation, which was in his drugstore. It was a special source of pride as the only post office controlled by their race in Tennessee. Martin had every reason to bask in his own success. According to a report in 1940 of Dun & Bradstreet, he had "an established business to which he is attentive, has a wide acquaintance locally, and has always had a good turnover. … A WELL MANAGED BUSINESS, AFFAIRS ARE IN GOOD CONDITION."[1]

Martin's involvement in the GOP grew in tandem with his businesses. He was a delegate to every national GOP convention except one between 1912 and 1940. Throughout this period, his main political mentor was Robert R. Church Jr., a wealthy black entrepreneur. Church's father had amassed a small fortune in Memphis real estate. The elder Church had generally abstained from politics, but his son was a longtime chair of the Shelby County Republican Party. One of the younger Church's friends and allies was US Representative J. Will Taylor, a white Republican and powerbroker in the state party from eastern Tennessee. Besides Church, Martin's closest associate in the local party was George W. Lee, an officer of the Atlanta Life Insurance Company who, in 1934, authored the widely acclaimed book *Beale Street: Where the Blues Began*. By the time Martin became politically active, GOP politics in most of the South had morphed into petty patronage turf battles between the integrated black and tan and racially exclusive lily-white factions. In Shelby County, the black and tans remained firmly entrenched (though sometimes effectively challenged by lily whites on the state level) and African Americans still voted in large numbers. The durability of this arrangement depended on a kind of "devil's bargain" they made with Boss Crump.[2]

Crump was unique among big city bosses in his ability to consistently control local events whether he was in or out of office. He was mayor only from 1910 to 1915, and for less than a single day in early 1940, but he dominated Memphis political life well into the late 1940s (and in some ways still later). His only other office was a stint in the US House from 1931 to 1935. Unlike many machine politicians, Crump was a successful businessman before, and after, his introduction to politics. Although he grew up in Mississippi, where white supremacy governed daily life in nearly all aspects, Crump allowed Church and others considerable leeway to register black voters and sometimes even arranged to have their poll taxes paid. In exchange for these favors, the local black and tan leadership mobilized African American voters for Crump's organization in crucial Democratic primaries. Crump also relied on the black and tans as a conduit to get the benefits of federal patronage during Republican presidential administrations. For African Americans, the advantage of the devil's bargain included some targeted governmental services, such as the segregated W. C. Handy Park. In addition, Crump both tolerated and encouraged black participation in various underground enterprises, which subsidized his machine functionaries, including numbers, bootlegging, and prostitution.[3]

Individual black and tans also gained personally from the bargain. Martin, for example, was both a "special officer" of the Memphis Police with the power to make arrests and an unlicensed (but Crump-sanctioned) bondsman authorized to release prisoners from the city jail. Similarly, Church received exemption from property taxes for long periods. But Crump could always jerk away any favor from those who did not toe the line. If that was not enough, he had the means to destroy their livelihood and the discretion to banish African Americans from the city. While the devil's bargain brought ordinary blacks some benefits, via parks and other amenities, some perspective is in order. Throughout the 1930s, there was not a single black policeman or fireman in Memphis.[4]

The bargain gradually unraveled during the 1930s. As an arrangement, it proved no match for the emerging close alliance between Roosevelt and Crump that started in 1931 when Crump became an early endorser of the future president. This support did not flag for the rest of Roosevelt's life. "I never make a second choice," Crump exulted early on, "I am for Franklin D. Roosevelt." Roosevelt also came to depend on Crump. At the 1932 convention, Crump was instrumental in getting FDR all of Tennessee's votes on the first ballot. Crump's ground floor status and consistent fealty to Roosevelt brought him great influence. Beginning in 1933, he became the key gatekeeper for any local federal funds for Memphis and, to some extent, for Tennessee as a whole. As a member of the US House, of course, he backed the New Deal down the line. Crump's national star rose still higher with his appointment to the Democratic National Committee in 1936, working under Frank Hague, vice chairman and fellow machine boss. His direct pipeline to the administration made superfluous any further help from Church and other Republican leaders.[5]

Historians have sometimes exaggerated the extent and generosity of Crump's largesse (much of it dispersed through the New Deal) to African Americans. There was no getting around the fact that the amounts were paltry. Of the more than $300,000 spent by the Memphis Park Commission in 1937, for example, only $3,000 went to African Americans, though they were nearly 40 percent of the population. To be sure, as total spending rose, in great part because the federal government sometimes picked up half the tab, those on the receiving end generally received more in absolute terms. But this must not obscure a very unpleasant reality. In Memphis, it was whites who reaped far greater rewards in both relative and absolute terms, including exclusive power to determine how the money was used.[6]

Moreover, Crump (and often, by extension, Roosevelt) extracted a steep price in return for these subsidies. Federal public housing projects, for example, had multiple dark sides, many of which were intentionally engineered. Because Crump made sure to place them in black neighborhoods only, the result was to perpetuate and extend segregation. Another negative consequence was the razing of whole neighborhoods, including black-owned businesses and one of the few black colleges in the city, to make way for these projects. In this respect, Memphis fit a national pattern, as documented by Richard Rothstein, of governments clearing away space for these projects by demolishing viable black neighborhoods in pursuit of strategies to extend residential segregation.[7]

There was an even more pronounced sign of African American retrogression during the New Deal period. In the 1920s, 77 percent of the letter carriers in Memphis (courtesy of Church's patronage influence) were African Americans, but by the end of the 1930s, whites had moved into the majority. If the impact of the New Deal proved a mixed affair for racial justice, it was most empowering for the Crump organization, which could at election time call on the services of some fifteen thousand county, city, and federal workers.

The result was to reinforce the machine's army of ward heelers, which enabled Crump-approved candidates for mayor to win almost 99 percent of the vote throughout the 1930s.[8]

The 1936 election campaign was a turning point in local politics. Nationally, and to a lesser extent in Memphis, black Republicans flexed their muscles. Landon entrusted Church, assisted by Martin, to coordinate Midwestern outreach to African Americans. The busy Church also made extensive efforts for that purpose on the East Coast and worked alongside Joseph N. Pew Jr., a prominent industrialist and member of the American Liberty League. The same year that Crump won his spot on the Democratic National Committee, Church became the first black member of the executive committee of the Republican National Committee in forty years. During the campaign, Church and Martin repeatedly charged that the New Deal had caused great harm for African Americans. Roosevelt's reliance on regressive excise taxes on basic products, ranging from hairpins to cars, in Martin's view, had mainly served to "fatten gluttonish politicians and high moguls in alphabet agencies, many of them filled to the gills with color prejudice." Church stressed that "the Negro is fundamentally a Republican because the Republican party is the party of rugged individualism and the Negro is an incipient capitalist."[9]

As Crump severed ties with the black and tan faction, New Deal funds enabled him to directly harness the voting power of African Americans. One of his conduits was the recently created Colored Democratic Club, which he subsidized. The relationship between Crump and the club was one of patron and supplicant. David Tucker summed it up well: "Mr. Crump did things *for* Negroes but not *with* them." His ward heelers, who usually doubled as governmental employees, mined detailed voter registration lists featuring such information as church membership. On a typical election day, every element of Crump's polling bureaucracy swung into action. Meals were lavished on prospects who were transported to the polls on condition that they vote the right way. The organization also mobilized the electoral pull of clergymen beholden to it for such favors as getting permission to spring parishioners from jail. Everyone, wrote an observer, had his "duties laid out before him. [T]he workers were busy, as in all other 51 wards. As voters came to the polls they ticked off their names. Those who didn't come were called. Those who still didn't come were sent for." These efforts paid off. In 1936, a record majority of the city's African Americans voted for Roosevelt.[10]

Despite this seismic voting shift away from the GOP, several postelection trends fueled black resentment against the Crump organization. First on the list was a series of police killings in 1937, underscoring, as Ralph Bunche put it, the brutal reality that the "only connection Negroes have had with the Memphis police force has been Negro heads colliding with nightsticks in the hands of white policemen." Also stoking African American anger was Crump's overt political use of the New Deal bureaucracy by, for example, deploying WPA supervisors to pay the poll taxes of employees. One supervisor even boasted that he had piles of affidavits pledging "100 percent" for the ticket. This heavy-handed approach prompted one woman to complain to WPA head Harry Hopkins that "they treat all colored peoples just like doges [sic] down here ... Miss Rosella Clink told us if we didn't vote for Mr. Crump we could lose our job."[11]

These mounting grievances gave an opening for Church's black and tan faction to make a comeback. Despite suffering an electoral shellacking in 1936, the group still had latent power because most African Americans retained their Republican Party registration. Church made his first major move in 1938 by calling for his followers to support the Democratic primary reelection of Governor Gordon Browning, who had alienated himself from the organization, over Crump's favorite, Prentice Cooper. Although Browning lost, he did unusually well among black voters in Shelby County. This was more than Crump could stomach.[12]

Crump ceased almost all pretense of cultivating the black electorate in the run-up to the scheduled end of state prohibition in 1939. Anticipating that this legal change doomed his lucrative reliance on bootlegging, he abandoned the de facto policy of toleration through an opportunistic campaign to "clean up" the city's image by cracking down on Beale Street's vice, much of it African American controlled. He shuttered brothels and gambling, including carnival bingo. It was no longer possible for those targeted by police raids to get out of jail by proving payment of poll taxes. When the dust settled, Crump's organization had squeezed African Americans almost completely out of the officially tolerated vice market. "The gambling joints are in the hands of whites," wrote Bunche in 1941, "who are at the same time precinct captains for Edward H. Crump's political machine." To compensate for the loss of the black vote, Crump focused on boosting the white percentage by, for the first time, emphasizing crude racist appeals.[13]

The retribution-minded Crump centered most of his ire on Church, however. In 1938, the city revoked a long-time informal tax exemption and sold off twelve pieces of his property for seven years of back taxes. Added to this were stepped up citations for building code infractions. As Roberta Church, Church's daughter, later put it, "[I]f you put in a fire escape after the fire inspectors had been to your property, then they'd find some trouble with the electrical wiring; after you got the electrical wiring repaired, there'd be some troubles with the exits. ... It was one constant thing after another, so that you always had to be spending money for repairs." The consequences, as historian Elizabeth Gritter points out, "left Church in a state of financial disaster given that his real estate was his main source of income." By then, he was spending most of his time outside of Memphis and pretty much had moved out. Crump twisted the knife again by renaming Church Park (as in Robert R. Church Sr.) to Beale Avenue Park. Some years earlier, Joseph E. Walker's Colored Democrats had taken control of the Memphis NAACP, thus neutering most of its civil rights potency.[14]

Church struck back by making his boldest move yet, albeit from afar. In early October 1940, he handed over the reins of the Shelby County GOP to his longtime political protégé, J. B. Martin. Martin shared Church's vision of a multiracial and assertive Southern GOP. Risking Crump's wrath to achieve this goal was a tremendous gamble, but the potential payoff was almost incalculable if Willkie won. The GOP platform of 1940 more forthrightly backed civil rights, including "universal suffrage," than its Democratic counterpart. Willkie spoke out against discrimination in federal employment and the military, and championed antilynching legislation. Taking on an issue that struck very close to home, he slammed Roosevelt's cozy ties to Democratic bosses, naming Crump as a key offender. The Republican state convention in Nashville piled on, proclaiming that there was "a real Hitler and Mussolini in Shelby County." Willkie himself boasted that among his supporters "there isn't a Mayor Hague nor a Mayor Kelly nor a Crump on the list."[15]

Martin took heart from several encouraging signs that Willkie might just pull off an upset. By late October, polls showed a tight national race, and it seemed possible, though unlikely, for the GOP to repeat its state victories of 1920 and 1928. If that happened, Tennessee's blacks might again be the balance of power. Also encouraging the pro-Willkie optimists was news that African Americans had turned out in unusually large numbers in the Shelby County GOP primary in August to elect delegates to the state convention. But even if Martin failed to tip the scales in Tennessee, a Willkie victory nationally held out the prospect of a friend in the White House and a protector of the black and tans from Crump's wrath.[16]

Martin kicked off his campaign on October 21 with a multiracial rally of as many 1,500. Although the vast majority of the crowd was black, several prominent white Republicans, including the wife and daughter of C. Arthur Bruce, the GOP candidate for governor, were also there. A. B. Clapp, a Crump subordinate and head of the social welfare division for the city of Memphis, reported back that speakers of both races depicted a Willkie victory as a "foregone conclusion," called for abolition of the poll tax, and belittled the Colored Democratic Club as Crump's puppet organization. They also demanded the hiring of black police officers and firefighters. Clapp advised Crump that the speakers "cause[d] trouble" because they "preached race equality without any reservations," and he expressed surprise that Martin, who he thought "was for us," was the master of ceremonies.[17]

In response to the first rally and a second one the following day, Crump tasked Shelby County Attorney General Will Gerber, who was second-in-command in the organization, to instruct Martin's black and tan comrade, George W. Lee, to intercede. Mayor Walter Chandler of Memphis was essentially a bystander in the whole process. When Gerber met with Lee, he laid it on the line: "Mr. Crump is boiling over. He is going to move in on Martin if Martin doesn't stop the meetings." Although Lee had served Church loyally, he did not intend to stick his neck out this time. He later explained that he preferred dying "in a town where my 'roots' are, near the grave that I have prepared for my body." Assuring Martin that Crump would "stoop to do anything," Lee said he had until Friday to call off a scheduled third rally on Monday, resign as chair of the county Republican organization, and close Willkie headquarters. If he refused, his drugstore would be "policed." Martin tried to be diplomatic but left no doubt of his intention not to comply.[18]

Crump, his finger always on the trigger if Martin did not relent, began the process of retaliation just after the Friday deadline. Two police officers appeared outside the drugstore. To remove any mystery about why they were there, Lee phoned to let Martin know that the policing had begun. In two eight-hour shifts, the officers, covering the working hours of the store, frisked everyone entering, including such influential whites as the GOP gubernatorial candidate. In comments to the press, Joseph P. Boyle, commissioner of public safety and vice mayor, avowed that the "policing has nothing to do with politics" but was intended to "break up Negro dope peddling." There were no warrants. Boyle used the thinnest of pretexts for the search, citing a dismissed case against Martin for buying a stolen shipment of aspirin. Although the frisking dragged on for weeks, it failed to net even a single marijuana cigarette. [19]

Martin was not the only one in Crump's sights. On Saturday, police also started to frisk the business patrons of Elmer Atkinson, another key black Republican, who owned a pool parlor, restaurant, and taxi stand on Beale Street. Boyle slyly implied (without evidence) that Atkinson and Martin were conspiring together in a "dope business." When Atkinson asked his wife's white priest to come to the store, the police ordered him to remove his shoes and socks before entering. The day after the policing began, Martin, Atkinson, and other black Republican activists (as well as several black journalists) received typed letters threatening bloodshed unless they quit "talking social equality." Another letter went to Rev. G. A. Long of Beale Street Baptist Church, a particularly energetic speaker at the Willkie rallies. Ever defiant, he reiterated that he stood "firmly for the Republican party" and wondered how "any Negro in the South with good sense can afford to vote for the Democratic ticket." [20]

Crump responded to Martin's persistence by ratcheting up the pressure. Soon after the third, and final, preelection rally of October 28, the city denied permission to hoist a banner at Shelby County GOP headquarters proclaiming, "Our Own Joe Louis [the world heavyweight champion] is for Willkie." The official explanation by Robert S. Fredericks, the director of the city department in charge of signs, was all too transparent: "I talked it over with the Mayor this morning, and he agreed with me that only candidates should have their names on signs." An article in the *Chicago Defender* reported that at about the same time, Governor Prentice Cooper (D-TN), a close Crump ally, had hectored a black delegation that the United States was "a white man's country." By contrast, C. Arthur Bruce, his Republican opponent, encouraged Martin to stand firm.[21]

Emblematic of Martin's increased isolation was the desertion of his own brother, W. S. (William) Martin, a co-owner with J. B. of the Memphis baseball team, who wrote an obsequious letter to Crump on November 1 lamenting that J. B. had made a "serious mistake" in backing Willkie. He pledged support for "the entire democratic ticket from President Roosevelt on down" and offered a reminder that he was a vice chairman of the Colored Democratic Club. He underlined his impeccable pro-Crump credentials, tracing them back to the time thirty years earlier when he bought a buggy from him. Just to make sure that Crump fully appreciated this zeal, he characterized FDR as a "true friend to the colored people," citing the construction of "3 colored housing projects, the W.P.A., the [C.]C.C. Camps, etc."[22]

Squeezed hard on every side by Crump, Martin struggled for a middle ground. Only a few days before the election, he made a personal appeal to Will Gerber, who assured him that "everything will be all right" if Martin both called a mass meeting to announce that he was resigning and shuttered GOP headquarters. Responding that this was not feasible so late in the campaign, Martin crafted a compromise that he unveiled the day before the election. He publicly instructed his workers that their only mission was to help Willkie and Bruce, not challenge the current city administration. "We consider Mr. Crump our political leader and boss," he added for good measure. These assurances, however, did nothing to appease Gerber, who later complained that Martin had "doublecrossed" him.[23]

Although Willkie's defeat both nationally and in Tennessee sealed Martin's unhappy fate in Memphis, his African American supporters had made a gamble that was not at all unreasonable. In addition, they had successfully repelled Crump's attempt to scare them away from the polls. While there is no precise information on the alignment of the black vote that year in Shelby County, the overall support for Willkie there was more than two times higher than for Landon in 1936 and more than three times higher than for the GOP candidate for governor in 1938. Nationally, the black Republican percentage moved up significantly over 1936, perhaps reaching as high as 50 percent.

But these gains were not enough to offset overwhelming victories in the state for Roosevelt and Cooper and were a far cry from predictions that victory for Willkie and Bruce was a "foregone conclusion." Gone was Martin's and Church's dream of any protection from the federal government under a new president.[24]

Walker's Colored Democrats wasted no time in gulping up any leftover patronage crumbs. Two days after the election, they successfully petitioned the Crump organization to replace George W. Lee and the rest of the Republican majority on the Colored Board of the Memphis Park Commission and give them unanimous control. By this measure, and others, Lee gained little for his fealty to the organization, and his reputation among African Americans suffered greatly because of his betrayal of Martin. The purge of Republicans in favor of Walker's group also extended to the Colored Housing Committee.[25]

More significantly, Crump's policing of the drugstore continued to push ahead at full speed. The frisking came to include kindergarteners seeking to buy ice cream. According to a news story, the police "ran their hands over little dresses and poked into the pockets of knickers." On the pretext of eliminating "undesirables," Commissioner of Public Safety Joseph Boyle oversaw raids in the Beale Street area. Police arrested sixty-five people in one evening alone, many on charges of carrying illegal weapons, a broadly defined category that included penknives. In a letter to Roscoe C. Grant, a black Republican and NAACP activist in Nashville, Martin complained that "local influential persons are absolutely afraid to help me in my case. … It has practically closed my business with exception of telephone calls. Help will have to come from some other place and I will have to have relief immediately or I can't stand it. I can't even get a good lawyer here to take the case."[26]

Crump's harsh measures were getting some local pushback, however. The absurdity of the situation was too much to tolerate, even for Memphis's normally quiescent white dailies. On November 21, for example, the *Commercial Appeal* broke editorial silence, complaining that the "blockade of a man's business plainly flouts the very principles of freedom. … If Dr. Martin has committed a crime, arrest him." The editorial pulled its punches somewhat by adding that the "Commercial Appeal is not defending Dr. Martin, but the law itself." More firmly, the *Memphis Press-Scimitar* declared that "[n]ot even a ten year old child will believe that this public search has law enforcement as its object." Ordinary Memphians, black and white, expressed solidarity for Martin by patronizing his drugstore. To stem this, however, the police stepped up their harassment by requiring everyone to present driver's licenses and, in some cases, tearing up their cigarette packs and dumping the contents in the hats of the owners. After one white man quipped, on being told to "move on," that he "thought the streets were free," a policeman arrested him, retorting, "We'll show you how free they are."[27]

In contrast to their quiescent elders in the local NAACP, the Memphis NAACP Youth Council protested strenuously. In a letter to Mayor Chandler, it condemned the recent dragnet arrests for violating the Fourth Amendment's prohibition of illegal searches and the Fourteenth Amendment by destroying "private business in Memphis by means of a police blockade." Instructors from the all-black LeMoyne College dismissed whole classes to allow students to visit Martin's drugstore in groups. The *Atlanta Daily World* estimated that the store's patronage actually ticked up in the first few weeks of policing.[28]

Almost immediately after the policing began, several white Tennessee Republican leaders lodged protests on behalf of Martin. The most prominent was the very conservative, but pro–civil rights, US Representative B. Carroll Reece from eastern Tennessee, who brought the matter up to the Department of Justice. One of Martin's most vigorous white Republican defenders was Ray H. Jenkins, the state party manager, who later went on to be the special counsel of the US Senate Subcommittee on Investigations during the Army-McCarthy hearings. In late October, Jenkins accused Crump of a "Reign of Terror" and of violating "practically every one of the rights listed in the Bill of Rights." His actions, he added, amounted "to a confiscation of a person's property ... the most deadly way in the world to put a man out of business." Not about to take this silently, Boyle warned Jenkins to "keep your hands out of Memphis." He also pushed a line of argument that nobody took seriously, asking (in reference to Martin), "[D]o you realize you are defending one who is a common fence dealing in stolen property whose police record is notorious in this community and further has been the subject of a narcotic investigation?"[29]

Black Republicans nationally were some of Martin's earliest and most unswerving supporters. One week after the election, Roscoe Conkling Simmons, a longtime GOP ally of Church and a nephew of Booker T. Washington, compared Crump to Hitler. In Memphis, he asserted, it was almost as easy to convict a black person with a trumped-up crime as "getting up 'charges' against Jews in Germany." He quipped, "Maybe Mr. Roosevelt will give less attention to Germany and more, at least briefly, to Memphis. He might say, on the other hand, the election being over, let bygones be bygones."[30]

But from Martin's perspective, the extent of this backing was either too isolated or too tepid to turn the tide. Moreover, both Republicans and Democrats were in a postelection lull and thus inclined to give Martin's plight relatively little play. A couple of weeks after the election, Martin began an extended visit to Chicago, which eventually became permanent, after hearing that Crump was planning to prosecute him for bonding prisoners without a license. Martin, who had exercised this privilege for years with Crump's approval, privately confided, "They're trying to put me in the workhouse, and I couldn't stand that." At about the same time, Elmer Atkinson sold his poolroom, cafeteria, and taxicab service and fled from Memphis.[31]

Hoping that Crump might be in a more forgiving mood because the election was over, the Commission on Interracial Cooperation, a group of white and black ministers, gently asked for easing up the harassment. They had no success and, if anything, spurred the Crump organization to take a harder line. African Americans, Boyle warned on December 4, were "not going to carry on and conduct themselves in Memphis as if they lived in Chicago, Pittsburgh and Philadelphia," stressing that "after all, this is a white man's country." He made plain his intention not to sit idly by if black newspapers continued to "write this character of stuff." As to Martin, he was nothing less than "a minister of evil, fence for thieves, buys stolen property, has been a professional bondsman, extorts money from the poor and unfortunate." This response sufficiently intimidated the white members of the Commission on Interracial Cooperation that they volunteered, in the words of Mayor Chandler, "approval of the city's law enforcement program and assured us that their sole desire is to cooperate whenever possible."[32]

When a delegation of Colored Democrats, led by Joseph E. Walker, spoke up on Martin's behalf, albeit somewhat timidly, Crump did not let them get a word in edgewise. He unleashed a racist screed akin to Boyle's, accusing Martin of aiding and abetting Church, who, now safely in the North, was "spreading ideas of social equality." This must stop, Crump emphasized, and "Negroes might as well learn their places."[33]

Even as Boyle and Crump got on their racist soapboxes, the city readjusted the methods of harassment on December 5. "We are going to police the store," Boyle proclaimed mysteriously, "in a different way." In place of the searches, uniformed officers in their patrol cars visited on an hourly basis. But this change did not mean any mitigation of the harassment. On December 11, the police began mass roundups of black men on trumped up charges of "loitering." Boyle left no doubt that the underlying goal was political intimidation. In addition, Crump called in the editors of the two local black newspapers and ordered them to cease all articles stirring up "race hatred." They largely complied.[34]

As he initiated a new wave of arrests, Boyle announced that he had his eyes "on five Negro preachers, four Negro doctors, one Negro barbecue and restaurant operator, two Negro postmen, five Negro newspaper writers, one Negro drugstore operator, one Negro undertaker, who have been fanning race hatred." Four on this target list belonged to the Commission on Interracial Cooperation. These and related threats motivated L. O. Swingler of the *Memphis World*, the main African American paper in the city, to scuttle a plan to carry articles defending Martin.[35]

Crump's audaciousness did more than any other factor to keep the Martin case in the news. His antics were too much even for many of those normally complacent about the evils of Jim Crow. A few (though just a few) stories broke into the mainstream national press, including a brief one in *Time*. "Anyone who tried to enter either place," it noted, "was frisked. Holy Joe [Boyle] declared that they were looking for dope. Negroes who protested were arrested, fined." In late December, NAACP head Walter White sent a telegram to Attorney General Robert H. Jackson urging an investigation of Boyle's threats against newspapers and attempts to dictate editorial content. The protest of the Southern Conference for Human Welfare, an activist pro–New Deal organization, was much more vigorous. In a letter to Roosevelt, Howard Lee, the group's conference secretary, accused Crump of "a systematic campaign of intimidation against the Negro citizens because some of them dared to vote for a presidential candidate other than the one dictated to them by Ed Crump."[36]

If there was any possibility of federal intervention, the likely vehicle was the new Civil Liberties Unit of the Department of Justice. Its creation in 1939 by Attorney General Frank Murphy was a byproduct, in part, of the Jersey City free speech case. The unit derived its power from two Reconstruction Era statutes, Sections 51 and 52 of Title 18 of the Federal Criminal Code. Section 51 allowed federal criminal charges against anyone conspiring to deprive "any citizen" of constitutional rights. Section 52, which was perhaps even more applicable to Memphis, extended federal jurisdiction to cover local officials who committed these offenses, including police officers who "under color of any law, statute, ordinance, regulation, or custom" violated "any rights, privileges, or immunities secured or protected by the Constitution."[37]

In January 1941, the Department of Justice gave Martin and Church a glimmer of hope. In response to the mounting pressure, Amos W. W. Woodcock, special assistant attorney general, arrived in Memphis to look over the situation. The Justice Department, however, carefully denied that this constituted an "investigation," and subsequent events bore out the truth of that denial. Woodcock stayed in the city just two business days and did not interview Martin or even a single black witness, though he met with Commissioner Boyle and United States District Attorney William McClanahan, a man with demonstrated racial biases. While Woodcock purportedly reminded Boyle of the federal "Civil Rights Code," he otherwise accepted the official explanation of Crump's "policing" at face value and concluded that "the federal government has no jurisdiction over the behavior of the police toward Negroes or anyone else." Not without reason, the black press dismissed the inquiry as a "whitewash."[38]

If the federal government had wanted to prosecute Crump and his associates (which it did not), it would have had a reasonable chance of success, both on the legal merits and in the court of public opinion. It had at its disposal overwhelming evidence of Crump's brazen violation of free speech, assembly, and Fourth Amendment rights. Like Hague, he had openly flouted the public forum doctrine, which the Supreme Court had laid down in *Hague v. Committee for Industrial Organization*. Also, like Hague, Crump made liberal use of what historian David E. Bernstein calls "facially neutral" laws and rules that "had a plausible public health or welfare justification." In theory, these provisions applied to everyone equally, but in Memphis, they were a politicized means of retribution and reward. Examples of facially neutral laws and rules used by Crump included discriminatory application of sign and meeting hall permits, tax assessments, prescription drug laws, and building code regulations.[39]

A more compelling argument for prosecuting Crump and his hench-men from the standpoint of those interested in promoting the interests of the Roosevelt administration was one of political expediency. The situation in Memphis, unlike many others in the South, did not directly impinge on those hot-button issues of segregation and race-based disfranchisement that Roosevelt had so habitually shunned. As Sven Hutchins Dubie observes, prosecutions were far more likely under FDR's Department of Justice; "[I]f African Americans were the incidental beneficiaries of federal civil rights enforcement policies, in no way were the civil rights of black Americans the central preoccupation of the Department's lawyers." While Crump's actions had a clear racist subtext, the legal questions they raised were, much like those in Jersey City, centered primarily on free speech and assembly. A prosecu-tion of Crump (again following the precedent set by *Hague v. Committee for Industrial Organization*) might have offered a low-cost way to win favor from African American voters as well as those "civil liberties–conscious" Americans (to use a term coined by Henry A. Schweinhaut, the head of the Civil Liberties Unit) who had fought Hague and Minton. Not least of all, key personnel in the Unit had hands-on experience in the Hague case, which had focused on closely related questions.[40]

While Section 52 required a high bar of proving willful intent to deny the rights of free speech and assembly, this too may not have presented an insurmountable obstacle. Few politicians in the United States looked guiltier under that standard than Crump. His over-the-top and brazen methods had the makings of a dream case for a prosecutor. The prospects for prevailing in the broader court of public opinion were also promising. Like Hague, Crump was not a particularly sympathetic figure. Outside of Memphis, he had rela-tively few defenders, even among the most vocal segregationists. But against all of this, the political reality was that Crump was reliably in Roosevelt's corner and an important political asset for him.[41]

In retrospect, the choice of Woodcock as an investigator showed a clear lack of seriousness. Woodcock's many career accomplishments had little direct connection to civil rights, not to mention free speech and assembly issues. As the former director of the Bureau of Prohibition under Herbert Hoover, Americans knew him, if they knew him at all, as "the dry czar," due his zealous enforcement of an increasingly unpopular law. Another factor accounting for the perfunctory nature of the inquiry was Woodcock's competing life priorities in 1941. A highly decorated World War I officer, Woodcock had secured a brigadier general commission from the governor of Maryland in 1936. During the first three or four years, his duties were mainly ceremonial, but by 1941 they increasingly preoccupied him as the United States mobilized. In the aftermath of Woodcock's visit, the first inclination of the powers-that-be in the Department of Justice was to depict the whole Memphis matter as closed. When asked how long Woodcock was in the city, Acting Assistant Attorney General Wendell Berge testily answered, "No good purpose would be served in furnishing you this information."[42]

Even as local African Americans expressed dismay about Woodcock's uneventful sojourn, the Crump organization seemed emboldened. "The process of intimidating Negroes goes on unabated in Memphis," lamented Collins C. George, a professor at LeMoyne College, to NAACP counsel Thurgood Marshall. "The incidents are small in themselves but their totality is startling. Police enter any Negro café or pool-room at any time, force the patrons to raise their hands, then proceed to paw over them, male and female, searching for God-knows what!" Crump, according to George, had erected "a most complete espionage service," which permitted holding anyone "incommunicado" for days.[43]

Few worked more tenaciously to fight Crump's onslaught than Claude Barnett, the founder and head of the Associated Negro Press. Before and after Woodcock had left, Barnett sent a deluge of letters to both the federal government and well-placed fellow Republicans. He personally appealed to Willkie, saying that there was no better way for the "Republican party to show its interest in the Negro Republican than for it to seek to protect this Negro Republican leader who is being crucified for the party's sake." He also pressed both Emmett J. Scott, the president of the Tuskegee Institute and a prominent national Republican, and Perry W. Howard, a black member of the Republican National Committee, to call for an investigation by the US Senate Special Committee to Investigate Presidential, Vice Presidential, and

Senatorial Campaign Expenditures (commonly known as the Gillette Committee): "Either we are going to prove to the Negro voter that the Republican party is interested absolutely in his welfare or we must admit the futility of our hopes."[44]

By the end of January, despite Woodcock's "whitewash," momentum was building for revisiting Martin's plight. In response to Barnett's entreaties, Scott and Howard promised to bring the matter up at the Republican National Committee's upcoming meeting in March. Perry W. Howard (belying his later reputation among historians as a complacent conservative) volunteered that he had observed "no more pronounced evidence of the failure of Democracy than the Nordic outburst at Memphis." Providing additional reinforcement, Thurgood Marshall wrote again to Attorney General Robert H. Jackson, dismissing Woodcock's investigation as "one-sided to say the least."[45]

These efforts appeared to bear fruit in early March when Henry A. Schweinhaut, the head of the Civil Liberties Unit, took depositions in Washington, DC, from both Martin and Church. Even before he met them, he concluded that the department had "sufficient justification under the suggestions above made to warrant invoking the investigative jurisdiction of the department." One of the possible precedents he cited for moving forward was *Hague v. Committee for Industrial Organization.* A factor in his thinking was, as Schweinhaut put it, the "open, notorious, public and continuing search of all patrons of a business establishment." When Martin, backed up by Church, gave his deposition on March 12, 1941, he related a grim, detailed, and credible history of harassment by the Crump organization. Schweinhaut nurtured the hopes of Martin and Church when he openly pondered in their presence the possible timing of grand jury indictments.[46]

Due in great part to these positive signals, Church purposefully derailed the long-awaited resolution on the agenda of the March 23 meeting of the Republican National Committee. That meeting came and went without any action. The following day Perry W. Howard related, somewhat cryptically to Barnett, that he had not proposed the resolution because "Church asked me not to do so inasmuch as it might hurt some work that is brewing in Dr. Martin's interest."[47]

Church's hopes proved to be in vain. The federal government ultimately did nothing. Attorney General Robert H. Jackson's lack of enthusiasm for the Civil Liberties Unit (later renamed Civil Rights Section) no doubt had something to do with why. Jackson, according to a lawyer for the unit, "paid very little attention to our work and the old guard [in the department] made it frustrating for us." Schweinhaut himself had always prioritized the rights of labor union members over African Americans. Finally, as the nation headed for war, the Roosevelt administration wanted more than ever to skirt anything that might get too close to the race issue. The only readily apparent result of federal inaction was to empower the Crump organization with a heightened sense of invulnerability. In December 1941, for example, the city pried away Church's last foothold in Memphis by selling off his family home, including crystal chandeliers.[48]

No better illustration of the irony involved was the airing during that same month of a special radio broadcast, "We Hold These Truths," to mark the 150th anniversary of the Bill of Rights. Commissioned by the federal government, the show was simultaneously broadcast on all four networks just a week after Pearl Harbor. "We Hold These Truths" had the largest audience, almost half the American population, up to that time for a dramatic show. An all-star cast, including Orson Welles, James (Jimmy) Stewart, Walter Huston, and Marjorie Main, acted out both the origins of the Bill of Rights and its continuing application. In one scene, Edward G. Robinson portrayed a political activist who was in jail on "trumped up" charges by the mayor because he had campaigned for the opposition party. The scene was clearly modeled after events in Jersey City circa 1938. The Robinson character defiantly declared, "Getting out on bail tomorrow, and when I'm finally tried, it will be by jury and in public. None of this Gestapo stuff, not that they wouldn't try it if they could." When asked why he was in jail by narrator James Stewart, he recounted that his political party had hired a hall "but they took away our permit, said the building was unsafe under an old fire ordinance, so then we went down to Garrison Square, where no permit is required to speak in public, and within ten minutes we were on our way to the police station on charges of blocking traffic, disturbing the peace, and inciting to riot."[49]

The scene ended on an optimistic flourish as the character played by Robinson vowed, "We'll beat him [the mayor]. He's scared of us. He's scared that people will find out the truth and with good reason because when they do, he's finished. That's why he doesn't want us to be heard. It's only the crooks and the frightened little big shots who need to shut up their opponents. That may work all right in some other countries but not here. ... There are such things as rights on our side, and not even the mayor's machine is powerful enough to stop us. We'll fight that fight on every front, carry it to the highest court if necessary and we'll win." Capping off the broadcast was a speech by Roosevelt himself that was equally upbeat. "We will not, under any threat, or in the face of any danger," the president proclaimed, "surrender the guarantees of liberty our forefathers framed for us in our Bill of Rights."[50]

One wonders what Martin thought of this broadcast if he heard it while in exile from Memphis where he no longer enjoyed the Bill of Rights protections so celebrated in "We Hold These Truths." No "higher" court was ever to hear his case against the "little big shot" who ruled Memphis. The future prospects at the time of the broadcast for African Americans in the city appeared bleak. According to a poll in 1942, 75 percent of blacks in Memphis expected better treatment if Japan won the war.[51]

Despite these disappointments, Martin was building a successful life in Chicago. Reelected as head of the Negro American League, he purchased the Chicago American Giants, a black team, in 1942. After an unsuccessful run for Cook County commissioner a year later, he won election in 1946 as a Republican to become the first African American trustee of the Sanitary District Board. His Memphis drugstore continued operation, at least until the 1950s, under the leadership of one of his brothers.[52]

Success in Chicago or not, Martin really did not have a choice on whether to stay in Memphis, where he was pretty much a public enemy. More confirmation of his lowly status there came in 1943 when he came back to throw out the first ball at an All-Star Game of the Negro American League. Three detectives entered his box, arrested him, and whisked him off to a holding cell. Finally, Police Chief Carrol B. Seabrook ordered Martin to leave town by the next day, and he complied. After recounting his plight to US Attorney General Francis Biddle yet again, Martin asked him to "advise" him on the possibility of coming back to Memphis temporarily to settle up some old business affairs, but "knowing the situation as I do, I am afraid to return." Though the request was modest, it met a firm rebuff. Writing on Biddle's behalf, Assistant Attorney General Tom C. Clark, who eventually assumed the top job, summarily replied that he did not see that the treatment of Martin constituted "any violation of federal law.[53]

Less than a month after Martin's expulsion from Memphis in 1943, however, the cause of free speech in that city found a powerful new champion: A. Philip Randolph. Unlike Martin and Church, Randolph, as the head of both the national Brotherhood of Sleeping Car Porters and the March on Washington Movement, had the necessary financial muscle and immunity from local pressures to wage a war of attrition.

The first phase in the hostilities centered on Randolph's scheduled speech at the Mount Nebo Baptist Church on November 7, 1943, under the sponsorship of the Memphis branch of the Brotherhood of Sleeping Car Porters. Crump, who kept track of national newspaper reports about Randolph, smelled trouble and acted swiftly. On the day before the speech, County Sheriff Oliver Perry called in more than a dozen black leaders, including Joseph E. Walker, George W. Lee, and Blair Hunt. Hunt was the principal of Booker T. Washington High School and a self-described "little brown nut in the Crump machine." Covering all the bases, Crump had included the head of the local chapter of the Brotherhood of Sleeping Car Porters in the proposed delegation. Perry, accompanied by Shelby County Attorney General Will Gerber, led the group to a cell and promised to put them at the top of his arrest list if there was any trouble resulting from the speech. "[I]f you don't want to meet him at the train and tell him," he specified, "I will." As instructed, they met Randolph at the train station to pass on the bad news.[54]

Although denied the pulpit at the Mount Nebo Baptist Church, Randolph had no intention of folding up his tent. By staying put, he was able to tap into a lingering spirit of local resistance. Within a few days, he appeared at both the White Stone Baptist Church and at LeMoyne College. Not coincidentally, LeMoyne had been a hub of support for J. B. Martin. In his speech at the White Stone Baptist Church, Randolph unleashed a torrent. "If American soldiers of both races fight for the right of free expression and free assembly," he declared, "it is our duty on the home front to keep … those democratic principles." He took a parting shot at the "spineless Negro stooges" who had met him at the train station.[55]

The verbal slugfest between Crump and Randolph continued long after Randolph left. Warning Randolph and other "outsiders" to butt out, Crump put a racial spin on Oliver Wendell Holmes Jr.'s famous justification for limiting the First Amendment. "Free speech," the Memphis boss asserted, "does not mean that anyone has a right to holler 'fire' in a crowded theater, nor does it mean that anyone, white or black, has a right to incite race trouble." In his response, Randolph gave as good as he got. He retorted that Crump's statement read "like a page from Hitler's Mein Kampf" but also pointedly deplored the failure of the federal government to respond. Randolph asked how the Tennessean US Secretary of State Cordell Hull could proclaim his intention to extend the four freedoms to other countries "when there is no right to freedom of speech and assembly in Memphis, a city of his own state?"[56]

As he was battling toe-to-toe with Crump, Randolph was privately reaching out to Eleanor Roosevelt. This may well have been a game changer had he won her support. On November 24, he urgently appealed to the First Lady "to speak out against this species of fascism in our Country. Memphis, it appears to me, is the head front of a native variety of fascism. If we can expose this unamerican and undemocratic rule of Boss Crump, it will help democracy at home and abroad. If Boss Crump can get away with this attack upon one of our Four Freedoms in Memphis, it may become epidemic in America." After a wait of three weeks, the First Lady sent a most discouraging, and uncharacteristically abrupt, reply. It read in full: "I referred your letter to a friend of mine when I received it and I am sorry it has not been answered before. I was advised not to do anything, as it might do more harm than good."[57]

If the truth be told, this brush-off was not entirely surprising. While the First Lady had a well-deserved reputation for fighting racial injustice, considerations of political calculus were usually present in the background. This was true in even the most famous example of her outspokenness: her 1939 resignation from the Daughters of the American Revolution in protest of the denial of a performance venue to singer Marian Anderson. Less well known was her intentional silence at the time about the simultaneous decision of the District of Columbia Board of Education to also bar Anderson from performing at an auditorium of the all-white Central High School. The District's presidentially appointed commissioners held the purse strings for the board and might, in theory at least, have exerted pressure. Political calculus was also a factor in 1941 when the president's wife ran interference for the administration by urging Randolph to call off the proposed March on Washington. Randolph turned her down and only relented because FDR issued Executive Order Number 8802 prohibiting discrimination in war industries. A similar calculus was arguably in play in the Crump case. More than likely, she regarded any involvement as politically unwise and potentially costly for the president. Taking a stand might also jeopardize the cordial relationship that she herself had cultivated with Crump.[58]

Spurned by the First Lady, Randolph continued to pursue other possible avenues of support. His reliable corner man in this fight was Robert R. Church Jr. The two repeatedly compared notes and discussed strategy on how to keep the controversy at the forefront. "I am back in New York," Randolph exuded to his Republican coconspirator, "and am busy building fires under Boss Crump and his reprehensible gestapo." Black newspapers played up the conflict, as did national periodicals such as the *New Republic*. In a letter in March 1944 to Roy Wilkins berating the NAACP for failing to do more, Church characterized it as the "hottest issue in the South today." Church's accusations prompted Wilkins's lengthy and rather defensive response, in which he tried to explain that it was "not strictly true that the NAACP did nothing on this subject." He listed several actions, including a letter by Walter White to Cordell Hull several days after Randolph had singled Hull out for admonishment. But Church had undeniably struck a nerve. The NAACP did indeed seem again to be more going through the motions rather than making a determined fight, perhaps sensing that any hint of rocking the boat might endanger its good relations with the Roosevelt administration during wartime.[59]

Intending to smoke Crump out again, and thus hopefully advance the cause of free speech and racial justice, Randolph publicly served notice in January 1944 that he was returning to Memphis, this time to address a joint mass meeting of the Southern Tenant Farmers Union and the American Federation of Labor. The precise location was still undetermined. Simultaneously, he urged Biddle to open an investigation on whether Assistant District Attorney Charles Mooney of Memphis was "intimidating Negro leaders" to sign statements endorsing Crump's claim that canceling the speech in 1943 had headed off a race riot. Meanwhile, Walker, the head of the Colored Democrats, provided cover for Crump by calling Randolph a "demagogue."[60]

Randolph made his much-anticipated speech on March 31, 1944, to an overflow crowd of more than one thousand at the Beale Street Baptist Church, pastored by the indefatigable Rev. G. A. Long. Long had given over the church for one of Martin's election eve pro-Willkie GOP rallies in 1940. In an open letter to Crump in the aftermath of the speech, Randolph ferociously denounced Crump as "a symbol of Southern fascism" and dismissed his boasts of giving largesse to African Americans as unwanted "Jim Crow charity." Randolph adroitly baited the boss as well as made a broader political point about integration. He dared Crump to debate him at the Memphis Municipal Auditorium on the condition that people "sit wherever they wish without any segregation or interference." If Randolph expected to provoke Crump and his henchmen to spout outrageous vitriol in response, he more than succeeded. Sheriff Perry fumed that if he had known what Randolph planned to say, he would have personally pulled him down from the pulpit. Other than Randolph, however, the main target of Perry's anger was his local enabler, Rev. Long: "[T]he blood of his race is on his altar in the House of God. He has desecrated it."[61]

Not long after Randolph's appearance in Memphis, an editorial in the generally complacent *Memphis World* defended Randolph's "freedom of speech and assembly rights" and lamented the cancellation of the earlier speech. Carefully hedging, however, it then tried to appease Crump by criticizing the least inflammatory parts of the speech. On an even more plaintive note, the editorial ended with a wish "that the matter be forgotten" and went on record against Randolph's continuing threats to stage a March on Washington sometime in the future.[62]

But the Crump organization had no intention of forgetting. Using the levers of the welfare state, it set out to undermine Randolph's planned local appearance at a celebration of his birthday on April 20 at the Foote Homes, a federal public housing project. The Ladies Auxiliary of the Brotherhood of Sleeping Car Porters had reserved the hall and was preparing to decorate it for the occasion. The Crump organization, which had loaded up the federal housing bureaucracy with patronage jobs over the previous decade, sprang into action. It passed the word to Henry E. Oates (a black Crump loyalist), the manager of Foote Homes, who dutifully revoked the permission. The rationalization resembled in absurdity that used four years earlier by Robert S.

Fredericks to prohibit the GOP from unfurling the pro-Willkie Joe Louis banner. Oates said that housing authority rules barred outside clubs from observing "celebrations" in recreation halls, not mentioning that others had used the same facilities for that purpose without incident. Oates also did not respond to allegations that the housing authority had recently evicted Brotherhood members who were residents of Foote Homes.[63]

During the same period, the Crump organization was also working to counter Randolph through manipulation of the regulatory state. Only six days after Randolph's speech, a reporter spied District Fire Chief A. J. Schaefer, flashlight in hand, poking around Long's church. When asked why he was there, he responded, "I'm just looking around." It proved to be the beginning of endless pestering. Ultimately, various code citations brought the church more than $5,000 in bills. Neither Long, who made only $25 per week, nor his impoverished congregation, had the money to pay them. Randolph's union was able to advance the church $1,000, but that was not nearly enough, especially after creditors demanded early payment. The harassed Long finally fled to Detroit.[64]

Through it all, the Roosevelt administration maintained a deafening silence, and its alliance with the Crump organization was none the weaker. In the run-up to the 1944 election, Crump promised an "all-out" campaign for the ticket rather than a "half-hearted, pussyfooting fight. … Who wants to return to the Hoover-Republican old days–apple selling?" Crump was as good as his word. Roosevelt carried Shelby County by a margin of nearly five to one, compared to three to one for the entire state.[65]

As this was happening, Randolph continued to be rankled by the federal government's failure to uphold his free speech rights. In January 1945, he complained that the Department of Justice had ignored his pleas to do something about "this outrageous fascist action." While he focused criticism on Assistant Attorney General (soon to be Attorney General) Tom C. Clark, he also charged that "Francis Biddle himself has not done all that he could have to make the Civil Liberties Section under Victor W. Rotnem [Schweinhaut's successor] effective for the protection of the rights of minority American citizens."[66]

The ultimate undoing of Crump's control came not from the Roosevelt or Truman administrations but from below. Years of second-class treatment finally had pushed African Americans to the breaking point. The memories of the intimidation and humiliation experienced by so many because of the Martin/Randolph free speech cases had still not completely faded away. Other provocations in the immediate postwar years included city censorship of films that depicted African Americans in nonstereotypical roles and several highly publicized incidents of police abuse. On top of these was the city's decision to bar the "Freedom Train," which featured documents of America's founding because the sponsoring group, the American Heritage Foundation, required integrated viewing. All of these sources of resentment culminated in 1948 when black voters turned out in large numbers in the Democratic primary for US Senate. They dealt Crump a severe blow by rejecting the organization's candidate for US Senate in favor of Estes Kefauver. For the first time, leading black Democrats, including Joseph E. Walker, deserted the organization.[67]

Parallels between the Memphis controversy of the 1940s and that which dominated Jersey City in the late 1930s are readily apparent. In both cities, Democratic political bosses selectively used broad powers, from denial of parade and sign permits to manipulation of building codes, personal intimidation of the press, and outright expulsion, to maintain control. Each of the two bosses had a cordial and reciprocal relationship with Roosevelt's New Deal, which brought them, in return for services rendered in elections, a constant flow of federal funds and extremely malleable regulatory powers. As with Hague, the Roosevelt administration valued its alliance with Crump so highly that its first inclination was to overlook obviously egregious violations of free speech. In each city, President Roosevelt acted (if he did anything at all) only when the political costs had become too high and, then, half-heartedly. As historian Preston Lauterbach aptly puts it, Attorney General Jackson (or for that matter Biddle) "didn't need Roosevelt to tell him not to pursue indictments against an FDR-friendly organization in Memphis. Crump had been good to Roosevelt, and a scandalized Crump could only harm the president."[68]

Instrumental in the final weakening of Crump was pressure exerted from diverse ideological bedfellows, including conservatives, civil rights activists, and civil libertarians. In Memphis, the compact between the conservative Robert R. Church Jr. and the socialist A. Philip Randolph closely resembled that several years earlier between Alfred Landon and Norman Thomas. Like Thomas, Randolph (who had started as Thomas's close associate) consciously took on the role of a high-profile agent provocateur pushing the limits of free speech and assembly in a hostile local environment. Church, like his old mentor Landon, did his best to build bridges to fellow conservatives. All four men had in common an ability to temporarily put aside other differences, draw on their comparative strengths, and cooperate to achieve shared goals.

The contrasts between Memphis and Jersey City were also instructive. Hague's outrages, though in some ways milder than Crump's, brought a groundswell that made headlines throughout the United States. News and editorial coverage of J. B. Martin and A. Philip Randolph, by contrast, rarely extended beyond the confines of the local press and the national black press. At least one key player in Jersey City, the American Civil Liberties Union, was largely missing in action in Memphis, while the NAACP, its nearest counterpart, pulled its punches.

Common threads in the Hague, Minton, and Crump cases were Roosevelt's inaction and his unwillingness to jeopardize useful political ties. It was only political pressure from a segment of his embarrassed and discontented New Deal base that finally forced the president to act against Hague, though in a mostly milquetoast way. Aside from the largely pro forma Woodcock inquiry and the stillborn federal follow-up, he did indeed leave Crump alone. Most of all, the Memphis experience revealed the disparate and uneven legacy of *Hague v. Committee for Industrial Organization*. While the implementation of that ruling had forced Hague to back off on restricting free speech, the precedent it established was a nonfactor in Memphis. Despite much flowery, and often unreflective, prose about the four freedoms, the overall effect of World War II only empowered Crump, at least for the duration. While a small group of free speech and civil rights advocates aggressively sought to depict Martin and Randolph as victims of an American version of fascism, they had little effect because of the relative timidity, often for reasons of wartime political expediency, of the ACLU and NAACP.

Ultimately, however, public pressure was crucial in undermining free speech restrictions in both cities, yet here too there were major contrasts. A major brake on Hague was an increasingly shared belief across the political spectrum by the late 1930s that free speech, at least in theory, protected all comers. Intervention by the courts and, to a lesser extent, the Department of Justice provided extra insurance and speeded the process. The free speech victory in Memphis, by contrast, was more incremental and resulted almost entirely from public opinion, as expressed by pressure from African Americans both from within, and without, Memphis, rather than from the Roosevelt administration. Though often hoped for and anticipated, a federal cavalry never rode to the rescue.

The harassment of J. B. Martin and A. Philip Randolph reveals the underside of New Deal machine politics, including its complicity in politicized racism. Politicians and bureaucrats at all governmental levels manipulated such diverse tools as building codes, tax assessment, and licensing to quash dissent, reward supporters, and, in the case of Memphis especially, bolster segregation. More positively, the stories of Martin, and before him Church, illustrate the largely unheralded importance of entrepreneurs as torchbearers of civil rights and voting rights in the decades before Martin Luther King Jr. Because they had some wealth behind them, they had certain advantages in taking risky stands. Their generally uncredited efforts brought genuine advances for ordinary African Americans as well. Business wealth and success, however, sometimes became a liability when confronted by political leaders determined to retaliate with the full force of the welfare and regulatory state. The Martin affair also gave a small preview to, and illustration of, the wartime racism and racial insensitivity at the top levels of the Roosevelt administration, a racism that became even more notorious in early 1942 in one of the greatest violations of civil liberties in American history.

7

"Persons Whose Removal Is Necessary": FDR's Concentration Camps

ROOSEVELT'S INTERNMENT OF Japanese Americans stands as a glaring exception in the historical literature's general neglect of his civil liberties record. No other single deprivation of the Bill of Rights has generated more books and articles. Of course, this attention seems merited in a general sense if measured by the standard of proportionality. In one fell swoop, the federal government had snatched away the First through Tenth Amendment protections from some 120,000 men, women, and children, two-thirds of them American citizens.

Although Roosevelt played a pivotal role in this process, historians have often conveyed a different impression. According to one specialist on the topic, studies of internment have focused so much on subordinates, "almost to the point where history absolved him of any responsibility. In this way, time has been kind to FDR." Survey texts have subtly cast Roosevelt as a victim of circumstance in an environment of hysteria created by others. Over and over again, they leave the impression of two very distinct Roosevelts. The first was the Roosevelt of the New Deal and World War II foreign policy: decisive, bold, humane, and dedicated to advancing the four freedoms. The second was the Roosevelt of internment: a passive and reactive, and somewhat clueless, prisoner of events.[1]

Despite continuity in Roosevelt's dismissiveness toward ensuring the protections of the Bill of Rights, his decision to implement internment was obviously different both in scale and in its defining feature of federally institutionalized racism. This policy did not represent a sudden change in attitudes. Roosevelt had long considered Japanese Americans to be a suspect group. As a young politician in New York, he had favored the policies of his cousin, Teddy, who had negotiated a series of gentlemen's agreements with Japan in 1907 and 1908 to cut off future immigration except for the wives, children, and parents of immigrants who had already arrived. While President Theodore Roosevelt, in return, headed off a proposal by San Francisco to segregate Japanese American schoolchildren, he promised that if Japan did not keep its part of the bargain, "the United States would at once pass an exclusion law."[2]

In the 1920s, Franklin D. Roosevelt, then in the political wilderness between his run as Democratic vice-presidential candidate in 1920 and his tenure as New York governor from 1929 to 1933, elaborated on his views on Japanese immigration as a columnist for the *Macon* [GA] *Telegraph*. The future president wrote that "[a]nyone who has travelled in the Far East knows that the mingling of Asiatic blood with European or American blood produces, in nine cases out of ten, the most unfortunate results." Regarding state laws on the West Coast banning land ownership by Japanese noncitizens, Roosevelt asserted that "Californians have properly objected on the sound basic grounds that Japanese immigrants are not capable of assimilation into the American population."[3]

In his first two terms as president, Roosevelt rarely returned to these issues, but when he did, he sometimes foreshadowed what came later. In 1935, he told a White House delegation that aggression "was in the blood" of Japanese leaders. He was in an even more provocative frame of mind the following year after reading a report by the chief of naval operations suggesting possible responses to a future Japanese attack on Hawaii. Regarding contacts between Japanese sailors and the local Japanese American population, Roosevelt suggested that "every Japanese citizen or non-citizen on the Island of Oahu who meets these Japanese ships or has any connection with their officers or men should be secretly but definitely identified and his or her name placed on a special list of those who would be the first to be placed in a concentration camp."[4]

Although racist attitudes toward Japanese Americans still persisted both in and outside of the Oval Office in 1940, conditions on the West Coast for them were better than ever before. Given the enormous obstacles in their way, the economic gains of Japanese Americans were nothing short of spectacular. Of the 126,948 in the continental United States in 1940, 93,717 were in California. Some two-thirds (the Nisei) were born in the US. Their immigrant parents (the Issei), who could not legally become citizens, constituted the rest. In just eleven years, the acreage owned by Japanese Americans in that state had more than quadrupled. They produced about one-fourth of all fresh vegetables, including nine-tenths of the strawberries. Japanese Americans also made inroads into governmental employment, and three hundred worked for the city of Sacramento alone. In 1937, along with their white allies, they showed sufficient political muscle to stop five bills in California and Washington restricting the rights of aliens.[5]

The assimilation process by 1940 was rapidly accelerating, and the Issei often found inventive ways to evade discriminatory land legislation by registering titles in the names of their children. Nearly all the American-born Nisei had attended integrated schools and frequently had participated in such routine activities as the Girl Scouts and organized sports. They also made major gains in higher education attendance. As the social and economic bonds between the Nisei and their white neighbors grew stronger, so too did evidence of a wider acceptance by the majority. The assimilation process in Hawaii, which had a much higher Japanese American population, was also making major strides. In August 1941, Robert Shivers, who headed the Honolulu office of the FBI, assured Assistant Attorney General Norman M. Littell that no more than 1 percent of the Nisei were disloyal. "You can scratch it off," he underscored. "Just forget the problem." This assessment echoed that of the Military Intelligence Division of the Army, the Office of Naval Intelligence, and the Office of Strategic Services.[6]

While the Japanese government tried mightily to strengthen the ever-weaker ties between the Nisei and the homeland, the results were disappointing. One of the most significant efforts was a campaign to give them financial inducements to study in Japan. More than nine thousand took advantage of this opportunity prior to the war. The Japanese government also subsidized a network of social-welfare institutions and "Japanese language schools" to instill loyalty, including annual celebrations of the emperor's birthday, and to present the overall case for the Greater East Asia Co-Prosperity Sphere. In California alone, there were some 241 of these language schools in 1940. By one basic measure, these efforts were a resounding flop. According to credible estimates, fewer than 3 percent of the Nisei spoke more than rudimentary

Japanese. Prior to the war, Japanese American newspapers stated the case for Japanese foreign policy, including opposition to trade restrictions. Because they were all printed almost exclusively in the Japanese language (with the exception of some small English sections), they were inaccessible to the vast majority of Nisei.[7]

Roosevelt's personal secret intelligence unit stressed the overall benign nature of the Japanese American population. The head of the unit was pro–New Deal columnist and commentator John Franklin Carter (who had taken over Hugh S. Johnson's radio slot in 1938 under the pseudonym of Jay Franklin). The unit, which Carter immodestly dubbed "FDR's personal G2," drew from an impressive array of credible contacts in the military, business, and government. In a report to the president shortly after Pearl Harbor, Carter said that Japanese Americans were no "more disloyal than any other racial group in the United States with whom we went to war." Stolen documents from the Japanese Consulate made available to the administration revealed that Japanese officials regarded the Nisei and Issei as "cultural traitors" who were unsuitable for intelligence purposes. They preferred instead for purposes of espionage to rely on such groups as white anti-Semites, paid spies, or people brought over from Japan for intelligence purposes.[8]

Other official Japanese government documents, including the Operation Magic code intercepts, known to US leaders at the time corroborate this characterization. They also show a surprising, and short-sighted, failure, which was partly the result of bureaucratic infighting, to even develop local intelligence sources. "Despite widespread pre-war U.S. fears of 'fifth column' sabotage by Japanese residents," writes historian Max Everest-Phillips, "there had been no such plans, nor did Japanese agents play any role in the attack on Pearl Harbor."[9]

But Carter had underestimated the strength of his boss's deeply ingrained habit to cherry-pick when it suited his needs. In a pattern repeated many times, Roosevelt sought out, and then amplified beyond all proportion, statements or anecdotes that conveyed, at least in his own mind, a more negative impression. In reading one of Carter's reports, for example, Roosevelt immediately fixated on a passage stating that "[d]ams, bridges, harbors, power stations, etc. are wholly unguarded. The harbor of San Pedro [Los Angeles port] could be razed completely by four men with hand grenades and a little study at night." This so alarmed the president that he made sure to pass it on to Secretary of War Henry L. Stimson even as he glossed over the report's general conclusion that 90 percent of the Nisei "were completely loyal to the United States."[10]

Compared to what came later, Japanese Americans on the West Coast experienced relative calm in the two months after Pearl Harbor. Leading newspapers seemed more inclined to defuse rather than to fire up racist fears. The *San Francisco Daily News* declared that to "subject these people to illegal search and seizure, then arrest them without warrant to confinement without trial, is to violate the principles of Democracy as set forth in our Constitution." As late as January 23, the *Los Angeles Times* characterized the Nisei as good Americans who "deserve sympathy rather than suspicion." But more hostile attitudes were starting to take hold. On January 27, Democratic Governor Culbert Olson said that Californians wanted the Japanese moved out. He complained that they were too "inscrutable" for the authorities to determine their loyalty status. Meanwhile, Republican State Attorney General Earl Warren asserted that the "fifth column activities that we are to get, are timed just like the invasion of France, and Norway."[11]

Instead of taking steps to cool down this increasingly hostile climate, however, federal officials often did just the opposite. On December 15, Secretary of the Navy Frank Knox sensationally warned that "very active Fifth Column work" had occurred in Hawaii. The ever-persistent John Franklin Carter (who showed no comparative concern for protecting rights of the anti-FDR "fifth and sixth columnists") urged the president to use his bully pulpit to defend Japanese Americans as loyal citizens. But Roosevelt did nothing, illustrating once again a failure of presidential leadership at a crucial turning point. Had Roosevelt deployed his famous charm and eloquence, perhaps citing the four freedoms, he might have prevented much suffering. He did not behave like a president who was trapped by conditions or distracted by other issues (Carter kept him closely advised on the reality of the situation), but rather like a man who really did not care.[12]

The president's private conversations are some of the best gauges of his attitudes. When writer Louis Adamic defended the loyalty of Japanese Americans at a meeting with the First Couple, he did not find a sympathetic audience: "'But some of the Japanese on the Coast have been caught as spies of the Japanese government,' said Mrs. Roosevelt sharply. The tone and finality of her words surprised me. The President looked thoughtful but said nothing." Later that month, Roosevelt told journalist Quentin Reynolds that the Japanese were "treacherous people" and "hissed through his teeth," imitating stereotypical speech patterns.[13]

Daily front-page headlines about Japan's military successes in the Pacific and the Far East conspired together with Roosevelt's silence to allow a more repressive approach, sometimes encouraged by federal officials, to gain a following. Illustrative of this was Secretary of War Stimson's reaction to a letter from Representative Leland M. Ford (R-CA), urging that "all Japanese, whether citizens or not, be placed in inland concentration camps." Although Stimson did not endorse the idea outright, his response was just reckless enough to give Ford encouragement and his proposal more momentum. Stimson volunteered that "the Army is prepared to provide internment facilities in the interior to the extent necessary."[14]

A factor that did much to ratchet up tensions was the media coverage of a report by a presidential commission chaired by Supreme Court Justice Owen J. Roberts on January 23. Although the report focused on the Pearl Harbor attack, and never once mentioned Japanese Americans, some sloppy and vague verbiage about spies in Hawaii led to a media frenzy: "Some were Japanese consular agents and others were persons having no open relations with the Japanese foreign service." Few in the press seemed inclined to consider the possibility that this reference to "persons" may have meant, for example, paid Caucasians.[15]

By early January, the Western Defense Command (WDC) began pushing ever more vigorously for restricting the freedoms of Japanese Americans. Heading the WDC was Lieutenant General John L. Dewitt, a "bureaucrat in uniform," who had risen through the ranks because of his record as a supply officer. Some historians have depicted DeWitt as the determinative protagonist of internment, but this vastly exaggerates his role. At first, DeWitt, unlike the president, actually went on record against sending the Nisei to camps, calling it "damned nonsense." In late December, he wrote that "if we go ahead and arrest the 93,000 Japanese [in California], native born and foreign born, we are going to have an awful job on our hands and we are very liable to alienate the Japanese. ... An American citizen, after all, is an American citizen."

He also downplayed the possibility of a Japanese invasion of the West Coast. These were not just fleeting thoughts. It took several weeks before DeWitt came out formally for putting citizens in camps.[16]

DeWitt's ultimate endorsement of internment in late January was not too surprising, however. It not only complemented his well-documented racial biases and hair-trigger readiness to see fifth column threats but also aligned with the views of his main advisers, Provost Marshal General Allen W. Gullion and Captain Karl Bendetsen, a Stanford Law School graduate and head of the Aliens Division in Gullion's department. Added to the mix was the pressure from such local politicians as Governor Olson and the failure of either Stimson or Roosevelt to offer any objection or restraint. For the cautious and indecisive DeWitt, endorsing internment was the easiest policy choice.[17]

The highest official in the federal government who opposed internment was Attorney General Francis Biddle. Despite excellent civil liberties credentials, his chief weakness was ineptitude in the game of power politics. Biddle confessed that he felt overawed and intimidated by the imposing Stimson, a fellow blue blood who was nearly twenty years his senior. When Biddle was confronted by "military necessity" arguments, his first inclination was to split the difference. In early January, for example, he complied without a fight to implement Gullion's request that he authorize warrantless raids on Japanese homes, including those with a citizen in residence. This meant, as Daniels points out, that "if a Nisei family had an Issei grandmother living with it, the Fourth Amendment constitutional protection against 'unreasonable searches and seizures,' no longer applied." Two of Biddle's subordinates opposed internment even more than he did and did their best to stiffen their boss's resolve: Assistant Attorney General James H. Rowe Jr. and Edward J. Ennis, the head of the Alien Enemy Control Unit for the Department of Justice.[18]

A cabinet meeting on January 20 displayed Biddle's shortcomings as a bureaucratic infighter. When Stimson immediately steered the discussion into the narrow topic of how to carry out a possible evacuation, Biddle not only failed to challenge the premise but meekly suggested "that the time might come that there would be certain areas where the president might suspend the writ of Habeas Corpus." Like John Franklin Carter before him, Biddle did not realize that temporizing in this way only undercut his own case. "Biddle's reassurance that the legal obstacles to removing citizens from restricted areas could be evaded in an emergency," Greg Robinson comments, "was an invitation to the President to ignore constitutional issues entirely."[19]

Perhaps feeling that he had proved too accommodative at the cabinet meeting, Biddle was much more steadfast two days later at a meeting with Gullion, Bendetsen, Rowe, Ennis, J. Edgar Hoover of the FBI, and John J. McCloy, the assistant secretary of war. Trying to seize the initiative, he drafted a proposed joint press statement for the secretary of war and the attorney general to cosign finding "no substantial evidence of planned sabotage by any alien" and affirming that "the present military situation does not at this time require the removal of American citizens of the Japanese race." McCloy, Gullion, and Bendetsen summarily rejected the proposal. When Biddle put forward constitutional arguments to justify the wording, McCloy quite memorably replied, "[W]hy the constitution is just a scrap of paper to me."[20]

Although Biddle did not always act like he knew it, he came from a position of great potential negotiating strength. He had a trump card that nobody, including DeWitt and Stimson, could match: the backing of J. Edgar Hoover, perhaps the most widely respected federal official. While Hoover's objections to evacuation and removal were primarily opportunistic and practical, they were still very real. As FBI director, he did not want to assume all the headaches involved in such a task. Hoover, also like Biddle, did not think that Japanese Americans posed a serious national security threat. "The necessity for mass evacuation," the FBI director advised Biddle, "is based primarily upon public and political pressure rather than on factual data." Biddle had an argument that seemed well calculated to appeal to his politically attuned boss in the White House: the lack of any public groundswell for tougher measures. According to a survey of the Office of Facts and Figures on February 4, a majority of Americans expressed satisfaction with existing governmental controls on Japanese Americans. Many years later Biddle even considered it doubtful "whether, political and special group press aside, public opinion even on the West Coast supported evacuation."[21]

Although he came from a position of strength in multiple ways, Biddle, somewhat inexplicably, continued to waver. On February 5, he handed his adversaries valuable ammunition when he told a Senate committee that evacuation by the army was constitutional if done for "military necessity." But Biddle, who was the "new boy" in the cabinet, continued to procrastinate about taking his concerns to the Oval Office. "I tried not to bother the President," he later wrote, "with anything that was not essential."[22]

Finally, when it was probably too late, Biddle presented his case directly to the president over a long lunch on February 7. He opened strongly, telling Roosevelt that he considered "mass evacuation at this time inadvisable, that the F.B.I. was not staffed to perform it; that this was an army job not, in our opinion, advisable; that there were no reasons for mass evacuation." However, after this fairly resolute statement he, quite predictably, appended disabling qualifiers that "the army should be directed to prepare a detailed plan of evacuation in case of an emergency caused by an air raid or attempted landing on the West Coast." Predictably, the cherry-picking Roosevelt saw what he wanted to see, and no more. His reply was also, characteristically, diversionary and cryptic. "Generally he approved," Biddle remembers, "being fully aware of the dreadful risk of Fifth Column retaliation in case of a raid."[23]

Not quite prepared to raise the white flag, Biddle made an appeal to Stimson on February 12. It was not an effective effort. Although he reiterated that the Department of Justice lacked legal authority to evacuate Japanese Americans, his wording lacked a certain firmness and clarity: "I have no doubt that the Army can legally, at any time, evacuate all persons in a specified territory if such action is deemed essential from a military point of view for the protection and defense of the area. No legal problem arises where Japanese citizens are evacuated; but American citizens of Japanese origin could not, in my opinion, be singled out of an area and evacuated with other Japanese." Biddle need not have bothered in any case. The president had already made his decision. On February 11, a "vigorous" Roosevelt, citing the military necessity justification, gave Stimson "carte blanche" and, in comments to McCloy, added, "Be as reasonable as you can."[24]

If there was any chance of a reversal by FDR, however, the appearance of a column on February 12 by Walter Lippmann endorsing "mass evacuation and mass internment" for Japanese Americans on the West Coast soon put that to rest. Few journalists enjoyed more regard across the political spectrum. Lippmann had unmatched prestige as an independent liberal who was zealous in defending the Bill of Rights. On occasion, he had also spoken out forcefully against such New Deal abuses of privacy and free speech as the Black Committee's telegram surveillance. One of his past hallmarks as a journalist was skepticism toward authority. In his column, Lippmann reported that he had seen alarming evidence of a "Fifth-Column problem" on the West Coast during a trip to California, using none other than DeWitt and Attorney General Warren as two of his main sources. "Nobody's constitutional rights," the purported civil libertarian sage proclaimed, "include the right to reside and do business on a battlefield. And nobody ought to be on a battlefield who has no good reason for being there." He uncritically repeated an argument often made by DeWitt that the current absence of sabotage was in itself "a sign that the blow is well organized and that it is held back until it can be struck with maximum effect."[25]

Lippmann received powerful reinforcement just three days later from Westbrook Pegler, a populist figure with his own widely circulated column. Like Lippmann, Pegler was sometimes supportive, sometimes critical of the administration, though more often the latter. "What Lippmann says I accept as truth based on his reputation," he wrote, "and if it is the truth we are just sitting around waiting for the enemy to stab us in the back." If Lippmann had put his prestige on the line to say there was an imminent threat, Pegler concluded, it was essential to take "preventive action" and accept the reality that "the Japanese in California should be under armed guard to the last man and woman right now and to hell with habeas corpus until the danger is over."[26]

The government had only a few final steps left before starting the machinery of internment. On February 14, DeWitt issued the "Final Recommendation." This document did not shy away from racially charged references to "an enemy race [not nationality] and while many second and third generation Japanese born on United States soil, possessed of United States citizenship have become 'Americanized,' the racial strains are undiluted." On February 17, Roosevelt delegated Stimson and McCloy to work out the wording for an executive order. Only then did the president inform Biddle that he had made his decision. On hearing this, the Attorney General immediately surrendered. At a meeting that evening, Gullion read a slip of paper authorizing the War Department to remove citizens and aliens. When Biddle sat silently and made no protest, Rowe recalled, "Ennis almost wept. I was so mad that I could not speak at all myself and the meeting soon broke up." Compounding his capitulation, Biddle assured the president that the administration did not need "further legislation" because the executive order fell under the president's "general war powers."[27]

Many years later, Biddle showed considerable regret and, to his credit, resisted the temptation to rationalize it. Admitting that he had fallen short in defending democratic principles at a major turning point in American history, he also refused to excuse the president. Unlike some modern historians, Biddle did not depict the decision as an inevitable by-product of hysteria. Roosevelt, Biddle speculated, "could probably have withstood the popular pressure without loss to the tenacity of his leadership—pressure of a highly vocative minority in the West. If Stimson had stood firm, had insisted, as he apparently suspected, that this wholesale evacuation was needless, the President would have followed his advice. And if, instead of dealing almost exclusively with McCloy and Bendetsen, I had urged the Secretary to resist the pressure of his subordinates, the result might have been different. But I was new to the Cabinet, and disinclined to insist on my view to an elder statesman [Stimson], whose wisdom and integrity I greatly respected." But Biddle, like many admirers of the president, was an accomplished compartmentalizer. The same autobiography that features a searing indictment of the president's disdain for constitutional protections in wartime was also dedicated to the "memory of Franklin Delano Roosevelt."[28]

Had Biddle strenuously resisted down to the last minute, or even threatened to publicly protest or resign, he might have found some powerful allies. In August 1942, Roger N. Baldwin and Alexander Meikeljohn of the ACLU reported that "[p]ractically all of the officials who commented on the evacuations" agreed that it was done "without the approval of the government agencies most directly concerned. The statement was made repeatedly by one official or another that the F.B.I., Naval Intelligence and Army Intelligence all disapproved of it." One could add to the list Archibald MacLeish, the director of the Office of Facts and Figures and the Librarian of Congress, who urged a policy of restraint. It was Roosevelt himself who was, in the words of George W. Bush, the "decider." Greg Robinson puts it well: "[T]he President was willingly misled. He had access to reliable information, which he ignored, from sources he trusted, notably the FBI, that the Japanese-Americans did not represent a danger. ... By contrast, the President lent credence to the wildest and most unsubstantiated anti-Japanese rumors."[29]

Roosevelt's Executive Order 9066 of February 19, putting an official stamp on evacuation and all that followed, was deceptively bland in its wording. It authorized the Secretary of War to prescribe "military areas" and "determine, from which any or all persons may be excluded" and "to provide for residents of any such area who are excluded therefrom, such transportation, food, shelter, and other accommodations as may be necessary, in the judgment of the Secretary of War or the said Military Commander, and until other arrangements are made, to accomplish the purpose of this order." The text did not mention any specific group or place but, initiating a stratagem of banality, featured such code words as "any and all persons excluded" to describe those to be evacuated. In this respect, the wording had parallels to the Constitution's well-known coded euphemism "other persons" to refer to slaves. Like those who wrote the "Three Fifths" and fugitive slave clauses, the purpose of the code words in Executive Order 9066 was to obscure the true nature of what was taking place.[30]

Claims that assert or imply that Executive Order 9066 was an unavoidable response to the neutral dictates of military necessity cannot stand scrutiny. Military necessity was never a sacrosanct doctrine to Roosevelt when it did not suit his needs. He always reserved the right to pick and choose whether to accept policy proposals recommended on that basis. For example, the president vetoed DeWitt's request to also remove Italian and German aliens from the West Coast under Executive Order 9066. He also gave thumbs-down to a plan to remove all Japanese from the East Coast. Even when listening to advisers on the topic of evacuation and internment, he was highly selective. While he chose to take advice from DeWitt and Stimson, he did not bother to seek out credible military sources who might have contradicted them, such as George Marshall, US Army chief of staff, or his deputy, Mark Clark (who did not think internment was necessary). As someone who considered himself an "old navy man," Roosevelt was singularly uncurious about hearing the views of such well-informed naval officers as Lieutenant Commander Kenneth Ringle, who had organized a successful espionage break-in at the Japanese Consulate, and regarded internment as unnecessary and who, like Admiral Harold R. Stark, argued that defenses of the West Coast were perfectly adequate.[31]

The vagueness and open-endedness of Executive Order 9066 was also an indicator that the president had still not made up his mind on what to do about Japanese Americans in Hawaii. At one-third of the population of the islands, confining them in camps presented enormous logistical and financial obstacles; yet even after he signed Executive Order 9066, Roosevelt still wanted to do it. On February 26, 1942, he informed Secretary of the Navy Knox that he had "long felt that most of the Japanese should be removed from Oahu to one of the other Islands." While Roosevelt conceded that such an undertaking involved "much planning, much temporary construction, and careful supervision of them when they get to the new location," he did not "worry about the constitutional question—first, because of my recent order and, second, because Hawaii is under martial law." He called for Knox to work with Stimson and "go ahead and do it as a military project."[32]

Despite Roosevelt's push for Hawaiian internment, the proposal soon collapsed of its own weight. This included the expense of diverting so many ships and personnel from fighting Japan in the Pacific theater to overseeing the transportation, housing, and guarding of over one hundred thousand inmates. Hawaiian internment also entailed major political risks. In contrast to California, Japanese Americans in Hawaii could raise a major political ruckus, no small danger to a president so attuned to public relations. Ultimately, the failure of the Hawaiian plan, which would have doubled the Japanese American concentration camp population in the United States, can be attributed to the resistance of one determined man. Unlike DeWitt, the local commander, General Delos Emmons, opposed the idea, arguing that the removal of Japanese labor would serve to decimate the local economy. While Emmons never openly defied his superiors, he ultimately prevailed through bureaucratic finesse, including creative foot dragging, as well as persistently and logically pointing out potential drawbacks to higher-ups. Emmons, unlike Biddle, had the requisite leadership skills to outmaneuver subordinates, peers, and superiors and the tenacity to follow through to a successful conclusion.[33]

While Roosevelt's executive order had not mentioned race, nationality, or a specific place, the various public proclamations that followed it most certainly did. Each specified that the requirements applied only to "any person of Japanese ancestry." If the "slave codes" of the states served to translate or define the "other persons" code phrase in the Constitution, DeWitt's proclamations did the same for the "any and all persons" wording in Executive Order 9066. Moreover, because only DeWitt's name appeared at the bottom of all the enforcement orders, he became the public face of internment, thus serving a politically and legally useful purpose for the administration. Purging any mention of race or ancestry from the text of the executive order could, and did, help insulate the administration from perceived culpability. That omission may have also contributed in subtle ways to the failure of historians to hold Roosevelt more accountable. Any professor who assigns Roosevelt's Executive Order 9066 as a reading for students will likely encounter blank stares over the meaning and implications, but not so with DeWitt's public proclamations.

Bit by bit, DeWitt's proclamations enforcing Executive Order 9066 tightened the noose around the freedom of movement of Japanese Americans. Public Proclamation No. 1 of March 2 created two zones, Military Area 1 (the western parts of Washington, Oregon, and California, and the southern half of Arizona) and Military Area 2 (the eastern portions of Washington, Oregon, and California). Public Proclamation No. 2 required Japanese Americans who were moving their residences to fill out change-of-address notices. The establishment of the Wartime Civil Control Administration (WCCA) on March 11, via DeWitt's General Order 35, laid out the procedure for "the evacuation of all persons of Japanese ancestry from Military Area No. 1 and the California portion of Military Area No. 2 of the Pacific Coast with a minimum of economic and social dislocation." DeWitt promoted Bendetsen, a pioneering advocate of internment, to colonel and gave him command of the new agency. Within a very short time, Bendetsen began to scout locations for "reception centers," each projected to have about ten thousand inmates.[34]

The second and final presidential order dealing with Japanese American evacuation and removal was Executive Order 9102 on March 18, which established the War Relocation Authority (WRA). Returning to the same code word euphemisms of Executive Order 9066, the stated purpose of Executive Order 9102 was to "provide for the removal from designated areas of persons whose removal is necessary in the interest of national security." Using circuitous legerdemain that led nowhere, it defined these "persons" as "the persons or classes of person designated under" Executive Order 9066. Roosevelt appointed Milton Eisenhower, a brother of the future president, as the WRA's director.[35]

Meanwhile, somewhat belatedly, Secretary Stimson drafted and sent to Congress a bill specifying legal punishments for anyone violating the new rules. It had the same coded wording as Roosevelt's two executive orders: "[W]hoever shall enter, remain in, leave, or commit any act in any military area or military zone prescribed, under the authority of an Executive order of the President [shall] … be guilty of a misdemeanor and upon conviction shall be liable to a fine of not to exceed $5,000 or to imprisonment for not more than one year, or both, for each offense." The only debate, if it can be called such, came after Senator Robert R. Reynolds (D-NC), the chair of the Committee on Military Affairs, introduced it on Stimson's behalf. Reynolds opened by spouting a litany of ridiculously sensational anecdotes, including one that the cane fields in Hawaii on December 7 "were cut in the form of arrows pointing to military objectives." A faint glimmer of dissent that quickly died came from Senator Robert A. Taft (R-OH), who called the proposal "probably the 'sloppiest' criminal law I have ever read" and charged that, if literally enforced, it might be applied against any American. Taft understood, however, as did everyone else in Congress, the meaning of the coded language and was not going to press the point "because I understand the pressing character of this kind of legislation for the Pacific coast today." The bill, which took effect on March 24 as Public Law 503, won unanimous support in both the House and Senate.[36]

But at least some members of Congress had private misgivings. In his autobiography in 1962, Senator Burton K. Wheeler stated that he had "protested to various high-level government officials," including his friend Under Secretary of War Robert P. Patterson, asserting that internment violated the "principles of the Four Freedoms." He warned that if the government "can get away with such treatment of citizens of Japanese descent, it can do the same to any minority." As of yet, no evidence from the time has surfaced to corroborate Wheeler's recollections.[37]

On the same day that Congress gave its final approval, DeWitt's command imposed a draconian curfew confining "all persons of Japanese ancestry residing within said Military Areas and Zones" to their homes, except if at their place of employment or in transit "within a distance of not more than five miles from their place of residence." It also prohibited Japanese Americans from possessing firearms, ammunition, radio transmitters, or cameras. Public

Proclamation No. 4 made the noose still tighter by banning people of Japanese ancestry "from leaving that area for any purpose until and to the extent that a future proclamation or order of this headquarters shall so permit or direct."[38]

With his quarry now in the trap, DeWitt issued the first of more than one hundred geographically specific exclusion orders beginning on March 24. All followed the same template. First, the WCCA posted announcements in newspapers and handbills in such high-visibility spots as telephone poles. These gave "Instructions to All Japanese" living in the area. Those who failed to comply within a week were liable for criminal prosecution. The future inmates were only allowed to take what they could carry, not including pets, which often had to be destroyed. The racism involved took on a life of its own. When asked about the fate of Nisei kids in orphanages, Colonel Bendetsen replied that "if they have one drop of Japanese blood in them, they must go to camp." Evacuees often had to dispose of their property at cut-rate prices. The financial losses added up to somewhere between $67 million and $116 million (more than 2.7 billion in 2023 dollars). From the reception and assembly centers, the WCCA sent the evacuees to one of ten WRA concentration camps (euphemistically described as internment or relocation camps). These were all east of the Sierra Nevada, eight in Western states and two in Arkansas.[39]

The aid provided by the US Census Bureau was absolutely essential in ensuring the success of internment. In the *Final Report*, DeWitt credited the 1940 Census, including punch cards on Japanese Americans, as the "most important single source of information" and as "the basis for the general evacuation and relocation plan." In addition, the WCCA obtained extensive confidential data from the Census Bureau on Japanese-owned businesses. In a shocking breach of personal privacy, though authorized by the Second War Powers Act of March 1942, the bureau also made available copies of individual census schedules, giving the name, family members, addresses, occupation, and citizenship status of Japanese Americans.[40]

When he took the helm as WRA head, Milton Eisenhower had hoped to rapidly disperse Japanese Americans into "subsistence homesteads" in the nation's interior and then, eventually, move them into private sector jobs. He soon gave this up, however, after a stormy meeting with Western governors in Salt Lake City. For example, on hearing Eisenhower's plan, Governor Nels H.

Smith (R-WY) "growled through clenched teeth" that Japanese brought into his state "will be hanging from every tree." The only governor willing to welcome the migrants was Ralph Carr (R-CO). "If we put American-born Japanese in concentration camps," he charged, "we abrogate their constitutional rights."[41]

By August, nearly all Japanese Americans on the West Coast were inmates in concentration camps, each characterized by guard towers and armed military patrols. By then Eisenhower was long gone as director. Never a firm believer in evacuation or removal, he had resigned in disgust in early June. He advised his successor, Dillon S. Myer, to only take the job if he could both accept the responsibilities and "sleep at night." Myer, a practitioner of progressive methods of expertise and "human conservation," replied that he was sure that he could do both. Although he eventually developed major misgivings, Myer, dubbed by his biographer the "Keeper of Concentration Camps," carried out his often unsavory duties. Under his watch, the camps were frequently characterized by racist double standards, labor exploitation, brutality by white internal police, and denial of due process.[42]

While conditions for Japanese Americans were a world apart from those in Nazi death camps, the label "concentration camp" still applies. The overwhelming majority of those incarcerated cooperated fully, but the WRA and the military did not hesitate to use force for those who did not. The rules were extensive, including one that all inmates had to stay at least ten feet from the fence. In all, soldiers shot and killed seven unarmed inmates, mostly for failure, either real or perceived, to obey often trivial instructions such as walking on a paved sidewalk. Only one of the shooting victims had actually attempted to escape. Kanesaburo (aka Kensaburo) Oshima, age 58, homesick for his family in Hawaii, was shot in the back for trying to climb the barbed wire. Although several of the soldiers doing the shooting were subject to legal proceedings, all either were found innocent or received only nominal punishment.[43]

Despite WRA pretensions to institute "self-government," the "camp councils" of the inmates had no real power. All incoming and outgoing mail went first to a New York postal facility, where more than a hundred censors opened and read everything. "The censors used scissors," Richard Reeves writes, "so letters looked like Swiss cheese or paper dolls." The government also banned all Japanese-language literature and restricted telephone calls to the outside to emergencies. The desert climate often had severe extremes (for good reason, nobody has lived in many of those areas ever since), and the cramped quarters offered little privacy. Conditions were particularly severe at the Tule Lake Camp facility in California, where 1,200 combat-equipped soldiers, along with 500 administrators, policed 18,000 inmates. Although deemed a camp for the disloyal, it became, according to one local ACLU observer, "a dumping ground for misfits, anti-administration leaders, embittered youngsters, and a lot of old people who just wanted to return to Japan."[44]

While the American military and national security states, as well as the Bureau of the Census, were obviously instrumental in enabling internment, so too was the New Deal welfare state. By far, the most important example was the Works Progress Administration (WPA). From March to the end of November 1942, that agency spent $4.47 million on removal and internment, slightly more than the $4.43 million spent by the Army for that purpose during that period. In terms of scale, this endeavor ranked perhaps as the most gigantic single "WPA project" of all time. Contrary to Roosevelt's statement in 1943 that "Dr. New Deal" had given way to "Dr. Win-the-War," both were still very much on the job. Dr. New Deal, in fact, took an intimate part in helping "Dr. Win-the-War" with removal and internment. As Jason Scott Smith observes, "[T]he eagerness of many WPA administrators to place their organization in the forefront of this wartime enterprise is striking."[45]

The WPA was on the ground helping with removal and relocation even before the creation of the WRA. On March 11, Rex L. Nicholson, the WPA's regional director, took charge of the "Reception and Induction" centers that controlled the first thirteen assembly centers. Nicholson's old WPA associates played key roles in the administration of the camps. A leading example was Clayton E. Triggs, the first manager of the Manzanar Relocation Center in California, a facility that, according to one insider, was "manned just about 100% by the WPA." Drawing on his experience running New Deal road camps, Triggs made sure to install such signature concentration camp trappings as guard towers and spotlights. Secretary of Commerce Harry Hopkins, considered the father of the WPA, was proud of his agency's involvement. In a letter to Roosevelt on March 19, he lauded the current director of the WPA

Senators James Davis, Hugo L. Black (chair of the Black Committee, later a Supreme Court justice), Lewis B. Schwellenbach, and Sherman Minton (chair of the Minton Committee). Minton, like Black and Schwellenbach, was a committed FDR loyalist and proposed a bill to censor the press.

Source: Library of Congress, Prints & Photographs Division, photograph by Harris & Ewing, LC-DIG-hec-23881.

"The Night Riders: An Old Southern Custom," *Chicago Daily Tribune*, March 7, 1936. When the pro–New Deal Black Committee searched through millions of private telegrams (using authorization granted by the Federal Communications Commission), the *Chicago Daily Tribune* highlighted evidence that the committee chair, Southern Senator Hugo L. Black (D-AL) (1886–1971), had belonged to the Ku Klux Klan. His Klan ties were fully confirmed in the rest of the press a year later after he took his seat on the Supreme Court in 1937.

Source: ©1936 Chicago Tribune All rights reserved. Distributed by Tribune Content Agency, LLC.

Few were more zealous in defending civil liberties—including for such key targets of New Deal vituperation as Japanese Americans, the anti–New Deal newspaper *Boise Valley Herald*, and the Sedition Trial (1944–1945) defendants—than perennial Socialist Party presidential candidate Norman Thomas. After Jersey City Mayor Frank Hague's Democratic machine forcibly ejected Thomas in 1938 from Jersey City, Thomas's former Republican opponent in the 1936 presidential election, Alfred Landon, offered his support to Thomas, and the two became lifelong friends.

Source: Library of Congress, Prints & Photographs Division, photograph by Harris & Ewing, LC-DIG-hec-28779.

FDR's fireside chats, which, along with his other speeches, the networks carried at an "instant's notice," enabled the president, in unprecedented fashion, to be, in the words of media historian Betty Houchin Winfield, "the newsgatherer, the reporter, as well as the editor." Roosevelt was thus able to bypass what he called the "poisonous propaganda of the conservative press."

Source: National Archives.

Stephen Early (left), the president's press secretary, warned that, in the event of war, radio must prove itself a "good child"—or the government might have to teach it "manners." He served as a key intermediary between FDR and Boake Carter's corporate sponsors in a secret, and ultimately successful, collusive effort to force that highly rated anti–New Deal commentator off the air.

Source: National Archives.

J. B. Martin (far left), chair of the Republican party of Shelby County in 1940, in front of his South Memphis drugstore, with other owners of the Memphis Red Sox (a black baseball team). After Martin refused to call off a rally for 1940 Republican presidential candidate Wendell Willkie, Memphis pro–New Deal Democratic Party boss Ed Crump ordered the "policing" of Martin's store. Despite pleas from the NAACP and many Republican leaders, FDR did nothing to stop Crump's extralegal, racist harassment.

Source: Memphis and Shelby County Room, Memphis Public Library & Information Center.

Pro–New Deal Democratic Party boss Ed Crump. Through a combination of extralegal racist property seizures, building-code regulations, and intrusive "policing," Crump forced out of Memphis two successive African American chairs of the Shelby County GOP, Robert R. Church Jr. and J. B. Martin. FDR, who was Crump's close political ally, turned a blind eye to these illegal and unconstitutional activities.

Source: Library of Congress, Prints & Photographs Division, photograph by Harris & Ewing, LC-USZ62-72846.

Major Lemuel B. Schofield (left), Solicitor General (and future Attorney General) Francis Biddle (center), and Attorney General (and future Supreme Court justice) Robert Jackson (right), in 1940. Biddle opposed FDR's internment of Japanese Americans but cooperated with the implementation of the policy. In 1944, while on the Supreme Court, Jackson cast one of the dissenting votes against the majority decision (authored by Hugo L. Black) in *United States v. Korematsu*, which upheld Japanese American internment.

Source: Library of Congress, Prints & Photographs Division, photograph by Harris & Ewing, LC-DIG-hec-28807.

Cissy Patterson was the first woman to publish a major metropolitan news-paper, the *Washington Times-Herald*. Cissy and her brother Joe, publisher of the *New York Daily News*, had reliably backed Roosevelt, until a falling out in early 1941 over foreign policy. FDR and his supporters dubbed them part of the "Patterson-McCormick Axis" and wanted to prosecute them, along with their more conservative cousin, Robert R. McCormick, publisher of the *Chicago Daily Tribune*.

Source: Library of Congress, Prints & Photographs Division, photograph by Harris & Ewing, LC-DIG-hec-25972.

"Waiting for the Signal From Home," *PM Magazine*. February 12, 1942. In his cartoons for *PM Magazine*, a pro–New Deal newspaper, Theodor Geisel—more commonly known today as Dr. Seuss—often depicted opponents of the New Deal as "fifth columnists." In this cartoon, Geisel depicts Japanese Americans in that category.

Source: Special Collections Library, University of California, San Diego.

Japanese Americans arrive from San Pedro at the Santa Anita Assembly Center in April 1942. Within a month, they had been moved into concentration camps in the nation's interior.

Source: Central Photographic File of the War Relocation Authority.

Anti–New Deal Governor Ralph L. Carr (left) (R-CO), with former president Herbert Hoover (center) and Governor Raymond E. Baldwin (R-CT) (right), at a Yale football game in October 1939. "If we put American-born Japanese in concentration camps," Carr charged, "we abrogate their constitutional rights." Carr's support of Japanese Americans cost him reelection in 1942. For his part, in 1938, Hoover had accused FDR of betraying "true liberalism," because FDR, according to Hoover, had empowered Jersey City Mayor Frank Hague (D-NJ) and US Senator Minton (D-IN, later a Supreme Court justice), who both favored the abrogating of those rights.

Source: Denver Post Collection, History Colorado. Accession #86.296.577.

During World War II, the FBI unsuccessfully pressured the increasingly anti-FDR journalist and writer George S. Schuyler to tone down the content of his columns for the *Pittsburgh Courier*. Schuyler also bravely opposed the 1944 Sedition Trial and urged African Americans to fight against Japanese American internment.

Source: Library of Congress, Prints & Photographs Division, Carl Van Vechten Collection, LC-USZ62-95999.

Using the Espionage Act, the Department of Justice and the Post Office Department revoked the third-class mailing rights of the *Boise Valley Herald*. The paper not only covered local news in the small town of Middleton, Idaho, but also promoted antiwar and anti–New Deal views as well as the rights of African Americans and Japanese Americans. From right to left: Adelbert Cornell; his wife, Bessie; and an unidentified man.

Source: Brent Cornell.

for the "building of those camps for the War Department for the Japanese evacuees on the West Coast."[46]

Despite the WPA's now generally unremembered significance in making internment possible, Roosevelt announced termination of the agency in December 1942. In part, he was responding to mounting criticism from members of Congress who regarded the WPA as a boondoggling New Deal anachronism. Misfires by the WPA leadership were another reason for FDR to pull the plug. Nicholson had thoroughly alienated Eisenhower and Bendetsen after a failed ploy to secure de facto WPA control of the reception centers and internment camps. Roosevelt's termination statement praised the WPA for a "job well done" in the development of New Deal public works projects but, significantly, left out its then still ongoing role in the building and management of concentration camps. Although the WPA wound down final operations in February 1943, former employees of the agency formed the backbone of the new WRA and provided it with needed expertise.[47]

During the initial period when the government was building and populating the camps, it encountered few obstacles from objectors. Sentiment against internment was sparse, scattered, uncertain, and poorly organized. The best, indeed really the only, hope for any critics was the American Civil Liberties Union. Unfortunately for those critics, the ACLU dithered and debated while crucial federal policies were being set in stone. On March 2, after the ACLU board discussed various options, including a possible test case, it deferred action. Baldwin publicly expressed misgivings about evacuation but then, inexplicitly, characterized the order as "undoubtedly legal in principle." On March 9, the ACLU pondered a possible letter to the president but voted to put it off it until the next meeting.[48]

The subsequent debate within the board on whether to send the letter sparked a factional struggle for control that continued throughout the duration of internment. Leading those who did not want to send any letter of protest at all was Morris Ernst, ACLU general counsel and a Roosevelt confidant and wire puller. His allies included Corliss Lamont, a pro-Soviet sympathizer and heir to a railway fortune. They were joined in these objections by Raymond L. Wise, a New Dealer and former federal prosecutor. The Ernst faction also included more corporatist elements such as the members of two well-connected Wall Street law firms: Walter Frank (vice chairman of the board) and Whitney North Seymour Sr., who was the board's lone Republican. Opposing the Ernst group were several old-line civil libertarians led by Arthur Garfield Hays, the other general counsel of the ACLU, and included Baldwin (who could not vote as a board member), John Haynes Holmes, Norman Thomas, Oswald Garrison Villard, and future US Supreme Court justice Thurgood Marshall. The Hays faction charged that internment both violated the Bill of Rights and perpetuated racism. Like the Ernst faction, most of the members were on the political left, but, unlike them, they also often had pacifist and quasi-anarchist sympathies or, in the case of Villard, classical liberal origins. Nearly all those in the Hays faction, including Thomas, were strongly anti-Communist.[49]

The debate between members of the board over the letter followed a pattern to be repeated many times. At one point, Ernst told Baldwin that he did not see "any possible constitutional question if there is military necessity." Lest Baldwin not get the point, he added, "and I assume the ACLU does not pretend to know anything about military necessities." Taking up the same theme, Lamont warned that "the Civil Liberties Union should not set itself up as capable of judging what is military necessity." But this time, the Hays faction prevailed, and the letter went out, albeit more than a month after Executive Order 9066.[50]

In addition to well-known old-line civil libertarians, signers of the Hays letter also included key California ACLU officers and local attorneys, who were already scouting out test cases. The wording of the letter itself lacked a certain forcefulness, however, in part because the Hays faction was trying to appease middle-of-the-roaders on the board. It shied away from a direct condemnation of Executive Order 9066, instead focusing on its "execution," including the "wholesale evacuation of citizens as well as aliens," as undemocratic and playing into the hands of Axis propagandists. It appealed to the president to ensure that "any American citizens ordered out of the zone, be evacuated only after individual examinations before or after removal." That particular recommendation had no discernable impact on Roosevelt's thinking.[51]

For the next two months, the ACLU board did almost nothing to follow up on the recommendations made in the letter. Quite simply, almost none of the members had the stomach for a full court confrontation with the administration. This reluctance also applied to Baldwin himself, who often seemed oblivious to, and forgiving of, Roosevelt's dark side. The president, he said decades later with lingering naïveté, was "so much our man there's no use mentioning him. Everyone was our friend in the White House in those days." Baldwin and other officers often attended official administration events and social functions and cultivated ties with high officials, including such active ACLU members as Supreme Court Justice Felix Frankfurter, Assistant Secretary of State Adolf A. Berle, and Secretary of the Interior Harold L. Ickes. These revolving-door relationships between the ACLU and the federal government almost inevitably nurtured double loyalties and blunted any critical edge.[52]

To a great extent, the divisions in the board mirrored the broader divisions among American leftists toward internment. A key difference for leftists outside the ACLU is that most had the luxury of remaining silent. The promoters of internment among New Dealers often came from the same group most ready to enact restrictions against the "isolationist" press. A visible example was novelist Rex Stout, the president of the Friends of Democracy and chairman of the War Writers' Board. In September 1942, he tangled with Norman Thomas in a radio debate on the issue. "Here and now I say," Stout declared flatly, "that Japanese-Americans include more fifth columnists than any other comparable group in the United States." When Thomas condemned the military's role as a "disgrace to our democracy" and comparable to "the powers of totalitarian dictators," Stout responded dismissively that moving "Japanese-Americans inland hardly constitutes Totalitarianism."[53]

Further to the left, the Communist Party perfunctorily concluded that internment was "unfortunate but vital," while the closely allied National Lawyers Guild refused to back any test cases challenging the policy. The small number of Nisei Communists went on record defending internment as a contribution to democracy and the war effort as members of the party's Japanese American Committee for Democracy. Representative Vito Marcantonio (American Labor Party-NY), who generally hewed to the party line, commented on the nefarious role of the Japanese "Fifth Column" in Hawaii, but he too (like his Communist allies) put more emphasis on attacking mainstream noninterventionists.[54]

A good guide to the overall attitudes of leading left-of-center opinion leaders can be found in the pages of three of the most influential proadministration periodicals, the *Nation*, the *New Republic*, and *PM*. In the period before Roosevelt's executive order, the situation on the West Coast was very much a sideshow compared to the high priority these publications all shared of putting restraints on right-wing criticism. The *Nation* had some initial commentary expressing sympathy for the plight of Japanese Americans and ran a few articles warning about the dangers of hysterical overreaction.[55]

When Roosevelt issued Executive Order 9066, however, the *Nation*, the *New Republic*, and *PM* went silent on the issue. The *Nation* broke from this pattern somewhat in June when it featured a hard-hitting article (though not an editorial), "Citizens Behind Barbed Wire," by Charles Iglehart, a former missionary who had spent many years in Japan. Iglehart condemned the evacuation as "unnecessary" and "deliberately fanned by interested persons and organizations until a conflagration was threatened, but at any time could have been quenched if the authorities had shown proper firmness." While conceding that internment was an "accomplished fact," he urged that some way be found to extricate Japanese Americans from this racist policy. But although Iglehart's article was unusual in condemning removal and relocation, it did not find specific fault with the president nor mention him by name.[56]

At the *New Republic*, the writer who had the most to say about the topic was Carey McWilliams, who was also California's commissioner of housing and immigration. At first a defender of removal and relocation, he eventually became very uncomfortable with the policy but, even then, treated it as a fait accompli and never strayed from seeing the president's motivations as benign. Hence, McWilliams hailed Executive Order 9102, which created the War Relocation Authority, for upholding a more "humanitarian" approach. An editorial in the *New Republic* went even further: "The intelligence with which the War Relocation Authority has approached the problem of resettling the 120,000 Japanese-Americans of the West Coast is changing that disagreeable necessity into what may turn out to be a constructive and nationally useful project."[57]

The pattern was similar for *PM*, a daily newspaper in New York founded in 1940 primarily for the purpose of defending the New Deal. Only days after Pearl Harbor, it featured a long sympathetic article about the Nisei, trying to humanize them as loyal citizens. Its coverage of Japanese Americans then lapsed into an almost total blackout for nearly a year and a half. A spectacular exception was a prominently featured cartoon on February 13 by Theodor Geisel (better known as Dr. Seuss). Captioned "Waiting for the Signal from Home," it depicted bucktoothed stereotypical Japanese Americans lining up in an "Honorable Fifth Column," stretched along the West Coast waiting to pick up packs of dynamite. Geisel's other cartoons during the war generally mirrored Roosevelt's hostility toward the unpatriotic "sixth columnists" in the press and their allies, such as Norman Thomas, Charles Lindbergh, John Haynes Holmes, and Burton K. Wheeler, who had fought the president's foreign policy. *PM* (though a daily newspaper) had no story or editorial on Executive Order 9066. By contrast, *PM* kept up a regular drumbeat for prosecuting, or otherwise restricting the rights of, allegedly seditious noninterventionists.[58]

Although the *Nation*, the *New Republic*, and *PM* were culpable in enabling internment and, indeed, were often Roosevelt's most loyal servants, they were not especially zealous in pushing that policy either. There is little reason to believe they would have faulted the president in any significant way had he avoided that step. These periodicals certainly did not put any noticeable "pressure" on him to act tougher on that front. By contrast, they exerted intense pressure against the administration's perceived slowness in limiting the rights of prewar noninterventionists.

Like their counterparts on the left, most conservative publications were either silent or silently complicit toward internment. The editorial pages of the *Chicago Daily Tribune*, normally so ready to rake the Roosevelt administration over the coals, barely mentioned the issue. Standing out among conservatives and libertarians was publisher R. C. Hoiles, the owner of a small chain of newspapers, who condemned internment as both unconstitutional and a violation of "the inherent rights that belong to all citizens." On the opposite extreme, the more populist and super-patriotic Hearst press considered the government to be excessively lenient and called for tougher measures toward Japanese Americans.[59]

African American leaders generally strived to stay on the sidelines. As in the Martin and Randolph cases, the NAACP feared rocking the boat during wartime and, like the ACLU, wanted to maintain the good will of the Roosevelt administration. Probably the best publicized, and most vociferous, black critic of internment was George S. Schuyler, an opinion columnist and associate editor at the *Pittsburgh Courier*, who returned to the topic often. "This country probably has as many of its citizens in concentration camps," he thundered in May 1943, "as has Germany." He dismissed accusations that Japanese Americans, whom he described as industrious and thrifty, presented any sort of genuine national security threat. Schuyler admonished African Americans to look beyond their own grievances, because "if the Government can do this to American citizens of Japanese ancestry, then it can do this to American citizens of ANY ancestry. ... Their fight is our fight."[60]

The Bill of Rights Committee of the American Bar Association, founded to such fanfare in 1938 to defend individual rights for all comers, showed no interest in the plight of Japanese Americans. If Grenville Clark and the committee as a whole were silent on internment, Clark became downright hostile to the rights of noninterventionists accused of subversion. His goal of a united front behind the president for the duration overrode everything else. Despite its weaknesses, the ACLU did not sink nearly as low as the Bill of Rights Committee in betraying its stated principles.[61]

Frustrated by the efforts of Ernst and other "totalitarian liberals" on the ACLU board to run interference for the administration, Norman Thomas launched a rare but impressive effort to mobilize the scattered forces against internment. In April 1942, he assembled a distinguished roll of prominent American religious leaders and educators to send a protest letter to Roosevelt. The signers, in addition to the old-line civil libertarian faction in the ACLU such as John Haynes Holmes and Oswald Garrison Villard, also included the famous American philosopher and educational reformer John Dewey, the prominent Protestant leader Harry Emerson Fosdick, educator George S. Counts, leading protestant missionary Sherwood Eddy, African American poet and a key figure in the Harlem Renaissance Countee Cullen, and theologian Reinhold Niebuhr. The appearance of Niebuhr's name merits special comment. Only three months earlier, as will be discussed in chapter 8, Niebuhr had criticized Baldwin for his rigidly "absolutist" belief in civil liberties for prewar noninterventionists. The Thomas letter was much more assertive than that recently sent by the ACLU and, unlike it, openly condemned Roosevelt's executive order. "Enforcing this on the Japanese alone," it warned the president, "approximates the totalitarian theory of justice practiced by the

Nazis in their treatment of the Jews." It demanded individual hearings before civilian boards and a right of return for those found to be loyal.[62]

Four days after the Thomas joint letter, John Finerty, one of Thomas's allies on the ACLU board, tried to break the logjam in the organization. To remove any further ambiguity, he proposed a resolution to put the ACLU on record against evacuation and, in effect, against Executive Order 9066. If Finerty's goal was to force a resolution of this issue, he failed, at least in the short term. The board punted by sending the resolution to members of the much larger ACLU Corporation to decide in a referendum, also appending a possible second resolution endorsing the government's right "to establish military zones and to remove persons, either citizens or aliens ... when their presence may endanger national security."[63]

During this interim period prior to the referendum, the ACLU board was pondering, albeit at glacial speed, possible test cases. One of the most promising involved college student Gordon Hirabayashi, a past conscientious objector, whose parents had converted to Quakerism in Japan. He turned himself in to the FBI office in Seattle on May 16 for violating the curfew order and announced that he planned to disobey a forthcoming removal order. He received help from lawyer, state senator, and local ACLU member Mary Farquharson, who on her own set up a fund to pay for his defense.[64]

A second case was from the San Francisco Bay area and centered on Fred Korematsu, who had tried to enlist in 1940 but was rejected as 4-F because of gastric ulcers. After failing to report to an assembly center, he was arrested in San Leandro, California, on May 30 (Memorial Day). Ernest Besig, the executive director of the Northern California Branch of the ACLU, recruited the legal services of Wayne Collins, a First Amendment fundamentalist, who was equally comfortable defending the free speech rights of radicals, Communists, or fascists. According to historian Robert Drinnon, Collins had "a boundless contempt for those he saw conniving with monumental injustice," including some of his fair-weather allies in the ACLU. Collins's "shotgun" approach featured almost every possible argument against the constitutionality of internment, including a contention that the seizure of guns and ammunition under curfews violated the Second Amendment.[65]

The referendum of the seventy members of the ACLU Corporation, when tabulated on June 16, brought a resounding victory to the president's defenders. By a two to one vote, they approved the second resolution endorsing the constitutionality of removal and relocation. This pro-administration triumph permanently sidelined the old-line civil libertarians and put the ACLU on record for Executive Order 9066. According to Norman Thomas, it meant that the ACLU had adopted the completely absurd position of "supporting the Presidential order of February 1942, and then somewhat reluctantly and ineffectively opposing most of the things done under that order."[66]

But Baldwin had become something of an ACLU "company man," and the board had spoken. In line with the policy shift, he informed the West Coast branches that they were not free "to sponsor cases in which the position is taken that the government has no constitutional right to remove citizens from military areas." The only legal actions that might be supported were those against proposals to specifically single out Japanese Americans for their race. Throwing a very small bone to backers of Hirabayashi and Korematsu, Baldwin suggested that suits for them might be funded through independent committees "without using the name of the Civil Liberties Union." Local ACLU members and officials involved in the embryonic test cases found it hard to contain their fury. Farquharson was "shocked" and complained that the "legal hair-splitting involved seems artificial to me and unreal as far as any actual merit is concerned. If the cases are worth fighting at all why not fight them in whatever ways are most practicable and effective." When a jury in King County, Washington, in October 1942 took just ten minutes to convict Hirabayashi of violating curfew and exclusion orders, the national ACLU board seemed unable to decide whether to even file an amicus brief for an appeal.[67]

The board was equally ruthless in cracking down on Korematsu's backers. When the board chastised the Northern California Branch of the ACLU for its continuing attack on the constitutionality of Executive Order 9066 and refusal to push aside Collins, Ernest Besig, the executive director of the branch, hit back: "We will not trim our sails to suit the Board's vacillating policy." When asked about it many years later, Besig showed no sympathy for Baldwin's eventual expression of remorse: "There were many friends of Roger's who were part of the administration under the Roosevelt regime. Roger used to go the rounds in Washington and meet with all these guys, and he was more of a government representative than he was an ACLU representative for a while."[68]

After Korematsu's conviction for violating the exclusion order in July 1942, Baldwin and the board reiterated that any appeal "must be disassociated" from any challenge to Executive Order 9066, admonishing the Northern California Branch to "concentrate the attack entirely on the order of General DeWitt." But the standoff entered a new phase as Collins, with Besig's backing, went ahead anyway and filed the appeal in the name of the Northern California Branch. The defiant Collins also filed a separate amicus brief in the Hirabayashi case challenging the constitutionality of the president's executive order. The board retaliated by formally disavowing the ACLU from any brief filed by Collins on behalf of Hirabayashi and Korematsu and threatened to expel the branch. The board only pulled back from this extraordinary punishment after the branch chair, Edward Parsons, abjectly apologized for the disobedience of Collins and his executive director, Besig. Deprived of ACLU financial support, lawyer Wayne Collins paid much of the legal costs out of pocket, some $10,000 dollars. A triumphant Ernst told Holmes, "You, and Roger and Art [Arthur Garfield Hays] … don't represent the Board any more."[69]

The ACLU's wartime abandonment of its role as champion of the Bill of Rights not only for Japanese Americans but for alleged seditionists inspired the contemporary saying "born in World War I and died in World War II." This abdication was deep and wide, and extended to some degree to the Hays faction as well. In November 1942, Baldwin, Holmes, and Hays signed off on an obsequious letter to DeWitt congratulating him "on so difficult a job accomplished with a minimum of hardship, considering its unprecedented character." Norman Thomas was merciless in his commentary. "Since the ACLU is going in for congratulating the army on being humane," he asked, "may I inquire whether you have yet practiced on a letter to Colonel Lanser who … is an officer of the German Army of occupation in Norway? He also tried to be humane."[70]

Meanwhile, as the deadline drew near for the Supreme Court hearings, several top officials in the War Department were up to their eyeballs in what Peter Irons has characterized as "a legal scandal without precedent in the history of American law." Had the details come to light at the time, the result might have torpedoed the government's case. The catalyst was the arrival at McCloy's Pentagon office of two copies of General DeWitt's more than six-hundred-page *Final Report*. McCloy panicked after reading the contents.

Particularly worrisome was a statement that it was "impossible" to determine the loyalty of Japanese Americans once they were in assembly centers because they were a "tightly-knit racial group." This contradicted DeWitt's earlier memo to the War Department that "there was time to determine loyalty." The wording also gave lawyers for the plaintiffs a basis to allege wrongful denial of due process because of race.[71]

The officially engineered cover-up, destruction of relevant documents, and evidence tampering moved forward swiftly. McCloy ordered the burning of all the original published drafts (along with galley proofs and relevant memoranda), thus violating a legal requirement to provide the other side with all "published material." He also persuaded DeWitt to sign off on a new version of the cover letter, dated June 15, 1943, as though his original letter of April 15 had never existed. The only copies of the originals were kept in a file marked "confidential" in Bendetsen's San Francisco office. "Not a single piece of paper," writes Peter Irons, "was left in the Pentagon to show that an earlier version of the Final Report had ever existed."[72]

The Supreme Court's ruling in *Hirabayashi v. United States* in June 1943 was a shut-out victory for the government. Because of the ACLU's earlier intervention, it only tested the parameters of the curfew regulations. In finding for the government, the court repeatedly cloaked itself in the "military necessity" rationale. Justice William O. Douglas wrote in a concurrence that "we cannot sit in judgment on the military requirements of that hour." The court's skirting of the obvious racism of the policy so bothered Justice Frank Murphy that he had originally intended to file a dissent, but his colleagues persuaded him to make it a concurrence. Nevertheless, he expressed vigorous misgivings: "Today is the first time, so far as I am aware, that we have sustained a substantial restriction of the personal liberty of citizens of the United States based upon the accident of race or ancestry. ... It bears a melancholy resemblance to the treatment accorded to members of the Jewish race in Germany."[73]

But the court's involvement with internment litigation was far from over. In addition to *Korematsu*, the Supreme Court still had *Endo* on its docket for 1944. The plaintiff, Mitsuye Endo, had the advantage of defying many common stereotypes. Raised as a Methodist in Sacramento, she did not speak any Japanese. Along with all other Japanese Americans in the city, she had lost her government job not long after Pearl Harbor. Once in the concentration camp, she secured representation from civil liberties attorney James C. Purcell, who filed a habeas corpus petition for her release. Hers was the only case that had full support from the national ACLU, but the motivations for that support were highly opportunistic. Backing Endo was a convenient way to make a distinction between the executive orders and the initial removals (which it did not want to challenge) and the subsequent incarceration.[74]

By late 1943, the government's "military necessity" defense for internment, to the extent it ever resonated, was losing its force. US counterattacks had pushed back Japan on all fronts, and perceived threats to the West Coast had disappeared. Moreover, the exploits in the European theater of Nisei volunteers in the 442nd Regimental Combat Team greatly impressed Americans from across the political spectrum. It was in this context that top administration officials urged Roosevelt to start winding down internment. One of the earliest who weighed in was Biddle. In December 1943, he wrote to the president warning that the "present practice of keeping loyal American citizens in concentration camps on the basis of race for longer than is absolutely necessary is dangerous and repugnant to the principles of our Government." Ever the political animal, however, Roosevelt did not want to rock the boat on the eve of the 1944 campaign and did nothing.[75]

Moreover, Roosevelt's private comments during this period do not indicate that he had greatly moderated his views toward the Japanese, including Japanese Americans. His assistant, William D. Hassett, recounted that in August 1942, "the President related an old Chinese myth about the origin of the Japanese. A wayward daughter of an ancient Chinese emperor left her native land in a sampan and finally reached Japan, then inhabited by baboons. The inevitable happened and in due course the Japanese made their appearance." In private conversations with friends during the same period, Roosevelt speculated that the Japanese were inferior to whites because their less developed skulls had accentuated "devious and treacherous" traits. That idea so fascinated him that he asked his friend, the eminent anthropologist Aleš Hrdlička, "Could that be dealt with surgically?"[76]

Roosevelt's amateur eugenicist musings covered wide ground. At a cabinet meeting in August 1944, he pondered the merits of sterilizing fifty thousand German leaders. He followed up by telling Secretary of the Treasury Henry

Morgenthau that "[y]ou either have to castrate the German people or you have got to treat them in such a manner so they can't go on reproducing people who want to continue the way they have in the past." A similarly twisted mixture of humor and sincerity (it is impossible to say which was which) characterized the president's comments to White House aides that the best way to solve Puerto Rico's "excessive" birth rate was to emulate "the methods which Hitler used effectively. ... It is all very simple and painless—you have people pass through a narrow passage and then there is a brrrrr of an electrical apparatus. They stay there for twenty seconds and from then on they are sterile."[77]

As the election drew nearer, the president was as inflexible as ever in rebuffing proposals to phase out internment. When Secretary of the Interior Ickes suggested closing the camps, FDR's first reaction was to cite the political problems involved. On June 12, he told Ickes: "The more I think ... of suddenly ending the orders excluding Japanese Americans from the West Coast, the more I think it would be a mistake to do anything too drastic or sudden. ... I think the whole problem, for the sake of internal quiet, should be handled gradually." Seemingly reading the president's mind after reporting to him that Stimson and McCloy also wanted to end internment, Under Secretary of State Edward R. Stettinius Jr. (who agreed with them) interjected: "The question appears to be largely a political one, the reaction in California, on which I am sure you will probably wish to reach your own decision."[78]

In September, pushed to ever greater anger about FDR's obfuscation, Ickes lamented that it was "the President himself who has insisted that the ban not be lifted until after the election and in the meantime we are having the devil's own time trying to persuade people in the Middle West and in the East that the Japanese are perfectly safe in those areas when they cannot be trusted in California." FDR's icy cynicism of intentionally leaving Japanese Americans to languish behind barbed wire during this period is impossible to explain away. Despite appeals from the Secretary of War and other top officials, including Ickes and the head of the WRA, Roosevelt continued the status quo because of election fears. His decision to keep Japanese Americans in the camps, writes Peter Irons, so as "to gain partisan advantage in the 1944 elections—provides a final count in the indictment of his political leadership."[79]

As the president was spurning the advice of his top subordinates, lawyers for the government were happening upon a startling discovery. Edward Ennis and his colleague John Burling found that DeWitt had ignored extensive evidence contradicting the *Final Report*'s findings of communication between illegal West Coast transmitters and the Japanese government. The FCC, for example, had no evidence of suspicious prewar radio transmissions. "[T]here wasn't a single illegal station and DeWitt knew it," concluded George E. Sterling, the head of the FCC's Radio Intelligence Division. Agreeing with the overall assessment of J. Edgar Hoover, Ennis and Burling concluded that the *Final Report* contained "false and erroneous statements about shore-to-ship signaling in the period before evacuation."[80]

The pair proposed inserting a footnote in their brief to acknowledge these flaws and even threatened not to sign if it did not appear. It read as follows: "The Final Report of General DeWitt is relied on in this brief for statistics and other details concerning the actual evacuation and the events that took place subsequent thereto. The recital of the circumstances justifying the evacuation as a matter of military necessity, however, is in several respects, particularly with reference to the use of illegal radio transmitters and to shore-to-ship signaling by persons of Japanese ancestry, in conflict with the information in possession of the Department of Justice. In view of the contrariety of the reports on this matter, we do not ask the Court to take judicial notice of the recital of those facts contained in the Report."[81]

McCloy and Solicitor General Charles Fahy vetoed the modification, and Ennis and Burling, like so many before them who were troubled by the government's policy, backed down. They signed the brief without the suggested footnote. "The Roosevelt administration," writes Robert Drinnon, "stacked the deck against the handful of Japanese American test cases by suppressing, altering, and destroying evidence critical to their defense." But subsequently, Ennis, plagued with guilt, tried to undo the damage wrought by "these lies." Exposing his career to considerable potential risk, he took the extraordinary private step of urging Roger N. Baldwin to have the ACLU intervene in Korematsu's defense. Ennis, in effect, was trying to throw his own case.[82]

Meanwhile, instead of intervening to support *Korematsu*, Baldwin rallied the ACLU to focus on *Endo*. This strategy allowed it to sidestep the constitutionality of Executive Order 9066 and the subsequent removal and, instead, concentrate on the issues of long-term incarceration and DeWitt's racist role. For the pro-FDR-minded officials who dominated the ACLU, this approach had the advantage of shielding the president from any implication of blame. The arguments before the Supreme Court for both *Korematsu* and *Endo* were in October, and they were decided on December 18, 1944.[83]

A divided Supreme Court sustained the government in *Korematsu* (6 to 3) in contrast to the united one in 1943 that had upheld the conviction of *Hirabayashi*. The majority opinion, written by Justice Black, was a study in denial and tortured reasoning. Side-by-side with assurances that race did not motivate exclusion were words contradicting those denials. "Regardless of the true nature of the assembly and relocation centers," it declared, "and we deem it unjustifiable to call them concentration camps with all the ugly connotations that term implies—we are dealing specifically here with nothing but an exclusion order. To cast this case into outlines of racial prejudice, without reference to the real military dangers which are presented, merely confuses the issue. Korematsu was not excluded from the Military Area because of hostility to him or his race." To rationalize this distinction, Black said that "evidence of disloyalty by some" created a situation where "the need for action was great, and time was short."[84]

Each of the three dissenters—Owen J. Roberts, Robert H. Jackson, and Frank Murphy—wrote separate opinions. The most quoted in later years was Murphy's, which excoriated the wholesale exclusion of Japanese Americans as both unconstitutional and falling into "the ugly abyss of racism." Brushing aside rationalizations of military necessity as rife with "misinformation, half-truths and insinuations," Jackson asserted that, even if true, this legal standard was contrary to the American tradition of judging each person on an individual basis rather than as a member of a collective racial group. He regarded this "legalization of racism" as "utterly revolting among a free people who have embraced the principles set forth in the Constitution of the United States."[85]

But the dissents of Murphy and Jackson (both former attorneys general of Roosevelt) were also noteworthy for what they left out, or, more precisely, who they did not blame. "Murphy's dissent," Daniel observes, "did not look behind DeWitt and see the Secretary War, and behind him, Franklin D. Roosevelt. The Roosevelt Court did not often point accusing fingers at its creator but surely Murphy understood that FDR's Executive Order 9066 was what gave DeWitt authority to act." Jackson (the future Nuremberg prosecutor) went to extra lengths to shift blame from Roosevelt to DeWitt. "Neither the Act of Congress nor the Executive Order of the President nor both together would afford a basis for this conviction [of Korematsu]. It rests on the orders of General DeWitt."[86]

The ruling in *Endo*, which was decided the same day as *Korematsu*, brought a unanimous victory to the plaintiff, granting her petition for habeas corpus on the grounds that it was unconstitutional to continue to detain a "concededly loyal" citizen. Although Endo was the only plaintiff in an internment-related case who prevailed, it was not exactly a defeat for the government either. The administration had already made the decision to close the camps, so it had no legal effect.[87]

The majority opinion in *Endo*, written by Douglas, mirrored the arguments made in the ACLU's briefs. On the one hand, it upheld the constitutionality of removal and assembly, but, on the other, it struck down long-term incarceration. The majority opinion elaborated that "the original evacuation was justified, its lawful character was derived from the fact that it was an espionage and sabotage measure, not that there was community hostility to this group of American citizens." It drew a contrast between the acts of the WRA, which used "the language of detention," and the president's two executive orders and DeWitt's subsequent enforcements, which were allegedly silent on that issue. This unconvincing evidence served as a basis for the majority to conclude that as a legal matter the "detention in Relocation Centers was no part of the original program of evacuation but developed later."[88]

If the court's opinion in *Endo* cast the War Relocation Authority as a kind of villain, it seemed to nominate Roosevelt for the role of hero. To clinch its condemnation of racist enforcement, it quoted the following statement from the president: "Americans of Japanese ancestry, like those of many other ancestries, have shown that they can, and want to, accept our institutions and work loyally with the rest of us, making their own valuable contribution to the national wealth and well-being." Ironically, the source of the quoted passage, a fact not mentioned in the text itself, was Roosevelt's message to the US Senate from September 1943, which praised the often coercive methods of the WRA to "segregate" the loyal from disloyal internees. This was the same agency that the court had just depicted as an illegal jailer.[89]

Roberts had a reputation for decorum and restraint but apparently found it impossible to hold his peace after reading the majority opinion. The strained effort by the pro–New Dealers on the court to absolve the president of blame was just too much. Quite obviously, Roberts pointed out, the executive branch "not only was aware of what was being done but in fact that which was done was formulated in regulations and in a so-called handbook open to the public." Roberts piled on, calling it "inadmissible to suggest that some inferior public servant exceeded the authority granted by executive order in this case," and closing with an extra dig: "It is to hide one's head in the sand to assert that the detention of relator resulted from an excess of authority by subordinate officials."[90]

Through his contacts on the court, Roosevelt was privy in advance to the outcome in *Korematsu*, and perhaps he had found out even before Election Day. While the president had decided on November 10 to end the exclusion policy, he continued to hold off formal implementation. In the interim, however, he offered a typically Rooseveltian hint that something was in the offing at a news conference on November 21. When asked about the continuing incarceration of Japanese Americans, Roosevelt mused, "It is felt by a great many lawyers that under the Constitution they can't be locked up in concentration camps." The president's use of the term *concentration camps* at this late date contradicts the government's (and for that matter the Supreme Court's) sustained renaming effort to promote less sinister labels such as *internment* or *relocation camps*. When a reporter asked if the lack of espionage from Japanese Americans had made the orders unnecessary, the president answered in feigned innocence, "That I couldn't tell you because I don't know." He did know. He had secretly decided the issue long before he spoke.[91]

On December 17, just one day before the court handed down the *Korematsu* and *Endo* decisions, the War Department publicly announced what Roosevelt had already decided in early November. Japanese Americans in the camps who had passed loyalty screenings would, after January 2, 1945, be "permitted the same freedom of movement throughout the United States as other loyal and law-abiding citizens." The effect was to render both *Endo* and *Korematsu* almost entirely moot. By early 1946, the federal government had completely emptied the camps.[92]

The War Department's announcement blunted any negative (or for that matter positive) assessments of *Korematsu*. One conspicuous exception was the reaction of Westbrook Pegler, who in 1942 had wanted to put all Japanese Americans under lock and key. Without a hint of self-awareness, much less self-reproach, Pegler slammed *Korematsu* for upholding "three years of imprisonment" for Japanese Americans as well as "the sacrifice of their homes, business interests and property, to say nothing of their rights as loyal, native citizens." Pegler called special attention to the central drafting role in the opinion of Black, the ex-Klansman who, while head of the Black Committee in the US Senate, had "prowled the private telegraphic correspondence of countless American citizens indiscriminately searching for information of political value to his political boss." Pegler also underscored the irony that an immigrant, Felix Frankfurter, had joined "in the condemnation of an innocent man [Korematsu] legally qualified to be president of the United States, an office to which he can't even aspire."[93]

The aftermath of *Korematsu* led to much new soul searching about the wartime mistreatment of Japanese Americans. On the day of the decision, Earl Warren, elected governor of California in 1942, issued a welcome to Japanese Americans who wanted to return and promised to protect their constitutional rights. In 1948, California's voters handily rejected more restrictions on alien land ownership, and soon thereafter the legislature repealed the original law entirely. In 1950, Ralph Carr, who was using his past opposition to internment as a selling point, won the Republican nomination for governor in Colorado (he died before the election). Black, however, was unrepentant. In 1971, he asserted that "[p]eople were rightly fearful of the Japanese in Los Angeles. … They all look alike to a person not a Jap. Had they [Japan] attacked our shores, you'd have a large number fighting with the Japanese troops." Internment did not outlive, at least in substance, the man who was chiefly responsible: Franklin D. Roosevelt.[94]

The establishment of concentration camps for Japanese Americans was Roosevelt's greatest violation of individual liberty. Except for its scale and the depth of its institutional racism, it showed great consistency with his other civil liberties policies. Even if Roosevelt had never signed Executive Order 9066, his overall record in protecting the Bill of Rights ranks as the worst, or nearly the worst, of any president. If considered as a puzzle piece on the board, internment was an outsized piece, but it was still one piece among many. During the same period when the administration was putting Japanese Americans behind barbed wire, it was undermining the Bill of Rights in a multitude of other ways as well.

8

A "Good War" for Free Speech?

WITH THE NOTABLE exception of the internment of Japanese Americans, World War II continues to have a widespread reputation as a "good war" for civil liberties. This perception can be traced to the period of the war itself. Using none other than the ACLU as its source, a *New York Times* editorial expressed the prevailing opinion at the time by marking 1943 as a "Good Year for Civil Liberty." To back this assessment, the ACLU issued a press release stating that up to the end of August 1943 the federal government had initiated only 25 legal actions "for utterances or publications alleged to obstruct the conduct of the war" (involving about 130 people), compared to an estimated 1,000 such cases in World War I (involving over 1,500 people). Similarly, the authors of a leading history survey text published in 2019 observed that "Franklin Roosevelt had been a government official during World War I. Now presiding over a bigger world war, he was determined to avoid many of the patriotic excesses he had witnessed then: mobs menacing immigrants, the patriotic appeals to spy on neighbors, the raids on pacifist radicals."[1]

The findings of Richard W. Steele in the most comprehensive work on the topic, *Free Speech in the Good War*, however, render untenable a benign interpretation of civil liberties during World War II. The central figure in Steele's account is Roosevelt himself. "If one looks at the paucity of opposition to the war," writes Steele, "and the extraordinary efforts to suppress what little radical dissent there was, the administration's record is less restrained than the figures suggest." While no mass roundups of dissidents occurred on Roosevelt's watch, it was not because he was averse to the idea of mass roundups as such. The numbers of Japanese Americans interned, which exceeded several fold the combined arrests of suspected dissidents in World War I, shows as much. Instead, a mass roundup outside of that ethnic group, and other limits on free speech, were never in the cards for one simple reason: the "mass," if defined as vocal opponents of the war, had almost evaporated after Pearl Harbor.[2]

If Roosevelt, or others around him, wanted extensive prosecutions of political figures who had agitated for noninterventionism before the war, that too was not feasible, albeit for different reasons. There is no question that Roosevelt desired more vigorous action on that front, but resistance within the federal government repeatedly stymied him. At the bottom of this was a preexisting American civil-liberties consciousness that was traceable to memories of World War I excesses. This resistance had gained recent reinforcement by the Hague and Minton controversies as well as much-publicized examples in other countries.[3]

Roadblocks against potential overreach by the executive branch came not only from judges but also from lawyers in the Department of Justice. Even when egged on from above, more than a few gummed up the legal works by quibbling over technicalities and using other methods of delay. As Steele observes, this "stratagem [was] made effective by the fact that the laws at their disposal were of relatively limited application." Would-be prosecutors were well aware that the increased support for civil liberties had filtered down to ordinary Americans, including potential jury pools. These legal and popular constraints were highly imperfect but, taken together, provided a significant brake on administration discretion.[4]

Roosevelt, like his World War I mentor, Woodrow Wilson, combined a public persona as a champion of democracy and liberalism with a considerable private streak of vindictiveness. If anything, he outdid Wilson in vindictiveness by repeatedly pestering subordinates to take tougher action than they may have otherwise wanted. The comparatively passive Wilson more often took the role of a sometimes reluctant rubber stamp for zealous underlings. Throughout World War II, Roosevelt constantly probed the limits of his repressive power through such diverse schemes as sedition trials, tax audits, and a revival of lobbying investigations. Principle, lofty or otherwise, did not appear to impede him. "He was not much interested in the theory of sedition," recalled Attorney General Francis Biddle, "or in the constitutional right to criticize the government in wartime. He wanted this anti-war talk stopped." Echoing this, Steele concludes that although Roosevelt gave lip service to the principle of free speech, "he rarely interpreted it as preventing the executive branch from doing what was necessary to ensure his broadly conceived view of national security."[5]

While pre–World War II events in Jersey City and elsewhere had helped to create a cross-ideological pro–free speech coalition, loyalty to the president still retained a powerful hold on many New Deal elements in that coalition, powerful enough to overwhelm most qualms. More than one New Dealer let the president off the hook for federal abuses, often preferring instead to blame subordinates, such as FBI Director J. Edgar Hoover. The inclination to overlook these free speech infringements did not just stem from loyalty to one man, however. As Steele states, a key factor that "deflated [pro–New Deal] civil libertarian idealism was the faith its adherents placed in the federal government."[6]

Although Roosevelt generally faced more limits on his freedom of action than Wilson, his administration was the only one of the two to initiate a peacetime sedition case. In January 1940, the Department of Justice, in *United States of America v. John T. Prout Jr.*, prosecuted in the United States District Court in New York seventeen men associated with the Christian Front, a group that had close ties to Father Coughlin. Because the World War I Espionage Act did not quite apply, the government pegged its hopes on a "seditious conspiracy" law from 1861. The precise charges were conspiracy to "overthrow, put down and or to destroy by force, the Government of the United States" and steal government property, including ammunition. According to the prosecutors, the ultimate aim of the defendants was to establish a "fuehrer type" system. Raids by FBI agents netted 3,500 rounds of ammunition, seventeen guns, including one 1870s Springfield rifle, and a family heirloom sword. Director Hoover stated that the plotters intended to "knock off about a dozen Congressmen" and "blow up the goddam Police Department."[7]

Besides Hoover, the key figure pushing the prosecution was Attorney General Frank Murphy, a quintessential New Dealer. Although an ACLU member in good standing, he cited the notorious Palmer Raids as one of his models. He even went so far as to depict his World War I predecessors as too tolerant and promised "no laxity—no disorder—only action, action, and on time … we are not a soft, pudgy democracy." Murphy depicted *Prout* as the culmination of a determined campaign against "un-Americans" on both the left and the right.[8]

While prosecutors had overstated the breadth of the alleged conspiracy, historian Charles R. Gallagher persuasively argues that a small group among the defendants were, in fact, planning violent action. Their goal was not to overthrow the government as such but to stage a kind of false-flag operation by setting off bombs against such targets as the *Daily Worker*. The hoped-for result was to incite Communists and Jews to stage a revolution that, in turn, would provoke a governmental crackdown against them. According to Gallagher, the government, because of direct pressure by such figures as Bishop Thomas E. Molloy of the Diocese of Brooklyn, who had an extraordinary pre-trial meeting with the prosecution, pretty much undermined its own case by failing to address the profound ideological influence on the defendants of such mainstream Catholic doctrines as the mystical body of Christ. Had prosecutors publicized the links between the defendants and Catholic doctrine at such a high-profile trial, however, the Democrats may have suffered an adverse impact in the upcoming 1940 election.[9]

As the trial moved forward, serious doubts emerged in the press about the viability of the government's case. The *New Republic*, still fairly solicitous of free speech for both left and right, condemned the proceedings as "illegal and prejudicial" and as based on opinion rather than a genuine threat. It was, it concluded, impossible to "preserve anyone's civil liberties unless we scrupulously guard the liberties of those whose opinions we detest." In many ways, the government was its own worst enemy. The seditious conspiracy charge, for example, was misplaced since the plot, to the extent the defendants had motive, was not to overthrow government but rather to produce a backlash. The government's dubious reliance on highly paid informants also did not sit well with the jury.[10]

Even many individuals who would normally be regarded as most likely to back such a prosecution were inclined to dismiss the credibility of any serious threat from the defendants, even if some of the allegations were true. Taking office only a month after the arrests, for example, Attorney General Robert H. Jackson, who was more attentive to civil liberties than Murphy, regarded the charges as a "bit fantastic." Mayor Fiorello La Guardia of New York City quipped, "I don't think the United States Government is in much danger from eighteen guys like these." The jury apparently felt the same way. In late June 1940 (just two days after France's surrender to Germany), it acquitted nine defendants, and the judge declared a mistrial for the rest. Another defendant had committed suicide in the interim between arrest and trial.[11]

Even as the jury was deliberating on its verdict in the *Prout* case, Congress was debating the most significant revision of antisedition legislation since the World War I era. Much of the momentum for new legislation came from the Molotov-Ribbentrop Pact, which remained in effect from August 1939 to June 1941. During that period, New Dealers and conservatives alike were on the lookout for opportunities to root out perceived "Communazi" fifth columns. Most media and congressional commentary on the bill emphasized the new rules for registration and fingerprinting of aliens. Less publicized was the provision that lowered the bar for sedition prosecutions from action to advocacy of a conspiracy to overthrow the government by force or to cause insubordination in the armed forces. Supporters of the legislation, such as Representative Emanuel Celler (D-NY), regarded the maximum penalties of the 1861 law, six years in prison or $5,000, as too lenient. Although the legislation was sometimes depicted as a right-wing initiative, the Department of Justice had helped draft it, and the intelligence community was fully supportive.[12]

Excepting those from the ACLU, the main witnesses against the bill were from such Communist-friendly organizations as the CIO National Maritime Union (a group allied with radical labor leader Harry Bridges) and the National Lawyers Guild. Casually brushing aside the objections of these critics, the House gave overwhelming approval with only four voting against. One of those four was Vito Marcantonio (American Labor Party-NY), who usually hewed to the Communist Party line. In the Senate, opposition was so negligible that passage was by a voice vote. Roosevelt signed the new legislation, popularly known as the Smith Act, on June 28, just four days after the verdict in *Prout*. Both sides generally took for granted that the Communist Party, which had recently broken with the president's foreign policy, was the most immediate future target of the law.[13]

One of the few observers who showed an inkling that this might not be true was Zechariah Chafee Jr., the nation's top legal authority on free speech. He classified the Smith Act as "one of the most drastic restrictions on freedom of speech ever enacted in the United States during peace" and denied that the law reached only "really dangerous men." Chafee compared the legislation to "an inscription on a sword. What matters is the existence of the weapon. Once the sword is placed in the hands of the people in power, then, whatever it says, they will be able to reach and slash at almost any unpopular person who is speaking or writing anything that they consider objectionable criticism of their policies."[14]

As if to prove Chafee right, the maiden federal prosecution under the Smith Act was against members of the Socialist Workers Party (SWP), the main rival to the Communists on the Marxist left. The genesis of the case was an intraunion dispute in Minneapolis. The SWP, though a tiny group nationally, had captured control of Local 544 of the Teamsters. The local had angered the Roosevelt administration as early as 1939 by organizing federal relief workers. These tensions intensified in late 1940 when Hoover warned that Local 544 was planning to call a strike against major defense contractors and seeking to gain a stranglehold on transportation employment in the Midwest.[15]

When national Teamsters president Daniel J. Tobin, a close FDR ally, tried to quash the rebellion, Local 544 retaliated by switching affiliation to the CIO. Tobin alleged that the local had fallen under control of German double agents and wrote to the president urging him to step in. Roosevelt, in turn, promised to notify the relevant authorities about the matter. He also proclaimed, via presidential press secretary Stephen T. Early, that this was no time "for labor unions, local or national, to begin raiding one another for the purpose of getting memberships or for similar reasons."[16]

Two weeks later, the FBI raided SWP offices in Minneapolis, St. Paul, and New York, and a federal grand jury charged twenty-nine key party leaders with conspiracy to "overthrow of the government of the United States by force and violence" and promoting insubordination in the armed forces. The timing struck even pro-Roosevelt observers as suspicious, leading the *New Republic* to brand it as "a prosecution for opinion only."[17]

The alleged "seditious" language of the defendants was the usual Trotsky-ite boilerplate emphasizing the follies of capitalist wars. The armed militia, depicted as central to the plot, was a moribund union "defense guard." Most of the members were ordinary Democrats and Republicans, and the combined "arsenal" amounted to between ten and fifty guns. The group had last met to serve as ushers at a Christmas party for the Minneapolis Teamsters. Because some of the purported plotters had frequented a local burlesque club, I. F. Stone in the *Nation* dubbed their doings a "G-String conspiracy." If SWP literature constituted seditious advocacy, he added, "a man might be sent to jail for ten years because he circulated such un-American documents as the Declaration of Independence and Lincoln's Second Inaugural." Sharing this view, the ACLU pointed out that the allegations fell well short of the Holmes-Brandeis "clear and present danger" rule for restricting speech.[18]

In one of the most obvious of the many obvious double standards in its history, the Communist Party loudly cheered on the prosecution of the "pro-Nazi" Trotskyites, while its allied National Lawyers Guild (which had also spoken out against passage of the Smith Act) remained mum. Anti–New Dealers, by contrast, were generally ambivalent about the indictments, questioning both the government's motives and the role of the Communist Party, then aligned with Roosevelt. The *Chicago Daily Tribune* thought it "odd" that the federal government had attacked the marginal SWP yet left the pro-Stalin Communist Party unscathed: "Of the Trotskyites it can be said that they are few in number and had a position of advantage only in Minneapolis."[19]

Overseeing the government's case was then Solicitor General Francis Biddle, who was, like Murphy, a longtime ACLU member. In bringing the case, Biddle acted from a confused and contradictory amalgam of careerist, Machiavellian, repressive, and civil libertarian motives. Although he publicly defended the prosecution, his autobiography states that he had hoped, and expected, the Supreme Court to overrule any conviction and thus provide a powerful pro–civil liberties precedent. He recalled that he had not thought it remotely "conceivable" for any higher court to classify the SWP as a clear and present danger. But the contemporary record reveals more muddled sentiment. While Biddle gave ACLU director Baldwin the impression that he had misgivings, he actively opposed a petition to take the case to the Supreme Court and, after the convictions, refused to recommend a presidential pardon. Biddle himself later gave a more plausible explanation of his motives at the time by candidly admitting a desire to demonstrate "firmness" as the new man on the job.[20]

If, on the other hand, Biddle was indeed attempting, even if half-heartedly and erratically, to overturn the conviction of the Socialist Workers Party defendants, the strategy completely backfired. After a Minneapolis jury found eighteen of the defendants guilty less than a week before Pearl Harbor, the verdict weathered a challenge in the Eighth Circuit Court of Appeals in *Dunne v. United States*. After the US Supreme Court refused to consider the case, Biddle declared with some bitterness that this result "became a defeat for me," though he took some solace from the "comparatively short" sentences of one year to sixteen months. The financially devastated SWP, bereft of its main leaders, lost its hard-won foothold in the Teamsters.[21]

But to Roosevelt, *Dunne* was a sideshow compared to his priority of neutralizing more mainstream noninterventionists, particularly those associated with the America First Committee (AFC). That committee was a cross-ideological organization led by aviator Charles Lindbergh and drew support from such varied noninterventionists as Robert Wood of Sears, Roebuck and Company, Norman Thomas of the Socialist Party, and publisher Robert R. McCormick of the *Chicago Daily Tribune*. In 1940, Roosevelt ordered J. Edgar Hoover to monitor both the AFC itself and such key members and backers as Senators Gerald Nye (R-ND) and Burton K. Wheeler (D-MT). Hoover complied by passing on to the president regular reports about these individuals. Within limits, Attorney General Robert H. Jackson tried to restrain his boss's inquisitorial urges and reaffirmed the importance of civil liberties in policy and public statements. Most notably, Jackson cautioned in April 1940 that in "times of fear or hysteria, political, racial, or religious social and economic groups, often from the best of motives, cry for the scalps of individuals or groups because they do not like their views."[22]

In 1940, a favored electoral strategy of the Roosevelt presidential campaign was to imply that the GOP was soft on the Nazi Germany threat. Democratic vice-presidential candidate Henry A. Wallace memorably proclaimed that the "native totalitarian organizations are herding their members to vote for the man Hitler wants. ... I ask you: Is Hitler working for Roosevelt's election?" As the crowd roared "No," Wallace taunted Willkie further that, of course, the GOP candidate wanted "his Nazi support" to "be hushed up until he is elected and the bells are ringing in Berlin." Once secure in a third term, Roosevelt remained fixated on the noninterventionist threat posed by America Firsters and did not seem too worried about fine distinctions between the mainstream and the lunatic fringe.[23]

Most irritating of all to Roosevelt was the defection from his side over the lend-lease issue in December 1940 of the publishers Joseph Medill Patterson of the *New York Daily News* and his sister, Eleanor Josephine Medill "Cissy" Patterson, of the *Washington Times-Herald*. With their cousin Robert R. McCormick of the *Chicago Daily Tribune*, they owned the three highest-circulation dailies in the United States. Roosevelt had thought so highly of Joe Patterson (a consistent advocate of naval preparedness) that in May 1940 he had offered him the job of secretary of the navy. Patterson preferred to continue as publisher of the *Daily News* and turned him down. "Roosevelt had been his friend," writes Cissy's biographer Ralph G. Martin, "and no publisher in America had supported the President as long and as loyally as he had." Cissy had known Eleanor Roosevelt for decades and had often lauded her performance as First Lady. But like their cousin Robert, Cissy and Joe were deeply fearful of foreign entanglements, and, on that issue, the president had lost their trust. By 1941, the Pattersons and McCormick embodied to Roosevelt a quasi-treasonous "Patterson-McCormick Axis," which had to be defeated at all costs.[24]

When Roosevelt elevated Attorney General Jackson to the Supreme Court in June 1941, Solicitor General Francis Biddle (who was already filling the role of acting attorney general) had the inside track to officially replace him. But Biddle knew well Roosevelt's fear that he would be too lenient on dissent and took steps to counter that impression. On the same day that the press first revealed that Jackson was the likely new pick for the court, Biddle sent a loud signal that if selected as attorney general, he did not intend to be a civil libertarian pushover. In a speech to the National Conference of Social Work, which may have solidified Roosevelt's subsequent decision to name him as attorney general, he belittled Charles Lindbergh's "flabby" fear that war threatened civil liberties at home. The patriots who had fought in 1776 and 1861, Biddle stressed, "surely did not discuss their loss of civil liberties when they chose to fight." While the protection of civil liberties was essential, this did not justify becoming "confused, putting the cart before the horse: the right to freedom of speech before the preservation of democracy itself."[25]

Seemingly confirming that this tough talk was not just rhetoric, Biddle, while still acting attorney general, approved in July a grand jury investigation in the District of Columbia to investigate possible right-wing seditionists and seditious propaganda. The prosecutor in charge was William Power Maloney, a young trial attorney fresh off a stint at the Securities and Exchange Commission. Biddle later recalled that Maloney's eyes were "never off the headlines." Combative, prone to hyperbole, and inclined to cut legal corners, Maloney had Roosevelt's full confidence. The president wanted action and Maloney was made to order.[26]

Soon after Biddle officially became attorney general in August 1941, however, his sometimes-latent civil libertarianism came back to the surface. He implemented an official policy of requiring district and state attorneys general to get his personal approval for any sedition prosecutions. His goal was to avoid "the disgraceful hysteria of witch hunts." Statements such as this prompted Roosevelt to wonder whether Biddle was really "tough enough" for his job, and he stepped up pressure on the new attorney general to take a harder line. In November 1941, for example, he urged Biddle to launch "a Grand Jury investigation of the money sources behind the America First Committee" because it "certainly ought to be looked into and I cannot get any action out of Congress."[27]

But Biddle fought off this pressure, at least for the time being. If anything, he became even more forthright in standing up for civil liberties after the Pearl Harbor attack on December 7. Soon after the US entered the war, he proclaimed the need to make free speech and tolerance "a reality for others as well as for ourselves; yes for aliens, for Germans, for Italians, for Japanese; for those who are against us as well as those who are with us." More boldly, Biddle boasted that the department had dropped charges against three alleged right-wing subversives because "free speech as such ought not to be restricted." At the same time, however, the sedition investigation he had green-lighted was quietly slogging along.[28]

An almost immediate result of the Pearl Harbor attack on December 7 was the evaporation of the American antiwar movement. One day later, the president's three most powerful critics in the press, Robert R. "Bertie" McCormick, Cissy Patterson, and Joe Patterson, pledged support for the war effort. "Well, we're in it," Patterson declared in an editorial reprinted in Cissy's *Washington Times-Herald*. "God knows Americans didn't want it. But let's get behind our President and fight for America first." Soon after writing those words, Patterson, who had been a captain in World War I and was still physically fit, came to the White House to offer his services. When he entered the Oval Office, he stood waiting for several minutes while Roosevelt read through some papers. Finally, the president looked up and asked what his visitor wanted. "I am here, Mr. President," Patterson answered, "to see what aid I can be in the war effort." The president responded, "Joe, I want to give you one assignment. ... I want you to go home and read your editorials for the past six months. Read every one of them and then think what you have done." As Patterson was leaving, Roosevelt told him "to pass on the word to Cissy to behave herself." Hot with anger over this treatment, an anger soon shared by his sister, Patterson said later that he wanted nothing more than "to outlive that bastard." Even some of Roosevelt's close allies, like Postmaster General Frank C. Walker, thought that the president had needlessly thrown away an opportunity to enhance wartime unity. "Roosevelt could easily have converted both Pattersons to his cause," writes Cissy's biographer, Ralph G. Martin. "Instead, he created two bitter and powerful enemies."[29]

But Roosevelt was in a highly vindictive mood. He had never liked Biddle's gestures toward tolerance and liked them even less now. He urged Hoover "to clean up a number of these vile [right-wing] publications." When the president followed up later to urge more "action taken against publishers of seditious matter," Hoover complained that Biddle had blocked him "time and time again in case after case." So frustrated was Hoover that he asked the president to personally admonish the attorney general about "the need for such action." Roosevelt was running out of patience. He made it a practice to send Biddle clippings of articles about possible seditious incidents with such notes as "What about this?" or "What are you doing to stop this?" Eventually, the president's frustration spilled over into cabinet meetings. "His technique was always the same," Biddle remembered. "When my turn came, as he went around the table, his habitual affability dropped. ... He looked at me, his face pulled tightly together. 'When are you going to indict the seditionists?'" He continued to do this "the next week, and every week after that."[30]

Roosevelt was not alone in regarding Biddle as too weak-kneed. During the first half of 1942, a succession of high-profile articles by leading New Deal editors, publishers, columnists, and academics made similar complaints. These "militant liberals," as Steele calls them, "offered an aggressive defense of American nationalism … and, ultimately, a somewhat deflated view of free speech." One of the earliest in this wave of articles was a contribution in the January issue of the *Nation* by Reinhold Niebuhr, a well-known theologian, political pundit, and founder of the Union for Democratic Action (UDA), which was the forerunner of Americans for Democratic Action. His underlying theme was that liberals needed to abandon their unrealistic "absolutist" defense of civil liberty in favor of a more nuanced "relativist" approach. Doing so, he elaborated, was necessary for the cleansing of "recalcitrant and even traitorous elements" from the body politic. It was time, Niebuhr concluded, to put aside "the assumption that liberty is the only principle of democracy" and "recognize that community has as much value as liberty."[31]

But Niebuhr was a paragon of moderation compared to Freda Kirchwey, the editor and publisher of the *Nation* and a UDA board member. In an article two months after his, she proposed that profascist publications be "exterminated exactly as if they were enemy machine-gun nests in the Bataan jungle." Their "filthy slanders of the President, their lies about Jews, as well as the open aid and comfort they offer to the Axis" disqualified them from the protections of free speech. To Kirchwey, the continued dissemination of these ideas proved that the "happy peace-time techniques" of "[t]olerance, democratic safeguards, trust in public enlightenment" had failed. Unlike Niebuhr, she grouped such "fellow travelers" as the McCormick, Hearst, and Patterson newspapers into the same dangerous category. The defeatist articles by those publishers were, in fact, "more dangerous than those of the out-and-out fascists both because they are not out-and-out fascists and because the circulation of their papers is enormous." These individuals must be carefully watched, and "the moment they skid across the thin line that divides their doctrines from open treason they should face the full blast of the law." At the same time, Kirchwey favored continued legal toleration of Communist Party publications because the question of "whether or not Communists favor the violent overthrow of the government … can be settled at leisure when the war is over." She affirmed her rejection of traditional civil libertarianism by quitting the ACLU during this period.[32]

Joining the chorus for more restrictions on free speech was *New Republic* editor and the future publisher of the magazine, Michael Straight, who, like Niebuhr and Kirchwey, was an officer in the Union for Democratic Action.

He had also recently been a secret Communist. Straight characterized the "isolationist" newspapers owned by Patterson, Hearst, and McCormick as the "heavy battalions" of "Hitler's guerillas." He led off: "The New York Daily News lays the smoke screen ... Hearst ... brings up the artillery ... Social Justice ... adds its cannon." Straight thought it high time to impose the "censorship which wartime morale demands," such as closing off these publications to interstate commerce. The old clear and present danger doctrine needed to give way to a more general rule barring "destructive criticism."[33]

Less than a month after Straight's call to arms, William L. Shirer, accomplished CBS war correspondent and best-selling author, reiterated many of the same points in the *Atlantic*. While he conceded that Biddle's desire to avoid an "orgy of witch hunting" was a "noble sentiment," it was suicidal in a time of "savage war." Shirer asked, "Why can't a democracy be strong and tough enough to squelch a little minority which is out to destroy it?" Similar to Kirchwey and Straight, Shirer highlighted the fifth-column threat posed by "a few press lords," most notably McCormick, Hearst, and the Pattersons. As an antidote, he called for tightened enforcement of the Espionage Act. Shirer had championed an even harsher approach in March when he was one of three reporters who spoke before a crowd that included such luminaries as Supreme Court Justices Felix Frankfurter and Robert H. Jackson, and several cabinet members, at the Washington, DC, conference of the Overseas Writers Association. A report in the *New York Daily News*, later corroborated in the main details by other sources, including Shirer's diary, stated that "Roosevelt advisors ... applauded lustily such declarations as The American Senate must be taught the facts of life. ... The important thing is to put an end (to criticism of the Roosevelt administration) by whatever means may be necessary—be as ruthless as the enemy. ... Get him on his income tax or the Mann Act. ... Hang him, shoot him or lock him up in a concentration camp." Soon after that, Shirer met with Attorney General Biddle to urge prosecution of McCormick for his "highly treasonable" post–Pearl Harbor editorial commentary in the *Chicago Daily Tribune*. Biddle was cordial but noncommittal.[34]

Of all the articles that appeared in early 1942 urging sanctions against pre–Pearl Harbor critics of intervention, however, none reached a wider audience than "Voices of Defeat," appearing in *Life* magazine in April 1942. *Life* had a circulation of over three million, dwarfing the combined total of about

166,000 for the *Nation*, the *New Republic*, and the *Atlantic*. The lengthy, unsigned featured story centered on marginal Roosevelt-hating groups and individuals in Chicago. Crackpots or not, it asserted that toleration had become a costly luxury in a time of "all-out war for national existence." The article followed a now-familiar pattern of heaping scorn on "defeatists and disunionists," such as the *Chicago Daily Tribune*, for giving "aid and comfort" to these extremists: "[L]aws of free speech contain no provision which permits a little group of spiteful men to indulge in unbridled abuse and falsehood in any attempt to thwart this nation from winning victory over its enemies."[35]

ACLU Director Roger N. Baldwin met this anti–free speech barrage by waging a spirited, and virtually one-person, counterattack. It began with a letter to the editor of the *Nation* in February 1942, challenging the existence of Niebuhr's claimed dichotomy of relativist and absolutist approaches. Commenting wryly that "there just ain't any such animals as absolutists," he stated that nearly all civil libertarians were relativists in the sense that they favored restrictions when speech crossed the line into a clear and present danger. Perhaps with more hope than personal conviction, Baldwin lauded "the professed policy of an Administration which appears to comprehend the essential obligations of democratic liberty in wartime." His letter responding to Kirchwey dismissed her plan as contrary to the Bill of Rights and "as impracticable and dangerous as it is fantastic coming from *The Nation*."[36]

But Baldwin was just getting warmed up. He sent off another letter, which rejected Straight's attempt to lump together the views of outright fascists with those of the large metropolitan newspapers just because they had some argumentative overlap. Millions of mainstream Americans had raised legitimate questions about "whether this is a war to save the British Empire or to aid communism or promote the New Deal." Baldwin might, or might not, have agreed, but he considered such questions perfectly reasonable to ask. He reminded those readers who were inclined to view a negotiated peace as subversive that many pacifists "without a shadow of suspicion of being pro-Axis" also held that position. While "anti-democratic propaganda" was a genuine problem, the best response was ideological "counterattack and exposure."[37]

By this point, however, Baldwin's fight for free speech, backed up occasionally by ACLU counsel Arthur Garfield Hays, was not going well. Most worrisome from his perspective, Biddle was buckling to pressure not only from Roosevelt but from others. A turning point was a cabinet meeting in March 1942. After the president unleashed another tirade against "subversive sheets," Biddle was finally ready to appease him with a suggestion to revoke the second-class mailing status of selected publications under the Espionage Act. Roosevelt liked the idea but also wanted to go further, and quickly. At a press conference soon after the cabinet meeting, the president gave some indication of his mindset when he stated that several unnamed journalists present were "sixth columnists" who were, "wittingly or unwittingly," dupes of the Axis. Subversives of this type never prevailed, he added, unless they had "a vehicle to distribute their poison."[38]

On the next day, Biddle staged a press conference of his own. This was not another of his signature accolades for free speech. Instead, he announced that the Department of Justice intended to file sedition charges soon against publications to be named later. He dismissed the clear and present danger standard as outmoded and vowed, "We are now ready to shoot and we are going to shoot quickly." Biddle soon moved to pull the second-class mailing privileges of several right-wing publications. With one exception, their readership numbered no higher than the low thousands. That exception was Father Coughlin's *Social Justice*, which had a distribution of about two hundred thousand and, not coincidentally, Biddle gave it priority. Working closely with Biddle in this effort were Postmaster General Frank C. Walker and Archibald MacLeish, the head of the Office of Facts and Figures and the chief librarian of the Library of Congress. MacLeish's role, which provides something of a contrast to his comparative willingness to defend the rights of Japanese Americans, was to handle the publicity aspects and to give this campaign further intellectual heft.[39]

The main accusation against *Social Justice* was that it had violated the Espionage Act because of a "substantial contribution to a systematic and unscrupulous attack on the war effort of our nation, both civilian and military." The evidence to back this up was as broad and open-ended as any used by Postmaster General Albert S. Burleson and Attorney General Thomas Gregory, who in World War I had stripped second-class mailing privileges from dozens of publications for impugning "the motives of the government," "improperly" criticizing "our allies," or alleging that "Wall Street or the munitions makers" had undue influence in the government.[40]

With similar vagueness, Biddle cited examples of "parallelism" between *Social Justice* and the propaganda of Axis powers. More specifically, these included "disparagement of the intentions and motives of Great Britain and of the United States" and "frequent attacks upon the war policies of the present government," blaming the war on "international bankers," expressing doubts about the United Nations, or predicting that rationing presaged a totalitarian society.[41]

Despite rather obvious evidence of prosecutorial overreach by Biddle, the media response to this action was overwhelmingly favorable. An editorial in the *Christian Science Monitor* was, more or less, representative: "[T]he Government is not obliged to provide the facilities of distribution to any publication which seems to undermine it or which abuses the freedoms the Nation is fighting to preserve." The *Nation* depicted the case against *Social Justice* as open-and-shut: "Father Coughlin cannot possibly cry persecution, since every safeguard of the democratic process was put at his disposal." But almost no one doubted that Roosevelt had forced Biddle's hand. Popular columnist Drew Pearson, who had long assailed the attorney general for "temporizing with native Fascist champions," said that Biddle had only acted because of the president's "personal orders." Similarly, *Time* declared, "Finally, the President could wait no longer. He told Attorney General Biddle to rise up and smite all heathen idolaters. Francis Biddle, stiffening, lifted up his voice and spoke."[42]

A few prominent press outlets and public figures dissented from the near consensus. The *Los Angeles Times* saw it as "better to err on the side of liberality than of gag imposition." Similarly, columnist David Lawrence, the publisher of *U.S. News* (later *U.S. News & World Report*), asserted that the government's action created a climate of fear that "let all newspapers know that any of them may suddenly be denied the use of the mails if their editorial contents do not satisfy the opinions of the Postmaster General on national politics." New Deal apostate Raymond Moley, then a regular columnist for *Newsweek*, who had several years earlier assailed Black's seizure of private telegrams, warned of a further drift into "dangerous ideological waters."[43]

Predictably, the Communist Party and its allies were delighted with Biddle's turnaround and hoped for more. The time was opportune, according to a pamphlet published by the party, to jail Father Coughlin and expel from

Congress such "fifth columnists" as Hamilton Fish (R-NY) and Martin Dies (D-TX). For good measure, it proposed a crackdown on "the treasonable activity of the Norman Thomases and Trotskyites." The New York chapter of the National Lawyers Guild backed the action against *Social Justice*, as did Representative Marcantonio, who wanted to suppress all subversive talk from the "internal enemies of our war effort." Alongside pictures of McCormick, Hearst, and Patterson, who were "spreading defeatism and distrust of our President and Commander in Chief," an article in the *New Masses* asked, "What About Them Mr. Biddle?" Somewhat ironically, the publication was named in homage to the defunct magazine *The Masses*, which had fought a losing battle in World War I against federal restrictions on its mailing rights under the Espionage Act.[44]

MacLeish's contribution to Biddle's effort, though somewhat indirect, was perhaps the boldest of all. He laid it out in high-profile speeches before two major media forums: the American Society of Newspaper Editors (April 17) and the Associated Press (April 20). He said relatively little about *Social Justice* or other small right-wing publications but instead presented the case that the major anti-Roosevelt metropolitan newspapers were the most dangerous purveyors of subversive and seditious ideas.

The press liberally quoted MacLeish's characterization of the articles published by the "venal editors" of these "defeatist" newspapers as something "close to treason." He left no doubt that the main offender, in his view, was the *Chicago Daily Tribune*, a purveyor of "newspaper propaganda [which] aimed to divide our people from the Russian people or the British people at this moment of real and present danger." The *Tribune* lurked in "that ambiguous and doubtful shadow where freedom of expression darkens into treason." The "loyal and honest press" had a moral obligation to "police" the defeatist press through "journalistic ambush" and ostracism. While MacLeish denied that he favored suppression of these papers, his other comments, not to mention his past (but unpublicized) role in Biddle's revocation plan, indicate otherwise. Also indicating otherwise was his warning that if the press did not clean itself up, it might become a "necessity of a policing by government, which neither government nor the press desires."[45]

Not surprisingly, this broad-brush attack greatly alarmed civil libertarians and prewar advocates of nonintervention. They had warned that the prosecution of *Social Justice* was just an entering wedge and that the government had bigger game in its sights. Now, they appeared to have confirmation. In a letter to Arthur Garfield Hays, Raymond Moley confessed that MacLeish's comments gave him "cold shivers about this so-called liberal government." The most prominent objector was Senator Robert A. Taft (R-OH), who accused MacLeish of orchestrating "a suppression of critics, who admittedly do not violate the sedition law, by a species of Lynch law." The overarching goal, Taft alleged, was to chill dissent by casting aspersions on the patriotism of those daring "to suggest that the conduct of the war can be improved."[46]

The federal government's campaign against *Social Justice* was a major moment of truth for free speech, and the ACLU blinked. The only protest it was able to muster was a tepid letter from Baldwin and Hays to the postmaster general. In its lack of forcefulness, it resembled the equally weak protest letter criticizing anti-Japanese American policies less than a month earlier. While Baldwin and Hays carefully disassociated themselves from the content of *Social Justice*, they warned of a precedent for other kinds of censorship that went "beyond the merits of this particular case." The ACLU as an organization showed no inclination to go any further. If it had not purged Communist Party members from its leadership in January 1940, it might not have even managed this diluted defense of free speech. Some self-described civil libertarians did not want to do that much. The Massachusetts Civil Liberties Union, a group that, as the state affiliate of the ACLU, had included such civil liberties icons as Baldwin and Chafee, loudly praised the government's action on the creatively strained rationale that the procedure enabled *Social Justice* "to be tried before a jury."[47]

Much like it was doing with reference to the internment of Japanese Americans, the Hays and Baldwin faction continued to press the ACLU to stand up against the government's suppressive policies, but others in the organization stood in their way. A typical example of the latter was longtime ACLU supporter Henry S. Canby, who was also the editor of the *Saturday Review of Literature*. When Baldwin forwarded a petition protesting the government's measures against *Social Justice*, Canby responded that, while he normally opposed censorship, he favored "proper legal action being taken to stop a paper which repeats foreign propaganda." As with internment, the most serious obstacle to Baldwin, Hays, and their allies was the Morris Ernst faction. The very well-connected Ernst was a confidant of top administration officials, including Roosevelt, with whom he carried on a voluminous correspondence.[48]

Ernst's backstage machinations both diluted possible ACLU opposition to Roosevelt's suppressive tendencies and actively fostered those tendencies. Only days after Biddle had moved against *Social Justice*, Ernst reported to the president that, along with the attorney general and a Department of Treasury official, he had worked up a plan to examine the tax returns of "America First, Coughlin, et al." Preferring to stay in the background, he was "content if Biddle's boys can run the show, they will get a bunch of indictments before the Summer. And I don't mean of little people." Ernst portrayed tax probes as necessary adjuncts to the ongoing sedition investigation. In June, he reported to Roosevelt that Maloney, the prosecutor, "was delighted to learn that tax returns of these organizations were available." These plans came to naught, however, when Biddle informed a disappointed chief executive that the Department of the Treasury had found no irregularities.[49]

The *Progressive* magazine was exceptional on the left in standing against this trend for more restrictions on free speech. With the full backing of two of its columnists, Oswald Garrison Villard and Milton Mayer, it forcefully condemned Biddle's revocation as an entrée for "arbitrary censorship over any periodical delivered through the mails." Few publications were more assertive than the *Progressive* in upholding civil liberty during the war, including for Japanese Americans. This uncompromising stance was a stark contrast from the 1930s, when the magazine had belittled the free speech and privacy concerns of "reactionaries" who had stood in the way of the Black and Minton committees. One change in the interim was that the La Follette family, who continued to be foreign-policy noninterventionists until Pearl Harbor, had reasserted full control from the previous co-owner and editor, William Evjue, who had supported Roosevelt's foreign policy.[50]

Contrary to what most observers expected, the *Social Justice* case did not culminate in a dramatic showdown at the Post Office Department hearing between Coughlin and the government. Although the ever-truculent radio priest was spoiling for a fight, Biddle and others in the administration successfully conspired with Leo Crowley, a prominent Catholic friend of the president, to head him off. After Biddle warned that an indictment risked "a rift that would do infinite harm to the war effort," Crowley successfully interceded with church fathers to silence Coughlin. In May 1942, Coughlin's surrogate at *Social Justice* voluntarily surrendered the magazine's second-class mailing status without a fight.[51]

Meanwhile, Roosevelt kept pressing for harsher measures against his critics. On April 22, 1942, he cautioned Biddle about the "subversive mind of Cissy Patterson." Six days later, FDR's fireside chat underscored that "this great war effort … must not be impeded by a few bogus patriots who use the sacred freedom of the press to echo sentiments of the propagandists in Tokyo and Berlin." This was not mere rhetoric. The following day Assistant Attorney General James H. Rowe Jr., Biddle's protégé in the Department of Justice, who was also leery, at least compared to Roosevelt, of limiting civil liberties, fretted that "signs are clear our actions are far from satisfactory" to the president.[52]

A source of this tension was that Biddle and Rowe had different priorities than Roosevelt. Much more than them, the president regarded the suppression of *Social Justice* as a small opening act rather than the end goal. Sending Biddle some clippings from the *Chicago Daily Tribune*, the *New York Daily News*, and the Hearst newspapers, Roosevelt called for stepped-up sedition prosecutions so as "to let the whole country know the truth about these papers. The tie-in between the attitude of these papers and the Rome-Berlin broadcasts is something far greater than mere coincidence." Although Biddle tried to hold the president off, he later observed that the major outlets in "the isolationist press, particularly the Chicago Tribune," had published articles that were "probably as seditious as anything put out by *Social Justice*, although they were not anti-Semitic or rabble-rousing." After some presidential prodding, he had the Department of Justice conduct an analysis of the papers. It concluded that the articles did not reflect or follow German propaganda, and the government took no further action against the publications.[53]

There was a partial exception, however, to Biddle's reticence to prosecute the "big fish." In June 1942, the Department of Justice began investigating the *Chicago Daily Tribune* for possible violation of the Espionage Act. The case centered on a June 7, 1942, front-page story by reporter Stanley

Johnson that had also appeared in the Patterson-owned *Washington Times-Herald* and the *New York Daily News* on the Battle of Midway, revealing that American military authorities had advance knowledge of the size of the Japanese attack force. While the story did not report that the United States had broken the Japanese naval code, that was a natural inference for an enemy agent. Before submitting the story, Johnson asked the managing editor, Loy "Pat" Maloney, and Washington Bureau Chief Arthur Sears Henning if the content violated the Code of Wartime Practices, which governed censorship decisions. Henning, who was thoroughly familiar with the rules, assured him that it did not, as did Maloney. At the time, the code said nothing about the movement of enemy ships in enemy waters.[54]

Administration officials were not about to give publisher Robert R. McCormick the benefit of the doubt, however. In the heat of the moment, Roosevelt even wanted to deploy the Marines to occupy the Tribune Tower. At his suggestion, the Department of Justice empaneled a grand jury and selected a respected veteran prosecutor. The case imploded when the navy failed to provide promised evidence that Johnson's story had exposed "confidential information concerning the Battle of Midway." Much like his experience with the conviction of the Socialist Workers Party defendants, Biddle confessed years later that he "felt like a fool." Even had the case moved forward, prosecutors faced a high bar of proving willful intent.[55]

Biddle may have felt like a fool for overreach against the *Chicago Daily Tribune*, but he was still getting tremendous pressure not only from the president but also from the pro–New Deal press to do something about the "Patterson-McCormick Axis." No daily publication was more active on that front than *PM*. It showed particular animus toward its powerful rival in New York, Joe Patterson's *New York Daily News*, and, beginning in the summer of 1942, it became almost obsessive. On July 20, *PM* editorialized optimistically that the recent indictment of seditionists could provide "precedents" for action against that newspaper. Several weeks later, it featured a cartoon by Theodor Geisel (Dr. Seuss) depicting a tank (emblazoned on the front with the words "Cissy, Bertie, & Joe") mowing down people with the caption "Still Spraying Our Side with Disunity Gas!" According to historian Paul Milkman, the pages of *PM* during this period showed "an alarming absence of concern for civil liberties."[56]

Ironically, perhaps, until the summer of 1940, there had been some close parallels between the *New York Daily News* and *PM* in editorial content and political ideals, as well as in their tabloid format. Both had loyally supported the New Deal, and even on foreign policy, they were not entirely at odds. Until mid-1940, each generally backed the president but also, in some cases, expressed leeriness about deeper US involvement. Although *PM* and the *Daily News* rapidly diverged on foreign policy after mid-1940, each gave a preelection endorsement of Roosevelt. A key difference between the newspapers was in the size and nature of the subscriber base. The *Daily News*, at only two cents per issue and an average daily circulation of 2.25 million, was centered on the masses, while *PM*, at a nickel per issue and a daily circulation hovering at its height between 150,000 and 165,000, catered more to the New Deal elite. As Milkman details, "*PM* was read daily by at least three Supreme Court justices, by several cabinet officers, by the vice president, and by the first lady who plugged it in her newspaper column in the Scripps-Howard press." President Roosevelt was both an avid reader and a fan, so much so that he pressured a reluctant Biddle to amass a file of clippings from the newspaper as evidence for possible legal action against other publications. *PM*'s editor, Ralph M. Ingersoll, met privately with the president several times. In one hour-long conclave between the two, Roosevelt ordered his secretary to hold his calls so he could pitch stories to Ingersoll.[57]

Biddle continued to resist any legal moves against the *New York Daily News* and the rest of the "Press Axis," but, relying on the *Social Justice* precedent, he had the Department of Justice, in cooperation with the Post Office, move rapidly to revoke the second-class mailing status of three additional, and much smaller, publications: the *X-Ray*, *Publicity*, and the German language *Philadelphia Herold*. All, to varying degrees, mixed right-wing and anti-Semitic content with attacks on Roosevelt's conduct of the war. The government's standard procedure was, first, to summarily revoke second-class mailing status, second, to give the publisher a few days to "show cause" for reversing same, and third, to hold a hearing several weeks later before a special board of the Post Office Department in Washington, DC. It then ruled on any objections by publishers and decided whether to make the revocation permanent. Only one of the publications, the *X-Ray*, bothered to send a representative to any of these hearings, and he had no success. The hearing process, as Richard W. Steele points out, did not entail "an adversarial proceeding" and the results were predetermined. The government also banned individual issues of nine additional publications from the mail. By contrast, in the World War I era, Postmaster General Albert E. Burleson, with the assent of Attorney General Thomas Gregory, restricted the mailing rights of about seventy-five publications. Of these, the Post Office Department suspended the second-class privilege of twenty-two Socialist papers, four of them dailies.[58]

These comparatively lower numbers in World War II revocations, at least if taken in isolation, did not mean that the government had liberalized its standards for protecting free speech. There were just fewer likely prospects. L. M. C. Smith, the head of the Special War Policies Unit, commented after the first wave of revocations in early 1942 that the number of possible cases was becoming "thinner and thinner." Smith, who disagreed with Biddle's new tougher line, wanted to limit this punishment to publications that had willfully collaborated with the Axis.[59]

Illustrative of just how much the "seditionist" herd had thinned was the government's stated reasoning for revoking the second-class mailing rights of the *Boise Valley Herald* (September 1942) and the *Militant* (March 1943), the final two publications to endure this fate. Few legal actions during this period provide more compelling evidence of prosecutorial overreach, even by the standards of the time. Although each publication was marginal in circulation and influence, both have outsized importance when judging the accuracy of the "good war" characterization. Because of the weaknesses in the government's cases, and because both shunned anti-Semitism and racism, they were the only publications on Biddle's list that secured legal counsel from the ACLU.

By some measures, the *Boise Valley Herald*, a weekly from Middleton, Idaho (population 477 in 1940), was a typical small-town newspaper. Published by Adelbert Cornell (who also was the editor), assisted by his sons Irving and Boyd, the paper featured a stable of like-minded regular columnists. Adelbert, the self-described "daylight farmer and lamplight editor" of a "little village paper," ran daily operations while Boyd Cornell sometimes contributed copy. Most of the news consisted of such routine fare as births, deaths, and weddings. The Cornells were lucky when they broke even.[60]

The content of the paper showed no hint of the xenophobia or racism that generally characterized other publications on Biddle's revocation list. ACLU board member and attorney Dorothy Kenyon, later a mentor to Supreme Court Justice Ruth Bader Ginsburg, reported that the editor did not have "a scintilla of Nazism in his make-up, is neither anti-semitic, anti-international banker, pro-fascist, or any of the rest of the things that stamp him of being an agent of Hitler." Biddle himself never really claimed otherwise. Norman Thomas stated that based on his knowledge, "the editors are decent enough Americans, not in collusion with enemy powers." The *Boise Valley Herald*, in fact, was unusual among American newspapers, progressive or otherwise, in so vigorously condemning Japanese American internment. It also reprinted articles by such promoters of racial justice as Bayard Rustin, praised A. Philip Randolph's March on Washington Movement, and blasted discrimination against African Americans in the criminal justice system. According to Brent Cornell, his grandfather Adelbert "identified with them because the little people were facing an established regime that would stack the deck against them if someone wasn't calling attention to it."[61]

The political views of the Cornells are not easy to locate on a right and left spectrum. The paper's content had much to please, and much to alienate, people from all political persuasions. Responding to an ACLU query in 1942, Idaho Secretary of State George H. Curtis guessed that the Cornells were vaguely leftist, in part because they had helped him in an effort to repeal an anti-syndicalism law. The paper had praised Eugene Debs and Norman Thomas, though usually for their civil libertarianism and opposition to war. It also gave lip service to an eventual transition to "social ownership" but was not too specific on what this meant. At the same time, the editorials repeatedly attacked the New Deal for "Tammanyizing the nation" and imposing "regimentation" through such measures as the National Recovery Administration and the Agricultural Adjustment Act. The two most consistent themes, however, were support for civil libertarianism (Adelbert Cornell was a longtime ACLU member) and foreign policy noninterventionism. In the run-up to the US declaration of war, the paper favorably covered the efforts of the America First Committee.[62]

Despite their willingness to court controversy, the Cornells had achieved a high degree of respectability, and the *Boise Valley Herald* was a well-established source of local pride. Curtis guessed that the people of Middleton "understand the Cornells, like and honor them and pay little attention to their radicalism." Yet at least part of what they said resonated in the community. As Curtis reported, that area of Idaho "was something of a hot bed for America First propaganda last year." Brent Cornell elaborates that the "people in Middletown knew the Cornells as good people and they really didn't put a lot of emphasis on my granddad's opinion, but there were people who were resentful. Somebody threw some yellow paint on the front of the newspaper office." The fact that the Cornells were not just armchair crusaders might have sharpened the government's animus. Two of Adelbert's sons had gone to jail for refusing to register for the peacetime draft in 1940.[63]

Even a cursory reading of Biddle's arguments for pulling the second-class mailing rights of the *Boise Valley Herald* will do some damage to his reputation as a voice for tolerance and restraint. One of his main objections against the paper was that it opposed "all wars on religious and moral grounds." Biddle even went so far as to say that the paper's point of view far exceeded "in strength and inflammatory character" that of *Social Justice*. As illustration, he excerpted fourteen "representative" quotations from January 1942 to August 1942. These included claims that the US embargo on Japan had helped provoke the Pearl Harbor attack, that income tax withholding imposed an onerous burden on the poor, and that the wartime mobilization was suppressing "individuality." Also featured on Biddle's list were two editorials by Adelbert Cornell. One led off: "The nation is at war. War is national madness. Every day madness continues values of all kinds are being destroyed." Another attacked British policy in India for "safeguarding the investments of those who declare wars for subservient people and classes to fight."[64]

Biddle's allegations against the *Boise Valley Herald* were more reminiscent in character of those of a Burleson or Gregory than of a civil libertarian. A case in point was Biddle's reliance on the paper's statements opposing discrimination against Japanese Americans and internment (policies he himself had privately criticized) as evidence of sedition. One article from March 5, 1942, accused the FBI of "pulling a typical Nazi stunt in this section of Idaho in the form and manner of raiding and searching the homes of every Japanese resident within many miles of Caldwell." This was not an abstract issue for the Cornells, who had positive personal and business relationships with Japanese truck farmers in the area. Although Japanese Americans in Idaho, unlike those on the West Coast, were not interned, they still faced extensive discrimination.[65]

One of Biddle's "representative" excerpts on this issue, however, was a spectacular illustration of ripping a quotation out of context. Here is the entire selection from Biddle's report: "Thank you Japanese ladies. Even the acting officials of a 'spoiled' setup of political racketeering will usually feel the sting of their inferior department when brought face to face with true human dignity that sneaks in the kindly tone that is characteristic of the culture of our Japanese neighbors. If our young Americans would absorb more of Japanese culture, character and courage in maintaining their civic rights, there would be less servile obedience to obscene and oppressive laws and far more home for America's future national prestige."[66]

A casual reader might interpret this as a paean to imperial Japan, but that was not true. The whole point of the editorial, titled "Young Japanese Do Honor to Citizenship," was to laud the liberty-loving behavior of local Japanese Americans. The omitted introduction, which gave the necessary context, recounted an altercation between a policeman and two Japanese American women. After following their car for some time, the officer drove alongside and gave the signal to pull over. When the driver did not immediately respond, the officer sounded his siren until she complied. After he asked her where the two were going, she replied "that they were American citizens and were quite within their rights and being so were exercising their daily pursuits as law-abiding people. The official saw the point and excused and apologized."[67]

Because of the uncertainty created by the loss of the *Boise Valley Herald*'s second-class mailing status, frightened local postmasters sometimes denied mailings for third-class, and even first-class, status if a return address was visible. Nevertheless, Adelbert Cornell defiantly pressed forward, seizing the chance, though in a rather good-natured way, of doing his bit for free speech. He arranged delivery by hand (much of it done by other members of the Cornell family) for local readers and sent "boot-leg" copies without a return address and in sealed envelopes to out-of-towners. Contingent on sufficient interest, he hoped to collect together and reprint all of the alleged seditious content in pamphlet form. He suggested, half seriously, that it "might be valuable to writers who wish to avoid the pains and penalties of the law, as a hand-book of forms of what 'not' to write for publication."[68]

The *Boise Valley Herald* affair produced barely a ripple of media coverage. Just about the only national publication to oppose, much less comment on, the revocation was the *Socialist Call* of Norman Thomas's Socialist Party. Some of the kindest words for the Cornells in the press came from those who knew them best: the *Idaho Statesman* from neighboring Boise and the *Idaho Free Press* in nearby Nampa. The *Idaho Statesman* commented that the "cantankerous Cornells … are no traitors. … What damage can be done by a shoestring weekly in Middleton, Idaho? … Out in the open they are harmless. Leave them there to squawk." Similarly, though the *Idaho Free Press* had backed Roosevelt's foreign policy before Pearl Harbor, it defended protecting the free speech rights of the Cornells, "assuming that the U.S. Constitution is still in effect."[69]

When an ACLU-recruited lawyer, Sol L. Alpher, agreed to represent the paper before the Post Office Department Board, ACLU Chief Counsel Clifford Forster warned him what he was up against: "Apparently, the boys in Justice are dead set against the newspaper even though it is a relatively unimportant one." At the hearing, Alpher rejected the government's claims that the paper presented a clear and present danger, stating that it had not aided the enemy, nor had it tried to obstruct the war effort. Alpher mostly emphasized, however, that the *Boise Valley Herald* was too marginal a publication to have any impact on the war effort.[70]

After the largely pro forma hearing, the government not only reaffirmed the original decision but left unsettled the question of whether the paper still retained first- and third-class mailing rights. Finally, in December, Assistant Postmaster General Vincent M. Miles indicated that third-class mailings were permissible, though copies had to be sent to his office for review. But Miles stated that "should any violation of the law result from the deposit of this matter in the mails, the person who mailed or caused the matter to be mailed will have to bear full responsibility." He added cryptically that the paper's full rights might be restored upon removal of content deemed objectionable. On this point, Adelbert Cornell continued to hold to his original unyielding position: "I'm not going to appease an obscene law by religiously observing it. A man can't do so and preserve the dignity of man."[71]

Biddle may have felt special disdain for the *Boise Valley Herald* precisely because it was not an ordinary pacifist publication. Instead of putting priority on calling for pacifists to make purely symbolic gestures or to seek a special conscientious objection exemption, the paper aggressively pushed a specific pro-peace political agenda. The paper's radical pacifism challenged the foreign policy status quo through specific proposals such as "Peace Without Victory." It was equally assertive in exposing the underside of wartime mobilization such as racism and governmental regimentation. Brent Cornell speculates, but it is only speculation, that the governor, who had pronounced anti-Japanese American views, might have "ratted them out."[72]

When Biddle pulled the second-class mailing status of the *Militant*, he was attacking a familiar adversary: the Socialist Workers Party. As solicitor general, he had helped engineer the conviction of the leaders of that organization on sedition charges. Given Biddle's later expression of remorse for his role in that case, his readiness to revisit that matter seems strange. His rationale for revocation was almost the same as that used against the *Boise Valley Herald*. The *Militant*, according to Biddle, was "permeated with the thesis that the war is being fought solely for the benefit of the ruling groups and will serve merely to continue the enslavement of the working classes. ... the lines [quoted from the *Militant* in the government's complaint] also include derision of democracy, stimulation of race issues and other material ... appearing to be calculated to engender opposition to the war effort as well as to interfere with the morale of the armed forces."[73]

Following the pattern set by the *Boise Valley Herald*, the government's complaint reproduced twenty-six allegedly seditious quotations. Perhaps the most inflammatory, at least from the perspective of the attorney general and postmaster general, was from December 27, 1941: "When we state that this is an imperialist war, it follows that we cannot possibly support the administration in its war effort." Other quotations included criticisms of the four freedoms policy as a hypocritical ploy to protect the British Empire, wartime wage reductions, limits on labor organizing, and continuing racism toward African Americans. To Postmaster General Frank C. Walker, statements of this type represented "a consistent, sustained and systematic feature of many consecutive issues of this publication, which, by plain import of language, show clearly a purposed attempt 'to embarrass and defeat the Government in its effort to prosecute the war to a successful termination.'"[74]

Absent from these selected excerpts, as in the case of the *Boise Valley Herald*, was evidence of any incitement to insubordination, giving aid or comfort to the enemy, or promoting fascism. The paper's disparaging comments on the war were mainly abstract rather than a specific call to obstruct its conduct. For the *Militant*, the war was just another in a long line of fratricidal capitalist conflicts that impeded working-class unity. The ACLU contended that the government had failed to demonstrate that the *Militant* had encouraged "any obstruction to the draft," much less had shown "connection or sympathy with the enemy." Instead, it had expressed "long standing Marxist views."[75]

The press showed far more interest in, and sympathy for, the *Militant*'s plight than that suffered by the *Boise Valley Herald*. Rejecting out of hand any attempt to compare the *Militant* with *Social Justice*, the *Nation* stated that the former had merely stated in a general sense the theory that capitalistic wars led to "an imperialist bloodbath," while the latter had "hindered the war effort not by forthright opposition to it but the dissemination of pro-Axis propaganda, including anti-Semitism and deliberate lies." Forgetting, or more likely unaware of, the example provided by the *Boise Valley Herald*, the *Nation* considered the *Militant* "more directly comparable to that of the legitimate pacifist groups which the government wisely ignored." As with the *Socialist Workers Party* sedition case in 1941, the *Chicago Daily Tribune* was dubious about the government's intentions and pointed to the apparent double standard of giving a free pass to Communist publications yet suppressing the publications of their Marxist rivals. It concluded that the owners of and writers for the *Militant*, unlike those of the *Daily Worker*, were "genuine and honest expositors of Lenin communism and not agents of a foreign government."[76]

The hearing before the Post Office Department Board in March not only brought predictable defeat for the *Militant* but also put on full display the embarrassingly flimsy nature of the government's case. Post Office attorney William C. O'Brien branded an article as seditious solely because it accurately reported the carnage of a battle in the Solomon Islands. "It does not make any difference if everything the Militant said is true," he declared. "We believe that anyone violates the Espionage Act who holds up and dwells on the horrors of war with the effect that enlistment is discouraged by readers."[77]

This was too much even for the normally complacent *New York Times*, which commented that if "the O'Brien thesis is sustained, any criticism of the conduct of the war—for instance, the assertion that 'island-hopping' in the Pacific involves a needless waste of life—would be punishable." Nevertheless, the *Times* softened this criticism somewhat by expressing confidence that neither Biddle nor Walker shared this view. Had the *New York Times* further scrutinized the reasoning in the government's case against both papers, it may have revised that charitable assessment of both men.[78]

The official complaints against the *Boise Valley Herald* and the *Militant* will not make for pleasant reading for subscribers to the theory that World War II was a "good war," or at least not a bad war, for free speech. The accusations against them closely mirrored in character those leveled against numerous publications in World War I by Burleson and Gregory. The parallels were even closer in other ways. The *Boise Valley Herald* was in a category similar to the pacifist or moderately socialist pro-peace publications that the federal government repressed in World War I, such as the *Masses* and the *Milwaukee Leader*. It expressed a no-holds-barred peace perspective rejecting all wars as immoral, shunned violent revolutionary change (even in the abstract), and never showed any sympathy with the enemy. The *Militant*, on the other hand, approximated the same leftist and revolutionary mold as the *Industrial Worker* of the Industrial Workers of the World. The third category, represented by the likes of *Social Justice*, did not really exist in World War I.[79]

While the numbers show that far fewer publications in World War II had their mailing status revoked compared to World War I, this is a somewhat misleading metric because the standard for coming under the government's hammer was essentially the same in both wars. What had changed, however, was that after December 7, 1941, publications like the *Boise Valley Herald* and the *Militant* had become much more exceptional. Put another way, the federal government did not bring nearly the same number of cases because far fewer fish were available to be caught in the same nets.

As the federal government was taking legal action against the *Boise Valley Herald*, the *Militant*, and various right-wing publications, it was subjecting black newspapers, many with far higher circulation, to intense scrutiny and pressure. Historian Patrick S. Washburn, the leading authority on this topic, concludes that "the black press was in extreme danger of being suppressed until June 1942." It was not surprising that these publications came under legal pressure. Quite a few black newspapers had tirelessly documented Jim Crow conditions in the military, federal medical facilities, and defense industries, and acts of violence against black troops, as well as selective and hypocritical enforcement of the four freedoms. These were the stories their readers wanted. When William Hastie, who had been the first African American federal judge and was then dean of the law school at Howard University, asked fifty-six black leaders at a meeting in New York only a month after Pearl Harbor to summarize the general attitudes of African Americans, a stunning thirty-six said that most did not completely support the war effort.[80]

Both black journalists and activists had a determination to avoid a repetition of the uncritical "Close Ranks" strategy that W. E. B. DuBois had advocated in World War I. Even the more moderate *Crisis* magazine of the NAACP agreed that "now is the time not to be silent about the breaches of democracy here in our own land." This idea found its most concrete application a month later in the Double V campaign (fighting for democracy simultaneously at home and abroad) popularized by the *Pittsburgh Courier*. The tenor of this reporting was almost guaranteed to get under the skin of top administration officials. On April 27, 1942, Archibald MacLeish, always ready to volunteer to be a federal watchdog, forwarded to Biddle articles from the *Washington* (DC) *Afro American* that had "seditious implications." He suggested "a very useful preventive effect, if your department could somehow call attention to the fact that the Negro press enjoys no immunity." A month later, Roosevelt urged both Biddle and Walker to personally admonish black editors to cease "their subversive language."[81]

Matters came to a head when Biddle summoned John H. Sengstacke, the publisher of the *Chicago Defender* and the president of the National Newspaper Publishers Association (NNPA), an African American group. Placed on the table before him were copies of several leading black papers, including the *Defender*, the *Baltimore Afro-American*, and the *Pittsburgh Courier*. Characterizing these as seditious, Biddle warned that the government was "going to shut them all up." The discussion continued to heat up, but Sengstacke calmly held his ground. He then suggested a compromise. He said that the newspapers might be willing to tone down their criticism if the government agreed both not to issue indictments and to give black journalists more access.[82]

Biddle gave his verbal assent to this compromise, and for the rest of the war, the Department of Justice did not bring any indictments or other formal legal action. Black publishers fulfilled their part of the bargain. A federal study of content in the *Pittsburgh Courier*, for example, showed that the paper devoted considerably less space to the Double V campaign in April 1943 compared to August 1942. Moreover, the main targets of negative coverage over that period shifted to local government and private business and away from the federal government. Several months later, a Post Office Department inspector said that heightened federal scrutiny had led to a considerable weakening in "the vigorness [sic] of its complaints" about discrimination.[83]

The application of the Biddle–Sengstacke compromise proved one-sided in the government's favor, however. Contrary to Biddle's promise, the authorities did not become more cooperative in the sharing of information with the black press. In late 1942, Sengstacke complained that the attitude of "administrative officials in Washington to date is far from being encouraging." He was beginning to question if "the government really wants sincere cooperation or whether there are clandestine forces working against the interest of a section of the Negro Press."[84]

While federal authorities did not bring legal charges against the black press for the balance of the war, neither did they shift to a hands-off approach. To the contrary, they ratcheted up both intense monitoring and informal pressure. In the first half of 1942 alone, FBI agents visited leading black newspapers that had carried critical stories about the federal government. In addition, Post Office Department inspectors admonished both the *Chicago Defender* and *New York Amsterdam News* in June 1942 that the "benefits of citizenship" carried an obligation not to "'play up' isolated and rare instances in such a fashion as to obstruct recruiting and in other ways hamper the war effort."[85]

On occasion, the government came close to moving to the next stage of initiating more formal legal action. In early 1942, the Department of Justice complained to the Office of War Information (OWI) about George S. Schuyler's articles in the *Pittsburgh Courier*. Rated as particularly offensive was his complaint that the status quo offered no hope for "liberty, equality, and fraternity" and that the "Negrophobic philosophy, originating in the South, had become the official policy of the government." In commenting on the article, the department urged that OWI take "action" against the paper, though, apparently, it did not do this.[86]

In the end, however, informal pressure suited the government's purposes far better than outright legal punishment. Some evidence for this being true was a revealing observation in May 1942 by Lucius C. Harper, the executive director of the *Chicago Defender*. Harper concluded that if the *Defender* had voiced opinions that were as incendiary as those in the Patterson-McCormick papers, "it would be paid a visit from the postmaster general and told to tone it down considerably or find some other way to circulate the paper." Of course, at this time, there was much speculation about a sedition prosecution against the *Chicago Daily Tribune*.[87]

Informal pressure proved a win-win strategy for the federal government. A Department of Justice analysis concluded that the likely result of declaring unmailable "a paper as prominent and as respected by the Negro population as the Pittsburgh Courier" would be "further unrest and possibly [arousing] a spirit of defeatism among the Negro population." A highly public and contentious prosecution of a black newspaper posed risks of driving away black votes from Roosevelt in key Northern states. Because the *Courier* had the highest circulation of all black newspapers in the United States and had provided crucial past support for Roosevelt, the potential political risks of revoking its mailing status were much higher compared to more marginal outlets like the *X-Ray*, the *Boise Valley Herald*, or the *Militant*.[88]

The use of statistical measures to assess the comparative severity, or lack thereof, of press restrictions in World War II often obscures more than it reveals. Any free speech improvements compared to World War I usually occurred despite, not because of, the president's desires. Roosevelt was not demonstratively more protective of civil liberties than Wilson, and when it came to Japanese Americans, he was less so.

A more compelling explanation for the apparent greater federal tolerance in World War II was a paucity of remotely viable prospects for conviction.

A minute percentage of the press after Pearl Harbor was "seditious" by any criteria prevailing in the legal community. At the same time, the courts, reflecting the views of that community, were more likely than their World War I predecessors to constrain the more anti–free speech instincts of the administration in power. The government's first major case, *United States v. Prout*, failed spectacularly. While it was more successful in the second case, which was brought against members of the Socialist Workers Party, the effect generated much press criticism and the defendants received relatively light sentences.[89]

Although the Department of Justice resisted presidential pressure, Biddle did finally crack down on *Social Justice* and the smaller fry. After that, he considerably lowered the bar for determining guilt to a standard reminiscent of World War I to get successful outcomes. Some of Biddle's subordinates, such as L. M. C. Smith, were far more sensitive to civil liberties than he was. In both wars, most of the publications found to be seditious did not rise anywhere close to the "clear and present danger" level in seriousness. Also, Biddle's efforts to head off a revival of super-patriotic local vigilantism and aggressive local prosecution were not as civil libertarian as sometimes depicted. While these motivations were not entirely absent, another goal was to deter private organizations and local governments from challenging the federal "monopoly on repression," more than to protect free speech as such."[90]

When African American newspapers became too strenuous in attacking wartime discriminatory policies, the federal government, for both political and practical reasons, relied on informal pressure to keep them in line. This method was often more effective in blocking critical content. While the threat of newspaper bans and mailing revocations had greatly diminished by late 1943, the looming sedition mass trial, which was to have profound implications for civil liberties, was just starting to formally get underway.

9

The Forgotten Sedition-Trial Fiasco

JUST AS THE federal government's campaign (launched mainly at the behest of President Roosevelt) to deny mailing rights to allegedly seditious periodicals was petering out, the largest mass trial in the history of Washington, DC, *United States v. McWilliams*, was beginning. The trial, despite its ignominious conclusion, had long-lasting, but unintended, consequences. Over the subsequent decade, *McWilliams* served as precedent for high-profile investigations of Communists, which began soon after the *McWilliams* trial was over.

Although the judge did not gavel the trial itself to order until 1944, the genesis of the case was a pre–Pearl Harbor grand jury investigation under federal prosecutor William Power Maloney. The initial target was George Sylvester Viereck, a German American poet and essayist who, by the late 1930s, was the leading publicist for Nazi Germany in the US. In October 1941, the jury indicted him for filing improperly under the Foreign Agents Registration Act. Maloney used leads from that case to begin assembling a list of possible defendants in multiple states. He wanted to try them together in Washington, DC.[1]

But Maloney's ambitious plan had little chance without evidence that these individuals had worked together in a coordinated conspiracy occurring, at least in part, in Washington, DC. Enter Dillard Stokes, a reporter from the *Washington Post*. Stokes, with the committed backing of his employer, set out to help prosecutors make this link by gathering up allegedly subversive literature and writing sympathetic letters (postmarked in Washington, DC) to the authors. Under the aliases of Jefferson Breem and

Quigley Adams, he enticed the recipients to supply literature and various juicy tidbits for Maloney to use as evidence and to justify venue in Washington, DC.[2]

News of a grand jury indictment of twenty-eight defendants on July 23, 1942, created a national media sensation. The charges were conspiracy to "publish, to convey to and urge upon members of the military ... for the purpose of obstructing, and designed and intended to impede, obstruct and defeat the preparation" of the war effort. The defendants were a bizarre and diverse amalgam of ex-Bundists, anti-Semites, Roosevelt haters, and obscure right-wing cranks. Making the strongest impression nationally was probably Elizabeth Dilling, the author of hyperbolic red-baiting books. Another defendant was Prescott Dennett, a Washington publicist and chairman of the Islands for War Debts committee. He had worked with Viereck to distribute literature opposed to Roosevelt's foreign policy.[3]

More obscure, but probably more representative of the lot, was Elmer J. Garner (age 78), proprietor of *Publicity*, a small weekly in Wichita, Kansas, and one of the publications that lost its second-class mailing status under the Espionage Act. While Garner, like most of the other defendants, was anti-Semitic and Anglophobic, these views did not derive from Nazi influence but from his participation many decades earlier in the Farmers' Alliance and the Populist movements. He achieved some local prominence in the 1930s as a backer of Dr. John R. Brinkley's near-miss write-in campaign for governor. While Garner was a hardline prewar noninterventionist, he pledged support after Pearl Harbor for "OUR PRESIDENT and our leader in this extraordinary emergency." In the subsequent months, however, he occasionally faulted particular policies in the conduct of the war, such as the "Germany first strategy" favored by the Allies.[4]

As Baldwin, Hays, and other civil libertarians had feared, the indictment lumped together, and tried to put on an equal plane, such ideas as noninterventionism, criticisms of US allies, anti-Semitism, and sympathy for the Axis powers. The prosecutors charged, for example, that the defendants had sought to undermine the war effort by depicting the "United Nations" (a name given to the wartime alliance of allied countries) as "ineffectual," falsely claiming that "the United States was safe from attack, and that confidence in American public officials was misplaced and unwarranted," and of waging "a systematic campaign of personal vilification and defamation of the public officials of the United States government."[5]

The naming of William Griffin in the indictment was at odds with past pronouncements that prosecutors intended to target only the pro-Nazi lunatic fringe. Griffin's mainstream accomplishments set him apart from the other defendants. He was the publisher of the *New York Enquirer*, a tabloid focusing on crime and gossip that in later years became the *National Enquirer*. Griffin got his start as an associate of William Randolph Hearst, with whom he still had a business relationship. In part, the *Enquirer* functioned as a "stalking horse" to try out stories that might later be picked up by Hearst. No evidence was produced of anti-Semitism, and, indeed, Griffin had a long record of friendly ties with key figures in New York's Jewish community. In 1936, Roosevelt had appointed him to a commission to settle foreign policy disputes between the United States and Poland.[6]

In 1939, Griffin broke from the administration's foreign policy and became an active leader of the Keep America Out of War Committee and, in that capacity, spoke at rallies alongside such figures as Senators Burton K. Wheeler (D-MT) and Gerald Nye (R-ND). After the Japanese attack on Pearl Harbor, however, he proclaimed (much like Garner had) that the "debate is over; they struck a knife in our back—let's break theirs." Maloney dismissed Griffin's post-December 7 reaction as just a subterfuge to obscure the *Enquirer*'s key role as the most important in "a ring of seditious newspapers." His case centered on Griffin's prewar contacts with Viereck via Dennett. Maloney stressed that Viereck had influenced Dennett to place an article, "Are You an American?" in the *Enquirer* and had facilitated, at least in part, Griffin's trip to Germany. In answer to this, Griffin stated that his only motive was to get an interview with Hitler to urge him to stop persecuting Jews. He said that he had acted at the suggestion of Benjamin Greenspun, an influential Jewish leader in New York City, a claim later backed by Greenspun.[7]

The timing of the indictment, which coincided with the denouement of Griffin's libel suit against Winston Churchill, Roosevelt's closest international ally, raised some eyebrows. At issue was a 1936 article in the *Enquirer* that quoted Churchill as saying "America should have minded her own business and stayed out of the World War. If you hadn't entered the war the Allies would have made peace with Germany in the Spring of 1917," thus preventing the rise of Communism and fascism. Three years after the article appeared, Churchill, when asked about it, slammed the quotation as a "vicious lie," though he later remembered meeting Griffin for the interview after first denying it. Griffin hit back against the then British Prime Minister with a libel suit still ongoing in July 1942 at the time of his initial indictment. Three months later, a judge dismissed the case because Griffin, preoccupied with the sedition prosecution and a recent heart attack, never showed up.[8]

A widely shared belief among anti-Roosevelt critics was that a hidden purpose of the indictments was to create an entering wedge to implicate and smear more mainstream noninterventionists in Congress and the press. Especially ominous from their perspective was the prosecution's use of voluminous quotations, given without attribution, from members of Congress. Adding to these fears was a specific count in the indictment that pro-Axis individuals and organizations had "supported, used, controlled, or contributed to" the America First Committee and the Griffin-backed Keep America Out of War Committee.[9]

Maloney's rather unsubtle strategy of guilt by association and innuendo was nowhere more evident than in the case he assembled against Elizabeth Dilling. There was some irony, of course, since she was a pioneer in similar attacks on adversaries in her conspiratorial jeremiad, *The Red Network: A Who's Who and Handbook of Radicalism for Patriots*. That book had promiscuously smeared as Communists or dupes such prominent Americans as H. L. Mencken, William Allen White, and John Dewey, as well as her future noninterventionist allies, Senator Gerald Nye (R-ND) and Representative Jeanette Rankin (R-MT). Highlighted in the prosecution's evidence was a speech by Representative Clare Hoffman (R-MI) from the *Congressional Record* that Dilling's newsletter had reprinted. Hoffman had quoted complaints by American soldiers that they were short of bombers because the British had priority under Lend-Lease. Also presented in evidence was Dilling's article that any "professed servant of Christ who could aid the church-burning, clergy-murdering, God-hating Soviet regime belongs either in the ranks of the blind leaders of the blind or in the ancient and dishonorable order of Judas." Prosecutors were able to establish venue because she had mailed an anti-Lend-Lease cartoon to one of Dillard Stokes's aliases in the District of Columbia.[10]

If the government's hidden agenda was to ultimately snare the "big game," however, the prosecution's most exuberant boosters in the press expressed impatience that this had not yet happened. With some frustration, the *New Republic* asked, "Where is Lindbergh in this list? Where is Lawrence Dennis? Where is Gerald L. K. Smith?" It wondered why the prosecution was pursuing Griffin but leaving others who said much the same thing alone, commenting that the *New York Enquirer* was "not essentially different in what it said from the papers of the McCormick-Patterson family axis in Chicago, New York, and Washington."[11]

The ACLU's conflicted reaction to the indictment mirrored its response to the government's actions against Japanese Americans and publications like *Social Justice*. Despite the best countervailing efforts of the Hays faction, the ACLU went on record in July 1942 (only a month after it endorsed Executive Order 9066) as refusing to participate "in any way in the defense of these trials since all of the defendants are adequately represented." As was also true on the *Social Justice* issue, ACLU director Baldwin continued to be at loggerheads with the board and persisted without success in revisiting the issue. To sway the doubters, he reported that many elements in the Department of Justice had either opposed bringing the case or were lukewarm. For this reason, according to Baldwin, an official ACLU letter of protest to the attorney general "would strengthen those elements in the Department who would like to withstand that sort of pressure and who, like ourselves, are opposed to this sort of use of the conspiracy statute." He feared that a trial would unleash the same "spirit of witch-hunting" that Biddle had warned against. The defendants, in his estimation, were not parties in a grand conspiracy but were better described as "competitors in their respective rackets."[12]

Joined by Hays, John F. Finerty, Osmond Fraenkel, and other members of the pro–free speech faction on the ACLU's board endorsed Baldwin's suggestion to send a letter to the attorney general condemning the indictments. They immediately encountered objections from two important pro–New Deal liberals, Morris Ernst and Carey McWilliams, both of whom had also supported the suppression of *Social Justice*. McWilliams did not want to align the ACLU in any way with "crackpots" who represented "a hodgepodge of provocation." Because of the effective strategy of delay by Ernst and others, the debate dragged on for months. But Baldwin and his allies pressed on and proposed a watered-down letter of protest to be sent to the attorney general. After the board voted 15 to 4 against sending the letter, the critics of the trial made their last stand in January 1943, by circulating a petition to have the decision overturned by the much larger ACLU Corporation.[13]

The list of the signers of this appeal represented the hardest core of civil liberty advocates on the left during the war and showed considerable overlap with those in the organization who went on record against Japanese American internment. The signers were a diverse group: a future lawyer for the Rosenbergs (John F. Finerty), a leading feminist proponent of birth control (Dorothy Dunbar Bromley), a former assistant attorney general in New York, a lawyer for the Scottsboro Boys and Harry Bridges (Osmond Fraenkel), an alleged Communist and the treasurer of the NAACP (Ben W. Huebsch), the head of both the committee to defend the Scottsboro Boys and the NAACP Legal Defense Fund as well as a future professor of Martin Luther King Jr. (Allan Knight Chalmers), two past defense counsels of Sacco and Vanzetti (Finerty and Arthur Garfield Hays), a perennial Socialist presidential candidate (Norman Thomas), a cofounder of the NAACP and the most famous pacifist in the United States (John Haynes Holmes), and the lead counsel of the NAACP and a future US Supreme Court Justice (Thurgood Marshall). Rounding out this list was Alfred M. Bingham, a founder of the premiere heterodox magazine for the literati, *Common Sense*.[14]

Those aligned with the Ernst faction who opposed sending the letter countered that it would only jeopardize the ACLU's good relations with the Department of Justice by needlessly calling into question "the comparative restraint and wisdom which it has so far shown" as well as confuse the public as to whether the ACLU supported the obnoxious views of the defendants. The best approach, according to the majority report, was for the ACLU to patiently wait for the promised forthcoming evidence "that all of the defendants were cooperating with, or acting on behalf of, the enemy and were parties to the conspiracy as charged." The petitioners who wanted to go on record against the sedition indictments failed to get enough votes to reverse the original decision. Out of ninety-five members of the corporation, thirty-five supported sending a letter to Biddle, forty-four were against, and the rest did not turn in ballots. As a result, the ACLU never took an official position on the indictments or the subsequent trial. The final major triumph of the Ernst faction in the ACLU Corporation referendum came six months after it had prevailed by an even wider margin on Japanese American internment.[15]

The effort by Baldwin and others to recruit civil libertarians outside of the ACLU to oppose the sedition trial was equally unsuccessful. The most disappointing response came from the ACLU's old tag-team partner during the Hague/Minton era, the Bill of Rights Committee of the American Bar Association. The committee, despite an appeal from Chafee, who called the charges "indefensible," refused to oppose the prosecution. The committee's leaders had shown signs of watering down their dedication to free speech for quite some time. In 1939, for example, Grenville Clark, who was then chair, endorsed the old axiom that "unbridled liberty degenerates into intolerable license." In the spring of 1941, Clark even pushed for an Espionage Act prosecution of Senator Wheeler and Robert E. Wood, the chairman of the board of Sears, Roebuck, and Company, two leading America Firsters. Under its new head, Douglas Arant of Birmingham, Alabama, the committee stopped publication of the *Bill of Rights Review* in 1943. Tellingly, the majority on the ACLU's board cited the committee's silence as a rationale for not backing the defendants.[16]

The sedition case was rife with ironies, but perhaps the greatest of them all was that lawyers in the Department of Justice sometimes showed greater sensitivity toward the rights of the defendants (as well as the rights of Japanese Americans) than either the ACLU's board or the ABA's Committee on the Bill of Rights. Just a week after the ACLU had voted to remain aloof, Baldwin, in his effort to persuade the board to reverse course, had helped to draft a confidential memorandum quoting lawyers in the Department of Justice directly involved in the sedition investigation. Their general opinion was to privately, but pointedly, dismiss claims of any clear and present danger from the defendants, who were better described as ineffectual "cranks or crackpots with little following after Pearl Harbor." Furthermore, the lawyers in the department denied that they had any intention of seeking a precedent and had only acted because of unbearable pressure coming from "such publications as PM, liberal journals and by a number of organizations." One "high official" in the department predicted that "history will probably hold that the Department was inconsistent and the victim of pressure and prejudice" so intense that (if not appeased) might have prompted Roosevelt to fire his attorney general.[17]

The relatively pro–free speech attitudes of so many in the Department of Justice probably stemmed, in great part, from a generational divide. The lower and middle ranks of the department had largely come of age in the interwar period, when the US Supreme Court had become more vigorous in defending the First Amendment and memories of the left/right cooperation against Hague and Minton were relatively fresh. Those educated in leading law schools had at least some exposure to Chafee's widely applauded *Free Speech in America*, in which he had mounted a full-throated defense of the First Amendment. The cumulative impact of landmark court rulings and commentary from respected jurists had done much to spread and legitimize pro–free speech perspectives among lawyers in the department.[18]

Although Roosevelt ranked "freedom of speech and expression" as the highest in his "four freedoms" proclamation of January 1941, his application of that concept at home left much to be desired. As historian Leo P. Ribuffo observes, antisedition indictments "were not secured by irresponsible subordinates ... on the contrary, he [Roosevelt] personally intervened to curtail far-right expressions ... [and] the president's enthusiasm for Maloney as prosecutor in 1942, combined with his earlier order to investigate the America First Committee and congressional isolationists, suggest that he expected the sedition prosecution to discredit reputable critics of New Deal foreign policy." Revenge and vindictiveness continued to be major drivers for the president, especially in relation to Hearst, the Pattersons, and McCormick. In October 1942, he derailed Ernst's plan to send out peace feelers to Joe Patterson of the *New York Daily News*. Instead, Roosevelt proposed that Ernst throw down the gauntlet and challenge Patterson with the question of "whether freedom of the press is not essentially freedom to print correct news and freedom to criticize the news on the basis of factual truth. I think there is a big distinction between this and freedom to print untrue news." This bellicosity was too extreme even for the Machiavellian Ernst, who appealed to the president, without apparent effect, that Patterson "was too deep and great a friend of yours for years to allow us to let him stay lost." Two months later, Roosevelt "awarded" a German Iron Cross by mail to John O'Donnell, Washington correspondent of the *Daily News*, because of an innocuous aside describing attitudes of the troops on wartime censorship.[19]

Joe's daughter Alicia Patterson, publisher of the popular and award-winning *Newsday* of Long Island, who did not share her father's prewar noninterventionism, summed up the motivations of Roosevelt and many of his hardline supporters: "Isolationism was a dead issue so far as my father was concerned, but it apparently wasn't with a lot of pre-Pearl Harbor interventionists … [these] fanatics stumped the country from end to end denouncing anyone who happened to have believed before the war that America should have looked before she leaped. … [I]t is true that my father from time to time criticized the Administration. Does that make him a traitor? If it does, then anyone who questions the policies laid down in Washington is likewise treasonable."[20]

Two organizations were especially vigorous in mobilizing support for the prosecution and extending it, if possible, to cover pre–Pearl Harbor noninterventionists: the Non-Sectarian Anti-Nazi League (NSANL) and the Friends of Democracy (FOD). They cooperated in a symbiotic relationship. Best known for pushing for a highly punitive peace with Germany, the NSANL had its own private intelligence arm for domestic surveillance. Before Pearl Harbor, it had conspired with the FOD and British Security Co-ordination in New York, a covert organization under William Stephenson, to get the United States into the war. A key NSANL priority was to discredit noninterventionist organizations in the eyes of the public. In September 1941, former Boston University professor James H. Sheldon, chair of the group's board of directors, vowed that the "America First Committee must be destroyed just as Adolf Hitler must be destroyed."[21]

Directing the NSANL's intelligence operation was Richard Rollins, who had served in that capacity for the House Special Committee on Un-American Activities, co-chaired by Representative Samuel Dickstein (D-NY). NSANL's stated goal was to expose "propaganda in the twilight zone between seditious activities and violations of the Espionage Act, on the one hand, and good Americanism on the other." The public face of the organization was the *Anti-Nazi Bulletin*, which repeatedly tried to conflate mainstream noninterventionists with extremists.[22]

Founded in the late 1930s by Rev. L. M. Birkhead, who continued to run day-to-day operations, the FOD had an energetic new president as its public face beginning in 1942, novelist Rex Stout. In addition to authoring the Nero Wolfe detective series, Stout had edited the book *The Illustrious Dunderheads* (1942), which lampooned pre–Pearl Harbor congressional obstructionists of Roosevelt's foreign policy. Relying on the familiar tactics of guilt by association and innuendo, NSANL/FOD deployed private snoops to dig up dirt on prominent noninterventionists so as to prove that the America First Committee (AFC) was the "Axis Transmission Belt." The FOD's well-connected informants included the daughter of Cissy Patterson. During the same period, Stout was speaking up in favor of Japanese American internment.[23]

With little success, top NSANL/FOD officers tried to cultivate a friendly relationship with the ACLU in the hope of both reshaping and redirecting attitudes on civil liberty. In correspondence with Roger N. Baldwin, Birkhead, in a joint letter with FOD's research director, Roy G. Tozier, asserted that excessive American allegiance to "the anarchy of speech, press and assembly" threatened to paralyze action against the fifth column. They questioned, perhaps to Baldwin's discomfort, whether the ACLU was as rigidly committed to free speech principles as it claimed. As evidence, Birkhead and Tozier pointed to the ACLU's support for the National Association of Broadcasters (NAB) code forcing Coughlin off the air and to Morris Ernst's proposal to require "propaganda" organizations to register with the postal service. But Baldwin was unmoved by such arguments. When Sheldon tried a similar approach on him, he parried, "My own advice to you, if you want it, is none of these [right-wing] movements are strong enough to take too seriously—and they won't be!"[24]

Republican gains in the 1942 elections energized congressional and media critics of the prosecution. The Republicans advanced to numbers not seen in a decade, gaining forty-seven seats in the US House and nine in the Senate. This new clout enabled congressional antiadministration forces to take more chances. Sustaining their skepticism were credible, and headline generating, indications of Maloney's overreach and incompetence. At an early point in the case, defendant William Griffin produced a 1932 letter from then-Governor Roosevelt, on official stationery, asking Griffin to make a seconding speech for his presidential nomination at the Democratic convention in Chicago as well as praising Griffin's "fine spirit of fair play and good citizenship." Maloney's only response to this evidence was to complain that Griffin's attorney had needlessly "dragged" in the president's name and that the letter might be a forgery.[25]

The two main leaders of the new congressional pushback against the administration on civil liberties were Senators Robert A. Taft (R-OH) and Burton K. Wheeler (D-MT), who both wrote open letters to Biddle. Taft did not see "even a shadow of conspiracy between many of the individual defendants" and charged that the federal government had used the vagueness of the Smith Act to violate individual rights. He had known of several individuals in past conspiracy cases who were added into indictments "without any real proof of a connection with the guilty parties." Taking an even harsher tone, Wheeler characterized the proceedings as a "disgrace" and a scheme to smear members both of the America First Committee and of Congress. When Biddle answered that he had no intention of doing anything like that, Wheeler asked, then, why he had included the AFC in the indictment in the first place? Furthermore, "Why was my name, and the names of other Senators dragged in before the Grand Jury, and people asked if they knew me?" Wheeler also accused Maloney of underhanded tactics in establishing jurisdiction, by entrapping defendants to write letters to Washington, thus subjecting them to a jury "made up of Government workers, or people who are dependent upon the Government, either directly or indirectly."[26]

When Maloney's collaborator, Dillard Stokes, interviewed Wheeler for the *Washington Post*, fireworks were almost inevitable. Wheeler berated the reporter as "a stooge for the Department of Justice, a little newspaper spy," adding that "it's a dirty business you are in, and the time will come when you will all regret it." Stokes scored a parting shot, however, by titling his story "Wheeler Defends Sedition Suspects, Although Nazi Used Him as a 'Front.'" The *Nation* speculated that Wheeler's hyperbole was a smokescreen to hide his "guilty knowledge" that he might be prosecuted next. But Wheeler was not to be underestimated. It was he who had recruited Chafee to ask the ABA's Committee on the Bill of Rights take up the issue.[27]

The *Progressive* remained almost a lone dissenting voice on the political left. Columnist Milton Mayer advised readers that they were making a mistake if they thought that the precedent of a sedition prosecution, once established, only harmed the political right. If the government prevailed this time, next in the prosecution's crosshairs would be "every crank and every grafter, and finally every dissenter." Similarly, the editor of the *Progressive*, Morris H. Rubin, concluded that the investigation had "seriously disturbed Americans who are actually in the firing line for civil liberties."[28]

Administration insiders privately agreed that Maloney, because of his bungling of an increasingly unwieldy case, was becoming a liability. According to an internal memo from Assistant Attorney General James H. Rowe Jr., the prosecutor had alienated Department of Justice professionals through flamboyant pronouncements, ever more grandiose conspiratorial claims, and promiscuous leaks, including of grand jury testimony to such favored sources as Winchell, Stokes, and Pearson. Another of Maloney's offenses, according to Rowe, was that of "'tipping off' newspapermen that he was getting ready to indict Hoffman, Fish and even Wheeler and Nye (and when in fact the lawyers conversant with the case knew we had no case against these men)." As early as September 1942, the Court of Appeals for the District of Columbia, while upholding Viereck's conviction, had admonished as misconduct Maloney's inflammatory remarks to the jury.[29]

But Maloney had two powerful media giants in his corner: Winchell and Pearson. The combined audience of their broadcasts and columns was considerably larger than that reached by the so-called McCormick-Patterson Axis. On February 7, 1943, both commentators condemned Wheeler and his congressional allies for impeding the sedition investigation. Citing the NAB code's prohibition of controversial comments, the NBC Blue Network instructed Winchell and Pearson to refrain from "derogatory or insulting remarks about either House of Congress or any groups or members in either House or any Federal Agency or employee thereof." Claiming selective censorship, fans of the commentators swung into action. Somewhat ironically, considering L. M. Birkhead's earlier praise of the code, the FOD organized a mass campaign to defend the "fundamental American right to criticize those whom the American people have elected to office." Only a few days later, the network backed down and stopped censoring Winchell and Pearson on the sedition case.[30]

Unbeknownst to his two radio champions, Maloney, despite his hunger for the limelight, was in over his head and he knew it. He had even admitted to Rowe that "he was afraid of Wheeler, that Wheeler had the goods on him." The day after Pearson and Winchell had defended the prosecution in their broadcasts, Biddle finally put Maloney out of his private misery through a "promotion" to head the Trial Section of the Department of Justice. Unaware of the possibility that Biddle had done the besieged prosecutor a favor, Maloney's supporters protested vehemently. An editorial in the pro-prosecution *Washington Post* complained that Biddle had "appeased the congressional friends of the Nazi conspiracy" and was naïvely implementing the theory that "free speech, as such, ought not to be restricted." Although Maloney's excesses had alienated many in the Department of Justice, he still had a sympathizer in the White House. The president forwarded an article to Biddle complaining that Maloney had lost his job because of pressure from Wheeler and appended the question: "Att Gen. Why Maloney's removal?"[31]

Enthusiasts for the trial, however, soon warmed up to the new prosecutor, O. John Rogge. Efficient, methodical, and idealistic, he had made his name tackling vestiges of the Huey Long machine in Louisiana for income tax evasion. He brought in an accomplished trial lawyer, Joseph W. Burns, as his assistant. Rogge, who had voted for ACLU partisan Norman Thomas in 1932, also had friends among civil libertarians.[32]

Freed of the Maloney albatross, Rowe became increasingly upbeat about the prospects for the sedition case, "*which must be won at all costs*" (emphasis Rowe's). Making a major revisionist leap, he even depicted Maloney's removal as an "excellent tactical maneuver" because it meant that "we have silenced the isolationists." Rowe's theory was if any of them began to gripe about Rogge, the public would discount their complaints as hypocritical pretexts to "kill the case." He was partly right. On March 1, the US Supreme Court bore out the wisdom of removing Maloney by overturning his main handiwork, the conviction of Viereck. According to the court, Maloney's closing remarks to the jury had jeopardized the defendant's right to a fair trial by indulging "in an appeal wholly irrelevant to any facts or issues in the case, the purpose and effect of which could have been to arouse passion and prejudice."[33]

But Rowe's hopes to the contrary, Maloney's removal did not bring respite to the prosecution. Many of the problems were Rogge's own doing. His missteps began early when he naïvely stated his intention to go to trial in a month. Rogge ran up against the same essential dilemma as Maloney, the impossibility of linking all the defendants into one grand conspiracy. The investigation dragged on for month after month, and promises of new evidence became increasingly threadbare.[34]

A major obstacle for the prosecution was the waning of the same war hysteria that had initially propelled the case. When Representative Dickstein proposed a bill in March 1943 barring any literature from mails causing "racial or religious hatred, bigotry or intolerance," it died in committee. More significant was the fate of the War Security Bill proposing the death penalty for "hostile acts" against the United States. The opposition focused on the so-called snooper section, criminalizing failure to report others who might be guilty. Despite the full support of the Department of Justice, a broad coalition of past opponents of Roosevelt's foreign policy were able to kill the "Gestapo bill" in Senate committee.[35]

Adding to the problems for Rogge were GOP gains in Congress, which provided some check on the administration's freedom of action. The judicial branch was also becoming more assertive. Even if Roosevelt had wanted to be another Wilson, and Biddle another Palmer, the courts were making that impossible. The bleak experiences of World War I, combined with the influence of prominent civil libertarians in the legal academy, such as Chafee, had made a deep impression both on lawyers in the Department of Justice and on judges. Finally, of course, allied battlefield victories since 1942 had considerably cooled the previous climate of fear.

While the more obvious threats to free speech had abated, at least temporarily, Roosevelt appeared as determined as ever to silence or, at least muffle, dissent, albeit through more subtle, clandestine, and informal methods, including repeated use of the Bureau of Internal Revenue. This approach was not completely new, of course. In 1938, Frank Knox, the publisher of the *Chicago Daily News* and future secretary of the navy, had written, "Let a person of prominence speak up in criticism [against the president's policies] and any one of three things—or, all three! –is likely to happen to him. 1. In due time he will find himself before a legislative committee in Washington. 2. He will be publicly castigated by a federal officeholder; or 3. He will be put on the calling list of the Internal Revenue Department."[36]

During World War II, however, various forms of selective and politicized tax monitoring and harassment became increasingly routine. A friendly police lieutenant, who was an expert on bugging, found four separate taps on the home phone of Walter Trohan, the Washington, DC, editor of the *Chicago Daily Tribune*: naval intelligence, military intelligence, the FBI, and the Anti-Defamation League. In addition, the federal government kept careful watch on Robert R. McCormick's taxes and rationed the newsprint of his publications, while his chief local rival, the pro–New Deal Marshall Field III, publisher of the *Chicago Sun*, was left alone.[37]

Morris Ernst, working in tandem with the president and top officials, helped to implement monitoring of a wide range of administration critics. He boasted in September 1942 that the Department of the Treasury had finally set up a unit "to start going over the tax returns of America First, et al." and that he had provided it with "the names of the big shot oil men who contributed large sums of money to Gerald L. K. Smith. I am turning over a similar list to Randolph Paul who might get help in his tax fight on oil reserves." Also in the tax crosshairs was John L. Lewis, the head of the United Mine Workers. When Biddle reported in 1943 "no income tax violation," Roosevelt urged him to speed up another investigation of the labor leader's taxes. In contrast to many in the ACLU, who opposed releasing any tax return without a subpoena, Ernst advocated their automatic disclosure as a means of enforcing greater "publicity."[38]

Meanwhile, the ACLU was as inert as ever on the sedition case, gaining ever diminished solace from governmental promises of forthcoming evidence that the defendants had taken money from the German government. This allegation was in itself an attempt by the prosecution to shift the goalpost from the question of causing insubordination in the US military to the acceptance of German money. Frustrated by the ACLU's standoffishness, Senator Wheeler implored in April 1943, "[W]hy in the name of the Lord was it that you people didn't get into the handling of these cases … is beyond my comprehension." While Baldwin responded evasively by restating the ACLU's official position, he privately regarded the indictments as "monstrous."[39]

Public interest in the sedition investigation, which had ebbed throughout most of 1943, received a sudden surge of energy after a blockbuster book appeared in August. Written under the pen name of John Roy Carlson, Arthur (born Avedis) Derounian's sensationalist *Under Cover: My Four Years in the Nazi Underworld of America—The Amazing Revelation of How Axis Agents and Our Enemies Within Are Now Plotting to Destroy the United States* rocketed to the top of the nonfiction best-seller ranking. The NSANL and the FOD went all out to promote the book, while the Department of War boosted already considerable sales by ordering five thousand copies. Much of Derounian's evidence came from his surreptitious work as the FOD's "chief investigator." For its part, the NSANL's *Anti-Nazi Bulletin* advertised *Under Cover* as "Democratic Dynamite."[40]

Billed as an account of how "our enemies within are now plotting to destroy the United States," *Under Cover* conveyed the message that noninterventionists, such as Wheeler, Nye, Edward Rumely, Frank Gannett, and Norman Thomas, had, wittingly or unwittingly, aided the same sinister fascist, or quasi-fascist, conspiracy. Derounian put a great emphasis on shared (often casual) acquaintances and hyped up occasions when a genuinely pro-Nazi publication had praised or republished the speeches of mainstream noninterventionists. Stressing urgency, he proclaimed that the "day had passed when we can afford to be tolerant with our enemies inside or outside the country and inside or outside of public office."[41]

For the time being, the appearance of *Under Cover* blindsided critics of the sedition investigation and created an additional dilemma for them. Did they question the contents of a best-selling and highly praised book, and thus be rendered suspect for pro-fascist sympathies, or did they remain silent? John T. Flynn, former *Nation* columnist and past head of the New York chapter of the America First Committee, framed the problem succinctly, commenting that *Under Cover* "'exposes' a lot of subversive groups like the Bund, Crusaders for America, etc. Nobody wants to take up the cudgels for them. ... [Its] object is to smear and intimidate everybody opposed to Roosevelt's foreign adventures."[42]

Perhaps influenced by the success of Derounian's methods, Rogge revamped the sedition case yet a third time in January 1944 when a revised indictment, now styled as *United States v. McWilliams*, charged that the defendants had collaborated with Nazi Germany in a worldwide conspiracy to "destroy democracy" in favor of a "national socialist or fascist" regime. A particular weakness in this allegation, of course, was that many of the defendants did not even know, much less like, each other. Rogge's response to this obstacle was to broaden the definition of the alleged conspiracy to include participation in a common "movement" to advance shared beliefs.[43]

Rogge conveyed the impression that several, often distinct, ideas were inseparably combined into a single package. These included theories that "Communists, International Jews, and plutocrats" controlled the government and that the laws passed by Congress "are illegal, corrupt, traitorous and in direct violation of the Constitution of the United States," that American political leaders had "deliberately planned" the war "with the ultimate aim of promoting our enslavement by British Imperialism and International Communism." Downplaying the specific acts of the defendants, Rogge instead set out to educate the jury about the history of the "worldwide Nazi movement." He entered into evidence speeches by Hitler, copies of *Mein Kampf*, and histories of Germany. All this material proved almost impossible for defense lawyers, much less the jury, to digest and opened numberless rabbit holes for debates about history and its meaning for the case.[44]

The effect of taking this approach, however, was sometimes to undermine Rogge's own, if somewhat grudging, pledge to avoid portraying mainstream opponents of Roosevelt's prewar foreign policy as culpable in the conspiracy. If nothing else, the Supreme Court's chastisement of Maloney demonstrated that trying to directly implicate these elements was a losing legal strategy. An indicator of Rogge's skittishness was his decision to drop William Griffin and the *New York Enquirer* from the indictment counts. While Rogge never gave his reasons, there were some obvious risks to putting the publisher in the dock, such as explaining pro-Griffin statements from such diverse figures as former presidential candidate Al Smith, US House Speaker William B. Bankhead (D-AL), and Senator Robert F. Wagner (D-NY). Representative Sol Bloom (D-NY), a supporter of Zionism, had once praised him as an ideal mayoral candidate. Moreover, according to a confidential NSANL report, "publishers and newspaper outfits are expected to back Griffin to the limit."[45]

While the prosecution dropped Griffin and ten others from the indictment, it added eight, including four German Americans associated with the Bund, Joseph McWilliams, who had run for Congress in 1940 under the banner of the rightist/nationalist American Destiny Party, and Lawrence Dennis, a Harvard-educated veteran of the American foreign service. The highly polished Dennis stood out in the mostly motley group. After graduating from Harvard, he had a short career in the Foreign Service, a post that he left in protest of continuing gunboat policies. The theme of one of his books, *The Coming American Fascism*, as he later explained, was that because of the war economy and decay of capitalism, the United States "would go Fascist" and that it "should recognize the inevitability of this trend, try to develop a nice Fascism without the bad features which went with Fascism abroad." Dennis's prose had the style of a detached observer implying a doctrine of inevitability. On the strength of the book, he gained a reputation as America's "leading intellectual fascist" and appeared in forums with the likes of William Z. Foster of the American Communist Party and the liberal theorist Max Lerner. Unlike most of the other defendants, Dennis did not indulge in anti-Semitic appeals. He was more of an intellectual scribbler commenting on world events than an activist, much less the leader of a "movement."[46]

The judge, Edward C. Eicher, was a longtime Roosevelt loyalist. Representing Iowa in the US House from 1933 to 1938, he had the reputation of a New Deal "wheelhorse" backing such controversial initiatives as the public utility "death sentence" and court packing. In 1938, he had run for the Senate but lost in the Republican wave. An appreciative Roosevelt appointed him, first, to the Securities and Exchange Commission (which he eventually chaired) and then, as chief justice of the District Court of the United States for the District of Columbia. When the sedition case came up, Eicher apparently took the initiative to put it on his docket. He gaveled the trial to order on April 17, 1944, in the US District Court of the District of Columbia to much media fanfare. Twenty-five reporters and twenty-two defense lawyers (plus prosecutors) crowded into the courtroom, leaving only twenty seats for spectators.[47]

Given a boost by *Under Cover*'s media plaudits and robust sales, the reaction of newspapers toward the trial was overwhelmingly favorable. Typical editorial themes included the contrast between the due process afforded to the defendants and the treatment of dissidents in totalitarian societies. As they had in other stages of the process, leftist publications and organizations were the most supportive of the prosecution. If they had any qualms, it was that Rogge had not gone far enough. The *New Masses* admonished the prosecutors to stop fixating on the "small fry" and "lay hands on the main culprits." No wonder, the *Daily Worker* commented, that "this trial makes the [New York] Daily News nervous. After all, the defendants are being tried for publishing the kind of material in which the Daily News specializes." An article in the official publication of the National Lawyers Guild proclaimed, "No democracy can permit its institutions to be used against it." The *Chicago Sun* rejected out of hand any possibility that the defendants were on trial for "entertaining certain social or political beliefs."[48]

The regular broadcasts and columns of Winchell and Pearson remained the prosecution's most powerful media assets. Both commentators, in their own unique ways, became part of the proceedings. Defense attorney James J. Laughlin attempted to subpoena Pearson to testify on possible inside information about Roosevelt's personal interest in furthering the prosecution. In addition, defense lawyers routinely asked jurors if they had listened to Winchell's broadcasts or had read *Under Cover.*[49]

Pro–free speech foes of the sedition trial on the political left, vastly outnumbered, struggled to make their presence felt. Although the ACLU always stayed on the sidelines, Baldwin discreetly searched for a way "to terminate the trial." The *Progressive* gave no quarter in championing the free speech rights of the defendants. Columnist Oswald Garrison Villard stated that although he "had the honor" of winning a place on Dilling's list of subversives in her best-known book, *The Red Network,* he considered it a travesty to charge her for holding anti-interventionist opinions that were shared, in varying degrees, by many millions of Americans. Free speech, he asserted, "does not mean merely the right to tell the truth. It means the right to talk nonsense, to spread falsehoods." The theory behind the prosecution, he added, "threatens the extinction of all criticism and takes us far along the road toward that complete suppression of public opinion which is one of the things that we abhor most in Germany and Japan."[50]

George S. Schuyler, recently under FBI scrutiny for his hard-hitting articles in the *Pittsburgh Courier,* was a rarity in depicting the plights of the sedition trial defendants, Japanese Americans, and African Americans as all analogous and interdependent. The Roosevelt administration, according to Schuyler, was persecuting the defendants for what they "said and wrote," and had presented no evidence of collusion or participation in a conspiracy. If these individuals could be put on trial for opposing the policies of Roosevelt or his subordinates, he asked (following the same approach as his defense of Japanese Americans), "[T]hen who is safe? I may be nabbed for speaking harshly about Brother Stimson's treatment of Negro lads in the Army."[51]

In the first week or so of the proceedings, the sometimes jaw-dropping antics of the defendants gave the reporters good copy. As a movie camera captured the moment on film, a photographer snapped pictures of Lois de Lafayette Washburn (who claimed to be descended from the famous Frenchman) thumbing her nose at the Capitol Building and giving a stiff-armed fascist salute. She also slapped a photographer and proclaimed, on hearing her name called in court, "Lafayette we are here to defend what you gave us—our freedom from tyranny."[52]

The novelty of all this soon wore off, however, as thirty often vulgarly rambunctious defendants, most represented by separate counsel, jockeyed for position and the limelight. Lawyers and defendants alike came forward with multiple objections. Especially memorable was a motion by the "suave, dark-skinned" Dennis to convene a sanity hearing for Prescott Dennett, Lois de Lafayette Washburn, and Edward James Smythe, and a separate trial for the rest. He did so on the grounds that the trio were "incapable of understanding properly the nature of the trial and of conducting for themselves a proper defense." Just before this, the 80-year-old Elmer J. Garner had died in his sleep, reducing the ranks of the defendants to twenty-nine.[53]

With the jury selected after four weeks, Rogge gave his opening statement for the prosecution. Downplaying the main official charge of military insubordination, he pressed the more sensationalistic claim that the defendants were foot soldiers in a "worldwide Nazi movement." To bring about this revolution, they had emulated "the same tactics the Nazis used to seize power in Germany in 1933." His presentation elicited cat calls and derision not necessarily helpful to the prosecution. When Rogge said the defendants had "picked out" a fuehrer to rule them, their chanted response was "Who? Who?" They appeared amused when he named retired General George Van Horn Moseley, former second in command in the army, though no evidence was presented that any defendant had contact with him after 1939. In later weeks, Rogge hedged a bit by saying that Moseley had only rated as a "possible" fuehrer. Howls of laughter greeted Rogge's characterization of Lawrence Dennis as "[t]he Alfred Rosenberg of the movement in this country."[54]

While Rogge stipulated that "many Americans in good faith" had opposed preparation for war, he put the defendants in a different category. Their motivation did not stem from patriotism but from a desire to promote "the Nazi cause throughout the world." Although Rogge (much like Boss Crump in Memphis seven months earlier) quoted Oliver Wendell Holmes Jr.'s famous dictum that free speech did not apply to a false shout of "'fire' in a crowded theater in order to cause a panic," he never really attempted to make a case that any of the defendants rose to that level of threat.[55]

The easygoing and affable judge simply was not up to the task. As Glen Jeansonne observes, Eicher (age 65) "lacked the stamina and temperament to preside over the rowdy McWilliams case, his first major criminal trial." Although his rulings almost reflexively favored the prosecution, he never got control of the situation. The courtroom disorder became ever more tedious for all concerned. After less than a week of trial maneuverings, Kenesaw M. Landis II of the pro–New Deal *Chicago Sun*, himself a former prosecutor, confessed that he felt like he was "in a zoo, with the Judge a rather careless keeper."[56]

Defenders of the government invariably blamed the chaos on the defendants and their lawyers for using tactics closely paralleling "the Nazis in their bid for national and international power." Although Eicher levied stiff fines and elicited a letter of support from Secretary of the Interior Harold Ickes, his sanctions were mostly in vain. Former Senator George W. Norris (Independent-NE), who long ago had shed his sympathies for noninterventionism, lamented that "every lawyer in the land who has the proper ideal of the nobility of his profession ought to rise up in holy horror and condemn in the severest of terms the attitude that has been taken by lawyers in that case." A few in the press were beginning to find morbid amusement in the situation. "Sebastian," a character in a cartoon published by the *Chicago Sun*, predicted that "defense tactics insure the sedition trial a longer run than 'Life With Father,'" a hit Broadway play that had been running since 1939.[57]

Less appreciated, however, was the prosecution's crucial role in prolonging the trial. Rogge's extended lectures on the history and characteristics of worldwide National Socialism presented all-too-inviting opportunities for twenty-two defense lawyers to challenge and question his claims. And, indeed, in the seven months of the trial, by putting into the record thousands of often unlabeled exhibits, he gave them plenty to object to. The mounds of paper rose so high that the government was unable to supply enough copies for the defense lawyers. Losing all sense of proportion, Rogge vowed to call over one hundred witnesses and thus keep adding to the stacks of evidence "if it takes forever." Even many of the hardened "New Deal lawyers" appointed by the court as defense counsels were increasingly disdainful of the prosecution's case and acted accordingly.[58]

The judge had a golden opportunity to call a halt to the proceedings after the US Supreme Court's ruling in *United States v. Hartzel* in June 1944. Because evidence fell well short of a clear and present danger or an attempt to cause insubordination in the armed forces, the court threw out the conviction under the Espionage Act of a man who had expressed opinions that were every bit as extreme as the defendants'. The ruling held that "an American citizen has the right to discuss these matters either by temperate reasoning or by immoderate and vicious invective." Owen J. Roberts cast the deciding vote. Later that year, he issued his acerbic concurring dissent in *Korematsu v. United States*. In some ways, Roberts had returned to his New Deal–era roots as a truth-teller to executive authority. But Judge Eicher declined to take the potential escape hatch and soldiered on. *McWilliams* was still valid, he ruled, because the defendant in *Hartzel*, unlike those in *McWilliams*, had acted alone rather than in an alleged conspiracy.[59]

Long before this, the daily "dreary farce," as Biddle privately called it, had dropped from the front pages. By July, the number of newspapers and other publications covering the trial, once as high as twenty-five, had fallen precipitously, leaving only a few stalwarts, including the *Daily Worker*. The most monumental of the dropouts was the *Washington Post*, which had played a major role as instigator. In a complete turnabout, the paper compared the proceedings to the Moscow purge trials engineered by Stalin in the late 1930s and as "a black mark against American justice for many years to come." Asked why he had taken the *Post*'s reporter off the case, the managing editor quipped that he did not want him "tied up on a lot of baloney."[60]

The final phase of the trial gave little comfort to prosecutors. It was only in October that Rogge presented his first, and only, witness to address the charge of trying to subvert the military. It did not go well. The witness, Hubert Schmuederrich, testified that he had mailed to soldiers a few hundred pamphlets given to him by a defendant. Cross examination, however, revealed that the content had nothing to do with advocating insubordination and that the defendant did not even know that Schmuederrich had mailed them. The day after the testimony came a new round of defense motions for a mistrial after a radio broadcast by Roosevelt condemned "fear propaganda" by "silver shirts and others on the lunatic fringe." The other witnesses during October and November were equally unhelpful to the prosecution.[61]

Appalled by what he was seeing in the courtroom, Baldwin desperately, and futilely, stepped up his maneuvering to find a way to end the case or "it will drag on for another year." He was also making it plain that he no longer gave any credence to the government's promises of forthcoming new evidence. By this time, supporters of the prosecution were much diminished in number, isolated, and dispirited.[62]

The end (or de facto end) was dramatic. On November 30, 1944, Judge Eicher, "worn out and unhappy," died of a heart attack in his sleep. No wonder. Rogge had barely begun to present his case and had some two hundred witnesses lined up. Among those slated eventually to testify were Representative Martin Dies (D-TX), the chair of the House Special Committee on Un-American Activities, as well as the prosecution's superstar Derounian. Most observers jumped to the conclusion that this meant that it was all over. The *Saturday Evening Post* spoke for many in an editorial, "Let It Be Our Last Mass Trial," when it commented that "only the death of Judge Eicher availed to release American justice from an exhibition far more appropriate to the court rooms of Berlin and Moscow than to those of the United States."[63]

Even Landis of the *Chicago Sun*, an early friend of the prosecution, was glad that it was over. "Most of the acts charged," he pointed out, "occurred before we were at war, and the same theory would have put all Communists in jail, and might have endangered a few British propagandists, if we had later found ourselves at war with Britain." According to Landis, the conspiracy basis of the prosecution had almost inevitably "broken down" when it became apparent that so many "of the defendants had never seen each other, and some of them weren't on speaking terms." The de facto collapse of the sedition trial occurred less than a month before the federal government announced the end of Japanese American internment.[64]

The remaining true believers still nursed hopes that the Department of Justice would appoint a new judge or retry the case. Prominent in this remnant were the Communist Party, some labor unions, *PM*, the *Nation*, and the FOD/NSANL nexus. John P. Lewis, the managing editor of *PM*, proclaimed that "the defendants should be retried, and their cases pushed to a final conclusion, if it takes 10 years." Winchell never lost his zeal. "Dammit," he wrote in June 1945, "it is about time we made certain that American soldiers do not fight and die to turn American street corners into fascist bases of operations!" A weary and frustrated Rogge leaned toward resuming in some form, perhaps by prosecuting a smaller number of the defendants in separate groups. The *Nation* backed the idea of a slimmed-down prosecution targeted to "the most dangerous of the defendants individually." No longer did it promote grandiose dreams of landing the big fish.[65]

In 1946, Rogge made one last try to revive the flagging prosecution. In an interview, he vented about the "liberal lawyers" who stubbornly clung to the outmoded ideal of a "market-place of opinion." He headed off to Germany hoping to dig up evidence about elusive money links and came up dry. Rogge's plans ended abruptly after an impolitic speech in October. In highly inflammatory prose, he declared that the "Nazis always preferred the one who opposed President Roosevelt. They preferred in turn Landon, Willkie, and Dewey." The result of this bombast was an immediate firing by Attorney General Tom C. Clark.[66]

But the case still lingered on, though it pretty much only had a nominal existence. Finally, in November 1946, Chief Justice Bolitha J. Laws of the US District Court of the District of Columbia threw out the charges, calling any possible retrial a "travesty of justice." In 1947, after the US Circuit Court of Appeals upheld the Laws ruling, Attorney General Clark dropped the matter entirely.[67]

This news elicited relatively little commentary because most of those interested thought that the case had ended long before that, and, really, it had. One observer who was paying attention, however, was George S. Schuyler of the *Pittsburgh Courier*. He took time to celebrate the dismissal of "the end of the first political trial a la Moscow in this country." In Schuyler's view, "Roosevelt and his henchmen were eager to convict this group chiefly in order to establish a precedent" eventually allowing them to go after "the Patterson-McCormick newspapers, the Hearst newspapers, Norman Thomas, Oswald Garrison Villard, the Rev. John Haynes Holmes, and others whose opposition has been vindicated by subsequent events." Those most potentially endangered were African American journalists who, among them, had caused more "insubordination than anything any of these people on trial said or wrote." The only reason the administration had not attempted such prosecutions, according to Schuyler, was "the undoubted mass reaction of the Negroes in and out of uniform to such an action." In stark contrast to Schuyler's jubilation, Winchell bemoaned that a worthy trial had floundered "in a swamp of petty legalisms" capped off with the injustice of Rogge's firing.[68]

The demise of *McWilliams* did not mean that the federal government had given up the whole enterprise of sedition trials. Only months after Eicher's death, the Department of Justice began to build a case against the Communist Party under the Smith Act. Ironically, the new crop of defendants eventually secured the legal assistance of O. John Rogge. The former prosecutor lamented that although people in the past had commonly associated sedition with fascists, "anti-fascists" were becoming the new targets. Thus, it was essential "that civil liberties must be safeguarded, regardless of whether a man who might properly belong in jail goes free." Although Rogge later conceded that he might not have brought *McWilliams* had it been his choice, he never repudiated the validity of the prosecution.[69]

While the sedition trial ended in fiasco, it may have also served a broader Roosevelt administration goal, at least temporarily, of intimidating critics. Few Americans wanted to be associated with such disreputable characters, and others, including African American journalists, may have pulled their punches for fear of being next if they crossed certain boundaries. But it is also true that the trial backfired in the long term for many of those who had wanted it so much. Almost as soon as it began, New Deal liberals were having second thoughts, and conservatives were starting to mobilize against the "New Deal Witch hunt." Memories of the trial survived for quite some time in the conservative and libertarian subculture. More than once over the next decades, many rationalized their McCarthyism by bitterly reminding critics that they had once been the victims.[70]

The collapse of the sedition trial did not dull the appetites of many New Dealers to investigate the political opposition. Instead of relying on massive show trials, they returned to the methods once used by the Black and Minton committees. In 1944, just as the sedition trial was entering its final phase, the

Anderson Committee launched yet another investigation into lobbying. The committee's main target was the same organization that had so bedeviled Senator Minton in 1938.

Conclusion

EVEN AS THE sedition trial was in the headlines, the US House Committee on Campaign Expenditures was immersing itself in a far less publicized investigation. The committee (also known as the Anderson Committee, named for its chair, Representative Clinton Anderson [D-NM]) fixed its gaze on the Committee for Constitutional Government (CCG), which had shortened its name in 1941 from the old National Committee to Uphold Constitutional Government (NCUCG). In a multitude of ways, this investigation represented continuity to the congressional lobbying investigations of the 1930s. As of yet, there was not going to be a ceasefire in the New Deal ideological war, as initiated by Roosevelt. While the Anderson Committee eventually came (more or less) to naught, it indirectly spawned the Buchanan Committee of 1950. Considerable overlap existed between those investigations and the sedition trial, and all three, in their own ways, had a lasting impact. An important legacy of the Buchanan Committee was a precedent-setting US Supreme Court decision on free speech and privacy.

From the late 1930s to the early 1950s, the Committee for Constitutional Government (CCG) had ranked high as a nemesis for New Dealer and Fair Dealer pundits and activists. Throughout this period, Edward A. Rumely remained the de facto head of the organization, and Frank Gannett was the main financial backer. After Gannett resigned as chair in 1940 to run for the Republican Party presidential nomination, Samuel B. Pettengill, a self-described "Jeffersonian" and former US House Democratic representative from Indiana, took over. Succeeding him in 1942 was the well-known religious leader and best-selling author Norman Vincent Peale. By 1944, the main office in New York City hummed with activity. The CCG had thirty-four employees, not including "men in the field," and in the first eight months of that year had receipts of $255,000 (about $4.2 million in 2023).[1]

During World War II, the CCG was repeatedly a roadblock for the administration on such issues as labor legislation, rent control, public housing, and national health insurance. Most worrisome of all for supporters of the New Deal, however, was the CCG's push in the states for a constitutional convention to limit federal taxes to 25 percent on incomes, gifts, and inheritance. By 1944, only one year after the effort began, the proposed amendment had received the backing of seventeen of the necessary thirty-two states.[2]

Many of the same people who cheered on the sedition investigation were becoming anxious about the CCG's rapid successes. These concerns came to a head in 1944 when the CCG established a presence in the congressional district of Representative Wright Patman (D-TX). The feisty New Deal populist dismissed as cynical camouflage the CCG's explanation that its goal for coming there was to educate youth about the Bill of Rights through such methods as sponsoring essay contests for Texas high school students. The real reason, he charged, was to turn him out of office, and in July 1944, he launched a one-man war on the CCG's "Quisling reserves," the "most sordid and most sinister lobby ever organized." Patman attacked the CCG from the House floor upward of twenty-nine times over the next seven years.[3]

One month after Patman had fired his volley at the CCG, Sidney Hillman, the head of the powerful Political Action Committee (PAC) of the Congress of Industrial Organizations (CIO), came to his aid. In 1944, while appearing as a witness before the House Committee on Campaign Expenditures, Hillman called for an investigation of several conservative and free-market organizations, including the CCG. A receptive Anderson came to Hillman's office to formulate strategy, along with two of the CIO-PAC's lawyers, Lee Pressman and John J. Abt (still a secret Communist).[4]

No labor leader was closer to Roosevelt's ear than Sidney Hillman. Shortly after the Democratic convention, Arthur Krock of the *New York Times* reported that the president had quipped, "Clear everything with Sidney," before selecting Harry S. Truman as his running mate. While the accuracy of this story is in dispute, no one doubted that Hillman wielded great influence in administration and other New Deal circles. Throughout the 1944 campaign,

Republicans made the phrase "Clear it with Sidney" into one of their favorite talking points. The CIO-PAC mobilized in full force to reelect Roosevelt as well as other Democratic candidates.[5]

CCG representatives who testified before the Anderson Committee may well have felt a sense of déjà vu. Nearly all of them had appeared before the Minton Committee in 1938. The questions and responses were also similar. As in 1938, Sumner Gerard, the treasurer of the CCG, denied any partisan agenda: "We did not advocate the election of anybody. We wanted to stop certain tendencies that we saw were encroaching upon our constitutional form of government." Alleging a double standard, Gannett depicted the creation of the CIO-PAC as a New Deal ploy to raise funds through "coercive" pressure over sometimes unwilling members. CCG officers also complained that the Internal Revenue Service had allowed groups such as the CIO-PAC to receive tax-deductible contributions.[6]

The Anderson Committee hearings of 1944 followed another familiar pattern. They started with a dragnet subpoena for "the books, papers, records, and documents of the Committee for Constitutional Government" plus the names of contributors for 1944 "of $100 or more." Also, as before, Rumely virtually dared a contempt citation by refusing to divulge the names of contributors. Championing the "constitutional right of privacy," he did not want the "partisan snoopers and smearers" to have a "precedent to demand the names of the purchasers of books of any publisher, the contracts made with any advertisers, the names of supporters of trade, business and professional organizations advocating any divergent economic theory or political philosophy." Former chair Pettengill, backing up Rumely, considered it foolhardy to expose CCG financial backers to the prying eyes of Winchell and *PM*. He blamed the New Deal for creating a "sort of reign of terror in this country now for some years." Americans "are afraid of the N.L.R.B. [National Labor Relations Board]. They are afraid of the S.E.C. [Securities Exchange Commission]. They are afraid of the Federal Communications Commission." According to Pettengill, prospective CCG donors had repeatedly asked, "'Will our names be given; will we be exposed?' And we have said, 'No, you will not be exposed.'"[7]

At first, the odds against Rumely were enormous, but of course that was also true in 1938. With only the lone Republican present dissenting, the Anderson Committee approved a contempt citation, and Speaker Sam Rayburn (D-TX) sent it on to federal prosecutors. The US House did not bother to vote on the matter. To justify his refusal to comply, Rumely appealed to the theory of Justice Brandeis that the right of privacy took priority. Gannett chimed in that if a committee "dominated by a New Deal zealot, can force us to comply with its demands, then it can demand the names of every advertiser of any newspaper, the names and contributors to any organization, church or charitable institution." Much like in 1938, the *Nation* dismissed the CCG's rhetoric as a hypocritical smokescreen to shield a secretive and nefarious organization and considered it overdue to turn "the spotlight on these rightest and often subversive movements." It continued: "[T]ermites," like Rumely, "cannot operate with immunity in the United States."[8]

But Rumely, fortified with Gannett's money, legal team, and experience, dug in for a war of attrition. He lost the first engagement. One week after Rayburn certified the resolution, a federal grand jury indicted Rumely for contempt. After a quick arraignment, a series of delays followed, and a trial date became ever more distant.[9]

Meanwhile, the Anderson Committee was morphing into a cloak-and-dagger operation. In August, the Non-Sectarian Anti-Nazi League (NSANL) successfully inserted one its employees, Sallie M. Connolly, as a mole in the CCG's New York office. Not only did her duties put her in close proximity to Gerard, but, at the suggestion of her NSANL handlers, she widened her reach by volunteering to do various errands. Taking advantage of this access, she passed on internal documents, including brand-new copies of the CCG's publications, so recent that the ordinary members had not yet seen them. The NSANL, in turn, gave everything she found to the Anderson Committee. What was still lacking, however, was a smoking gun to implicate either Rumely or any other officer in illegal activity.[10]

At about the same time as Rumely's contempt citation, a matter of pure luck enabled the CCG to turn the tables. An "intelligence officer in the Federal government" informed Gerard that someone ensconced in the CCG was leaking confidential documents that were then making their way to the Anderson Committee. An ex-FBI agent hired by Gerard to investigate soon identified Connolly as a suspect and trailed her making forays to NSANL headquarters. Confronted with the evidence, Connolly confessed to the whole thing, expressed remorse, and signed a detailed affidavit on October 17, 1944. "I am very sorry because I feel it was really a wrong thing to do," she stated, "and I intended to stop. I was going to tell them [NSANL] last week I couldn't do it any longer." Gerard and Rumely decided for the time being to keep their discovery quiet from the public. Seeking to prove a pipeline from the CCG to the Anderson Committee, they recruited the remorseful Connolly to act as a double agent. They had her, as their bait, convey a memorandum from Rumely to Gerard (dated October 18), describing an ongoing CCG project costing $14,102. Gerard and Rumely made the wording sufficiently obscure to pique curiosity from Connolly's handlers. The memo described the funds as "one special commitment" and featured a cryptic notation from Gerard at the bottom, reading, "Owing to the present situation we must move cautiously. I suggest I see you first (confidentially) to talk it over."[11]

As Rumely and Gerard had gambled, the Anderson Committee took the bait. In separate letters to Gerard and Rumely, Anderson reproduced for the press the most provocative quotations from the purloined memo and implied a serious election violation. He demanded that the organization explain the wording, pointedly stating that failure to report spending for partisan purposes constituted guilt under the Corrupt Practices Act. Anderson followed up by publicly airing his charges. Meanwhile, James H. Sheldon, the chair of NSANL's board of directors, not suspecting that he was one of the victims of a CCG sting, boasted to Anderson that this disclosure would "certainly get some results" and enclosed, per Anderson's previous request, five additional photostats of the original.[12]

Gerard was careful not to tip his hand in his response to Anderson. While he pleaded innocence in a very general way, he did not offer specifics or express any outrage. Instead, he coyly requested a photostat of the memo from the Anderson Committee, stating that he had no record of it in his files. Probing a bit further, Gerard inquired if the committee intended to charge Rumely with perjury. He launched his counterattack with full force only after Anderson sent on the requested photostat. The CCG released an official statement accusing the committee of attempting to defame it with a "stolen document" about a routine transaction that had no connection with electioneering. The true purpose of the $14,102, it explained, was to defray the costs of printing 200,000 copies of the Bill of Rights in multiple colors and languages suitable for display in churches and schools. Somewhat at a loss to respond, Anderson denied any theft of the document but also did not explain how he got it. More importantly, he disputed the CCG's claim that the money was for a routine expense. He also stressed that (contrary to rumors) the committee had no intention of charging Rumely with perjury. For the time being, Gerard and Rumely let the matter slide and so did Anderson.[13]

This was not the only bombshell that had turned out to be a dud for the Anderson Committee. In November 1944, the Stern-owned and NSANL-allied *Philadelphia Record* had reported that the Anderson Committee had found that Joseph N. Pew Jr., a Philadelphia industrialist and CCG contributor, had "financed the distribution of at least 1,000,000 anti-Semitic postcards" abusing Sidney Hillman and urging the election of Thomas E. Dewey. Pew denied this and publicly demanded a retraction. Forced on the defensive, Anderson explained that the story had misquoted him and told the *Record*'s reporter that Pew had, in fact, fully cooperated with the investigation.[14]

Although the CCG pretty much won these two skirmishes, the adverse publicity seriously set back the fight for the tax limitation amendment, a measure increasingly depicted as a "millionaire's amendment." At the beginning of 1944, seventeen out of the necessary thirty-two state legislatures had called for a convention. Less than a year later, this momentum had shifted into reverse as several states rescinded their ratifications, reducing the total to fourteen. To former Roosevelt adviser Lowell Mellett, this trend was a hopeful sign that the "tide of reaction in his country seems to be receding." To top it off, the CCG suffered some longer-term financial damage. In a pattern similar to the aftermath of the Black and Minton committees, gun-shy donors closed their wallets. The CCG also was on the receiving end of a legislative defeat, or so it seemed. The Lobbying Act of 1946 required disclosure of all donors of $500 or more. The law gave a sweeping definition of lobbying as encompassing any attempt to influence the passage of legislation.[15]

In early 1945, as a trial date for Rumely still had not been set, Anderson was moving on other fronts as well. He urged the Bureau of Internal Revenue to deny the CCG's tax deductibility because of "its vicious, malicious political slander of top characters in public life such as the President." He charged that the CCG had shown its partisan colors by entering "Patman's district for the sole purpose of destroying him politically." Even as Rogge was searching for Nazi ties to incriminate the sedition defendants, Anderson was imploring Assistant Attorney General Wendell Berge to find out if Rumely was communicating with "his old friends in Germany." There is no record of a response from Berge. Along with the sedition defendants, Rumely had figured prominently in the list of alleged subversives in John Roy Carlson's NSANL/FOD–supported exposé, *Under Cover.*[16]

Much like Hugo L. Black nearly a decade earlier, Anderson depicted himself as a crusader for full transparency: "Enforced disclosure by purveyors of political propaganda thus becomes as necessary for the protection of the public as it has in the past been recognized to be in the case of food and drugs, and in the case of securities." Through forcing transparency, Anderson hoped to expose the CCG as "a bad outfit, not necessarily bad because of some of the people who are connected with it but turned to very bad channels I think by its executive director, Dr. Rumely."[17]

The Rumely case did not go to trial in the US District Court until March 1945, five months after the indictment, and it finally came to a close in October because of a hung jury. Government prosecutors moved to try him again but fared even worse. In April 1946, a jury in the US District Court gave Rumely a full acquittal on the contempt charge. Drew Pearson later complained that "in the long history of the United States, Rumely is one of only three cases who has thumbed his nose at Congress and got away with it."[18]

After the acquittal, Gerard considered it opportune to reveal to Anderson, who had become secretary of agriculture under Harry S. Truman in June 1945, the full story of NSANL's mole. According to Gerard, these revelations so bothered the former congressman that he retracted his allegation to the Bureau of Internal Revenue that the CCG was a partisan organization. Anderson's 1947 letter to Joseph P. Kamp of the Constitutional Educational League (a smaller, right-wing nationalist group), also targeted by the probe, does indeed reveal a change in attitude. He reserved special disdain for James H. Sheldon, the head of the "special interest ... so-called Anti-Nazi League." Anderson related to Kamp that Sheldon had not only tried to dictate the nature of the inquiry but made an ethically dubious offer to reveal "for a price" the complete copy of the CCG's financial records. Anderson said that he turned Sheldon down but did not acknowledge the extent of his past collaboration with NSANL. Anderson was probably sincere in his regrets, however.

His record was not that of a reflexive New Deal loyalist of the Minton type. Almost from the time he took office as secretary of agriculture, he played a central role in successfully encouraging President Truman to reach out to former president Herbert Hoover, then still a pariah to many on the left, to work together on food relief for Europe.[19]

With the Anderson Committee defunct for well over a year, the 1946 congressional elections showed that Mellett was somewhat premature in predicting that the "tide of reaction" had receded. The Republicans won their largest majorities in both houses since the 1920s. In this new political atmosphere, the CCG had an unprecedented opening to influence debates on such issues as labor legislation and governmental health insurance. Well-fortified with funds, the CCG, according to the *Congressional Quarterly*, ranked second to the AFL as a leading big-spending "pressure group."[20]

After Truman's upset victory in 1948, bringing Democratic majorities in the House and Senate, however, the victors promised again to scrutinize lobbies widely blamed for the previous Republican triumph. The CCG was high on their list. The *New Republic*'s first postelection issue declared triumphantly that the "New Deal is again empowered to carry forward the promise of American life" and that it was high time to investigate "the great lobbies and the millions they have spent … to defeat social legislation." The American Federation of Labor (AFL) and the CIO agreed on this goal, as did Pearson, Winchell, and Truman himself. The president's speeches during the 1948 campaign had stressed the dangers of lobbies. Less than a week before the election, he had blasted the current Republican Congress as the "most thoroughly surrounded Congress with lobbies in the whole history of this great country. … It's disgraceful, and you ought not to let that happen again."[21]

Truman threw his administration's full weight behind the call for an investigation. Shortly after the election, he opined in a letter to Eric Peterson, the general secretary and treasurer of the National Association of Machinists, that "a thorough investigation of lobbying activities would have a very salutary effect." Peterson's initial letter to Truman blamed both the CCG and the International Association of Manufacturers for seeking "to block your legislative program."[22]

Haggling over the details of a joint Senate/House committee, however, greatly slowed the promised investigation. The prospect of prominent anti-

Truman Senator Pat McCarran (D-NV) as chair led the US House finally to go it alone. In August 1949, it authorized a seven-member select committee under Representative Frank Buchanan (D-PA), who had long regarded the CCG as a stumbling block to causes he favored, such as public housing and labor legislation. At his urging, the House defined the Lobbying Committee's mission sweepingly to include investigation of "all lobbying activities intended to influence, encourage, promote or retard legislation."[23]

If the CCG's officers felt under siege as a result, they did not show it. Although the group had registered protest under the Lobbying Act of 1946, it was resourceful in finding ways around the reporting requirement. Instead of accepting cash contributions of over $490, it took them in the form of book orders. The CCG first used this method in a major way to promote John T. Flynn's full-bore assault on the New Deal, *The Road Ahead: America's Creeping Revolution* (1949). Flynn had warned that leftist pressure groups were edging the United States into socialism through an incremental Fabian strategy as had happened in Britain. Harper and Brothers sold the book for $2.50, but the CCG slashed the price to $1.00 and even lower in bulk, thus creating an incentive for mass purchases by groups such as the American Medical Association.[24]

Flynn's message reached a still greater audience when *Reader's Digest*, which had a circulation of nine million, carried a condensed version in February 1950. From 1949 to 1950, more than a million copies of the book turned up in the offices of doctors, dentists, and professional people throughout the country. "In neat piles on waiting room tables," wrote a critic of the CCG, "where they could not escape the attention of the bored and the apprehensive alike, reposed countless copies of a book that became, if not the most widely read book of the year, one that was at least the most widely distributed." Similarly, the Friends of Democracy described this effort as one "of the largest propaganda drives in recent years."[25]

Meanwhile, the CCG's stalled campaign for a constitutional limit on taxes was making a comeback. Beginning in 1950, after a long lull, several more state legislatures approved the proposed amendment, reaching a new high of twenty-two the following year. The CCG was proving a resilient enemy to New Dealers, and to Harry Truman's Fair Dealers, and, in some ways, was emerging from the reverses suffered during the Anderson Committee investigation more powerful than ever.[26]

As the CCG was gaining traction and Flynn's treatise found its way into nearly every congressional district, the Buchanan Committee finally began to gear up through a probing questionnaire sent to more than 170 businesses and organizations. The wording defined lobbying in the broadest possible terms to also include groups responsible for the indirect formation of political ideas. Buchanan vowed to play no favorites and said that the only goal was information and transparency, but few of the questionnaires went out to businesses or groups led by New Dealers or Fair Dealers. Especially revealing was the question asking to "include all expenditures in connection with" eight, and only eight, named organizations. All but one of these groups were either right-wing or libertarian in orientation: the CCG, the American Enterprise Association (the predecessor of the American Enterprise Institute), America's Future, Inc. (a conservative outlet for Robert R. McCormick of the *Chicago Daily Tribune*), the Constitution and Free Enterprise Foundation, the Economists National Committee for Monetary Policy (pro–gold standard), the libertarian Foundation for Economic Education (FEE), and the Constitutional Educational League. The lone exception to this pattern was the Public Affairs Institute, a left-of-center group that promoted a larger welfare state.[27]

The most glaring omissions on the Lobbying Committee's target list were the CIO-PAC as well as businesses allied with the administration, such as Kaiser, Latex Corporation, Consolidated Vultee, and Ed Pauley's oil interests. Buchanan himself revealed some explicit bias early on when he said that three out of the eight organizations under fire advocate "a brand of American Fascism; they are against those who believe in a free, progressive America."[28]

Buchanan's failure to consult with, or even inform, the Republican minority on the committee until well after sending out the questionnaire came to dog him in the coming months. From the beginning, the Republican members were suspicious. Nevertheless, everything went smoothly for the committee during the first phase of hearings in April and May, which centered on assorted witnesses from the "real estate lobby." Although some Republicans grumbled about overreach, they all cooperated. The most publicized episode came when Buchanan and other Democrats put Herbert U. Nelson, the executive vice president of the National Association of Real Estate Boards, into the spotlight because of a letter he had had sent in 1949 to the incoming president of the organization, T. H. Maenner. Nelson had declared, "I do not believe in democracy. I think it stinks." The Republicans charged that someone on the committee had leaked and quoted out of context Nelson's "private correspondence," thus contradicting Buchanan's vow of an unbiased investigation. Nelson emphasized that his letter had also specified support for a "republican form of government" with limited powers, but the overall effect of the imbroglio put detractors of the Buchanan Committee on the defensive.[29]

By this time, the investigation was starting to scare away CCG contributors. On this matter, both friend and foe agreed. "Book sales by the Committee for Constitutional Government," declared the *UAW-CIO Ammunition* with some encouragement, "have fallen off substantially since the committee's activities have had some light put on them." More somberly, Rumely admitted to John T. Flynn that "the Buchanan Committee has cost us heavily."[30]

Even so, in another repetition of what had happened to Minton and Anderson, the tide was starting to turn against the investigation in other ways. The first signs of trouble for the Buchanan Committee came on June 5, when William C. Mullendore, the president of the Southern California Edison Company and a trustee of FEE, publicly refused to answer the questionnaire. Mullendore blasted the inquiry as an intimidating threat to "the right of free speech by millions of citizens in opposing or supporting proposed legislation" and "a brazen attempt at thought control." Mullendore's defiance, seconded by Clarence B. Randall, the president of the Inland Steel Company, probably stiffened Rumely's resolve as he prepared to testify the next day. Rumely, never shying from a good fight, had already decided in May not to comply, opining to Frank Gannett that "[t]hirty or sixty or ninety days in jail in a fight for principle are not without real compensation." A grimly determined Buchanan repeatedly pressed the witness, but Rumely retorted (much as he had at previous congressional inquiries) that he had no intention of giving "the names of the people who bought books." His promise to answer all of the other twenty-five questions did not appease the Democratic majority. After rebuffing Rumely's request to enter a statement of explanation into the record, Buchanan curtly dismissed the witness.[31]

In contrast to Rumely, two other key targets of the Buchanan Committee, the National Economic Council (a right-wing nationalist organization headed by Merwin K. Hart) and the FEE (headed by Leonard Read), chose to cooperate. Joseph P. Kamp of the Constitutional Educational League testified that he was willing to comply but did not know what Buchanan expected of him. Both Hart and Read made no secret that they appeared under protest. Prior to Read's testimony, Mullendore had privately warned him that he was "going against a bunch of cut-throats who have very vicious motives."[32]

But Read, ever the sunny optimist, sought to turn adversity into opportunity, stating to Mullendore that if "the intention is purely for information, enlightenment and philosophy on freedom vs. licensing, then a careful statement is in order." In the end, the amiable and erudite Read acquitted himself well, though he stipulated that he thought the committee was exceeding its authority. After listening to Read, Buchanan, then very much in the opposition's crosshairs, diplomatically stated that the FEE was not "a propaganda mill" but rather "strictly a research and educational institution, according to your viewpoint."[33]

Read's conciliatory testimony received little publicity compared to the energetic counterattack by Mullendore and Rumely. Their resistance threw the Buchanan Committee back on its heels permanently. Media commentary, which had generally ignored the investigation, turned abruptly hostile. The committee faced a barrage of unrelenting press attacks in the two weeks after Rumely's testimony. One of the first salvos, an editorial from the *Plain Dealer* (Cleveland, OH), stressed the selectivity of the investigation, alleging that Buchanan had purposely ignored corporate "pets of the administration" such as the Henry Kaiser enterprises. Similarly, the *Nashville (TN) Banner* wondered why the Americans for Democratic Action (ADA) and the CIO-PAC had not received the committee's questionnaire, and the *Richmond (VA) News Leader* advised Buchanan to "take a long running jump in[to] the nearest convenient lake." Even Buchanan's hometown paper, the *Pittsburgh (PA) Post-Gazette*, condemned the probe. More than a few opponents demonstrated elephantine memories through a background analysis of the investigation's history and backers. The *Chicago Daily Tribune* made a direct comparison to Hugo L. Black's "infamous inquisition into lobbying" during the 1930s and emphasized the behind-the-scenes "assistance in his smearing campaign" by "a poison pen outfit misnamed 'Friends of Democracy.'"[34]

In contrast to the media response to the Anderson Committee, this first wave of anti–Buchanan Committee commentary also included several prominent establishment outlets. For example, *Editor and Publisher* called the inquiry "an invasion of the guaranteed right of the American people to own, hire or use a printing press without interference," and Marquis Childs, a popular syndicated columnist with impeccable pro–New Deal credentials, had this to say in the *Washington Post*: "Such a precedent is exceedingly dangerous to all of us who cherish the freedoms that have made this Nation great." True to form, but more isolated than in the past, Winchell consistently championed the committee, remarking that the "pompous" Rumely was being "coy about handing over the names of the dupes" who supported him. Joining Winchell in this stance was the *CIO News*, which had published several editorial cartoons belittling the CCG as a puppet of wealthy interests.[35]

As the press gave ever-increasing cover to Republican minority members on the committee, those members become more confident in challenging Buchanan. In an academic account, which was highly favorable to the investigation, political scientist Karl Schriftgiesser summed up the tenor of the partisan divide:

> Two members of the minority, Representatives Brown and Halleck, were obsessed with the thought that the committee members, and particularly the chairman, were intent upon absolving all "left wing" lobbies of wrongdoing, and equally intent upon condemning all "right wing" lobbies. If by "right wing" is meant organizations dedicated to all antidemocratic measures that have come before Congress since 1932, and if by "left wing" is meant labor unions, small business organizations, minority groups, consumer lobbies, and the like, the charge has some validity.[36]

Thrown off balance by all the unanticipated flak, Buchanan scrambled to regain the high ground. In a confrontation on the House floor with Representative Clare Hoffman (R-MI), one of the most vocal congressional detractors of the committee, he announced his intention to send questionnaires to the CIO-PAC, the ADA, and key Democratic corporate donors such as Consolidated Vultee and the Kaiser interests. Furthermore, Buchanan reemphasized that he did not want to single out anyone. This gesture led Hoffman (who was similarly prominent six years earlier in denouncing the sedition trial) to quip that, had the committee included the named organizations in the original probe, "there might not have been so much criticism."[37]

Buchanan's reassurances did not impress the critics, who dismissed it as mere window dressing. To the extent that Buchanan's new strategy was sincere, his efforts to implement it may even have rebounded against him. He sent questionnaires to, and scheduled hearings for, the pro–New Deal ADA and the hard-left Civil Rights Congress (CRC), a group aligned with the Communist Party. The naming of the CRC prompted the *Daily Worker*, which a decade earlier had demanded prosecuting Rumely for sedition, to blast the investigation as a "witchhunt." Whereas ADA leader Francis Biddle, who had authorized the sedition trial of 1944 as attorney general, fully cooperated and supported mandatory disclosure of contributors and purchasers of books, the head of the CRC, William L. Patterson, took the opposite approach. The Buchanan Committee eventually sent a questionnaire to the CIO, the AFL, and key Democratic corporate donors, including Consolidated Vultee and the various Kaiser-owned interests, but did not call witnesses or hold hearings on these groups. The reasons for not doing so are unclear but may have included Buchanan's desire to wrap things up before the election in 1952 and his increasing weariness of the whole enterprise.[38]

Patterson of the Civil Rights Congress was Rumely's political opposite, but the nature of his confrontation with the committee was strikingly similar. So too was the reaction it produced. The Democratic majority was uniformly hostile, albeit for somewhat different reasons. Because of the rise of McCarthy earlier that year, besieged New Dealers were not going to give any quarter to an alleged Communist. By putting Patterson through the wringer, they also gained cover to demonstrate that they had not singled out the political right.

Like Rumely, Patterson attacked the committee's definition of "indirect lobbying" as overly broad and denied that the CRC, though it took stands on legislation, fell within it. When pressed by Representative Henderson Lanham (D-GA) and Buchanan Committee counsel Benedict F. Fitzgerald for the names of contributors, Patterson answered much like Rumely would have:

MR. FITZGERALD: And you refuse to furnish any list of contributors?

MR. PATTERSON: I do. If I am defending my civil rights, as I think I am right now, it's a question of defending their civil rights—

MR. LANHAM: Let's not get into that. We are not interested in that. Now answer the question.[39]

But it was another, more fiery, exchange with Lanham about lynchings in Georgia that generated the most headlines. The most explosive moment never made it into the official record, though African American and leftist newspapers reported on it. Lanham was so incensed by Patterson's testimony that the Capitol Police had to restrain him as he lunged at the witness, calling him a "black son-of-a-bitch." A deluge of racially charged fan letters from constituents poured into Lanham's office. While Lanham, a self-described "progressive" who had first ridden to office with CIO backing, expressed some regret, he generally defended his actions as justified "because of the provocation from this contemptable [sic] chocolate covered Communist."[40]

In the aftermath of the Lanham–Patterson brawl, Aubrey Grossman, the CRC's national organizational secretary, sounding again like Rumely, stressed that the potential threat to the CRC went beyond a single racial incident. He accused the Buchanan Committee of scheming to intimidate CRC donors by requiring "the names and addresses of contributors from Mississippi, Georgia and other Southern states for the defense of Willie McGee [a black man sentenced to death on rape charges in Mississippi], the Martinsville Seven, and other similar victims of southern 'justice.'" Perhaps because of controversies like this, committee staffers passed the word on to Truman that Buchanan planned to step down as chair once the committee had completed its report.[41]

Rumely's conservative defenders had diverse reactions when confronted with accusations that the methods of the Buchanan Committee and the Mc-Carthy Committee were analogous. The CCG avoided the issue entirely. For his part, John T. Flynn (who had become a defender of McCarthy) rejected any comparison out of hand. According to Flynn, ongoing congressional anti-Communist investigations, unlike that of the Buchanan Committee, had "nothing to do with the right of Communists to write books" but rather focused on "the behavior of men who are Communists—who refuse to admit they are Communists—and who sneak into the State Department, the Intelligence departments and the public schools and at public expense corrupt the minds of American children against their government." Like Flynn, such important figures on the right as Representative Clare Hoffman and former Representative John McDowell, who had served on the House Committee on Un-American Activities, pointed out that many of the same leftists declaiming against red-hunters for violation of civil liberties had egged on the sedition prosecution.[42]

In August 1950, the Buchanan Committee referred three separate contempt resolutions to the House for a floor vote. The first, and most publicized, centered on Rumely, the second on Patterson, and the third on Joseph P. Kamp. In the floor debate, Democratic majority leader Representative John W. McCormack (D-MA) went to bat for the Buchanan Committee. In language as incendiary as any uttered by Senator Joseph McCarthy, he excoriated Rumely as "a spy in World War I, and a man who is nothing but a Fascist, who is an opponent of American institutions and American Government." As dogged as ever, Wright Patman said a "cancer on the American body politic, Rumely, and the coterie of blind Tories that support him are sending across the Nation a book written by a psychopath named John T. Flynn." Although Buchanan avowed again that his investigation was completely evenhanded, he undercut this somewhat by characterizing the CCG as an un-American "anti-Fair-Deal propaganda mill for reaction" that was "seeking to kill off the liberal-labor movement in America."[43]

Just about the only opponents of the Rumely contempt resolution were conservatives. The most notable exception was Representative Vito Marcantonio (American Labor Party-NY). Marcantonio portrayed himself as a free speech absolutist even for a "Fascist" such as Rumely. If Rumely's conservative defenders were sincere in their calls to uphold the First Amendment, Marcantonio contended, consistency dictated a vote against the Patterson contempt resolution. This rhetorical flourish aside, Marcantonio's record on free speech was at best mixed. During World War II, for example, he had not only applauded prosecuting the political right for sedition but urged even tougher action. The final vote on the resolution citing Rumely for contempt was close, 183 to 175. Nearly all Republicans opposed it, joined by Marcantonio and forty-two Democrats; almost everyone in the latter group was from the South. Most Southern Democrats, however, supported the Rumely resolution. The overall alignment in the vote citing Kamp for contempt, which received much less publicity, was similar, though more lopsided, 215 to 115.[44]

The Patterson contempt resolution also passed, but by a far more sizable majority compared to the one centering on Rumely. Although the debate took place during the height of McCarthyism, Republicans cast virtually all the 106 votes against it. This outcome prompted the *Daily Worker*, which had once demanded hauling up Rumely for sedition, to cautiously praise the Republican–Marcantonio alignment as evidence that the "logic of Marcantonio's words had an effect." Or perhaps, it added, "some Republicans were worried by having to explain their vote in defense of this avowed reactionary propagandist for Wall Street."[45]

By contrast, Southern Democrats who opposed citing Rumely for contempt voted for the Patterson resolution even though the charges were essentially the same. For the Southerners and twenty-eight Republicans who backed it, race or anticommunism, and sometimes both, trumped all other considerations. Representative John Rankin (D-MS), perhaps the most notorious racist in Congress, justified his split vote by characterizing the CCG as an organization "for constitutional government" but the CRC as a "Communist outfit" advocating "the overthrow of Government." Most Southern Democrats—including, of course, Lanham—voted to cite Rumely for contempt. To Lanham, "those at the extreme right [including those who subscribed to Rumely's "peculiar brand of Fascism"] are almost as dangerous to our way of life as those to the extreme left."[46]

Although the Buchanan Committee swayed a narrow House majority against Rumely, its campaign to win over the press was proving futile. If anything, Rumely's steadfastness was making him a more sympathetic figure. "We believe," charged the *Wall Street Journal* in language that was becoming a staple of the critics, that "the Buchanan committee's course, now approved by a bare majority of the House members present, is objectionable and even dangerous." The Lobbying Committee's defenders outside the halls of Congress fought an uphill battle to stem the tide against it. In an article for the *Nation*, Willard Shelton praised the committee's "first-rate job," including the "biting" prose of its final report, which had characterized *The Road Ahead* as a "moody panegyric to the eighteenth-century."[47]

In the months following the vote, interest in the Buchanan Committee gradually died down, with one notable exception: the columns of Westbrook Pegler. Pegler's acerbic, over-the-top, increasingly right-wing populist commentary reached millions of readers during the 1940s and 1950s. At first, Pegler, though suspicious of the Buchanan Committee, paid relatively little attention to it. After Congress cited Rumely for contempt, however, he went into attack mode and never let up. In column after column, he depicted the Buchanan Committee as the culmination of a New Deal suppressionism stretching back to the Black Committee of 1936.

Pegler's line of argument had some idiosyncratic aspects. His main concerns were not free speech or even partisan angles. Rather, his fixation was on the hidden and, in his view, sinister role in the investigation of an interlocking network that included the NSANL, the FOD, and the Society for the Prevention of World War III (a group that favored a harsh peace toward Germany). He branded the investigation as an "absolute fake" because it "deliberately exempted" any consideration of these groups. Buchanan's real goal, Pegler charged, was to put "into hostile hands the names of the anti-Communist, nationalistic patriots including many who had bought John T. Flynn's anti-socialist and anti-communist book." The cast of characters in Pegler's columns were largely absent from most other commentary during the period. They included Sheldon, Birkhead, and Isadore Lipschutz, the financial angel of both the NSANL and the Society for the Prevention of World War III.[48]

Pegler's preoccupation with conspiracy was famously obsessive but was not entirely off base and thus elicited some discomfort in these groups. During the same month that the US House cited Rumely for contempt, Birkhead urged the Department of Justice to prosecute the columnist for sedition under the Smith Act because of comments critical of US involvement in the Korean War. But while the role played by NSANL/FOD in helping the Buchanan Committee, as it had the Anderson Committee, certainly merits more scrutiny, it can be overdone. Anderson and Buchanan, and before them Black, quite consciously were carrying on an anti-lobbying investigative tradition that predated the formation of these groups.[49]

The next major legal round after the contempt vote went against Rumely. In April 1951, US Federal District judge Richmond B. Keech gave him a six-month suspended sentence for contempt and a $1,000 fine, saying that he would have sent the 68-year-old defendant to jail save for his advanced age. Rumely was unmoved: "I already had given them 95 percent of what they wanted. But on that one point—'who bought your books?' we would not yield." Winchell exulted that he had gotten "real satisfaction out of the conviction last week of Edw. A. Rumely. ... A convicted pro-German agent." Only a few newspapers or columnists expressed agreement with Winchell, though the *Washington Post* editorialized that the ruling put everyone on notice that they "can withhold information from Congress only at their peril." Even the *New Republic* and the *Nation* as well as Pearson, who had cheered on Buchanan at the beginning, were generally silent.[50]

Buchanan was unable to savor his apparent vindication in the courts for long. Only days after Rumely's conviction, Buchanan, only 48, died from a postoperative internal hemorrhage. Representative Lanham had "no doubt but that the misrepresentation and vilification to which he was subjected contributed to his untimely death." Pegler was predictably less charitable, wondering why Buchanan had launched his lobbying crusade in the first place: "Maybe one of Lipschutz's gum-shoe men had uncovered his past and put the heat on him."[51]

The combined pressure from Congress and the courts, however, had seriously, and perhaps permanently, damaged the CCG. The investigation created a chilling effect as money dried up from formerly dependable contributors, expressing fear of being named. Rumely complained that donors had become money-shy because of the congressional investigation, "causing heavy financial loss for the Committee." The inner circle of the Truman administration agreed, albeit from a different perspective, that the investigation had scared away donors. In August 1950, administrative assistant to the president David D. Lloyd, who had previously worked as research director of the liberal ADA, observed that "[c]ontinuing disclosure of the financial sources of the anti–Fair New Deal propaganda which is now flooding the country would, of course, be welcome during the Fall." He praised Buchanan's discovery of "a new undercover Liberty League" run by wealthy interests. Truman himself, shortly before the election of 1952, had singled out the CCG as a "reactionary group" that "specializes in calling progressive legislation communistic."[52]

Despite these setbacks for Rumely, the next round went to him in a big way. In 1952, the Court of Appeals of the District of Columbia Circuit Court overturned his contempt conviction. The ruling demolished the entire foundation of the Buchanan Committee by holding that "indirect lobbying" was not "an evil and a danger" but was "the healthy essence of the democratic process." When the case reached the US Supreme Court one year later, Rumely won again. In a narrowly applied decision holding that the mere dissemination of political literature did not constitute lobbying, the court unanimously overturned the conviction. Justice Sherman Minton, because he had led the Senate investigation of Rumely and his associates in 1938, recused himself.[53]

A concurring opinion by the two most liberal justices, William O. Douglas and Hugo L. Black, endorsed Rumely's free speech and privacy rights in no uncertain terms. The opinion described the Buchanan Committee's demands as "the beginning of surveillance of the press." A jubilant Rumely could not have asked for more favorable phrasing, and the CCG quoted it repeatedly. Writing to his wife, he boasted, "I broke up the Black–Minton Committee by my opposition and yet Hugo Black writes an opinion in my favor! Once more my lifelong experience with our American courts is confirmed—they do justice!" This was quite a turnabout for a man who only a few years earlier had been repeatedly condemned as a fascist, federal convict, and German spy.[54]

In the short term, after the collapse of the Buchanan probe, congressional committees continued to be aggressive in deploying the contempt power against uncooperative witnesses. The most zealous of all was the House Committee on Un-American Activities (HCUA), often misidentified as "HUAC," which became a standing (permanent) committee in 1945. Empowered with a broad mandate, not unlike that of the Black Committee, HCUA had the stated mission to simultaneously investigate "un-American" and "subversive" behavior using standards that defied precise definition and discernable restraining limits. Between 1945 and 1957, it was responsible for a remarkable 135 contempt citations, more than the total number issued by either house of Congress up to that time in American history. During the first two years, the lion's share of these contempt citations involved subpoenas *duces tecum* for the records of various Communist and alleged Communist front organizations. After that, they centered on the refusal of witnesses to testify or related to their appeal for immunity under the self-incrimination provision of the Fifth Amendment.[55]

Even before the Supreme Court handed down *United States v. Rumely*, some prominent liberal Democrats were losing their appetite for investigative crusades against the right. One reason for this was that they were too busy beating back McCarthyism. By upholding Rumely's free speech, they could better undermine charges of hypocrisy. As early as 1950, the pro–New Deal columnist Marquis Childs held him up as illustration that the First Amendment protected "the extreme right" just as much as it protected Communists. Later, two victims of McCarthyism, the American Orientalist scholar and former head of the Pacific area of the Office of War Information, Owen Lattimore, and ACLU board member Corliss Lamont (1954), cited *United States v. Rumely* in their defense.[56]

The victory in the Supreme Court did little to improve the CCG's prospects. It was already fading out as an organization because of years of litigation and a fall-off in contributions, even from its main patron, Frank Gannett. Another factor was that the elderly Rumely no longer showed the same vigor or creativity. Libertarian journalist Frank Chodorov had seen it coming. Not long after the ruling, Chodorov, who considered "Buchananism" to be a species of "thought control," concluded that the "Buchanan Committee achieved its purpose of reducing the revenues of a dissident organization."[57]

The CCG had become little more than a paper organization when the US Supreme Court issued four landmark rulings on June 17, 1957. Taken together, they represented an important turning point in the history of congressional investigations. Critics dubbed the day they were handed down as "Red Monday" because the litigants on the winning side were Communists or other leftists. The rulings, however, had implications for investigations of all types. Most notably, in *Watkins v. United States*, which involved HCUA, the court made it more difficult for congressional committees to force witnesses to answer questions about their political stances or associations. The court declared: "There is no congressional power to expose for the sake of exposure where the predominant result can be only an invasion of the private rights of individuals." A precedent cited in this case was *United States v. Rumely*.[58]

One year later, it also became a precedent in the fight for civil rights. In *NAACP v. Alabama* (357 U.S. 449 [1958]), the court upheld the NAACP's challenge to an Alabama state requirement to turn over membership lists. Specifically appealing to *United States v. Rumely*, the court elaborated that "[c]ompelled disclosure of membership in an organization engaged in advocacy of particular beliefs is of the same order. Inviolability of privacy in group association may in many circumstances be indispensable to preservation of freedom of association, particularly where a group espouses dissident beliefs." In another parallel to *United States v. Rumely*, the court cited the dangers of retaliation and a possible chilling effect. A mandated disclosure of the membership list, it declared, is "likely to affect adversely the ability of petitioner [the NAACP] and its members to pursue their collective effort to foster beliefs which they admittedly have the right to advocate, in that it may induce members to withdraw from the Association and dissuade others from joining it because of fear of exposure."[59]

When the New Deal wars on privacy and free speech were finally winding down or, at least, leading to another phase, the reputation of the man who had started those wars seemed unassailable. If Roosevelt's civil-liberties reputation meant anything to mainstream Americans at the end of the 1950s, it was not for witch hunts against gays in the navy, mass surveillance of private telegrams, crackdowns on free speech, inquisitorial investigations, sedition prosecutions, or the internment of Japanese Americans in concentration camps. Far more central in the memories of most was his authorship of the four freedoms and the Fair Employment Practices Committee and his appointment of Black and Douglas to the Supreme Court. But that was not the whole truth, or even the beginning of the whole truth.

Notes

Introduction

1. Andrew Soergel and Kaia Hubbard, "How Historians Rate Presidents," *U.S. News & World Report*, November 6, 2019, accessed December 18, 2020, https://www.usnews.com/news/special-reports/the-worst-presidents/articles/how-historians-rate-presidents; and Historical Rankings of Presidents of the United States, Wikipedia, accessed December 18, 2020, https://en.wikipedia.org/wiki/Historical_rankings_of_presidents_of_the_United_States.

2. The following US history survey textbooks were examined: John Mack Faragher et al., *Out of Many: A History of the American People*, combined volume (Boston: Pearson, 2020), 565; John Henretta et al., *America's History, Since 1865*, vol. 2 (Boston: Bedford/St. Martin's, 2014), 787; David M. Kennedy and Lizabeth Cohen, *American Pageant: A History of the American People* (Boston: Wadsworth, 2013), 799–800; Eric Foner, *Give Me Liberty: An American History*, vol. 2 (New York: W. W. Norton, 2014), 878; James L. Roark et al., *The American Promise: A History of the United States, From 1865*, vol. 2 (Boston: Bedford/St. Martin's, 2020), 751; David Emory Shi, *America: A Narrative History*, vol. 2 (New York: W. W. Norton, 2019), 1240–41; Carol Berkin et al., *Making America: A History of the United States* (Belmont, CA: Wadsworth, 2014), 642–43; Alan Brinkley et al., *The Unfinished Nation: A Concise History of the American People* (Boston: McGraw Hill, 2016), 637–38; Rebecca Edwards et al., *America's History, Since 1865*, vol. 2 (Boston: Bedford/St. Martin's, 2018), 766; and Robert Divine et al., *America: Past and Present*, combined edition (London: Pearson, 2013), 652.

3. Daniel T. Rodgers, *Atlantic Crossings: Social Politics in a Progressive Age* (Cambridge, MA: The Belknap Press of Harvard University Press, 1998), 76–108; and Thomas C. Leonard, *Illiberal Reformers: Race Eugenics and American Economics in the Progressive Era* (Princeton, NJ: Princeton University Press, 2016), 17.

4. Leonard, *Illiberal Reformers*, 11–16; Richard M. Gamble, *The War for Righteousness: Progressive Christianity, the Great War, and the Rise of the Messianic Nation* (Wilmington, DE: ISI Books, 2003), 64; American Economic Association, *Report of the Organization of the American Economic Association*, vol. 1, no. 1, March 1886 ([Baltimore]: Publications of the American Economic Association, 1886), 6–7; and Sidney Fine, *Laissez-Faire and the General Welfare State* (Ann Arbor, MI: University of Michigan Press, 1956), 240.

5. James MacGregor Burns, *Roosevelt: The Lion and the Fox* (1956; repr., San Diego, CA: Harcourt Brace Jovanovich, 1984), 25–26, 33–34; and Burton W. Folsom Jr., *New Deal or Raw Deal? How FDR's Economic Legacy Has Damaged America* (New York: Simon & Schuster, 2008), 16–21.

6. Frank Freidel, *Franklin D. Roosevelt: The Apprenticeship* (Boston: Little, Brown and Company, 1952), 135; and Burns, *Lion and the Fox,* 30.

7. Burns, *Lion and the Fox,* 47–53.

8. Kenneth S. Davis, *FDR: The Beckoning of Destiny, 1882–1928: A History* (New York: G. P. Putnam's Sons, 1972), 512; and Freidel, *Apprenticeship,* 333–34.

9. Irwin F. Gellman, *Secret Affairs: FDR, Cordell Hull, and Sumner Welles* (New York: Enigma Books, 1995), 235; Sherry Zane, "'I Did It for the Uplift of Humanity and the Navy': Same-Sex Acts and the Origins of the National Security State, 1919–1921," *New England Quarterly* 91, no. 2 (June 2018): 279–82, 285, 289.

10. Gellman, *Secret Affairs,* 236; and Zane, "Uplift of Humanity," 300–301.

11. Herbert Croly, *The Promise of American Life* (1909; repr., Boston: Northeastern University Press, 1989), 26; and David M. Rabban, *Free Speech in Its Forgotten Years* (Cambridge, UK: Cambridge University Press, 1997), 232–37.

12. Zane, "Uplift of Humanity," 282, 302–303, 305; Davis, *Beckoning of Destiny,* 643; and Ted Morgan, *FDR: A Biography* (New York: Simon & Schuster, 1985), 244.

13. Francis Biddle, *In Brief Authority* (1962; repr., Westport, CT: Greenwood Press, 1976), 219; and Burton W. Folsom Jr. and Anita Folsom, *FDR Goes to War: How Expanded Executive Power, Spiraling National Debt, and Restricted Civil Liberties Shaped Wartime America* (New York: Simon & Schuster, 2011), 211.

14. Curt Gentry, *J. Edgar Hoover: The Man and His Secrets* (New York: W. W. Norton, 1991), 217–18; American Radio Works, The President Calling, accessed [August 19, 2022], http://americanradioworks.publicradio.org/features/prestapes/notebook.html; and Transcripts of White House Office Conversations, 08/22/1940-10/10/1940, President Roosevelt and His Aide Lowell Mellett Talk. Side 2, 0–821 (pt. 1) 821–1640 (pt. 2), sometime between August 22 and August 27, 1940, Franklin D. Roosevelt Presidential Library and Museum, accessed March 27, 2022, http://docs.fdrlibrary.marist.edu/transcr6.html; and Steve Neal, *Dark Horse: A Biography of Wendell Willkie* (Garden City, NY: Doubleday, 1984), 44.

Chapter 1: New Deal Mass Surveillance: The "Black Inquisition Committee"

1. Graham J. White, *FDR and the Press* (Chicago: University of Chicago Press, 1979), 10; and Gary Dean Best, *The Critical Press and the New Deal: The Press Versus Presidential Power, 1933–1938* (Westport, CT: Prager, 1993), 1–7.

2. Betty Houchin Winfield, *FDR and the News Media* (Urbana, IL: University of Illinois Press, 1993), 40–42; White, *FDR and the Press,* 35; Best, *Critical Press,* 17; and Melvin G. Holli, *The Wizard of Washington: Emil Hurja, Franklin Roosevelt, and the Birth of Public Opinion Polling* (New York: Palgrave, 2002), 66.

3. Frederick S. Lane, *American Privacy: The 400-Year History of Our Most Contested Right* (Boston: Beacon Press, 2009), 103–8; Laura Weinrib, *The Taming of Free Speech: America's Civil Liberties Compromise* (Cambridge, MA: Harvard University Press,

2016), 216–17; Michael Stephen Czaplicki, "The Corruption of Hope: Political Scandal, Congressional Investigations, and New Deal Moral Authority, 1932–1952" (PhD diss., University of Chicago, 2010), 19–105; Athan G. Theoharis, *Spying on Americans: Political Surveillance from Hoover to the Huston Plan* (Philadelphia: Temple University Press, 1978), 66–70; Ellen Schrecker, *Many Are the Crimes: McCarthyism in America* (Princeton, NJ: Princeton University Press, 1998), 102–9; and Anthony Gregory, *American Surveillance: Intelligence, Privacy, and the Fourth Amendment* (Madison, WI: University of Wisconsin Press, 2016), 38–41. It is true, however, that the FBI had access to information from the often-extensive systems of surveillance of local and state police agencies. Nick Fischer, *Spider Web: The Birth of American Anti-Communism* (Urbana, IL: University of Illinois Press, 2016), 257.

4. Czaplicki, "Corruption of Hope," 56–58; and Arnold Markoe, "The Black Committee: A Study of the Senate Investigation of the Public Utility Holding Company Lobby" (PhD diss., New York University, 1972), 37–47.

5. Czaplicki, "Corruption of Hope," 39, 57; Markoe, "Black Committee," 92; David D. Lee, "Senator Black's Investigation of the Airmail, 1933–1934," *Historian* 53, no. 3 (Spring 1991): 439–41; and Amity Shlaes, *The Forgotten Man: A New History of the Great Depression* (New York: HarperCollins, 2007), 254–55, 268, 280–82.

6. 74 Cong. Rec., S11003 (Daily ed., July 11, 1935); and Czaplicki, "Corruption of Hope," 58, 253.

7. Czaplicki, "Corruption of Hope," 58; and Roger K. Newman, *Hugo Black: A Biography* (New York: Fordham University Press, 1994), 228.

8. Czaplicki, "Corruption of Hope," 43–47, 79, 83; Michael Perino, *The Hellhound of Wall Street: How Ferdinand Pecora's Investigation of the Great Crash Forever Changed American Finance* (New York: Penguin Press, 2010), 283–86; Carl Beck, *Contempt of Congress: A Study of the Prosecutions Initiated by the Committee on Un-American Activities, 1945–1957* (New Orleans, LA: The Hauser Press, 1959), 6–9, 212–14; and Donald A. Ritchie, "What Makes a Successful Congressional Investigation?" *OAH Magazine of History* 12, no. 4 (Summer 1998): 21.

9. Newman, *Hugo Black*, 178–80; Czaplicki, "Corruption of Hope," 79; and Markoe, "Black Committee," 95–96.

10. Markoe, "Black Committee," 100; Jamie C. Euken, "Evil, Greed, Treachery, Deception, and Fraud: The World of Lobbying According to Senator Hugo Black," *Federal History*, no. 6 (January 2014): 73–74.

11. Markoe, "Black Committee," 105–6; Euken, "Evil, Greed, Treachery," 74; and "Executive Defends His Utility," *New York Times*, August 13, 1935, 1.

12. *Diaries of Henry Morgenthau Jr.*, July 24, 1935, 122C, Franklin D. Roosevelt Presidential Library and Museum; and Czaplicki, "Corruption of Hope," 96–97.

13. Marjorie E. Kornhauser, "Shaping Public Opinion and the Law: How a 'Common Man' Campaign Ended a Rich Man's Law," *Law and Contemporary Problems* 73, no. 1 (Winter 2010): 125–45; and Black to J. A. Smith, March 25, 1935, Treasury Department Legislation (1935), Income Tax Returns Publicity, Box 223, Folder 9, Senatorial File, Hugo L. Black Papers, Library of Congress, Washington, DC.

14. Czaplicki, "Corruption of Hope," 96–99.

15. McGrain v. Daugherty, 273 U.S. 135, 175 (1927); Czaplicki, "Corruption of Hope," 34, 46–48; "The Power of Congressional Investigating Committee to Issue Subpoena Duces Tecum," *Yale Law Journal* 45, no. 8 (June 1936): 1505–8; Louis B. Boudin, "Congressional and Agency Investigations: Their Uses and Abuses," *Virginia Law Review* 35, no. 2 (February 1949): 170–72; and Jurney v. MacCracken 294 U.S. 152 (1935).

16. Euken, "Evil, Greed, Treachery," 74–75; U.S. Senate, 74th Cong., 2nd sess., *Alleged Seizures of Telegrams and Records and Telephone Communications*, Document No. 188 (Washington, DC: Government Printing Office, 1936), 3–5; Hearst v. Black et al., 87 F. 2d 68 (1936); Francis R. Stark to Black, March 16, 1936, Box 181, Folder 2, Senatorial File (Lobbying) Correspondence, Hugo L. Black Papers, Library of Congress, Washington, DC.

17. Copies of some of the telegrams are at Special Committee to Investigate Lobbying Activities, Records, US Senate, 75th Cong., Telegram Files, 1935–38, National Archives; Czaplicki, "Corruption of Hope," 98; Harry Y. Saint to Black, March 13, 1936 , Folder 6, Box 181 Senatorial File (Lobbying) Correspondence, Hugo L. Black Papers, Library of Congress, Washington, DC; and 74 Cong. Rec., S4495–96 (Daily ed., March 26, 1936).

18. 74 Cong. Rec., H3265 (Daily ed., March 4, 1936); and Felix Bruner, "Lobby Group Seeks to Find Wire Seizure Justification," *Washington Post*, March 5, 1936, 1.

19. William Doherty, "Court's Power Challenged by Black Group," *New York American*, March 27, 1936, 4; Paul C. Yates to Black, September 25, 1935, Box 181, Folder 2, Senatorial File (Lobbying), Correspondence, Hugo L. Black Papers, Library of Congress, Washington, DC; and Saint to Black, March 13, 1936, Folder 6, Box 181 Senatorial File (Lobbying) Correspondence, Hugo L. Black Papers.

20. Czaplicki, "Corruption of Hope," 98–99.

21. William Randolph Hearst v. Hugo L. Black et al., In the Supreme Court of the District of Columbia, "Brief of Plaintiff in Support of Motion for Injunction Pendente Lite and in Opposition to Motion to Dismiss for Want of Jurisdiction" [c. April 1936], 52, Folder: District of Columbia, Hearst vs. United States Senate Special Committee, 1935, Box B-48, Western Union Telegraph Company Records, Archives Center, National Museum of American History, Washington, DC.

22. Holli, *Wizard of Washington*, 67–68; Burton W. Folsom Jr., *New Deal or Raw Deal? How FDR's Economic Legacy Has Damaged America* (New York: Simon & Schuster, 2008), 178–79; and William E. Leuchtenburg, *The FDR Years: On Roosevelt and His Legacy* (New York: Columbia University Press, 1995), 101–2.

23. "Lobby Probe Aims at Liberty League," *Baltimore Sun*, January 29, 1936, 2; Newman, *Hugo Black*, 185; "New Lobby Hunt Begun," *Los Angeles Times*, January 29, 1936, 2; "Senators Open Fresh Quiz on New Deal Foes," *Chicago Daily Tribune*, January 28, 1936, 1; Arthur Sears Henning, "Terror Spread Among Enemies by New Dealers," *Chicago Daily Tribune*, February 9, 1936, 1; J. Fred Essary, "Senate Lobby Investigators Defied by Liberty League," *Baltimore Sun*, February 15, 1936, 9; and "Scores Lobbying Inquiry," *New York Times*, February 11, 1936, 10. Black's interest in the Crusaders, however, had started long before January 1936. On September 4, 1935, the committee had sent the group a "full and exhaustive questionnaire regarding the Crusaders, their structure, purposes and methods."

F. W. Blaisdell to Hugo L. Black, October 15, 1935, Folder: NRA, Black, Hugo, Committee, 1936, Series I-60, Box 57, Robert R. McCormick Papers, Colonel Robert R. McCormick Research Center, First Division Museum at Cantigny Park, Wheaton, IL.

24. Sears, "Terror Spreads," 8; "Liberty Leaguers Flay Senate Lobby Probe," *Atlanta Constitution*, February 15, 1936, 2; and Hugo L. Black, "Inside a Senate Investigation," *Harper's Magazine* 172 (February 1936): 275–76.

25. Mark Sullivan, "Stories Clash on Seizure of Telegrams," *Hartford Courant* (Hartford, CT), March 9, 1936, 18; Hearst v. Black et al., "Brief for Plaintiff," 52; "Crusaders Tell Tactics in Black Inquisition Here," *Chicago Daily Tribune*, March 8, 1936, 17; "Utility Inquirers Seize Files Here," *New York Times*, March 3, 1936, 7; and N. J. Neamy to Robert R. McCormick, March 12, 1936, Byron Price to McCormick, April 13, 1936, Special Committee to Investigate Lobbying Activities to McCormick, January 21, 1936, Folder: NRA, Black, Hugo, Committee, 1936, Series I-60, Box 57, Robert R. McCormick Papers, Colonel Robert R. McCormick Research Center, Wheaton, IL.

26. "Utility Inquirers Seize Files Here," *New York Times*, March 3, 1936, 1.

27. Silas H. Strawn v. The Western Union Telegraph Company, In the Supreme Court of the District of Columbia "Brief for Plaintiffs" [March 1936], 1–3, Folder: District of Columbia, Strawn v. Western Union, Western Union Telegraph Company Records, 1936, Archives Center, National Museum of American History, Washington, DC; "Silas Hardy Strawn, 1866–1946," *American Bar Association Journal* 32, no. 3 (March 1946): 164; Jeff Shesol, *Supreme Power: Franklin Roosevelt vs. the Supreme Court* (New York: W. W. Norton, 2010), 10; and Arthur Sears Henning, "Strawn Asks Court to Halt Lobby Snooping," *Chicago Daily Tribune*, March 3, 1936, 4.

28. William E. Leuchtenburg, "A Klansman Joins the Court: The Appointment of Hugo L. Black," *University of Chicago Law Review* 41, no. 1 (Fall 1973): 6–7.

29. "Washington: Black Inquisition," *Chicago Daily Tribune*, March 8, 1936, B7; Czaplicki, "Corruption of Hope," 87; "A Damaging Attitude," *New York Times*, March 22, 1936, E8; White, *FDR and the Press*, 31; Mark Sullivan, "Capitol Comment," *Centralia Sentinel* (Centralia, IL), March 6, 1936, 1; "Black Booty," *Time* 27, no. 11, March 16, 1936, 18; and Arthur Krock, "In Washington: Seizure of Telegrams May Be Campaign Issue," *New York Times*, March 6, 1936, 20.

30. "Black Group Gets Wires by the Millions," *Chicago Daily Tribune*, March 5, 1936, 1, 8; 74 Cong. Rec., S3328, S3331 (Daily ed., March 5, 1936); and 74 Cong. Rec., H3266 (Daily ed., March 4, 1936); and Kenneth W. Vickers, "John Rankin: Democrat and Demagogue" (MA thesis, Mississippi State University, 1993), 50–55.

Ira Katznelson documents how Southern Democrats (including racists such as Bilbo and Rankin) were instrumental to the creation and implementation of the New Deal. Katznelson, *Fear Itself: The New Deal and the Origins of Our Time* (New York: W. W. Norton, 2013), 84–91, 163.

31. 74 Cong. Rec., S3330–31 (Daily ed., March 5, 1936).

32. Walter Lippmann, "Today and Tomorrow: Legislative Inquisition," *Los Angeles Times*, March 7, 1936, A4; and Ronald Steel, *Walter Lippmann and the American Century* (Boston: Little, Brown and Company, 1980), 167, 216–19, 227–33.

33. Felix Bruner, "Borah Request Adopted," *Washington Post,* March 10, 1936, 1.

34. Newman, *Hugo Black*, 187–88; "Report of the Standing Committee on Communications to the American Bar Association," *Annual Report of the American Bar Association* 61 (1936): 644; "Senate Accepts Curb on Activity of Lobby Inquiry," *Christian Science Monitor*, March 12, 1936, 2; Black to Western Union Telegram Company and T. B. Kingsbury, 18 March 1936, Folder 7, Box 181, Senatorial File (Lobbying), Correspondence, Hugo L. Black Papers, Library of Congress, Washington, DC; and Arthur Sears Henning, "Halt Senate Wire Seizures," *Chicago Daily Tribune*, March 12, 1936, 8.

35. Ben Procter, *William Randolph Hearst: The Later Years, 1911–1951* (New York: Oxford University Press, 2007), 170–71, 190–91, 206; "Increased Fund Asked to Push Lobby," *Washington Post,* March 13, 1936, 2; 74 Cong. Rec., H3950 (Daily ed., March 18, 1936); and Arthur Sears Henning, "Black 'Terror' Fought in New Court Actions," *Chicago Daily Tribune*, March 13, 1936, 1.

36. Arthur Sears Henning, "New Suit Filed to Halt Black Wire Seizures," *Chicago Daily Tribune*, March 14, 1936, 1, 8; and "Hearst Files Suit on Lobby Inquiry," *New York Times*, March 13, 1936, 6.

37. Black to Western Union Telegraph Company and T. B. Kingsbury, March 18, 1936, Folder 7, Box 181, Senatorial File (Lobbying), Correspondence, Hugo L. Black Papers, Library of Congress, Washington, DC; and "Hearst Telegram Given Out in House," *New York Times*, March 19, 1936, 1.

38. 74 Cong. Rec., H3950 (Daily ed., March 18, 1936); and Black to Western Union Telegraph Company and Kingsbury.

39. 74 Cong. Rec., S4384 (Daily ed., March 26, 1936); 74 Cong. Rec., S4579 (Daily ed., March 30, 1936); 74 Cong. Rec., S4708 (Daily ed., April 1, 1936; and "Interest Is Taken in Schwellenbach Reply to Hearst," *Christian Science Monitor,* March 31, 1936, 2.

40. 74 Cong. Rec., S4650 (Daily ed., March 31, 1936).

41. Saint to Black, Folder 6, Box 181 Senatorial File (Lobbying) Correspondence, Hugo L. Black Papers; Arthur Sears Henning, "New Suit Filed," 1–2; and "Hearst Assailed as Real 'Dictator,'" *Baltimore Sun*, March 31, 1936, 6.

42. "Validity of Subpoena Issued by Senate Committee for All Telegraphic Correspondence over Named Period," *Columbia Law Review* 36, no. 5 (May 1936): 843; "An Obvious Red Herring," editorial, *Washington Post*, March 21, 1936, 8; "Raw Censorship," editorial (reprinted from *Editor and Publisher*), *New York American*, March 22, 1936, 8; and Arthur Krock, "In Washington: Black Committee Accused of Invading Court Functions," *New York Times*, March 27, 1936, 20.

43. 74 Cong. Rec., H5530–36 (Daily ed., April 15, 1936); and "House Delays Black Group's Defense Fund," *New York American*, April 3, 1936, 1.

44. Markoe, "Black Committee," 173.

45. William Anderson, *The Wild Man from Sugar Creek: The Political Career of Eugene Talmadge* (Baton Rouge, LA: Louisiana University Press, 1975), 136–40; "Photo Hitting at First Lady Is Revealed," *Hartford Courant* (Hartford, CT), April 16, 1936, 1; George Wolfskill, *The Revolt of the Conservatives: A History of the American Liberty League, 1934–1940* (Boston: Houghton Mifflin, 1962), 175–78; and Robert F. Burk, *The Corporate State and*

the Broker State: The Du Ponts and American National Politics, 1925–1940 (Cambridge, MA: Harvard University Press, 1990), 226.

46. Burk, *Corporate State,* 226; Alan J. Lichtman, *White Protestant Nation: The Rise of the American Conservative Movement* (New York: Atlantic Monthly Press, 2008), 86; Myron I. Scholnick, *The New Deal and Anti-Semitism in America* (New York: Garland Publishing, 1990), 182–83; and Jonathan J. Bean, ed., *Race and Liberty in America: The Essential Reader* (Lexington, KY: University Press of Kentucky, 2009), 175.

47. "Foe of A.A.A. Defies Quiz," *Los Angeles Times,* April 17, 1936, 2; "Farm Leader Won't Answer Lobby Probers," *New York American,* April 17, 1936, 1; "Lobby Group Witness Balks at Questions," *Washington Post,* April 17, 1936, 1; and US Congress, Senate, Select Committee to Investigate Lobbying Activities, *Hearings,* Part 65, April 14, 16, and 17, 1936, 74th Cong., 2nd Sess., 2012.

48. Jean Choate, *Disputed Ground: Farm Groups That Opposed the New Deal Agricultural Program* (Jefferson, NC: McFarland and Company, 2002), 84–87; and James C. Carey, "The Farmers' Independence Council of America, 1935–1938," *Agricultural History Society* 35, no. 2 (April 1961): 73.

49. "Court's Power Challenged by Black Group," *New York American,* March 27, 1936, 4; "Partial Retreat from Moscow," editorial, *Washington Post,* April 1, 1936, 8; and Czaplicki, "Corruption of Hope," 95. Even after the FCC ceased cooperation, however, Stanley Morse, executive president of the Farmers' Independence Council, alleged that a telegram sent on April 10 to E. V. Wilcox, the council's secretary who also testified that day, "apparently was in the hands of the Committee a few hours later." Stanley Morse to Member, 20 April 1936, Folder: I-60 NRA-Black, Hugo, Committee, 1936, Robert R. McCormick Papers, Robert R. McCormick Papers, Colonel Robert R. McCormick Research Center, Wheaton, IL.

50. "Report of the Standing Committee [American Bar Association]," 645; William A. Gregory and Rennard Strickland, "Hugo Black's Congressional Investigation of Lobbying and the Public Utility Holding Company Act: A Historical View of the Power Trust, New Deal Politics, and Regulatory Propaganda," *Oklahoma Law Review* 29, no. 3 (1976): 569; and Alice Roosevelt Longworth, "What Alice Thinks," *Los Angeles Times,* April 1, 1936, 5.

51. Newman, *Hugo Black,* 188; White, *FDR and the Press,* 95–96; "Senator Black Feeds on Poisoned Meet," editorial, *New York American,* April 28, 1936, 14; Cartoon, *New York American,* April 17, 1936, 22; and Berton Braley, "Sh-h-h-Sh-Shish," *New York American,* April 11, 1936, 10.

52. Berton Braley, "Go As Far As You Like," *New York American,* May 2, 1936, 14.

53. Arthur "Bugs" Baer, "Giving the Committee a Black Name," *New York American,* April 4, 1936, 4.

54. Czaplicki, "Corruption of Hope," 88–89; Newman, *Hugo Black,* 190; Black to Seba Eldridge, March 23, 1936, Box 181, Folder 6, Senatorial File (Lobbying) Correspondence, Hugo L. Black Papers, Library of Congress, Washington, DC; Roger N. Baldwin to Black, April 18, 1936, Hugo L. Black, Box 181, Folder 8, Senatorial File (Lobbying) Correspondence, Hugo L. Black Papers, Library of Congress, Washington, DC; and Black to Bald-

win, April 29, 1936, Folder: American Civil Liberties Union, Box 11, Special Committee to Investigate Lobbying Activities, Records, U.S. Senate, 75th Cong., National Archives.

55. "Hearst Assailed as Real 'Dictator,'" *Baltimore Sun*, March 31, 1936, 1; and "Better to Give Nation Back, Malone Says," *Baltimore Sun*, March 31, 1936, 2.

56. "Black Names Ex-Partner as Probe Counsel," *New York American*, March 23, 1936, 8; 74 Cong. Rec., H5540–41 (Daily ed., April 15, 1936); and "House, 153 to 137, Rebukes Senate Lobby Committee," *New York Times,* April 16, 1936, 2.

57. 74 Cong. Rec., H5543–5545 (Daily ed., April 15, 1936).

58. 74 Cong. Rec., S5832–33 (Daily ed., April 22, 1936; "A Setback for the Grand Snoop," editorial, *Chicago Daily Tribune*, April 17, 1936, 14; and "A Black Eye for Black," editorial, (reprinted from the *Chicago Daily News*), *New York American*, April 27, 1936, 13.

59. "Text of Attack on Black Group," *New York American*, April 23, 1936, 13; "Publishers Score Senate Committee for 'Gagging' Press," *New York Times,* April 23, 1936, 18; and Walter Lippmann, "Today and Tomorrow," *Los Angeles Times*, April 28, 1936, A4.

60. Arthur Sears Henning, "Terror Spread Among Enemies," 8; "The Senate Black Shirts," editorial, *Chicago Daily Tribune*, March 7, 1936, 10; and "The Night Riders: An Old Southern Custom," cartoon, *Chicago Daily Tribune*, May 7, 1936, 1.

61. Paul W. Ward, "Washington Weekly," *Nation*, March 25, 1936, 371–72; "The Liberty Leaguers Have Their Own Private Interpretation of the United States Constitution," *Progressive* 4, no. 176 (May 2, 1936): 1; and "The Progressive Repudiates Selfish Use of Freedom of the Press," *Progressive* 4, no. 171 (March 21, 1936): 1.

62. Harold Ickes, *The Secret Diary of Harold Ickes: The First Thousand Days, 1933–1936* (New York: Simon & Schuster, 1953), 555, 693; Michael J. Webber, *New Deal Fat Cats: Business, Labor, and Campaign Finance in the 1936 Presidential Election* (New York: Fordham University Press, 2000), 136–37; and James T. Patterson, *Congressional Conservatism and the New Deal: The Growth of the Conservative Coalition in Congress, 1933–1939* (Lexington, KY: University of Kentucky Press, 1967), 39, 50.

63. Raymond Moley, *After Seven Years* (New York: Harper & Brothers, 1939), 336–39.

64. "Court Rebukes the FCC," *New York Times*, November 10, 1936, 5; "Senator Black Maps Course with Liberals," *Washington Post*, September 11, 1936, 2; "Senate Votes Fund to Defend Black Quizzers," *Chicago Daily Tribune,* June 7, 1936, 10; "Strawn Wins Wire Suit," *New York Times,* June 26, 1936, 3; and "The Republican Party Platform of 1936," June 9, 1936, accessed May 24, 2017, http://www.presidency.ucsb.edu/ws/?pid=29639.

65. Folsom, *New Deal or Raw Deal?* 180; and Holli, *Wizard of Washington*, 74–75.

66. Choate, *Disputed Ground*, 87; and Burk, *Corporate State*, 243.

67. Hearst v. Black et al., 87 F.2d 68 (1936), 69–70, 72; and "Court Rebukes the FCC," *New York Times,* November 10, 1936, 5.

68. "Unlawful Snooping," editorial, *Washington Post*, November 11, 1936, X8.

69. Beck, *Contempt of Congress*, 213–15; U.S. Congress, Senate, Subcommittee of the Committee on Education and Labor, Hearings, Violations of Free Speech and the Rights of Labor, Part 3, 75th Cong., 1st sess., (1938), 733, 954–56; 75th Cong., 2nd sess., Part 15-D, [1938], 6929.

70. Arthur M. Schlesinger Jr., *The Politics of Upheaval, 1935–1936*, vol. 3, *Age of Roosevelt* (Boston: Houghton Mifflin, 1960), 323; and Gregory and Strickland, "Hugo Black's Congressional Investigation," 560.

71. Leuchtenburg, "Klansman Joins the Court," 6; Newman, *Hugo Black*, 190, 193; and Czaplicki, "Corruption of Hope," 3, 104.

72. Tony A. Freyer, *Hugo L. Black and the Dilemma of American Liberalism* (New York: Pearson Longman, 2008), 107–57; and Czaplicki, "Corruption of Hope," 100–01.

73. Lane, *American Privacy*, 108.

74. *Nardone v. United States*, 302 U.S. 381–82 (1937); *Nardone v. United States*, 308 U.S. 338 (1939); Hearst v. Black, 87 F.2d 69 (1936); Athan G. Theoharis, *The FBI and American Democracy: A Brief Critical History* (Lawrence, KS: University Press of Kansas, 2004), 56–57; and Colin Agur, "Negotiated Order: The Fourth Amendment, Telephone Surveillance, and Social Interactions, 1878–1968," *Information and Culture* 48, no. 4 (2013): 429–31.

Some congressional opponents of the Black Committee had charged, however, that the FCC had violated Section 605 by giving access to the telegrams. Arthur Sears Henning, "Asks Discharge of FCC for Aid in Wire Seizure," *Chicago Daily Tribune*, March 18, 1936, 6.

75. David Hochfelder, "Constructing an Industrial Divide: Western Union, AT&T, and the Federal Government, 1876–1971," *Business History Review* 76, no. 4 (Winter 2002), 725; United States, Congress, Senate, Committee on the Judiciary, Wiretapping for National Security: Hearings Before a Subcommittee of the Committee on the Judiciary, April 20, 28, 29, May 6 and 12, 83rd Cong., 2nd Sess. (Washington, DC: Government Printing Office, 1954), 15, 24; Alan F. Westin, *Privacy and Freedom* (New York: Atheneum, 1967), 173–83; Anthony Gregory, *American Surveillance*, 39, 44; Theoharis, *Spying on Americans*, 67–69, 99, 74; U.S. Senate, 83rd Cong., 2nd sess., Subcommittee on the Committee of the Judiciary, Hearings, 106–11; and Schrecker, *Many Are the Crimes,* 222–26, 259–60.

Chapter 2: The Minton Committee: An Anti–Free Speech Bridge Too Far

1. The quotation from the article in *Collier's* can be found in Leonard Baker, *Back to Back: The Duel Between FDR and the Supreme Court* (New York: Macmillan, 1967), 42.

2. Both quotations are shown in Arthur M. Schlesinger Jr., *The Politics of Upheaval: 1935–1936, The Age of Roosevelt* (Boston: Houghton Mifflin, 1960), 513, 639.

3. Baker, *Back to Back*, 8–9.

4. Richard Polenberg, "The National Committee to Uphold Constitutional Government, 1937–1941," *Journal of American History* 52, no. 3 (December 1965): 583; and Joanne Dunnebecke, "The Crusade for Individual Liberty: The Committee for Constitutional Government, 1937–1958" (master's thesis, University of Wyoming, 1987), 46–47.

5. Baker, *Back to Back*, 75, 81; and Laura Weinrib, *The Taming of Free Speech: America's Civil Liberties Compromise* (Cambridge: MA: Harvard University Press, 2016), 218.

6. Polenberg, "National Committee," 588.

7. Gary Dean Best, *The Critical Press and the New Deal: The Press Versus Presidential Power, 1933–1938* (Westport, CT: Praeger, 1993), 115, 124; and Richard W. Steele, *Propa-*

ganda in an Open Society: The Roosevelt Administration and the Media, 1933–1941 (Westport, CT: Greenwood Press, 1985), 49.

8. Robert S. Allen, "Roosevelt Fights Back," *Nation* 145, no. 140, August 21, 1937, 188; Graham J. White, *FDR and the Press* (Chicago: University of Chicago Press, 1979), 40; and Best, *Critical Press*, 18.

9. H. A. Blomquist to Theodore Francis Green, September 8, 1937, Blomquist to Minton, July 29, 1938, Office File: Committee Members, Records of the Special Committee on Lobbying, Miscellaneous Files, Folder: Newspaper Clippings–General, Box 106, U.S. Senate, 75th Congress, National Archives; and Carlisle Bargeron, "The New Senate Prosecutors," *Nation's Business* 25, no. 12 (December 1937), 16–17.

10. Elizabeth Anne Hull, "Sherman Minton and the Cold War Court" (PhD diss., New School for Social Research, 1976), 16–17; Linda C. Gugin and James E. St. Clair, *Sherman Minton: New Deal Senator, Cold War Justice* (Indianapolis, IN: Indiana Historical Society, 1987), 102; Bargeron, "New Senate Prosecutors," 119; and David H. Corcoran, "Sherman Minton: New Deal Senator," PhD diss., University of Kentucky, 1977), np, 77, 115, 130, 156, 176.

11. Drew Pearson and Robert S. Allen, "Merry-Go-Round," *Gazette* (Worcester, MA), August 26, 1937, 6.

12. Drew Pearson and Robert S. Allen, "Washington Merry-Go-Round, Roosevelt Holds Fighting Conference with Eight Senators," *Seattle Daily Times*, December 28, 1937, 6. In his dissertation on Minton, David H. Corcoran states that in November 1937, Minton conducted a "mini-purge" in cooperation with Roosevelt by intimidating Representative Samuel B. Pettengill (D-IN) into not running in 1938. Pettengill had opposed the president on court packing and other measures and later became an NCUCG officer. This view appears to be mistaken. It is true the two had a combative showdown in November when Pettengill charged that Minton was seeking "to tear down respect for the constitution" on the court issue, and Minton retorted that Pettengill had refused to appear at the Black Committee hearings because of his ties to utility lobbyists. But Pettengill had already announced in August, even before the Minton Committee first met, his decision not to seek renomination and return to his law practice. Corcoran, "Sherman Minton," 177, 191; and "Pettengill to Retire from Congress in 1938," *Evansville Courier & Press* (Evansville, IN), August 23, 1937, 4.

13. Robert Higgs, *Depression, War, and Cold War* (New York: Oxford University Press, 2006), 9; "Great Caesar Fell," *New Republic*, 95, no. 1236, April 13, 1938, 303; and Richard Polenberg, *Reorganizing Roosevelt's Government: The Controversy Over Executive Reorganization, 1936–1939* (Cambridge, MA: Harvard University Press, 1966), 41–42, 148–51, 169.

14. Polenberg, *Reorganizing Roosevelt's Government*, 149–51.

15. "Great Caesar Fell," 303; Polenberg, "National Committee," 589; and "Open Letter to the President on His Reorganization Plan," January 29, 1938, 4, Folder: Amos Pinchot, General Correspondence, Chronological File, 1938, February (4 of 4) Amos Pinchot Papers, Manuscript Division, Library of Congress, Washington, DC. Emphasis by Pinchot.

16. Polenberg, *Reorganizing Roosevelt's Government*, 109, 113–115, 120.

17. Charles G. Dunwoody, interview by Amelia R. Fry, November 26, 1966, Oral History Center, Bancroft Library, University of California, Berkeley, 18, 27–28; "Lobby Against U.S. Bureau Reform Bill Bared: Congress May Ask for Probe," *St. Louis Star-*

Times, March 8, 1938, 1; Paul Y. Anderson, "Fund Is Being Gathered for Bureau Lobby," *St. Louis Star-Times*, March 9, 1938, 1; and Polenberg, *Reorganizing Roosevelt's Government*, 114–17.

18. Edmund B. Lambeth, "The Lost Career of Paul Y. Anderson," *Journalism Quarterly* 60, no. 3: 401–06; Paul Y. Anderson, "'Tis of Thee," *St. Louis Star-Times*, October 31, 1938, 5; "Death Gets By-line on Last Story," *Hartford Courant* (Hartford, CT), December 7, 1938, 5; "Paul Y. Anderson a Suicide: Was Washington Correspondent," *New York Times*, December 7, 1938, 48; and Terry Ganey, "The Tragic End of Paul Y. Anderson, *Gateway Journalism Review*, September 27, 2013, accessed August 21, 2022, https://gatewayjr.org/6188/; Franklin D. Roosevelt, Press Conference, December 6, 1938, 284, Press Conferences of Franklin D. Roosevelt, 1933–1945, Franklin D. Roosevelt Library and Museum, Hyde Park, NY, http://www.fdrlibrary.marist.edu/_resources/images/pc/pc0073.pdf.

19. Paul Y. Anderson, "Lobby Against U.S. Bureau Reform Bill Bared: Congress May Ask for Probe," *St. Louis Star-Times*, March 8, 1938, 1.

20. Anderson, "Lobby Against U.S. Bureau Reform," 1; and Paul Y. Anderson, "Fund Is Being Gathered for Bureau Lobby," *St. Louis Star-Times*, March 9, 1938, 1.

21. Anderson, "U.S. Senate to Probe Lobby Bared, by Star-Times," *St. Louis Star-Times*, March 11, 1938, 1; and Paul Y. Anderson, "Lobbyist Against Bureau Changes has 250 'Key Men,'" *St. Louis Star-Times*, March 12, 1938, 2.

22. "Gannett Group Faces Senate Lobby Inquiry," *New York Times*, March 15, 1938, 14.

23. Dunwoody, interview, 22, 26.

24. Dunwoody, interview, 27–28.

25. Dunwoody, interview, 22, 60.

26. Dunnebecke, "The Crusade for Individual Liberty," 12–13; Isaac William Martin, *Rich People's Movements: Grassroots Campaigns to Untax the One Percent* (New York: Oxford University Press, 2013), 92–93; and Polenberg, *Reorganizing Roosevelt's Government*, 76.

27. Dunnebecke, "Crusade for Individual Liberty," 12–13; Isaac Martin, Rich People's Movements, 92–93; and Polenberg, *Reorganizing Roosevelt's Government,* 76.

28. Polenberg, *Reorganizing Roosevelt's Government*, 75; Committee for Constitutional Government, Inc., *Needed Now—Capacity for Leadership, Courage to Lead* (New York: Committee for Constitutional Government, Inc., 1944, 12; and "Elisha Hanson, Publishers' Aide: Ex-Counsel for A.N.P.A. Dies in Washington," *New York Times*, August 12, 1962, 81.

29. "The Black Inquisition Revived," editorial, *Chicago Daily Tribune,* March 24, 1938, 12; and U.S. Senate, *Hearings Before a Special Committee to Investigate Lobbying Activities*, Part 7, March 18, 23, and April 20, 1938, 75th Cong., 3rd Sess. (Washington, DC: Government Printing Office, 1938), 2121, 2139.

30. Amos Pinchot to Geoffrey Parsons, March 21, 1938, Folder: Amos Pinchot, General Correspondence, Chronological File, 1938, February (4 of 4), Amos Pinchot Papers, Manuscript Division, Library of Congress, Washington, DC; Paul Y. Anderson, "Lobby Director Defies Senate Investigation, Refuses to Give Up Files," *St. Louis Star-Times*, March 18,

1938, 3; U.S. Senate, *Hearings Before a Special Committee to Investigate Lobbying Activities*, 75th Cong., 3rd Sess. (1938), 2101, 2121, 2139; and Corcoran, "Sherman Minton," 210.

31. Pinchot to Parsons, March 21, 1938, Folder: Amos Pinchot, General Correspondence, Chronological File, 1938, February (4 of 4) Amos Pinchot Papers, Manuscript Division, Library of Congress, Washington, DC; "Wheeler Hits Lobby Group in Senate Speech," *Post-Crescent* (Appleton, WI), March 18, 1938; Kenneth Crawford, "Gannett Lobbyist Facing Contempt Action by the Senate," *New York Post*, March 19, 1938, 5; and Corcoran, "Sherman Minton," 211.

32. "Gannett Aid Again Ignores Lobby Subpoena," *New York World-Telegram*, March 23, 1938, vol. 1089, American Civil Liberties Cases, 1938, Federal Legislation, Clippings 2, American Civil Liberties Union Papers, Mudd Library, Princeton University, Princeton, NJ; and "Gannett Assails Lobbying Inquiry," *News and Courier* (Charleston, SC), March 21, 1938, 1; and "Senators Defied Again by Rumely," *New York Post*, March 25, 1938, 5.

33. Paul Y. Anderson, "Lobbyist Again Blocks Probe of His Records," *St. Louis Star-Times*, March 23, 1936, 2; Crawford, "Gannett Lobbyist Facing Contempt," 5; "The President Fights on Three Fronts," *New York Post*, March 24, 1938, 2, 6; and "The Shape of Things," *Nation* 146, no. 13, March 26, 1938, 342.

34. "The Black Inquisition Revived," 12; "Terrorism and the Senate," *New York Herald-Tribune*, March 24, 1938, vol. 1089, American Civil Liberties Cases, 1938, Federal Legislation, Clippings 2, American Civil Liberties Union Papers, Mudd Library, Princeton University, Princeton, NJ; and Frederic Nelson, "Pressure by 'Inquiry,'" *Baltimore Sun*, March 27, 1938, 8.

35. Hugh S. Johnson, "Open Letter to a Number of Senators," *Reading Times* (Reading, PA), March 29, 1938, 8.

36. Polenberg, *Reorganizing Roosevelt's Government*, 71; and "A Defeat for the Lobby," editorial, *St. Louis Star-Times*, March 29, 1938, 14.

37. "In Congress," *Newsweek* 11, April 4, 1938, 13; and "Minton to Avoid Citing Rumely," *New York Post*, March 24, 1938, 50.

38. John J. Abt, *Advocate and Activist: Memoirs of an American Communist Lawyer* (Urbana, IL: University of Illinois Press, 1993), 40–41, 72; and Memorandum for the Solicitor General by John J. Abt, Special Assistant to the Attorney General, Re Special Senate Committee to Investigate Lobbying Activities–Punishment of Edward A. Rumely for Contempt, March 26, 1938, 3, 8, Folder 13, Box 83, Robert H. Jackson Papers, Manuscript Division, Library of Congress, Washington, DC.

39. Memorandum for the Solicitor General by John J. Abt, 8; "Edward A. Rumely—A Traitor Then and a Traitor Now: An Editorial," *Daily Worker*, April 6, 1938, page number not identified, Folder: Newspaper Clippings–General, Records of the Special Committee to Investigate Lobbying Activities, Miscellaneous Files, Box 106, States Senate, 75th Congress, National Archives.

40. Paul Y. Anderson, "Lobby Group May Decide Soon on Contempt Action," *St. Louis Star-Times*, March 28, 1938, 11; "Rumely Will Not Be Cited Many Believe," *Rockford Morning Star* (Rockford, IL), March 31, 1938, 1; Paul Y. Anderson, "Let Gannett Explain," *Nation* 146, no. 14, April 2, 1938, 376; and Committee for Constitutional Government, Inc., "Needed Now—Capacity for Leadership, 13.

41. 75 Cong. Rec. H4622 (daily ed. April 2, 1938); Sherman Steele to Marvin McIntrye, April 2, 1938, J. Edgar Hoover to Homer S. Cummings, April 16, 1938, Franklin D. Roosevelt Papers, OF 3220—Rumely, Dr. Edward A., 1936-1938. Franklin D. Roosevelt, Papers as President: The President's Official File, Part 7: Of 3001–3500, Franklin D. Roosevelt Papers, Franklin D. Roosevelt Presidential Library, Hyde Park, NY.

42. Polenberg, *Reorganizing Roosevelt's Government*, 146, 180; "Ganging Up on the President," *New Republic* 95, no. 1236, April 13, 1938, 291; "White House Accepts Reorganization Defeat," *Los Angeles Times*, April 10, 1938, 1; Minton to Henry Morgenthau, Jr., March 26, 1938, U.S. Senate, 75th Congress, Special Committee to Investigate Lobbying Activities, General Files, 1-32 to 1-45, Box 2; U.S. Bureau of Internal Revenue, *Treasury Decisions Under Internal-Revenue Laws* 34 (Washington, DC: United States Government Printing Office, 1939), 254–55; Walter Lippmann, "Today and Tomorrow," *Los Angeles Times*, April 30, 1938, A4; and "Lobby Probers Can Use Income Tax Records," *Baltimore Sun*, April 22, 1938, 1.

43. Carl Tinney, "Man of the Week: Dr. Frank," *New York Post*, March 5, 1938, 6; and James L. Wright, "Tax Returns Inquisition Order Bared," *Hartford Courant* (Hartford, CT), April 22, 1938, 1.

44. William C. Murphy Jr., "Foes of New Deal Face Probe of Tax Returns on Roosevelt's Order," *Philadelphia Inquirer*, April 22, 1938, 7; "As to 'Personal Recrimination,'" editorial, *Philadelphia Inquirer*, April 23, 1938, 6; and "A Free Hand for Snoopers," editorial, *Los Angeles Times*, April 27, 1938, A4.

45. Walter Lippmann, "Today and Tomorrow," *Canton Repository* (Canton, OH), April 26, 1938, 4.

46. Grenville Clark to Roger N. Baldwin, April 27, 1938, Correspondence–Federal Legislation, vol. 1092, American Civil Liberties Union Papers, Mudd Library, Princeton University, Princeton, NJ; and Nancy Peterson Hill, *Very Private Public Citizen: The Life of Grenville Clark* (Columbia: University of Missouri Press, 2014), 81, 110, 114.

47. Hill, *Very Private Public Citizen,* 117–118; "Inquiry Backfires on Revenue Chiefs," *New York Times*, July 2, 1937, 22; William V. Nessly, "2 Officials Quit in Row on Tax Inquiry Method," *Washington Post*, September 17, 1937, 1; and "Courageous Resignations," editorial, *New York Times*, September 18, 1937, 18.

48. "Of Course! They Fear the Fate of the Liberty League!" editorial, *Progressive* 2, no. 18, April 30, 1938, 8.

49. White, *FDR and the Press,* 64; "We Know Who Makes Our Dishes—But Who Makes Our Ideas?" editorial, *New York Post*, April 20, 1938, 18; and "What Little Birdie Starts Those Telegrams?" editorial, *New York Post*, April 29, 1938, 18.

50. Diary of James A. Farley, April 22, 1938, Reel 4 of 54, James A. Farley Papers, Manuscript Division, Library of Congress, Washington, DC; Harold Ickes, *The Secret Diary of Harold L. Ickes* (New York: Simon & Schuster, 1954), 375; and Mordecai Lee, *Promoting the War Effort: Robert Horton and Federal Propaganda, 1938–1946* (Baton Rouge: Louisiana State University Press, 2012), 12.

51. Ickes, *Secret Diary,* 375; and Paul Y. Anderson, "Will Not Yield to Old Guard," *St. Louis Star-Times*, April 15, 1938, 1, 12.

52. "Spending and Recovery," *Nation* 146, no. 17, April 23, 1938, 456; and White, *FDR and the Press,* 130.

53. Grenville Clark, "The Relation of the Press to the Maintenance of Civil Liberty" (address, American Newspaper Publishers Association, New York City, April 27, 1938), Correspondence–Federal Legislation, vol. 1092, American Civil Liberties Union Papers, Mudd Library, Princeton, NJ; and "Press Affirms Freedom; Minton Asks Press Curb," *Chicago Daily Tribune*, April 29, 1938, 1.

54. "Dailies Must Oppose Use of Radio Against Democracy," *Editor and Publisher* 71, April 20, 1938, 18; and Bruce Robertson, "Radio Dominates Meeting of Publishers," *Broadcasting* 14, no. 9, May 1, 1938, 17.

Chapter 3: Senator Minton and Mayor Hague: The Dawn of a Left–Right Bill of Rights Coalition

1. "Here's Minton's Plan," *Progressive* 2, no. 20, May 14, 1938, 4; "Minton Offers Bill to Censor Hostile Press," *Philadelphia Inquirer*, April 29, 1938, 34; "Senator Hits Publishers for Combining Demand for Free Press with a Blow at President's Use of Air to State Views," *Washington Post*, April 29, 1938, 30; "New Dealer Blasts Publishers, Want to Put Editors in Jail if They Print Untruths," *Dallas Morning News*, April 29, 1938, 4; and "Minton Bill Asks Falsifying News Be Made Penalty," *Atlanta Constitution*, April 29, 1938, 9.

2. "The Periscope," *Newsweek* 11, no. 19, May 9, 1938, 7; Paul Y. Anderson, "Senator Minton Delivers Bitter Attack on Press," *St. Louis Star-Times*, April 29, 1938, 21; and "Senator Minton and American Journalism," *Christian Science Monitor*, May 6, 1938, 3.

3. David N. Atkinson, "From New Deal Liberal to Supreme Court Conservative: The Metamorphosis of Justice Sherman Minton," *Washington University Law Quarterly* 361 (1975): 382; and *Newsweek*, "Periscope," 7.

4. Press Conferences of President Franklin D. Roosevelt, 1933–1945, Series 1: Press Conference Transcripts, April 29, 1938, 399–400, Franklin D. Roosevelt Presidential Library & Museum, accessed June 1, 2018, http://www.fdrlibrary.marist.edu/archives/collections/franklin/?p=collections/findingaid&id=508.

5. Robert S. Allen, "False-News Bill Draws Ridicule From Roosevelt," *New York Post*, April 29, 1938, 11; "Minton Proposes Bill to Punish Papers That Print False News," *Courier-Journal* (Louisville, KY), April 29, 1938, 10; Robert S. Allen, "Senate Hears Press Lashed as Dishonest," *Philadelphia Record*, April 29, 1938, 1, 14; and 75 Cong. Rec., S5915 (daily ed., April 28, 16, 1938).

6. "To Undermine the Press," editorial, *Washington Post*, April 20, 1938, X8; "Now the Gag," editorial, *Milwaukee Journal*, April 30, 1938, 4; M. L. Annenberg, "The New Dealers Can't Muzzle the Inquirer: A Statement by M. L. Annenberg," *Philadelphia Inquirer*, April 30, 1938, 1; "Another 'Great Liberal' Hoists His Standard," cartoon, *Philadelphia Inquirer*, April 30, 1938, 6; "German News Agency Praises Minton's Plan," *Chicago Daily Tribune*, May 1, 1938, 9; and "Heil Minton!" editorial, *Philadelphia Inquirer*, May 3, 1938, 8.

7. Nelson Johnson, *Battleground New Jersey: Vanderbilt, Hague, and Their Fight for Justice* (New Brunswick, NJ: Rutgers University Press), 2014, 94–95.

8. Lyle W. Dorsett, *Franklin D. Roosevelt and the City Bosses* (Port Washington, NY: National University Publications, 1977), 101–5.

9. Laura Weinrib, *The Taming of Free Speech: America's Civil Liberties Compromise* (Cambridge: MA: Harvard University Press, 2006), 229, 231, 236–37; Dayton David McKean, *The Boss: The Hague Machine in Action* (Boston: Houghton Mifflin, 1940), 191; Johnson, *Battleground New Jersey*,107; and Dorsett, *City Bosses,* 103–5.

10. Weinrib, *Taming of Free Speech,* 236–37; "Socialist Chief Manhandled, Wife Struck," *Philadelphia Record*, May 1, 2018, 1; McKean, *Boss,* 236; and "The Shape of Things," *Nation* 146, no. 19, May 7, 1938, 518.

11. "Fight Against Fuehrer Hague Warming Up on Two Fronts," *New York Post*, April 30, 1938, 6, 10; and "Add It Up," cartoon, *New York Post*, May 2, 1938, 10.

12. Walter Lippmann, Today and Tomorrow," *Canton Repository* (Canton, OH), April 26, 1938, 4.

13. "Landon Writes Norman Thomas He's Behind His Jersey Fight," *Courier-Journal* (Louisville, KY), May 2, 1938, 1; W. A. Swanberg, *Norman Thomas: The Last Idealist* (Charles Scribner's Sons, 1976), 202; "The C.I.O. Forms on the Left," editorial, *Courier Journal* (Louisville, KY), May 3, 1933, 6; "Press Censorship Feared by Landon," *New York Post*, May 17, 1938, vol. 1089, American Civil Liberties Cases, 1938, Federal Legislation, Clippings, American Civil Liberties Union Papers, Mudd Library, Princeton University, Princeton, NJ; "Landon Assaults Press Gag Bill," *Huntsville Times* (Huntsville, AL), May 17, 1938, 4; and "Landon Insists F.D.R. Crack Down on Hague," *St. Louis Star-Times,* May 17, 1938, 7.

14. "Landon Is Leading in Jersey Pledges," *New York Times,* April 3, 1936, 14; Weinrib, *Taming of Free Speech,* 237; and Johnson, *Battleground New Jersey*, 50, 53, 108.

15. "Landon Writes Norman Thomas," 1; "Our Half-Pint Hitler," *New York Post*, May 2, 1938, 10; "Left Dress," editorial, *Courier Journal* (Louisville, KY), May 4, 1938, 8; and untitled editorial, *Courier Journal* (Louisville, KY), May 8, 1938, 8.

16. Richard L. Harkness, "Minton Abandons Bill to Gag Press; Wanted Publicity," *Philadelphia Inquirer*, May 3, 1938, 1; "Honest–I Was Only Kidding," cartoon, *Philadelphia Inquirer*, May 4, 1938, 11; "Franklin Discovers Lightning Again," cartoon, *Philadelphia Inquirer*, May 4, 1938, 10; Minton to James H. McGill, May 10, 1938, Folder: Newspaper Clippings–General, Records of the Special Committee on Lobbying, Miscellaneous Files, Folder: Newspaper Clippings–General, Box 106, U.S. Senate, 75th Congress, National Archives, Washington, DC; and "And No Back Talk!" cartoon, *Philadelphia Inquirer*, May 10, 1938, 6.

17. U.S. Senate, *Hearings Before a Special Committee to Investigate Lobbying Activities*, Part 8, May 6, 1938, 75th Cong., 3rd Sess. (1938), 2177, 2197–2198, 2211.

18. U.S. Senate, *Hearings Before a Special Committee to Investigate Lobbying Activities*, Part 8, May 6, 1938, 75th Cong., 3rd Sess. (1938), 2196–2198.

19. U.S. Senate, *Hearings Before a Special Committee to Investigate Lobbying Activities*, Part 8, May 6, 1938, 75th Cong., 3rd Sess. (Washington, DC: Government Printing Office, 1938), 2200, 2211; and "Dr. Frank Hushed at Senate Probe," *Macon* [GA]*Telegraph*, May 7, 1938, 1.

20. "Plenty of Work for Lobby Committee in Washington," *San Francisco Chronicle*, May 9, 1938, 8.

21. "Two May Quit Lobby Committee," *New York World-Telegram*, May 10, 1938, vol. 1089, American Civil Liberties Cases, 1938, Federal Legislation, Clippings 2; undated

article, American Civil Liberties Union Papers, Mudd Library, Princeton University, Princeton, NJ; "Purifying the Press," received May 11, 1938 (Box: Washington, Correspondence, 1938, L-M, Folder: Lobby Committee, Theodore F. Green Papers, Library of Congress, Washington, DC; William V. Nessly, "Frank Calls Lobby Quiz 'Terrorism,'" *Washington Post*, May 7, 1938, xi; and Chesly Manly, "Minton and His Probers Grill Farm Publisher," *Chicago Daily Tribune*, May 7, 1938, 1.

22. "A 'Free Press' Is Not a Privileged Class," editorial, *Courier-Journal* (Louisville, KY), May 8, 1938, 8; 75 Cong. Rec., A1991 (daily ed., May 16, 1938); and "Minton Continues Exposé of Frank's 'Rural Progress,'" *New Leader,* June 4, 1938, vol. 1089, American Civil Liberties Cases, 1938, Federal Legislation, Clippings 2, American Civil Liberties Union Papers, Mudd Library, Princeton University, Princeton, NJ.

23. "Spare the President from Such Friends," editorial, *Philadelphia Record*, May 7, 1938, 8.

24. "Muzzling the Press," editorial, *Chicago Defender*, May 21, 1938, 16.

25. Vernon L. Pedersen, "Jerry O'Connell, Montana's Communist Congressman," *Montana: The Magazine of Western History* 62, no. 1 (Spring 2012): 15–16; "Hague Foe Guilty in Election Case; Rally Plans Go On," *New York Times*, May 6, 1938, 3; and "800 Veterans Swinging Hoses Wait 2 Congressmen in Jersey," *Washington Post*, May 6, 1938, XI.

26. "Solons Abandon Jersey City Trip to Avert Rioting," *Atlanta Constitution,* May 8, 1938, 1A; "2 Congressmen Fail to Speak to Defy Hague," *Chicago Daily Tribune*, May 8, 1938, 3; "The Shape of Things," *Nation* 146, no. 20, May 14, 1938, 547; "O'Connell Will Defy Hague with Speech in Two Weeks," *Atlanta Constitution,* May 9, 1938, 1; "O'Connell Takes Up Hague Quarrel with White House," *St. Louis Star-Times*, May 10, 1938, 2; and "The President and Hague," editorial, *St. Louis Star-Times*, May 10, 1938, 14.

27. "Save the Democratic Party from the Hague Taint," editorial, *New York Post*, May 4, 1938, 10; and "C.I.O.," *National Republic* 25, February 1938, 11.

28. George E. Sokolsky, "We Don't Need You, Mayor Hague," *Ogden Standard-Examiner* (Ogden, UT), May 8, 1938, 22.

29. Arthur Garfield Hays to Joett Shouse, April 28, 1938, Arthur Garfield Hays to American Civil Liberties Union, May 20, 1938, William G. Fennell to Baldwin, May 10, 1938, Board of Directors, Minutes, May 16, 1938, Correspondence–Federal Legislation, vol. 1092, American Civil Liberties Union Papers, Mudd Library, Princeton University, Princeton, NJ; and Weinrib, *Taming of Free Speech,* 268.

30. Press Conferences of President Franklin D. Roosevelt, 1933–1945, Series 1: Press Conference Transcripts, May 10, 1938, 407–8, Franklin D. Roosevelt Presidential Library & Museum, accessed August 23, 2022, http://www.fdrlibrary.marist.edu/_resources/images/pc/pc0066.pdf.

31. 75 Cong. Rec., H6703–04 (daily ed., May 11, 1938).

32. 75 Cong. Rec., H6703–04 (daily ed., May 11, 1938).

33. Pedersen, "Jerry O'Connell," 16; James C. Duram, "Norman Thomas as Presidential Conscience," *Presidential Studies Quarterly* 20, no. 3 (Summer 1990): 584–85; and "Will Hague Be a National Issue?" editorial, *New York Post*, May 31, 1938, 10.

34. McKean, *Boss,* 234; Arthur Garfield Hays to American Civil Liberties Union, May 20, 1938; William G. Fennell to Baldwin, May 10, 1938, Board of Directors, Minutes,

May 16, 1938, American Civil Liberties Union, Press Release, May 19, 1938, American Civil Liberties Union, Press Release, June 2, 1938, Correspondence–Federal Legislation, vol. 1092, American Civil Liberties Union Papers, Mudd Library, Princeton University, Princeton, NJ.

35. Harry F. Ward, Arthur Garfield Hays, Roger N. Baldwin, John Haynes Holmes, and Osmond K. Fraenkel to Sherman Minton, May 27, 1938, Minton to Harry F. Ward, June 7, 1938, June 3, 1938, Correspondence–Federal Legislation, vol. 1092, American Civil Liberties Union Papers, Mudd Library, Princeton University, Princeton, NJ.

36. Paul Y. Anderson to American Civil Liberties Union, June 3, 1938, Correspondence–Federal Legislation, vol. 1092, American Civil Liberties Union Papers, Mudd Library, Princeton University, Princeton, NJ.

37. David H. Corcoran, "Sherman Minton: New Deal Senator" (PhD diss., University of Kentucky,1977), 216–17; Cong. Rec., S9589–90 (daily ed., June 16, 1938); and "Big Spending Congress Ends," *Jersey Journal*, June 17, 1938, 12.

38. McKean, *Boss,* 228.

39. "Bar Urged to Fight for Civil Liberties," *New York Times*, June 12, 1938, 2; and Nancy Peterson Hill, *A Very Private Public Citizen: The Life of Grenville Clark* (Columbia, MO: University of Missouri Press, 2014),126.

40. Hill, *Very Private Public Citizen,* 126–27.

41. Oswald Garrison Villard, "Issues and Men," *Nation* 146, no. 21, May 21, 1938, 589; "Mayor Hague's Long Shadow," *New Republic* 95, no. 1228, June 15, 1938, 144; and "The Shape of Things," *Nation* 146, no. 23, June 4, 1938, 631.

42. Fireside chat, June 24, 1938, accessed August 23, 2022, http://www.presidency.ucsb.edu/ws/index.php?pid=15662.

43. Fireside chat, June 24, 1938, accessed August 24, 2022, http://www.presidency.ucsb.edu/ws/index.php?pid=15662.

44. Weinrib, *Taming of Free Speech,* 239; and "Editorial," *Baltimore Sun*, June 26, 1938, 1.

45. "The President Reports," *New Republic* 75, no. 1231, July 6, 1937, 237–38; "The Shape of Things," *Nation* 147, no. 1, July 2, 1938, 2; Norman Thomas to Roosevelt, June 25, 1938, Thomas C. Corcoran Papers, Manuscript Division, Library of Congress, Washington, DC; and Norman Thomas, "The Menace of Hagueism," *Socialist Review* 6 no. 7, July-August 1938, 1–2.

46. "Press Menaced, Hoover Asserts," *New York World-Telegram*, July 6, 1938, vol. 1089, American Civil Liberties Cases, 1938, Federal Legislation, Clippings 2, American Civil Liberties Union Papers, Mudd Library, Princeton University, Princeton, NJ.

47. Ralph G. Martin, *Cissy* (New York: Simon & Schuster, 1979), 383; and "The Press and the President," editorial, *New York Daily News*, July 1, 1938, 23.

48. H. A. Blomquist to W. Lowrie Kay, May 14, 1938, Minton to H. A. Blomquist, July 25, 1938, "H. A. Blomquist to Minton, July 29, 1938, Folder: Office File: Committee Members, Records of the Special Committee on Lobbying, Miscellaneous Files, Box 106, U.S. Senate, 75th Congress, National Archives, Washington, DC.

49. "U.S. Bar Names 9 to Fight for the Bill of Rights," *Washington Post*, August 15, 1938, 7; and Weinrib, *Taming of Free Speech,* 249–50; and Jefferson G. Bell, "Bar Enters Civil Liberties Fight," *New York Times*, July 30, 1938, 1.

50. Linda C. Gugin and James E. St. Clair, *Sherman Minton: New Deal Senator, Cold War Justice* (Indianapolis, IN: Indiana Historical Society, 1987), 99; "Minton in Savage Attack on Nation's Newspapers," *Arkansas Gazette*, August 13, 1938, 1; George Seldes, *Lords of the Press* (New York: Julian Messner, 1938), 397; "Press Called 'Big Business': 'Monopoly' Practices Charged," *Christian Science Monitor*, August 13, 1938, 3; "Minton Criticizes Press," *New York Times*, August 13, 1938, 7; and Jon Byrne, "Delight and Dole," *Jersey Journal* (Jersey City, NJ), August 29, 1938, 9.

51. Westbrook Pegler, "Fair Enough," *Atlanta Constitution*, August 16, 1938, 4; Walter Winchell, "The New York Scene," *Hutchinson News* (Hutchinson, KS), August 23, 1938, 4; "Muddy Water," editorial, *Times-Picayune* (New Orleans, LA), August 20, 1938, 6; and Jon Byrne, "Delight and Dole," *Jersey Journal* (Jersey City, NJ), August 22, 1938, 9.

52. "Sen. Minton Declares News Monopoly Chokes U.S. Press," *Bakersfield Californian* (Bakersfield, CA), August, 13, 1938, 1; "Col. M'Cormick Assails Minton Blow at Press," *Chicago Daily Tribune*, August 28, 1938, 4; Frank Gannett, "Sen. Minton Would Destroy Our Free Press," as Broadcast Saturday, Sept. 24, to 1:30 p.m. over NBC Network, Transcript, 6, Box: Washington, Correspondence, 1938, L-M, Folder: Lobby Committee, Theodore F. Green Papers, Manuscript Division, Library of Congress, Washington, DC; "Gannett Charges Minton Lied in Press Attack," *Editor and Publisher* 71, October 1, 1938, 14; and "Minton Attacks Chicago Tribune in Radio Speech," *Chicago Daily Tribune*, September 18, 1938, 7.

53. Graham J. White, *FDR and the Press* (Chicago: University of Chicago Press, 1979), 35, 138; Franklin D. Roosevelt: "Letter of Congratulations to the St. Louis Post-Dispatch," *St. Louis Post-Dispatch*, November 2, 1938, The American Presidency Project, accessed September 3, 2011, https://www.presidency.ucsb.edu/documents/letter-congratulations-the-st-louis-post-dispatch.

54. Amos Pinchot to Franklin Dr. Roosevelt, May 17, 1938, Folder: Amos Pinchot, General Correspondence, Chronological File, 1938, May (4 of 4) Amos Pinchot Papers, Manuscript Division, Library of Congress, Washington, DC; "Discuss Wagner for Cardozo's Seat on Bench," *Chicago Daily Tribune*, July 11, 1938, 4; "Minton Mentioned Again for Bench," *New York Times*, August 22, 1938, 11; and Chesly Manly, "Three Radicals Considered for Supreme Court," *Chicago Daily-Tribune*, September 26, 1938, 12; and Joseph Alsop and Robert Kintner, "The Capital Parade," *Atlanta Constitution*, October 27, 1938, 6.

55. "Petition Urges Jersey City Probe," *Atlanta Constitution*, September 16, 1938, 8; "Decides Hague Did Not Break Federal Law," *Baltimore Sun*, September 8, 1938, 3; and "Hague Under Inquiry," *Washington Post*, September 13, 1938, X8.

56. Weinrib, *Taming of Free Speech*, 239–40; "Cummings Drops Inquiry on Hague; Mayor Is Cleared," *Washington Post*, September 8, 1938, X1; "Hague Under Inquiry," *New York Times*, September 13, 1938, X8; "Thomas Belittles Inquiry on Hague," *New York Times*, September 13, 1938, 14; Thomas Continues Drive on Democrats," *New York Times*, October 9, 1938, 33; and Albert Jay Nock, "State of the Union: Job-holders' Paradise," *American Mercury* 45, no. 177 (September 1938), 90–91.

57. Hill, *Very Private Public Citizen*, 129; Weinrib, *Taming of Free Speech*, 254; and Jeremy K. Kessler, "The Early Years of First Amendment Lochnerism," *Columbia Law Review* 118, no. 8 (December 2016): 1943–47.

58. Grenville Clark, "The Prospects for Civil Liberty," *American Bar Association Journal* 24 (1938): 833, 834, 836.

59. Clark, "Civil Liberty," 834, 858

60. Kessler, "First Amendment Lochnerism," 1948; and Clark, "Civil Liberty," 835, 836.

61. "Federal Judge Restrains Hague on Deportations," *Chicago Daily Tribune*, October 28, 1938, 6; and Weinrib, *Taming of Free Speech,* 242–44.

62. "The Shape of Things," *Nation* 148, no. 1, December 31, 1938, 3; and "Help for the Oppressed," editorial, *Chicago Daily Tribune*, August 10, 1938, 10.

63. Kessler, "First Amendment Lochnerism," 1925, 1926, 1930.

64. Kessler, "First Amendment Lochnerism," 1945, 1930.

65. Kessler, "First Amendment Lochnerism," 1919–20.

66. Kenneth O'Reilly, "The Roosevelt Administration and Black America': Federal Surveillance Policy and Civil Rights during the New Deal and World War II Years," *Phylon* 48, no. 1 (1st quarter, 1987), 15–19.

67. John W. Jeffries, *A Third Term for FDR: The Election of 1940* (Lawrence, KS: University Press of Kansas, 2017), 33; 92.

68. "A Forgotten Agency," editorial, *Washington Post*, June 5, 1938, B8; "Rise Is Voted in Emergency Council Despite Sharp Attacks in Senate," *New York Times*, June 1, 1938, 4; Frank R. Kent, "The Great Game of Politics," *Baltimore Sun*, June 22, 1938, 9; "New Deal Use of Publicity: Is It Justified? *Christian Science Monitor*, July 2, 1938, 1; "Inquiry Is Ordered as Langer Charges Vote Intimidation," *New York Times*, July 24, 1938, 1; and "Georgia RFC Chief Quits Under Orders," *New York Times*, August 19, 1938, 1.

69. Francis MacDonnell, *Insidious Foes: The Axis Fifth Column and the American Home Front* (New York: Oxford University Press, 1995), 146.

70. Hague v. Committee for Industrial Organization, 307 U.S. 496 (1939), accessed August 22, 2022, https://supreme.justia.com/cases/federal/us/307/496/case.html.

71. McKean, *Boss,* 196; and Weinrib, *Taming of Free Speech,* 265.

72. Joseph McBride, *Frank Capra: Catastrophe of Success* (New York: Simon & Schuster, 1992), 253–56, 401–5, 408–11.

73. Johnson, *Battleground New Jersey,* 46–62, 232–33; and Matthew C. Gunter, *The Capra Touch: A Study of the Director's Hollywood Classics and War Documentaries, 1934–45* (Jefferson, NC: McFarland, 2011), 39–40.

74. Dorsett, *City Bosses,* 110–11; and "Frank Hague" in "Jersey City Past and Present," New Jersey City University, accessed December 27, 2020, https://njcu.libguides.com/hague.

75. Corcoran, "Sherman Minton," 204–5; Frank R. Kent, "The Great Game of Politics," *Baltimore Sun*, July 21, 1944, 11; and Kessler, "First Amendment Lochnerism," 1983.

Chapter 4: The Necessary First Stage: Radio and the Quashing of a Free Speech Medium

1. Charlotte Twight, "What Congressmen Knew and When They Knew It: Further Evidence on the Origins of U.S. Broadcasting Regulation," *Public Choice* 95 (1998): 251; Hiram L. Jome, "Property in the Air as Affected by the Airplane and the Radio," *Journal*

of Land and Public Utility Economics 4, no. 3 (August 1928): 27–70; and James Patrick Taugher, "The Law of Radio Communication with Particular Reference to a Property Right in a Radio Wave Length," *Marquette Law Review* 12 (1928): 316.

2. U.S. Senate, Radio Control, Hearings Before the Committee on Interstate Commerce, on S. 1 and S. 1754, January 8 and 9, 1926, 69th Cong., 1st Sess. (Washington, DC: Government Printing Office, 1926), 24; Mark Arbuckle, "Herbert Hoover's National Radio Conferences and the Origin of Public Interest Content Regulation of United States Broadcasting: 1922—1925" (PhD diss., Southern Illinois University at Carbondale, 2001), 183; "U.S. Keeps Hands Off," *Seattle Daily Times*, May 30, 1925, 43; and "Sure, Let's Censor Some More," *Rockford Daily Republic* (Rockford, IL), April 4, 1924, 22.

3. "Radio Censorship Proposed at Albany," *New York Times*, January 27, 1927, 1; "Question of State Power Over Radio Studied," *Oregonian*, February 6, 1927, 60; and Arbuckle, "National Radio Conferences," 91.

4. "Censor Fanatics Turn to Radio," *Exhibitors Herald* 19, no. 6, August 2, 1924, 1.

5. Susan J. Douglas, *Inventing American Broadcasting, 1899–1922* (Baltimore: Johns Hopkins University Press, 1987), 288–89; Elaine J. Prostak, "'Up in the Air:' The Debate Over Radio Use During the 1920s" (PhD diss., University of Kansas, 1983), 30–33; and Misook Baek, "Public Interest and Technological Rationality Social Determinants of American Broadcasting, 1920–1927" (PhD diss., University of Iowa, 2003), 75.

6. Baek, "Public Interest," 168–69; and Janice Lyn Platt, "Taxation Proposals for the Funding of American Broadcasting, 1922–1926" (PhD diss., University of Missouri, 1981), 69–70.

7. David Gillis Clark, "The Dean of Commentators: A Biography of H. V. Kaltenborn" (PhD diss., University of Wisconsin, 1965), 301, 305–7.

8. David Gillis Clark, "H. V. Kaltenborn," 309–12; Erik Barnouw, *A Tower in Babel: A History of Broadcasting in the United States,* vol. 1 [to 1933] (New York: Oxford University Press, 1966), 139–41; and Baek, 177.

9. Louise Margaret Benjamin, "Radio Regulation in the 1920s: Free Speech Issues on the Department of Radio and the Radio Act of 1927" (PhD diss., University of Iowa, 1985), 275–79, 304, 483; and Gillis, "H. V. Kaltenborn," 318–19.

10. "Secretary Hoover Opens the Radio Conference," *Radio News* 7, no. 7 (January 1926): 1050, 1052; and "No More Licenses for Radio Stations," *New York Times*, November 11, 1925, 25.

11. *The Memoirs of Herbert Hoover: The Cabinet and the Presidency, 1920–1933* (New York: Macmillan, 1952), 139–41, 144; "Secretary Hoover Broadcasts His Views on Radio Situation," *New York Times*, April 13, 1924, XX17; and Herbert Hoover, "Secretary Hoover Opens the Radio Conference," *Radio News* 7, no. 7 (January 1926): 957, 1048, 1052.

12. Twight, "What Congressmen Knew," 250; and Thomas W. Hazlett, *The Political Spectrum: The Tumultuous Liberation of Wireless Technology—from Herbert Hoover to the Smartphone* (New Haven, CT: Yale University Press, 2017), 41–42.

13. Clifford J. Doerksen, *American Babel: Rogue Radio Broadcasters of the Jazz Age* (Philadelphia: University of Pennsylvania Press, 2005), 20; and Robert W. McChesney, *Telecommunications, Mass Media, and Democracy: The Battle for the Control of U.S. Broadcasting, 1928–1935* (New York: Oxford University Press, 1993), 14–15.

14. Doerksen, *American Babel*, 6–9; and Bill Kirkpatrick, "Localism in American Media, 1920–1934" (PhD diss., University of Wisconsin, 2006), 282–84.

15. Barnouw, *Tower in Babel*, 121–22; and Thomas Streeter, *Selling the Air: A Critique of the Policy of Commercial Broadcasting in the United States* (Chicago: University of Chicago Press, 1996), 90–91, 121; and Arbuckle, 62–63.

16. *U.S. House of Representatives, Hearings Before the Committee on the Merchant Marine and Fisheries on H.R. 7357, March 11, 12, 13 and 14, 1924, 68th Cong., 1st Sess.* (Washington, DC, United States Government Printing Office, 1924), 10–11; and Streeter, *Selling the Air,* 228.

17. Rufus D. Turner to W. E. Downey, December 3, 1925, Radio Division, General Records, 1910–1934 in records of the FCC, RG 173, National Archives, Washington, DC.

18. Barnouw, *Tower in Babel*, 174; "No More Licenses for Radio Stations," *New York Times*, November 11, 1925, 25; Frank S. Rowley, "Problems in the Law of Radio Communication," *University of Cincinnati Law Review* 1, no. 1 (January 1927): 5.

19. Barnouw, *Tower in Babel*, 180; Hazlett, *Political Spectrum*, 41; and United States v. Zenith Radio Corporation, et al., 12 T. 2d, 614–17.

20. *Harold N. Cones and John H. Bryant, Zenith Radio: The Early Years—1919–1935* (Atglen, PA: Shiffer Publishing, 1997), 43, 214; and U.S. Senate, Hearings before the Committee on Interstate Commerce, on S. 1 and S. 1754, January 8–9, 1926, 69th Cong., 1st Sess. (Washington, DC: Government Printing Office, 1926), 25.

21. Hazlett, *Political Spectrum*, 41–42; William J. Donovan, "Origin and Development of Radio Law, III," *Air Law Review* 2, no. 3 (July 1931), 353; and Twight, "What Congressmen Knew," 250, 256.

22. Thomas W. Hazlett, "Oak Leaves and the Origins of the 1927 Radio Act: Comment," *Public Choice* 95, nos. 3–4 (June 1998): 279; Hazlett, *Political Spectrum*, 42; Carl Zollmann, "Recent Federal Legislation, Radio Act of 1927," *Marquette Law Review* 2, no. 3 (April 1927): 123; and Carl Zollmann, *Law of the Air* (Milwaukee, WI: Bruce Publishing Company), 1927, 104.

23. "Radio Row May End in Courts," *Los Angeles Times*, July 17, 1926, 5; "More Radio Stations Jump Wave Lengths," *New York Times*, July 17, 1926, 15; "Court Forbids WGES to Hinder W-G-N Programs," *Chicago Daily Tribune*, October 10, 1926, 6; and Robert R. McCormick, "The W-G-N Story, Part I: The Station and Facilities," *Chicago Daily Tribune,* February 14, 1954, 24.

24. "Court Fixes Radio Rights on Air; W-G-N Wins," *Chicago Daily Tribune,* November 18, 1926.

25. "Radio Regulation," *Chicago Daily Tribune*, October 12, 1926, 10; "Radio Property Rights in the Air Recognized," editorial, *Chicago Daily Tribune*, November 26, 1926, 10; "Property Rights in the Ether," editorial, *Chicago Daily Tribune*, July 6, 1926, 10; "Injunctions—Protection of Broadcasting Status from Interference," *Georgetown Law Journal* 15, no. 469 (1927): 476; and "Fourteen Years Without a Change in Radio Legislation," *Radio Broadcast* 9, no. 5 (September 1926), 373.

26. Hazlett, "Oak Leaves," 280.

27. "Interim Report on Radio Legislation," *American Bar Association Journal* 12, no. 12 (December 1926): 848, 869.

28. W. Jefferson Davis, "The Radio Act of 1927," *Virginia Law Review* 12, no. 8 (June 1927): 612; Streeter, *Selling the Air,* 96–97; and American Bar Association, "Report of the Standing Committee on Radio Law," *Reports of the American Bar Association*, vol. 52 (1929), 444.

29. Taugher, "Property Right in a Radio Wave Length," 316; "Appendix [Public—No. 632 – 69th Congress] [HR 9971]," in Stephen Davis, *The Law of Radio Communication* (New York: McGraw Hill, 1927), 186; and Wallace White Jr., "Whys and Wherefores of Radio Legislation," *Broadcasting* 1, no. 2 (November 1, 1931): 8–9, 33.

30. Radio Act of 1927," accessed January 9, 2023, https://worldradiohistory.com/Archive-FCC/Federal%20Radio%20Act%201927.pdf; "Hoover Is Foe of Radio Monopoly," *Plain Dealer* [Cleveland, OH], May 28, 1925, 4; Twight, "What Congressmen Knew," 264; and "Progress on Radio Bill," *Los Angeles Times*, January 5, 1927, 4.

31. McChesney, *Telecommunications,* 13; and Arbuckle, "National Radio Conferences," 104–5; and Hoover, *Memoirs*, 145–47.

32. U.S. Senate, Radio Control, Hearings Before the Committee on Interstate Commerce, on S. 1 and S. 1754, January 8–9, 1926, 69th Cong., 1st Sess., 27, 31; Hazlett, *Political Spectrum*, 48–49; Steven Phipps, "'Order Out of Chaos': A Reexamination of the Historical Basis for the Scarcity of Channels Concept," *Journal of Broadcasting and Electronic Media* 45, no. 1 (2001): 66–67; "Stabilizing the Broadcast Situation," *Radio Broadcast* 11, no. 2 (June 27, 1927), 79; Twight, "What Congressmen Knew," 259; and Barnouw, *Tower in Babel*, 216.

33. McChesney, *Telecommunications,* 30–33; Barnouw, *Tower in Babel*, 209, 215; and U.S. Federal Radio Commission, *Second Annual Report of the Federal Radio Commission* (Washington, DC: United States Government Printing Office, 1928), 167.

34. American Bar Association, "Standing Committee on Radio Law," 459; "Hoover Is Foe of Radio Monopoly," *Plain Dealer* (Cleveland, OH), May 28, 1925, 4; Herbert Hoover, "Secretary Hoover Opens the Radio Conference," *Radio News* 7, no. 7 (January 1926), 1052; and Alan Wells, *Mass Media and Society* (Bethesda, MD: National Press Books, 1972), 126.

35. Leon Seymour Stein, "A Developmental Analysis of the Problem of Federal Regulation of Editorializing by Broadcast Licensees" (PhD diss., New York University, 1965), 113, 120–22, 135, 207; "Radio Censorship and the Federal Communications Commission," *Columbia Law Review* 39, no. 3 (March 1939): 448–49; McChesney, *Telecommunications,* 27; Louis G. Caldwell, "Freedom of Speech and Radio Broadcasting," *Annals of the American Academy of Political and Social Science* 177 (January 1935), 194–205; Patrick Farabaugh, "Carl McIntire and His Crusade Against the Fairness Doctrine" (PhD diss., Pennsylvania State University, 2010), 25, 27; and Federal Radio Commission, *Third Annual Report* (1929) (Washington, DC: United States Government Printing Office, 1930), 34.

36. McChesney, *Telecommunications,* 73; Doerksen, *American Babel*, 105, 107–09, 113.

37. McChesney, *Telecommunications,* 66–67; and Hazlett, *Political Spectrum*, 57–58.

38. McChesney, *Telecommunications,* 30–31; and Kirkpatrick, "Localism in American Media," 123, 323–24. Underlining in the original.

39. McChesney, *Telecommunications,* 20, 24, 257; Phipps, "'Order Out of Chaos,'" 69; and Barnouw, *Tower in Babel*, 218–19.

40. Kirkpatrick, "Localism in American Media," 233, 245, 327–29; and Louis G. Caldwell, "Principles Governing the Licensing of Broadcasting Stations," *University of Pennsylvania Law Review and American Law Register* 79, No. 2 (December 1930): 117.

41. Doerksen, *American Babel*, 115.

42. Doerksen, *American Babel*, 68, 85–86, 89; and Barnouw, *Tower in Babel*, 170–71.

43. Doerksen, *American Babel*, 88–89; Stein, "Editorializing by Broadcast Licensees," 91–92; and KFKB Broadcasting Association v. Federal Radio Commission, 47 F. 2d 670 (1931).

44. Eric B. Easton, "The Colonel's Finest Campaign: Robert R. McCormick and Near v. Minnesota," *Federal Communications Law Journal* 60, no. 2 (March 2008): 185, 196–98.

45. Easton, "McCormick and Near v. Minnesota," 185–90, 201; "Censorship of Radio," *Broadcasting* 1, no. 4 (December 1, 1931): 29; and "L. G. Caldwell Found Dead of Heart Attack," *Chicago Daily Tribune*, December 12, 1951, E9.

46. Easton, "McCormick and Near v. Minnesota," 198–204, 208–10, 221.

47. Mark Sumner Still, "'Fighting Bob' Shuler: Fundamentalist and Reformer" (PhD diss., Claremont Graduate School, 1988), 208–34, 255–62; D. J. Waldie, "Cathedrals of the Air: Sister Aimee, Fighting Bob, and Early L.A. Radio," June 24, 2016, History and Society, KCET, Lost LA, accessed October 26, 2020, https://www.kcet.org/shows/lost-la/ cathedrals-of-the-air-sister-aimee-fighting-bob-and-early-la-radio; and Robert Shuler, *Fighting Bob Shuler of Los Angeles* (Indianapolis, IN: Dog Ear Publishing, 2012), 98.

48. "Plea Filed by Shuler: Broadcast Ban Attack Opens," *Los Angeles Times*, December 1, 1931, 1; "Free Speech Plea in KGEF Appeal," *Broadcasting* 2, no. 7, April 1, 1932, 28.

49. Edward C. Caldwell, "Censorship of Radio Programs," *Journal of Radio Law* 1, no. 3 (October 1931): 462, 475.

50. Hazlett, *Political Spectrum*, 53; Caldwell, "Freedom of Speech," 199; and Reuel E. Schiller, "Free Speech and Expertise: Administrative Censorship and the Birth of the Modern First Amendment," *Virginia Law Review* 86, no. 1 (2000): 49.

51. Gordon W. Moss to Robert Shuler, November 14, 1931, Robert P. Shuler to Gordon W. Moss, November 18, 1931, American Civil Liberties Union, Correspondence–Organizational Matters, 1931–1933, vol. 510, American Civil Liberties Union Papers, Mudd Library, Princeton University, Princeton, NJ; and Still, "'Fighting Bob' Schuler," 169–72, 177–98.

52. Clifton J. Taft, "An Open Letter to Bob Shuler," *Open Forum*, November 28, 1931, American Civil Liberties Union, Correspondence–Organizational Matters, 1931–1933, vol. 510, American Civil Liberties Union Papers, Mudd Library, Princeton University, Princeton, NJ.

53. Trinity Methodist Church, South v. Federal Radio Commission, Court of Appeals of the District of Columbia, November 28, 1932, 62 F. 2d (1932), 853–54.

54. "Pastor Shuler Wages War to Lift Radio Ban," *Indianapolis Times*, December 3, 1932, 3; "Freedom of Radio Speech Beyond Any Personal Stake," *Springfield Republican* (Springfield, MA), December 25, 1932, 28; and Louis G. Caldwell to American Civil Liberties Union, January 17, 1933, Correspondence–Organizational Matters, 1931–1933, American Civil Liberties Union Papers, Mudd Library, Princeton University, Princeton, NJ.

55. Easton, "McCormick and Near v. Minnesota," 220–21; and Mary Welek Atwell, "Louis Brandeis," *The First Amendment Encyclopedia*, accessed November 5, 2020, https://www.mtsu.edu/first-amendment/article/1316/louis-brandeis.

56. A. L. Wirin to Baldwin, January 16, 1933, Louis G. Caldwell to American Civil Liberties Union, January 17, 1933, Correspondence–Organizational Matters, 1931–1933, American Civil Liberties Union Papers, Mudd Library, Princeton University, Princeton, NJ.

57. In the Supreme Court of the United States, no. 551, *Trinity Methodist Church, Petitioner v. Federal Radio Commission, Brief in Support of Petition for Rehearing*, February 10, 1933, 6–7, 13–14, American Civil Liberties Union, Correspondence–Organizational Matters, 1931–1933, vol. 510, American Civil Liberties Union Papers, Mudd Library, Princeton University, Princeton, NJ.

58. "Rev. Shuler Radio Fight at an End," *Daily Gazette* (Schenectady, NY), February 14, 1933, 3.

59. "Lawyers View Pastor's Fate as a Warning," *Springfield Republican* (Springfield, MA), September 10, 1933, 34; and Wallace White Jr., "Whys and Wherefores of Radio Legislation," 33.

60. Louis G. Caldwell, "Freedom of Speech," 195; James L. Baughman, *Same Time, Same Station: Creating American Television, 1948–1961* (Baltimore: Johns Hopkins University Press, 2007), 10; and Seymour N. Siegel, "Censorship in Radio," *Air Law Review* 7, no. 1 (January 1936): 19.

Chapter 5: A New Deal for Radio and a New Uniformity

1. "Radio Censorship and the Federal Communications Commissions," *Columbia Law Review* 39, no. 3 (March 1939): 447; and Robert W. McChesney, *Telecommunications, Mass Media, and Democracy: The Battle for the Control of U.S. Broadcasting, 1928–1935* (New York: Oxford University Press, 1993), 29.

2. Becky M. Nicolaides, "Radio Electioneering in the American Presidential Campaigns of 1932 and 1936," *Historical Journal of Film, Radio and Television* 8, no. 2 (1988): 116, 121.

3. Robert J. Brown, *Manipulating the Ether: The Power of Broadcast Radio in Thirties America* (Jefferson, NC: McFarland and Company, 1998), 14; McChesney, *Telecommunications,* 182; and Ruth Brindze, *Not to Be Broadcast: The Truth About Radio* (New York: Vanguard Press, 1937), 134.

4. Leon Seymour Stein, "Editorializing by Broadcast Licensees: A Developmental Analysis of the Problem of Federal Regulation of Editorializing by Broadcast Licensees" (PhD diss., New York University, 1965), 99; Orrin B. Dunlap Jr., "Talking to the People: Radio Devices in White House Give President Quick Contact with Populace from Coast to Coast," *New York Times*, March 19, 1933, XB; Minna F. Kassner, "Radio Censorship," *Air Law Review* 8, no. 97 (April 1937): 104; and Richard W. Steele, *Propaganda in an Open Society: The Roosevelt Administration and the Media, 1933–1941* (Westport, CT: Greenwood Press, 1985), 18–20.

5. McChesney, *Telecommunications,* 182; Steele, *Propaganda in an Open Society,* 19; and Brown, *Manipulating the Ether,* 14.

6. Gary Dean Best, *The Critical Press and the New Deal: The Press Versus Presidential Power, 1933–1938* (Westport, CT: Praeger, 1993), 25; Robert J. Brown, *Manipulating the Ether,* 14; James Ragland, "Merchandisers of the First Amendment: Freedom and Responsibility of the Press in the Age of Roosevelt, 1933–1940," *Georgia Review* 16 (Winter 1962): 382; and Steele, *Propaganda in an Open Society,* 18–19.

7. "Lafount Urges NRA Cooperation," *NAB Reports* 1, no. 26, August 19, 1933, 118–19; and Brindze, *Not to Be Broadcast,* 118–19.

8. Stein, "Editorializing by Broadcast Licensees," 100–01; Steele, *Propaganda in an Open Society,* 19; Brown, *Manipulating the Ether,* 14; and James L. Baughman, *Same Time, Same Station: Creating American Television, 1948–1961* (Baltimore: Johns Hopkins University Press, 2007), 10.

9. Brown, *Manipulating the Ether,* 14.

10. Nicolaides, "Radio Electioneering," 125–26; "Widespread Support for Radio in Political Broadcast Fracas," *Broadcasting* 10, no. 3, February 1, 1936, 8; and Franklin Delano Roosevelt, "State of the Union," January 3, 1936, accessed August 25, 2022, http://www.let.rug.nl/usa/presidents/franklin-delano-roosevelt/state-of-the-union-1936.php.

11. Nicolaides, "Radio Electioneering," 125–26, 133; and Lynn D. Gordon, "Why Dorothy Thompson Lost Her Job: Political Columnists and the Press Wars of the 1930s and 1940s," *History of Education Quarterly* 34, no. 3 (Fall 1994): 293.

12. Nicolaides, "Radio Electioneering," 127, 136.

13. Nicolaides, "Radio Electioneering," 125.

14. Stanley High, "No-So-Free Air," *Saturday Evening Post* 211, no. 33 (February 11, 1939), 8–9; and "Broadcasters Memorize This!" *Variety,* February 15, 1939, 1.

15. Elizabeth Fones-Wolfe, "Creating a Favorable Business Climate: Corporations and Radio Broadcasting, 1934 to 1954," *Business History Review* 73 (Summer 1999): 230; and Brindze, *Not to Be Broadcast,* 62–73.

16. F. W. Blaisdell to Hugo L. Black, October 15, 1935, Folder: NRA–Black, Hugo, Committee, 1936, Series I-60, Box 57, Robert R. McCormick Papers, Colonel Robert R. McCormick Research Center, First Division Museum at Cantigny Park, Wheaton, IL; "Scores Lobbying Inquiry," *New York Times,* February 11, 1936, 10; "Crusaders Tell Tactics in Black Inquisition Here," *Chicago Daily Tribune,* March 8, 1936, 17; "New Lobby Hunt Begun," *Los Angeles Times,* January 29, 1936, 2; Jamie C. Euken, "Evil, Greed, Treachery, Deception, and Fraud: The World of Lobbying According to Senator Hugo Black," *Federal History* 6 (2014), 80; Brindze, *Not to Be Broadcast,* 72–75; and Arnold Markoe, "The Black Committee: A Study of the Senate Investigation of the Public Utility Holding Company Lobby" (PhD diss., New York University, 1972), 181–84.

17. Fones-Wolfe, "Creating a Favorable Business Climate," 230–36; "New Deal Disk Series Aired by 223 Stations," *Radio Daily* 2, no. 23, August 3, 1937, 1; and "Radio Reports," *Variety,* July 22, 1936, 40.

18. Alan Brinkley, *Voices of Protest: Huey Long, Father Coughlin, and the Great Depression* (New York: Vintage Books, 1983), 91, 107–23, 134–39; and Patrick Farabaugh, "Carl McIntire and His Crusade Against the Fairness Doctrine" (PhD diss., Pennsylvania State University, 2010), 34.

19. Brinkley, *Voices of Protest,* 127, 261, 270; and Farabaugh, "Carl McIntire," 33.

20. Kathy M. Newman, *Radio Active: Advertising and Consumer Activism, 1935–1947* (Berkeley, CA: University of California Press, 2004), 80, 85–86; Fones-Wolfe, "Creating a Favorable Business Climate," 251; and David H. Culbert, "'Croak' Carter: Radio's 'Voice of Doom,'" *Pennsylvania Magazine of History and Biography* 97, no. 3 (July 1973): 303–4.

21. A. J. Liebling, "Boake Carter," *Scribner's Magazine*, 104, no. 2, August 1938, 8–9; Culbert, "'Croak' Carter," 293–94, 302; and Steele, *Propaganda in an Open Society*, 129.

22. Hoover to Carter, January 8, January 21, January 21, February 6, March 12, March 19, April 6, April 9, April 12, April 19, May 6, September 24, October 19, 1937, Boake Carter, FBI File; and Clyde Tolson to Hoover, January 20, 1937; Boake Carter, FBI File, Federal Bureau of Investigation, Washington, DC. The copy was obtained from the FBI through a Freedom of Information request.

23. Fones-Wolfe, "Creating a Favorable Business Climate," 236–41; Culbert, "'Croak' Carter," 305–6; and *Newman, Radio Active, 90.*

24. Culbert, "'Croak' Carter," 306–7.

25. Steele, *Propaganda in an Open Society*, 129–30; "'Boss' Agrees Marvin McIntyre Can Accept Degree Here," *Atlanta Constitution*, May 29, 1938, 13A; and Stanley High, "No-So-Free Air," *Saturday Evening Post* 211, no. 33, February 11, 1939, 76.

26. Joseph E. Davies to Stephen Early, February 8, 1938, C. M. Chester to Joseph E. Davies, January 25, 1938 (Enclosure: "Proposal for Method of Operation with Mr. Boake Carter"), Folder: President Roosevelt, 1938, Stephen Early Papers, Franklin D. Roosevelt Presidential Library, Hyde Park, NY; and Culbert, "'Croak' Carter," 307–10.

27. Harold L. Ickes, *The Secret Diary of Harold L. Ickes: The Inside Struggle, 1936–1939*, vol. II (New York: Simon & Schuster, 1954), 313; and Culbert, "'Croak' Carter," 308–9.

28. Culbert, "'Croak' Carter," 309–10; 75 Cong. Rec., H3320 (daily ed., March 14, 1938); Stanley High, "No-So-Free Air," *Saturday Evening Post* 211, no. 33, February 11, 1939, 76; Robert U. Brown, "Boake Carter Charges 'Gag' Attempt by U.S.," *Editor and Publisher*, March 12, 1938, 28.

29. Culbert, "'Croak' Carter," 313; Paul Y. Anderson, "Boake Carter's Radio Problem," *St. Louis Star-Times*, April 8, 1938, 5; and Jerre Mangione, *An Ethnic at Large: A Memoir of America in the Thirties and Forties* (New York: G. P. Putnam's Sons, 1978), 248.

30. Culbert, "'Croak' Carter," 305; Steele, *Propaganda in an Open* Society, 130; "But–Says Boake Carter," *Nevada State Journal (Reno)*, May 3, 1938, 8; "But—Says Boake Carter," *Augusta Chronicle*, May 18, 1938, Section A, 4; and "But–Says Boake Carter," *Augusta Chronicle*, May 19, 1938, 4.

31. Stanley High, "No-So-Free Air," *Saturday Evening Post* 211, no. 33, February 11, 1939, 76; "Carter, Quitting Air Reads Freedom Essay," *Editor and Publisher* 71, September 3, 1938, 10; and Newman, *Radio Active*, 91; and "Hampered on Radio, Says Boake," *Hartford Courant* (Hartford, CT), October 19, 1938, 12.

32. Hoover to Carter, January 21, May 2, Hoover to Carter, May 12, 1938, June 9, 1938, June 11, 1938, February 6, 1939, Carter, FBI File, Federal Bureau of Investigation, Washington, DC.

33. Albert Samuel Karr, "The Roosevelt Haters: A Study in Economic Motivation" (PhD diss., University of Southern California, 1956), 73–93; "Gen. Hugh Johnson Joins Radio Columnist Ranks," *Broadcasting* 13, no. 4, August 15, 1937, 47.

34. Steele, *Propaganda in an Open Society*, 128–29.

35. "FCC Attacked by Newspaper Writers for Rebuke to NBC in Mae West Case," *Broadcasting* 14, no. 3, February 1, 1938, 28.

36. Gene A. Coyle, "John Franklin Carter: Journalist, FDR's Secret Investigator, Soviet Agent?" *International Journal of Intelligence and Counterintelligence* 24 (2011): 148–72; Jay Franklin, "We, the People," *Wilkes-Barre Record* (Pennsylvania), May 9, 1938, 14; Stanley High, "No-So-Free Air," *Saturday Evening Post* 211, no. 33, February 11, 1939, 74; and Brown, *Manipulating the Ether*, 15.

37. "Paley's Speech on Federal Regulation Draws Favorable Comment from Press," *Broadcasting* 14, no. 8, April 15, 1938, 63.

38. Fones-Wolfe, "Creating a Favorable Business Climate," 228–29; Aaron Robertson Hatley, "Tin Lizzie Dreams: Henry Ford and Antimodern American Culture, 1919–1942" (PhD diss., Harvard University, 2015), 114–17; Edward Klauber to A. R. Barbier, December 14, 1939, Box 165, Folder: "Ford Sunday Evening Hour," 1934–1943, and undated, Fair Lane Papers, Benson Ford Research Center, Henry Ford Museum of American Innovation, Dearborn, MI; and Sol Taishoff, "Vital Changes Seen in FCC Control Foreseen," *Broadcasting* 14, no. 5, March 1, 1938, 60.

39. Sheldon Marcus, *Father Coughlin: The Tumultuous Life of the Priest of the Little Flower* (Boston: Little, Brown and Company, 1973), 154–61; and "Coughlin Storm Is Revived," *Broadcasting* 15, no. 12, December 15, 1938, 65.

40. "Flamm Explains Refusal to Broadcast Coughlin," *Broadcasting* 15, no. 11, December 1, 1938, 79; and "Three Stations Refuse Coughlin Talks for Allegedly Inciting Race Prejudice," *Broadcasting* 15, no. 11, December 1, 1938, 17.

41. "U.S. Radio Monopolistic? Sarnoff Starts String of Denials as FCC Inquiry Opens," *Newsweek* 12, no. 18, November 28, 1938, 19; "FCC Chairman Strikes Back at Assailants," *Baltimore Sun*, February 11, 1939, 15–20; "Bars Radio Censorship," *New York Times*, November 13, 1938, 42; and Laurence E. Neville, "Free Speech and Broadcasting," *Broadcasting* 16, no. 3, February 1, 1939, 40.

42. "Code Compliance Under Way," *NAB Reports* 7, no. 40, October 6, 1939, 3754–55; and Steele, *Propaganda in an Open Society*, 134–35.

43. "Press Comments on NAB Code," *Broadcasting* 17, no. 3, August 1, 1939, 46; and "Statement of the Code Compliance Committee," *NAB Reports* 7, no. 40, October 6, 1939, 3755–56.

44. Hugh S. Johnson, "Johnson Says," *Knoxville News Sentinel* (Knoxville, TN), July 14, 1939, 4.

45. David Lawrence, "Sees N.A.B. Ban as a Grave Mistake," *The Tablet* (Brooklyn, NY), October 21, 1939, 1, 12.

46. "Curb of Executive Power Over Radio Is Advocated," *Broadcasting* 17, no. 9, November 15, 1939, 79; and Frank E. Gannett, "No," *Washington Post*, December 17, 1939, B2.

47. Sol Taishoff, "NAB Adopts Code, Demands ASCAP Action," *Broadcasting* 17, no. 2, July 15, 1939, 8; Sol Taishoff, "First Code Action Brings Discord," *Broadcasting* 17, no. 8, October 15, 1939, 11, 72; "Code's Restrictions on Commentators Are Blow to Freedom, Patt Tells NAB," *Broadcasting* 17, no. 8, October 15, 1939, 12.

48. McChesney, *Telecommunications* 5, 80–83; and Clifton Reed, "Radio Censors Labor," *Nation* 141, no. 3664, September 25, 1935, 357.

49. Norman Thomas, "Yes," *Washington Post*, December 17, 1939, B2.

50. Sol Taishoff, "NAB Adopts Codes, Demands ASCAP Action," *Broadcasting* 17, no. 2, July 15, 1939, 14, 90; Stephen T. Early, "White House Secretary Lauds Radio," *Broadcasting* 17, no. 2, July 15, 1939, 19, 41; and "A United Industry Discovers Its Own Strength: An Editorial," *Broadcasting* 17, no. 2, July 15, 1939, 10; and "Voluntary Plan for War News Is Adopted," *Broadcasting* 17, no. 2, September 15, 1939, 77–78.

51. "Industry Accord Solves Code Crisis," *Broadcasting* 17, no. 9, November 15, 1939, 19; and Marcus, *Father Coughlin,* 176–77.

52. "Free Offers," *NAB Reports* 7, no. 17, April 28, 1939, 3446; "Free Offers," *NAB Reports* 7, no. 24, June 16, 1939, 3542; and "The American Family Robinson," *NAB Reports* 17, no. 32, August 11, 1939, 3657.

53. The listener can compare and contrast the initial "first series" of extant episodes from "The American Family Robinson" with the more placid entries in the "second series" of the program here: accessed August 25, 2022, https://www.oldtimeradiodownloads.com/drama/american-family-robinson/2.The final listing of "The American Family Robinson" in a radio schedule, according to newspapers.com, was in September 1941. "Complete Radio Programs," *Bakersfield Californian*, September 11, 1941, 24.

54. Newman, *Radio Active*, 105–06; and David R. Mackey, "The National Association of Broadcasters—The First Twenty Years" (PhD diss., Northwestern University, 1956), 411.

55. Mackey, "National Association of Broadcasters," 408–9.

56. Norman Thomas to Flynn, November 27, 1941, Folder: Thomas, Box 20, John T. Flynn Papers, Special Collections and University Archives, University of Oregon, Eugene, OR.

57. "FCC Chairman Commends Code," *NAB Reports* 7, no. 43, October 27, 1939, 3791–3794; Stein, "Editorializing by Broadcast Licensees," 180–90; "The Mayflower Doctrine Scuttled," *Yale Law School Journal* 39, no. 4 (March 1950): 764–65.

58. Brown, *Manipulating the Ether*, 243.

59. Stein, "Editorializing by Broadcast Licensees," 188, 206–13; and Lucas Powe Jr., *American Broadcasting and the First Amendment* (Berkeley, CA: University of California Press, 1987), 109–11.

60. Stein, "Editorializing by Broadcast Licensees," 113, 124.

61. Stein, "Editorializing by Broadcast Licensees," 246–47; and Paul David Lunde, "The Broadcast Editorial" (master's thesis, Northwestern University, 1958), 45.

62. Hatley, "Tin Lizzie Dreams," 114; "Ford Cancels CBC," *Broadcasting* 17, no. 9, November 15, 1939, 71; "The Cameron Case," *Los Angeles Times*, February 13, 1941, 36; 76 Cong. Rec., A200 (daily ed., January 21, 1941); and U.S. House, Select Committee on Immigration and Naturalization (Regarding the Alleged False Swearing of William J. Cameron During His Naturalization Proceedings), February 12, 1941, In the United States House of Representatives, 77th Cong., 1st Sess., 43–46. Hearing Id:HRG-1941-IMN-0080, [gated], accessed August 26, 2022, https://congressional-proquest-com.libdata.lib.ua.edu/congressional/docview/t29.d30.hrg 1941-imn-0080?accountid=14472.

63. "Ford Evening Hour on Radio Closes," *News-Palladium* (Benton Harbor, MI), March 2, 1942, 11; Erik Barnouw, *The Golden Web: A History of Broadcasting in the United States, 1933–1953* (New York: Oxford University Press, 1968), 60; "Program Policy Blue

Hearing Topic," *Broadcasting* 25, no. 11, September 13, 1943, 10; and Hatley, "Tin Lizzie Dreams," 111; and "Woods Shows Courage with Pearson—Also Fly on Blue," *Heinl Business Letter*, September 14, 1943, no. 1561, 1–2.

64. "Code Compliance Under Way," *NAB Reports* 7, no. 40, October 6, 1939, 3755; and Ken I. Kersh, *Conservatives and the Constitution: Imagining Constitutional Restoration in the Heyday of American Liberalism* (New York: Cambridge University Press, 2019), 188.

65. Arthur Garfield Hays, "Civic Discussion Over the Air," *Annals of the American Academy of Political and Social Science* 213 (January 1, 1941): 37, 45–46; David Goodman, *Radio's Civic Ambition: American Broadcasting and Democracy in the 1930s* (New York: Oxford University Press, 2011), 199–215; and Hugh S. Johnson, "Johnson Says," *Dothan Eagle* (Alabama), April 15, 1940, 4.

66. Richard W. Steele, *Free Speech in the Good War* (New York: St. Martin's Press, 1999), 74.

67. Steele, *Propaganda in an Open Society*, 144.

68. Steele, *Propaganda in an Open Society*, 144–45.

Chapter 6: "A Most Complete Espionage Service": Boss Crump Cracks Down on Dissent

1. Memorandum Regarding Police Persecution of Dr. J. B. Martin of Memphis, Tennessee, Because of Political Activities in 1940 Presidential Election, March 26, 1941, 2, National Association for the Advancement of Colored People Papers, Group II, Box A508, Library of Congress Department of Justice, Criminal Division, Memorandum Regarding Police Persecution of Dr. J. B. Martin of Memphis, Tennessee, Because of Political Activities in 1940 Presidential Election, March 26, 1941, 2, Group II, Box A508, National Association for the Advancement of Colored People Papers, Library of Congress, Washington, DC; and John B. Martin, Drugs, Memphis, Tennessee, Dun & Bradstreet report, May 20, 1940 [Capital letters are in the original], E. H. Crump Papers, Folder 1, Box 4, Series I, E. H. Crump Collection, Memphis and Shelby County Room, Benjamin L. Hooks Central Library, Memphis, TN, Memphis and Shelby County Public Library; and Miriam DeCosta-Willis, *Notable Black Memphians* (Amherst, NY: Cambria Press, 2008), 10, 216, 236–38.

2. Darius Jamal Young, "The Gentleman from Memphis: Robert R. Church Jr. and the Politics of the Early Civil Rights Movement" (PhD diss., University of Memphis, 2011), 45–47, 73–79, 114, 121, 126–27, 156; Roger Biles, "Robert Church Jr. of Memphis: Black Republican Leader in the Age of Democratic Ascendancy, 1928–1940," *Tennessee Historical Quarterly* 42, no. 4 (Winter 1983): 364; and David M. Tucker, *Lieutenant Lee of Beale Street* (Nashville, TN: Vanderbilt University Press, 1971), 68–69.

3. Tucker, *Lieutenant Lee*, 68; and Biles, "Robert Church Jr.," 371–73, 376; and Ralph J. Bunche, *The Political Status of the Negro in the Age of FDR* (Chicago: University of Chicago Press, 1973), 494–95.

4. Department of Justice, Criminal Division, Transcript of Deposition of J. B. Martin, 4, Washington, DC, March 12, 1941, Box 7, Folder 11, Robert H. Church Family Papers, Special Collections, McWherter Library, University of Memphis [Memphis, TN]; Department of Justice, Criminal Division, Memorandum Regarding Police Persecution of Dr. J.

B. Martin of Memphis, Tennessee, Because of Political Activities in 1940 Presidential Election, March 26, 1941, 1, Group II, Box A508, National Association for the Advancement of Colored People Papers, Library of Congress, Washington, DC; Tucker, *Lieutenant Lee,* 127; and Bunche, *Political Status of the Negro,* 495.

5. Lyle W. Dorsett, *Franklin D. Roosevelt and the City Bosses* (Port Washington, NY: National University Publications, 1977), 35–38; and Edwin A. Halsey, *Factual Campaign Information* (Washington, DC: United States Government Printing Office, 1939), 9, 13–14.

6. Bunche, *Political Status of the Negro,* 493, 496; and Elizabeth Gritter, *River of Hope: Black Politics and the Memphis Freedom Movement, 1865–1954* (Lexington, KY: University Press of Kentucky, 2014), 111–12.

7. Gritter, *River of Hope,* 112; and Richard Rothstein, *The Color of Law: A Forgotten History of How Our Government Segregated America* (New York: W. W. Norton, 2017), 19–24.

8. Biles, "Robert Church Jr.," 378; and Gritter, *River of Hope,* 115, 138. The term *ward heeler* is often used to describe a political operative at the district (ward) level in a city who works as an operative for a political party organization. Ward heelers often both received and dispensed patronage and other favors.

9. James J. Kenneally, "Black Republicans During the New Deal: The Role of Joseph W. Martin, Jr.," *Review of Politics* 55, no. 1 (Winter 1993): 130; Gritter, *River of Hope,* 122, 129–31; "GOP Notes," *Chicago Defender,* August 29, 1936, 5; and Biles, "Robert Church Jr.," 370.

10. Tucker, *Lieutenant Lee,* 145; and Gritter, *River of Hope,* 131, 139.

11. Bunche, *Political Status of the Negro,* 495; Gritter, *River of Hope,* 132; Biles, "Robert Church Jr.," 378; and Dorsett, *City Bosses,* 47.

12. Gritter, *River of Hope,* 132–34; and Biles, "Robert Church Jr.," 378.

13. Gritter, *River of Hope,* 134–35; Bunche, *Political Status of the Negro,* 495; Tucker, *Lieutenant Lee,* 124–25; and Biles, "Robert Church Jr.," 378.

14. Gritter, *River of Hope,* 115–16, 142–44; and Tucker, *Lieutenant Lee,* 126.

15. Department of Justice, Criminal Division, Transcript of Deposition of J. B. Martin, 4, Washington, DC, March 12, 1941, Box 7, Folder 11, Robert H. Church Family Papers, Special Collections, McWherter Library, University of Memphis, Memphis, TN; Biles, "Robert Church Jr.," 379; John W. Jeffries, *A Third Term for FDR: The Election of 1940* (Lawrence, KS: University Press of Kansas, 2017), 151–53; and Tucker, *Lieutenant Lee,* 127.

16. "Apathy in the South Capitalized by G.O.P," *Commercial Appeal* [Memphis, TN], November 1, 1940, 9; Kenneally, "Black Republicans," 132–33; Young, "Gentleman from Memphis," 121; "Republican Party Platform of 1940," June 24, 1940, The American Presidency Project, accessed December 1, 2020, http://www.presidency.ucsb.edu/ws/index.php?pid=29640; Burton Folsom Jr. and Anita Folsom, *FDR Goes to War: How Expanded Executive National Debt, and Restricted Civil Liberties Shaped Wartime America* (New York: Simon & Schuster, 2011), 44–50; George Gallup, "Gain in Key States Gives Willkie an Even Chance to Win Electoral Majority," *Washington Post,* October 30, 1940, 1; "Predictions on the Outcome of Tuesday's Voting in All Parts of the Country," *New York Times,* November 3, 1940, 53; and "Heavy Vote Cast in GOP Primary," *Atlanta Daily World,* August 6, 1940, 2.

17. Department of Justice, Criminal Division, Transcript of Deposition of J. B. Martin, 4, Washington, DC, March 12, 1941, 1, Box 7, Folder 11, Robert H. Church Family Papers, Special Collections, McWherter Library, University of Memphis, Memphis, TN; Biles, "Robert Church Jr.," 380; and A. B. Clapp to Guy Joyner, October 22, 1940, Folder: Joyner, Guy, 1940, Series IV, Box 175, E. H. Crump Collection, Memphis and Shelby County Room, Memphis Public Library and Information Center [Memphis, TN].

18. Department of Justice, Criminal Division, Transcript of deposition of J. B. Martin, 1–3, Washington, DC, March 12, 1941, Box 7, Folder 11, Robert H. Church Family Papers, Special Collections, McWherter Library, University of Memphis, Memphis, TN; Tucker, *Lieutenant Lee,* 127; and Elizabeth Gritter, "Black Politics in the Age of Jim Crow, Memphis, Tennessee, 1865–1954" (PhD diss., University of North Carolina, Chapel Hill, 2010), 236.

19. "Both Races Reported Disturbed Over 'Insult' to Negro Leader," *Atlanta Daily World,* December 18, 1940, 1; and Memorandum Regarding Police Persecution of Dr. J. B. Martin of Memphis, Tennessee, Because of Political Activities in 1940 Presidential Election, March 26, 1941, 2, 7, Group II, Box A508, National Association for the Advancement of Colored People, Library of Congress, Washington, DC; J. B. Martin to Francis Biddle, February 16, 1944, Department of Justice, Criminal Division, Class 144 (Civil Rights) Litigation Case Files and Enclosures, 1936–1997, Entry Number 72, Box 1, National Archives, Washington, DC; Jason Jordan, "'We Have No Race Trouble Here': Racial Politics and Memphis's Reign of Terror," in *An Unseen Light: Black Struggles for Freedom in Memphis, Tennessee,* ed. Aram Goudsouzian and Charles W. McKinney Jr. (Lexington, KY: University Press of Kentucky, 2018), 133; Department of Justice, Criminal Division, Transcript of Deposition of J. B. Martin, 2, Washington, DC, March 12, 1941, Box 7, Folder 11, Robert H. Church Family Papers, Special Collections, McWherter Library, University of Memphis, Memphis, TN.

20. "Searchings Continue at Negro Drug Store," *Commercial Appeal* (Memphis, TN), October 27, 1940, 7; Department of Justice, Criminal Division, Transcript of Deposition of J. B. Martin, 21–22, Washington, DC, March 12, 1941, Box 7, Folder 11, Robert H. Church Family Papers, Special Collections, McWherter Library, University of Memphis, Memphis, TN; Roscoe Conkling Simmons, "The Week," *Chicago Defender,* November 16, 1940, 15; Gritter, *River of Hope,* 142; and "Colored Memphians Threatened," *Atlanta Daily World,* October 29, 1940, 1.

21. "City Swings at a Beale Sign and Joe Louis Goes Down, Out," *Commercial Appeal* (Memphis, TN), November 1, 1940, 1; Memorandum Regarding Police Persecution of Dr. J. B. Martin of Memphis, Tennessee, Because of Political Activities in 1940 Presidential Election, March 26, 1941, 2, 5, Group II, Box A508, National Association for the Advancement of Colored People Papers, Library of Congress, Washington, DC, 5; "Governor Warns 'It's a White Man's Country!' Then Calls for Draftees," *Chicago Defender,* November 2, 1940, 4; and Tucker, *Lieutenant Lee,* 129.

22. W. S. Martin to Crump, November 1, 1940, Folder 14, Box 15, Arthur Webb Collection, Memphis and Shelby County Room, Memphis Public Library and Information Center [Memphis, TN].

23. Department of Justice, Criminal Division, Transcript of Deposition of J. B. Martin, 5–8, Washington, DC, March 12, 1941, Box 7, Folder 11, Robert H. Church Family

Papers, Special Collections, McWherter Library, University of Memphis, Memphis, TN; and "Negroes Are Warned Against Arguments," *Commercial Appeal* (Memphis, TN), November 5, 1940, 11.

24. Gritter, "Black Politics," 226; and Kenneally, "Black Republicans," 133–34.

25. J. E. Walker to J. B. Vesey, November 9, 1940, John B. Vesey to Crump, December 9, 1940, Series 3, Box 6, Watkins Overton Papers, Mississippi Valley Collection, Brister Library, Memphis State University, Memphis, TN.

26. Edwin T. Connell, "Store in Memphis Put in 'Quarantine' because Owner Defies Political Boss," *Pittsburgh Press*, December 6 or 7, 1940, Box A508, Group II, National Association for the Advancement of Colored People, Papers, Library of Congress, Washington, DC; Gritter, *River of Hope*, 147; Jordan, "No Race Trouble Here," 138; and J. B. Martin to Roscoe Grant, November 22, 1940, Box A508, Group II, National Association for the Advancement of Colored People Papers, Library of Congress, Washington, DC.

27. "We Defend the Law," editorial, *Commercial Appeal* [Memphis, TN], November 21, 1940, 6; Department of Justice, Criminal Division, Memorandum Regarding Police Persecution of Dr. J. B. Martin of Memphis, Tennessee, Because of Political Activities in 1940 Presidential Election, March 26, 1941, 2–6, Group II, Box A508, National Association for the Advancement of Colored People Papers, Library of Congress, Washington, DC.

28. Daniel D. Carter and Alma Miller to Mayor Walter Chandler, November 26, 1940, Box A508, Group II, National Association for the Advancement of Colored People Papers, Library of Congress, Washington, DC; Department of Justice, Criminal Division, Transcript of Deposition of J. B. Martin, Washington, DC, March 12, 1941, 3, Box 7, Folder 11, Robert H. Church Family Papers, Special Collections, McWherter Library, University of Memphis, Memphis, TN; and "Both Races Reported Disturbed Over 'Insult' to Negro Leader," *Atlanta Daily World*, December 18, 1940, 1.

29. B. Carroll Reece to R. C. Grant, November 20, 1940, Box A508, Group II, National Association for the Advancement of Colored People Papers, Library of Congress, Washington, DC; "Boyle Tells Jenkins to Keep 'Hands Out,'" *Commercial Appeal* [Memphis, TN], October 29, 1940, 20; Jordan, "'No Race Trouble Here,'" 142; and Tucker, *Lieutenant Lee*, 148.

30. Roscoe Conkling Simmons, "The Week," *Chicago Defender*, November 16, 1940, 1–5.

31. "Both Races Reported Disturbed Over 'Insult' to Negro Leader," *Atlanta Daily World*, December 18, 1940, 1; and Gritter, *River of Hope*, 148.

32. Memorandum Regarding Police Persecution of Dr. J. B. Martin of Memphis, Tennessee, Because of Political Activities in 1940 Presidential Election, March 26, 1941, 2, Group II, Box A508, National Association for the Advancement of Colored People Papers, Library of Congress, Washington, DC, 1, 7; and Racial Commission and City Fathers in Harmony," *Commercial Appeal* [Memphis, TN], January 20, 1941, 1.

33. Memorandum Regarding Police Persecution of Dr. J. B. Martin of Memphis, Tennessee, Because of Political Activities in 1940 Presidential Election, March 26, 1941, 2, 8, Group II, Box A508, National Association for the Advancement of Colored People Papers, Library of Congress, Washington, DC.

34. "Both Races Reported Disturbed Over 'Insult' to Negro Leader," *Atlanta Daily World*, December 18, 1940, 1; Department of Justice, Criminal Division, Memorandum Regarding Police Persecution of Dr. J. B. Martin of Memphis, Tennessee, Because of Political Activities in 1940 Presidential Election, March 26, 1941, 3, Group II, Box A508, National Association for the Advancement of Colored People Papers, Library of Congress, Washington, DC.; Jordan, "'No Race Trouble Here,'" 138; Carter to Marshall, January 8, 1941, Group II, Box A508, National Association for the Advancement of Colored People Papers, Library of Congress, Washington, DC; and Gritter, *River of Hope*, 148.

35. Tucker, *Lieutenant Lee,* 130; Department of Justice, Criminal Division, Memorandum Regarding Police Persecution of Dr. J. B. Martin of Memphis, Tennessee, Because of Political Activities in 1940 Presidential Election, March 26, 1941, 6–7, Group II, Box A508, National Association for the Advancement of Colored People Papers, Library of Congress, Washington, DC; Gritter, *River of Hope*, 148; and Carter to Marshall, January 8, 1941, Group II, Box A508, National Association for the Advancement of Colored People Papers, Library of Congress, Washington, DC.

36. "Tennessee: White Man's Country," *Time* 36, no. 24, December 9, 1940, 17; Department of Justice, Criminal Division, Memorandum Regarding Police Persecution of Dr. J. B. Martin of Memphis, Tennessee, Because of Political Activities in 1940 Presidential Election, March 26, 1941, 8, Group II, Box A508, National Association for the Advancement of Colored People Papers, Library of Congress, Washington, DC; Walter White to Robert H. Jackson, December 27, 1940, Box A508, Group II, National Association for the Advancement of Colored People, Papers, Library of Congress, Washington, DC; and "Ask Roosevelt to Halt Memphis Police Terror," *Chicago Defender*, December 28, 1940, 2.

37. Kenneth O'Reilly, "The Roosevelt Administration and Black America: Federal Surveillance Policy and Civil Rights During the New Deal and World War II Years," *Phylon* 48, no. 1 (lst Quarter, 1987): 15–19; and Henry A. Schweinhaut, "The Civil Liberties Section of the Department of Justice," *Bill of Rights Review* 1 (1941): 209–13.

38. Department of Justice, Criminal Division, Memorandum Regarding Police Persecution of J. B. Martin of Memphis, Tennessee, Because of Political Activities in 1940 Presidential Election, March 26, 1941, 2, 9–10, Group II, Box A508, National Association for the Advancement of Colored People Papers, Library of Congress, Washington, DC; "Justice Department Investigates Terrorism," *Atlanta Daily World*, January 15, 1941, 1; "Expect Whitewash of Memphis Terror," *Chicago Defender*, January 18, 1941, 1; and Wendell Berge to Thurgood Marshall, February 4, 1941, Group II, Box A508, Group II, National Association for the Advancement of Colored People, Papers, Library of Congress, Washington, DC.

39. Sven Hutchins Dubie, "Forging the Sword: The Formative Years of the Civil Rights Division, 1939–1961" (PhD diss., University of Delaware, 2004), 52, 64–66; and David E. Bernstein, *Only One Place of Redress: African Americans, Labor Regulations, and the Courts from Reconstruction to the New Deal* (Durham, NC: Duke University Press, 2001), 24.

40. Schweinhaut, "Civil Liberties Section," 206; and Dubie, "Forging the Sword," 32, 37–38, 50–51, 72.

41. Risa L. Goluboff, *The Lost Promise of Civil Rights* (Cambridge: MA: Harvard University Press, 2007), 117–18; and Geoffrey D. Berman, "A New Deal for Free Speech: Free

Speech and the Labor Movement in the 1930s," *Virginia Law Review* 80, no. 1 (February 1994): 302, 321.

42. Stephen C. Gehnrich, "General Amos W. W. Woodcock of Salisbury, Maryland (1883–1964)—Gentleman, Soldier, Scholar, and Good Citizen" (master's thesis, Salisbury University, 2008), 31–32, 35–38, 41, 50, 53–54; "General Woodcock Puts the 175th Through a Rigid Imposition," *Baltimore Sun*, February 5, 1941, 26; and Wendell Berge to John T. Risher, January 30, 1941, Department of Justice, Criminal Division, Class 144 (Civil Rights) Litigation Case Files and Enclosures, 1936–1997, Entry Number 72, Box 1, National Archives, Washington, DC.

43. Collins C. George to Thurgood Marshall, January 14, 1941, Group II, Box A508, National Association for the Advancement of Colored People Papers, Library of Congress, Washington, DC.

44. Kenneally, "Black Republicans," 134; Barnett to Wendell Willkie, January 11, 1941, Politics-General Correspondence, 1927–46, Claude A. Barnett Papers, Chicago History Museum, Research Center, Chicago, Illinois; Barnett to Emmett J. Scott, January 18, 1941, Republican National Committee News Releases, 342–45, C. A. Barnett Papers, Chicago History Museum, Research Center, Chicago, Illinois; and Barnett to Perry W. Howard, January 18, 1941, Republican National Committee News Releases, Claude A. Barnett Papers, Chicago History Museum, Research Center, Chicago, Illinois.

45. Emmett J. Scott, January 21, 1941, Perry W. Howard to Barnett, January 22, 1941, Republican National Committee News Releases, Claude A. Barnett Papers, Chicago History Museum, Research Center, Chicago, Illinois; and Thurgood Marshall to Robert H. Jackson, January 20, 1941, Group II, Box A508, National Association for the Advancement of Colored Papers, Library of Congress, Washington, DC.

46. Henry A. Schweinhaut to Wendell Berge, Memorandum, February 12, 1941, Department of Justice, Criminal Division, Class 144 (Civil Rights) Litigation Case Files and Enclosures, 1936–1997, Class 144 (Civil Rights) Litigation Case Files and Enclosures, 1936–1997, Entry Number 72, Box 1, National Archives, Washington, DC; and Transcript of Deposition of J. B. Martin, Washington, DC, March 12, 1941, 25–27, Box 7, Folder 11, Robert H. Church Family Papers, Special Collections, McWherter Library, University of Memphis, Memphis, TN.

47. Perry W. Howard to Barnett, March 25, 1941, Republican National Committee News Releases, 342–45, Claude A. Barnett Papers, Chicago History Museum, Research Center, Chicago, Illinois; and Kenneally, "Black Republicans," 134.

48. Goluboff, *Lost Promise,* 120; Gritter, *River of Hope,* 149; and Dubie, "Forging the Sword," 73–74; James H. Purdy, Jr., "Bob Church Home Sold in Memphis," *Chicago Defender*, December 6, 1941, 1; Gritter, *River of Hope*, 155; and Memorandum Regarding Police Persecution of J. B. Martin of Memphis, Tennessee, Because of Political Activities in 1940 Presidential Election, March 26, 1941, 1–2, Group II, Box A508, National Association for the Advancement of Colored People Papers, Library of Congress, Washington, DC.

49. Orson Welles, James Stewart, Walter Huston, Marjorie Main, Edward G. Robinson, et al., "We Hold These Truths" (radio broadcast), December 15, 1941, accessed August 27, 2022, https://archive.org/details/NormanCorwinWeHoldTheseTruthscombinedAmericanNetworks15December.

50. "We Hold These Truths."

51. "We Hold These Truths"; and Tucker, *Lieutenant Lee,* 127.

52. "Dr. J. B. Martin Runs for Office in Cook County," *Atlanta Daily World*, February 13, 1942, 2; "Martin Makes Political History in Chicago," *Chicago Defender*, November 30, 1946, 1; and Roi Ottley, "Memphis Row Is Boon to Chicago," *Chicago Daily Tribune*, September 26, 1954, N11.

53. J. B. Martin to Francis Biddle, February 16, 1944, Folder Ma, Series 4, Box 177, E. H. Crump Collection, Memphis and Shelby County Room, Memphis Public Library and Information Center [Memphis, TN]; and Tom C. Clark to Martin, February 26, 1944, 44-72-1, Criminal Division, Department of Justice, National Archives.

54. "A. Philip Randolph, Noted Labor Leader Speaks Here Sunday," *Memphis World*, November 5, 1943, 1; "Memphis City Officials Flayed by Randolph," *New Journal and Guide* (Norfolk, VA), November 20, 1943, 18; Gritter, *River of Hope*, 157–58; Jordan, "'No Race Trouble Here,'" 146; "Randolph Defies Boss Crump in Memphis," *Chicago Defender*, November 20, 1943, 3; and "Crump Bans Memphis Rally for Randolph," *Chicago Defender*, November 13, 1943, 1.

55. "Memphis City Officials Flayed by Randolph," *New Journal and Guide* (Norfolk, VA), November 20, 1943, 18; "Randolph Defies Boss Crump in Memphis," *Chicago Defender*, November 20, 1943, 3; "Randolph Speaks at STFU Conclave-Mass Meeting Cancelled," *Memphis World*, November 12, 1943, 1; and Jordan, "'No Race Trouble Here,'" 246.

56. "Crump Warns 'Outsiders' to Stay Out of Memphis," *Chicago Defender*, November 27, 1943, 1.

57. A. Philip Randolph to Eleanor Roosevelt, November 24, 1943, Eleanor Roosevelt to Randolph, December 18, 1943, 100-Personal Letters, Box 790, Eleanor Roosevelt Collection, Franklin D. Roosevelt Presidential Library, Hyde Park, New York. Many thanks to Joel Sturgeon for calling my attention to this correspondence. Also, see Joel Sturgeon, "You Will Be Policed: Boss Crump, the New Deal, and Price of Black Defiance in FDR's America," *Tennessee Historical Quarterly*, forthcoming in 2023.

58. Allan Keiler, *Marian Anderson: A Singer's Journey* (Urbana, IL: University of Illinois Press, 2002), 199–207.

59. A. Philip Randolph to Church, December 3, 1943, Randolph to Church, November 24, 1943, Church to Roy Wilkins, March 22, 1944, Roy Wilkins to Church, March 23, 1944, Folder 1, Carton 9, Series II, Church Family Papers, Special Collections, McWherter Library, University of Memphis, Memphis, TN; and Gritter, *River of Hope*, 158.

60. "Randolph Plans Memphis Speech," *Chicago Defender*, January 29, 1944, 18; A. Philip Randolph to Francis Biddle, March 10, 1944, Folder 1, Carton 9, Series II, Church Family Papers, Special Collections, McWherter Library, University of Memphis, Memphis, TN; and "How 'Boss' Crump's Stooges Rule Memphis," *Chicago Defender*, March 25, 1944, 4.

61. "Randolph Scores Attitude of Memphis Labor Leaders," *Memphis World*, April 4, 1944, 1; "Randolph Challenges Crump to Open Debate," *Chicago Defender*, April 15, 1944, 1; and "'Christ Not Crump, Is My Boss'—Rev. Long," *Chicago Defender*, April 15, 1944, 3.

62. "The Randolph Speech," editorial, *Memphis World*, April 6, 1944, 6.

63. "Crump Cancels Celebration to Honor Randolph," *Chicago Defender*, May 6, 1944, 1; and Dorsett, *City Bosses,* 45.

64. "Crump Starts Spite Work on Memphis Cleric," *Chicago Defender*, April 29, 1944, 1; Gritter, *River of Hope*, 163; and Tucker, *Lieutenant Lee*, 143.

65. Dorsett, *City Bosses,* 41–43.

66. "Must Watch Justice Dept. Says Randolph," *New York Amsterdam News*, January 6, 1945, A7.

67. Laurie B. Green, *Battling the Plantation Mentality: Memphis and the Black Freedom Struggle* (Chapel Hill, NC: University of North Carolina Press, 2007), 114–41, 183; and Gritter, *River of Hope*, 171–80.

68. Preston Lauterbach, *Beale Street Dynasty: Sex, Song, and the Struggle for the Soul of Memphis* (New York: W.W. Norton and Company, 2011), 302.

Chapter 7: "Persons Whose Removal Is Necessary": FDR's Concentration Camps

1. Greg Robinson, *By Order of the President: FDR and the Internment of Japanese Americans* (Cambridge, MA: Harvard University Press, 2001), 6. The following U.S. history survey textbooks were examined: John Mack Faragher et al., *Out of Many: A History of the American People,* combined volume (Boston: Pearson, 2020), 565; John Henretta et al., *America's History, Since 1865*, vol. 2 (Boston: Bedford/St. Martin's, 2014), 787; David M. Kennedy and Lizabeth Cohen, *American Pageant: A History of the American People* (Boston: Wadsworth, 2013), 799–800; Eric Foner, *Give Me Liberty: An American History,* vol. 2 (New York: W. W. Norton, 2014), 878; James L. Roark et al., *The American Promise: A History of the United States, From 1865,* vol. 2 (Boston: Bedford/St. Martin's, 2020), 751; David Emory Shi, *America: A Narrative History*, vol. 2 (New York: W. W. Norton, 2019), 1240–41; Carol Berkin et al., *Making America: A History of the United States* (Belmont, CA: Wadsworth, 2014), 642–43; Alan Brinkley et al., *The Unfinished Nation: A Concise History of the American People* (Boston: McGraw Hill, 2016), 637–38; Rebecca Edwards et al., *America's History, Since 1865,* vol. 2 (Boston: Bedford/St. Martin's, 2018), 766; and Robert Divine et al., *America: Past and Present*, combined edition (London: Pearson, 2013), 652.

2. Robinson, 17–20.

3. "Roosevelt Says," *Macon Telegraph* (Macon, GA), April 30, 1925, 4; and Theodore Roosevelt, *The Autobiography of Theodore Roosevelt* (Overland Park, KS: Digireads.com, 2019), 275.

4. Robinson, *By Order of the President*, 56, 120.

5. Roger Daniels, *Prisoners Without Trial: Japanese Americans and World War II* (1993; repr., New York: Hill and Wang, 2004), 8, 16; Frank J. Taylor, "The People Nobody Wants," *Saturday Evening Post* 214, no. 45, May 9, 1942, 64; and Roger W. Lotchin, *Japanese American Relocation in World War II: A Reconsideration* (Cambridge, UK: Cambridge University Press, 2018), 13–26.

6. Lotchin, *Japanese American Relocation*, 13, 20–23; and Norman M. Littell, *My Roosevelt Years* (Seattle, WA: University of Washington Press, 1987), 39.

7. Page Smith, *Democracy on Trial: The Japanese American Evacuation and Relocation in World War II* (New York: Simon & Schuster, 1995), 76–80; and Richard Reeves, *Infamy: The Shocking Story of the Japanese Internment in World War II* (New York: Henry Holt, 2015), 145.

8. Gene A. Coyle, "John Franklin Carter: Journalist, FDR's Secret Investigator, Soviet Agent?" *International Journal of Intelligence* 24 (2011): 167; Reeves, *Infamy*, 13, 16; and Robinson, *By Order of the President*, 78.

9. Brian Masaru Hayashi, "Kilsoo Haan, American Intelligence, and the Anticipated Japanese Invasion of California, 1931–1943," *Pacific Historical Review* 83, no. 2 (May 2014): 278, 283, 291–92; and Max Everest-Phillips, "The Pre-War Fear of Japanese Espionage: Its Impact and Legacy," *Journal of Contemporary History* 42 (2007): 249, 250, 259, 261. Hayashi, Everest-Phillips, and other historians persuasively challenge much higher estimates of Japanese American disloyalty by such writers as Roger Lotchin, *Japanese American Relocation*, and Michelle Malkin, *In Defense of Internment: The Case for 'Racial Profiling' in World War II and the War on Terror* (Washington, DC: Regnery Publishing, 2004). The term "fifth column" has become shorthand to characterize those in the homeland who secretly aid the enemy through methods such as sabotage. According to one account, it originated in 1936 in reference to the Spanish Civil War when Spanish rebel General Francisco Franco claimed that four columns of his troops preparing to attack Madrid could depend on a clandestine fifth column within the city. "Franco Fifth Column," *Christian Science Monitor*, April 22, 1949, 16.

10. Daniels, *Prisoners Without Trial*, 25.

11. Robinson, *By Order of the President*, 96; Richard Drinnon, *Keeper of Concentration Camps: Dillon S. Myer and American Racism* (Berkeley, CA: University of California Press, 1987), 32; Reeves, *Infamy*, 17, 33; and Daniels, *Prisoners Without Trial*, 37.

12. Robinson, *By Order of the President*, 77–79; and Jay Franklin [pseudonym for John Franklin Carter], "We, the People," *Seattle Star*, April 20, 1942. Carter even lauded Stalin's suppression of "seditionists" in the purge trials. Franklin, "We the People," *Seattle Star*, August 25, 1942, 4.

13. Robinson, *By Order of the President*, 93–94, 120.

14. Peter Irons, *Justice at War: The Story of the Japanese American Internment Cases* (New York: Oxford University Press, 1983), 39; "Stimson to Ford, January 26, 1942," in *American Concentration Camps*, vol. 2, January 1, 1942–February 19, 1942, ed. Roger Daniels (New York: Garland Publishing, 1989), np.

15. Robinson, *By Order of the President*, 94–96.

16. Irons, *Justice at War*, 25, 30; Daniels, *Prisoners Without Trial*, 29–32; Hayashi, "Kilsoo Haan," 292; and Robinson, *By Order of the President*, 86.

17. Irons, *Justice at War*, 26; Robinson, *By Order of the President*, 84–87; and Daniels, *Prisoners Without Trial*, 38.

18. Irons, *Justice at War*, 17, 31–34; and Daniels, *Prisoners Without Trial*, 32, 41–42.

19. Robinson, *By Order of the President*, 98–100.

20. "General DeWitt, General Gullion, and Major Bendetsen [Transcript], February 1, 1942" and Transcript of Telephone Conversation, General Gullion, General Clark, February 4, 1942, in *American Concentration Camps*, vol. 2, January 1, 1942–February 19, 1942, ed. Roger Daniels (New York: Garland Publishing, 1989), np.

21. Lorraine K. Bannai, *Enduring Conviction: Fred Korematsu and His Quest for Justice* (Seattle: University of Washington Press, 2015), 24; Irons, *Justice at War*, 52; Robinson, *By Order of the President*, 101; and Francis Biddle, *In Brief Authority* (1962; repr., Westport, CT: Greenwood Press, 1976), 224.

22. Irons, *Justice at War*, 17.

23. Robinson, *By Order of the President*, 104; and Irons, *Justice at War*, 53.

24. Robinson, *By Order of the President*, 105–6; and Biddle to Stimson, February 12, 1942, in *American Concentration Camps*, vol. 2, January 1, 1942–February 19, 1942, ed. Roger Daniels (New York: Garland Publishing, 1989), np; Daniels, *Prisoners Without Trial*, 44; and Audrie Girdner and Anne Loftis, *The Great Betrayal: The Evacuation of the Japanese-Americans During World War II* (London: MacMillan, 1969), 29.

25. Walter Lippmann, "Today and Tomorrow," *Oakland [CA] Tribune*, February 12, 1942, 32.

26. Westbrook Pegler, "Are We Asleep to the This Twin Menace on the Pacific Coast," *Knoxville News Sentinel* (Knoxville, TN), February 15, 1942, C2.

27. "Final Recommendation of the Commanding General, Western Defense Command and Fourth Army, Submitted to the Secretary of War," February 14, 1942, accessed November 24, 2021, http://www.sfmuseum.org/war/dewitt4.html; Robinson, *By Order of the President*, 107; and Irons, *Justice at War*, 62–64.

28. Biddle, *In Brief Authority*, 226.

29. Confidential Memorandum of Conversations with Officials at Washington on August 26, 1942, Dr. Alexander Meikeljohn and Roger Baldwin representing the Union, American Civil Liberties Cases, 1943, Sedition, Correspondence 6., vol. 2501, American Civil Liberties Union Papers, Mudd Library, Princeton University, Princeton, NJ; Archibald MacLeish to John J. McCloy, February 9, 1942, in *American Concentration Camps*, vol. 2, January 1, 1942–February 19, 1942, ed. Roger Daniels (New York: Garland Publishing, 1989), np; Daniels, *Prisoners Without Trial*, 44–45; and Robinson, *By Order of the President*, 113–15.

30. "Transcript of Executive Order No. 9066: Resulting in the Relocation of Japanese (1942)," accessed August 27, 2022, https://www.archives.gov/milestone-documents/executive-order-9066.

31. Robinson, *By Order of the President*, 64, 110–12; Daniels, *Prisoners Without Trial*, 44; and Irons, *Justice at War*, 61.

32. "Roosevelt to Frank Knox, Memorandum for the Secretary of the Navy, February 26, 1942," in *American Concentration Camps*, vol. 3, February 20, 1942–March 31, 1942, ed. Roger Daniels (New York: Garland Publishing, 1989), np.

33. Daniels, *Prisoners Without Trial*, 48; and Robinson, *By Order of the President*, 148–55.

34. Western Defense Command Public Proclamation No. 1 establishing military zones where Japanese residents are no longer allowed, March 2, 1942, accessed November 24, 2021, https://digitalcollections.lib.washington.edu/digital/collection/pioneerlife/id/15329; and Western Defense Command Public Proclamation No. 2 establishing military zones where Japanese residents are no longer allowed, March 16, 1942, accessed November 24, 2021, https://digitalcollections.lib.washington.edu/digital/collection/pioneerlife/id/15286/; Western Defense Command and Fourth Army United States, Final Report, Japanese

Evacuation of the West Coast, 1942 (Washington, DC: United States Government Printing Office, 1943), 41; and Irons, *Justice at War*, 68–69.

35. Robinson, *By Order of the President*, 130; and Executive Order 9102, Establishing the War Relocation Authority, https://www.presidency.ucsb.edu/documents/executive-order-9102-establishing-the-war-relocation-authority#axzz10yXFVV9p.

36. 77 Cong. Rec., S2722–26 (daily ed., March 19, 1942); and Western Defense Command and Fourth Army, Final Report, 30–31.

37. Marc C. Johnson, *Political Hell-Raiser: The Life and Times of Senator Burton K. Wheeler of Montana* (Norman, OK: University of Oklahoma Press, 2019), 322.

38. Western Defense Command and Fourth Army, Public Proclamation No. 3, March 24, 1942, 2–3, accessed November 22, 2021, http://www.javadc.org/java/docs/1942-03-24%20WDC%20Public%20Proclamation%20No3,8,14,15,16,17,21%20Establishes%20concuct%20of%20Japanesein%20WDC%20areas%20Pg13_ck.pdf; and Western Defense Command and Fourth Army, Public Proclamation No. 4, March 24, 1942, accessed November 22, 2021, http://digitalcollections.archives.csudh.edu/digital/collection/p16855coll4/id/12129/.

39. Daniels, *Prisoners Without Trial*, 55; Reeves, *Infamy*, 48; and Robinson, *By Order of the President*, 144.

40. Western Defense Command and Fourth Army, Final Report, 352; William Seltzer and Margo Anderson, "Census Confidentiality Under the Second War Powers Act (1942–1947)" (paper prepared for presentation at the session on "Confidentiality, Privacy, and Ethical Issues in Demographic Data," Population Association of America, New York, NY, [March] [29–31], 2007), 15, 21–25, accessed August 27, 2022, https://margoanderson.org/govstat/Seltzer-AndersonPAA2007paper3-12-2007.doc.

41. Daniels, *Prisoners Without Trial*, 56, 61; Stephanie Reitzig, "'By the Code of Humanity': Ralph Carr Takes a Stand for Japanese-American Rights in World War II," *History Teacher* 51, no.1 (November 2017): 108; and Adam Schrager, *The Principled Politician: Governor Ralph Carr and the Fight Against Japanese American Internment* (Golden, CO: Fulcrum, 2009), 205.

42. Robinson, *By Order of the President*, 131; Charles Wollenberg, *Rebel Lawyer: Wayne Collins and the Defense of Japanese American Rights* (Berkeley, CA: Heyday, 2018); *California*, California Historical Society, San Francisco, California, 2018, 43; and Drinnon, *Keeper of Concentration Camps*, 9–10, 21, 44, 151.

43. "Homicide in Camp," accessed December 6, 2021, https://encyclopedia.densho.org/Homicide_in_camp/; and Girdner and Loftis, *Great Betrayal*, 187–88.

44. Reeves, *Infamy*, 136, 203; and Girdner and Loftis, *Great Betrayal*, 187.

45. Jason Scott Smith, "New Deal Public Works at War: The WPA and Japanese American Internment," *Pacific Historical Review* 72, no. 1 (February 2003): 71, 92; and Franklin D. Roosevelt, Excerpts from a Press Conference, December 28, 1943, accessed November 22, 2021, https://www.presidency.ucsb.edu/documents/excerpts-from-the-press-conference-8.

46. Jason Scott Smith, "New Deal Public Works," 70, 72–75.

47. Jason Scott Smith, "New Deal Public Works," 71, 82–87; Franklin D. Roosevelt Letter to the Federal Works Administrator Discontinuing the W.P.A., December 4, 1942,

The American Presidency Project, accessed October 10, 2021, https://www.presidency.ucsb.edu/node/210274.

48. American Civil Liberties Union, Board of Directors, Minutes, March 2, 1942, March 9, 1942, March 16, 1942, Committee Matters, Correspondence, 1942, vol. 2356, American Civil Liberties Union Papers, Mudd Library, Princeton University, Princeton, NJ; and Drinnon, *Keeper of Concentration Camps,* 120.

49. Samantha Barbas, *The Rise and Fall of Morris Ernst, Free Speech Renegade* (Chicago: University of Chicago Press, 2021), 282; and Irons, *Justice at War,* 108–10.

50. Barbas, *Morris Ernst,* 282; and Corliss Lamont to Baldwin, May 14, 1942, Correspondence–Organizational Matters, 1942, vol. 2355, American Civil Liberties Union Papers, Mudd Library, Princeton University, Princeton, NJ.

51. "Hays, et al., to Roosevelt, March 20, 1942," in *American Concentration Camps*, vol. 3, February 20, 1942–March 31, 1942, ed. Roger Daniels (New York: Garland Publishing, 1989), np.; and Robinson, *By Order of the President*, 160–61.

52. Drinnon, *Keeper of Concentration Camps,* 124; and Barbas, *Morris Ernst,* 206.

53. "Should Japanese-Americans Be Returned to Normal Civilian Life? As Debated by Norman Thomas and Rex Stout," *Choctaw Advocate* (Butler, AL), September 17, 1942, 1.

54. Cheryl Lynn Greenberg, "Black and Jewish Responses to Japanese Internment," *Journal of American Ethnic History* 14, no. 2 (Winter 1995): 9–10; Drinnon, *Keeper of Concentration Camps,* 298; and Irons, *Justice at War,* 181.

55. Howard Costigan, "Plight of the Nisei," *Nation* 154, no. 7, February 14, 1942, 184–85; and "Hysteria Over the West Coast Japanese," *Nation* 154, no. 8, February 21, 1942, 206.

56. Charles Iglehart, "Citizens Behind Barbed War," *Nation* 154, no. 23, June 6, 1942, 649–51.

57. Reeves, *Infamy,* 67, 186; Takeya Mizuno, "The Civil Libertarian Press, Japanese American Press, and Japanese Mass Evacuation" (PhD diss., University of Missouri, 2000), 87–88, 101–6; and "Democracy and the Nisei," *New Republic* 107, no. 6, August 10, 1942, 158.

58. "U.S. Bred Japanese Show They're Good Americans," *PM*, December 11, 1941, 18; Paul Milkman, *PM: A New Deal in Journalism, 1940–1948* (Denver, CO: Outskirts Press, 2016), 318; and "Dr. Seuss" [Theodor Geisel], "Waiting for the Signal from Home," *PM*, February 13, 1942, 21. For some of Geisel's cartoons on the "sixth columnists" and their allies, see Richard H. Minear, *Dr. Seuss Goes to War: The World War: The World War II— Editorial Cartoons of Theodor Seuss Geisel* (New York: W. W. Norton, 1999), 19, 198, 217, 229, 231, 234.

59. "The Evacuation of the Japanese in Retrospect," *Santa Ana Register* (California), October 14, 1942, 15; and Robinson, *By Order of the President,* 200.

60. Greenberg, "Black and Jewish Responses," 10–11; George S. Schuyler, "The World Today," *Pittsburgh Courier* (Pittsburgh, PA), May 29, 1943, 1; and George S. Schuyler, "Views and Reviews," *Pittsburgh Courier* (Pittsburgh, PA), June 6, 1942, 6.

61. Nancy Peterson Hill, *A Very Private Public Citizen: The Life of Grenville Clark* (Columbia, MO: University of Missouri Press, 2014), 148–50, 242.

62. Alfred N. Bingham et al. to Roosevelt, April 30, 1942, Correspondence–Federal Departments, Japanese American Internment, 1942, vol. 2394, American Civil Liberties Union Papers, Mudd Library, Princeton University, Princeton, NJ.

63. Irons, *Justice at War*, 128–29; and Walter Frank, Arthur Garfield Hays, and B. W. Huebsch to the members of the Board of Directors, May 18, 1942, Committee Matters, Correspondence, 1942, vol. 2356, American Civil Liberties Union Papers, Mudd Library, Princeton University, Princeton, NJ; and Irons, *Justice at War,* 129.

64. American Civil Liberties Union, Board of Directors, Minutes, May 18, 1942, Committee Matters, Correspondence, 1942, vol. 2356, American Civil Liberties Union Papers, Mudd Library, Princeton University, Princeton, NJ; Irons, *Justice at War*, 88–92; and Mary Farquharson to Baldwin, March 11, 1943, Correspondence–Federal Departments, Japanese-American Internment, 1943, vol. 2470, American Civil Liberties Union Papers, Mudd Library, Princeton University, Princeton, NJ.

65. Bannai, *Korematsu*, 42–44, 58–59; Wollenberg, *Wayne Collins,* 20; and Drinnon, *Keeper of Concentration Camps*, 133.

66. Irons, *Justice at War*, 130–31; Walter Frank, Arthur Garfield Hays, and B. W. Huebsch to the members of the Board of Directors, June 19, 1942, Committee Matters, Correspondence, 1942, vol. 2356, American Civil Liberties Union Papers, Mudd Library, Princeton University, Princeton, NJ; and Norman Thomas, October 8, 1942, Memorandum to Civil Liberties Union, Correspondence–Organizational Matters, 1942, vol. 2355, American Civil Liberties Union Papers, Mudd Library, Princeton University, Princeton, NJ.

67. Irons, *Justice at War*, 130–31, 159; Wollenberg, *Wayne Collins,* 28; and American Civil Liberties Union, Board of Directors, Minutes, July 20, 1942, Committee Matters, Correspondence, 1942, vol. 2356, American Civil Liberties Union Papers, Mudd Library, Princeton University, Princeton, NJ; Farquharson to Lucille B. Milner, July 15, 1942, Correspondence–Federal Departments, Japanese-American Internment, 1943, vol. 2470, American Civil Liberties Union Papers, Mudd Library, Princeton University, Princeton, NJ.

68. Irons, *Justice at War*, 132, 360.

69. Wollenberg, *Wayne Collins*, 31; American Civil Liberties Union, Board of Directors, May 10, 1943, Correspondence–Federal Departments, Japanese-American Internment, 1943, vol. 2470, American Civil Liberties Union Papers, Mudd Library, Princeton University, Princeton, NJ; Irons, *Justice at War*, 194–95; Robert C. Cottrell, *Roger Nash Baldwin and the American Civil Liberties Union* (New York: Columbia University Press, 2000), 284; and "Notes on the Special Evening of the Board Held at Walter Frank's Home, October 12, 1942, Correspondence–Organizational Matters, 1942, vol. 2355, American Civil Liberties Union Papers, Mudd Library, Princeton University, Princeton, NJ.

70. Peggy Lamson, *Roger Baldwin: Founder of the American Civil Liberties Union, A Portrait by Peggy Lamson* (Boston: Houghton Mifflin Company, 1976), 237; and Cottrell, *Roger Nash Baldwin*, 292–93.

71. Drinnon, *Keeper of Concentration Camps*, 256; and Irons, *Justice at War*, 207–8.

72. Irons, *Justice at War*, 207–11; and Bannai, *Fred Korematsu*, 148.

73. Daniels, *Prisoners Without Trial*, 59; and Hirabayashi v. United States, 320 U.S. 81 (1943), accessed November 24, 2021, https://www.courtlistener.com/opinion/103875/hirabayashi-v-united-states/.

74. Wollenberg, *Wayne Collins*, 35; and Irons, *Justice at War*, 102–3.

75. Irons, *Justice at War*, 271; and Reeves, *Infamy*, 220–47.

76. Robinson, *By Order of the President*, 120; and Reeves, *Infamy*, 34.

77. Reeves, *Infamy*, 34; and Drinnon, *Keeper of Concentration Camps*, 255. Despite the president's statement, the federal government, in fact, actively promoted sterilization in Puerto Rico at the time. A survey in 1949, for example, indicated that 21 percent of Puerto Rican women had been sterilized. Bonnie Mass, "Puerto Rico: A Case Study of Population Control," *Latin American Perspectives* 4, no. 4 (Autumn 1977): 71.

78. Irons, *Justice at War*, 273; Drinnon, *Keeper of Concentration Camps*, 59; and Robinson, *By Order of the President*, 221.

79. Robinson, *By Order of the President*, 224; and Irons, *Justice at War*, 365.

80. Irons, *Justice at War*, 280–86.

81. Irons, *Justice at War*, 285–87.

82. Drinnon, *Keeper of Concentration Camps*, 256, 259; and Wollenberg, *Wayne Collins*, 34–35.

83. Wollenberg, *Wayne Collins*, 35.

84. Korematsu v. United States, 323 U.S. 214 (1944), accessed November 24, 2021, https://www.courtlistener.com/opinion/104040/korematsu-v-united-states/.

85. Korematsu v. United States, 323 U.S. 214 (1944).

86. Korematsu v. United States, 323 U.S. 214 (1944); and Daniels, *Prisoners Without Trial*, 62–63, 80.

87. Ex Parte Endo, 323 U.S. 283 (1944), accessed November 24, 2021, https://www.courtlistener.com/opinion/104043/ex-parte-endo/.

88. Wollenberg, *Wayne Collins*, 38; and Ex Parte Endo, 323 U.S. 283 (1944); and Daniels, *Prisoners Without Trial*, 63.

89. Ex Parte Endo, 323 U.S. 283 (1944); and Franklin D. Roosevelt, Message to the Senate on the Segregation Program of the War Relocation Authority, September 14, 1943, accessed December 2, 2021, https://www.presidency.ucsb.edu/documents/message-the-senate-the-segregation-program-the-war-relocation-authority.

90. Ex Parte Endo, 323 U.S. 283 (1944).

91. Reeves, *Infamy*, 232.

92. Bannai, *Fred Korematsu*, 105–6; Wollenberg, *Wayne Collins*, 39–40; and Daniels, *Prisoners Without Trial*, 72.

93. Westbrook Pegler, "Political Record of Justice Black, Who Wrote Supreme Court Korematsu Decision," *Carroll Daily Times Herald* (Carroll, IA), March 13, 1945, 2.

94. Daniels, *Prisoners Without Trial*, 89; Schrager, *Governor Ralph Carr*, 324; and Drinnon, *Keeper of Concentration Camps*, 259.

Chapter 8: A "Good War" for Free Speech?

1. "Good Year for Civil Liberty," *New York Times*, June 13, 1943, E8; "Civil Liberties Union Praises War II Record," *Christian Science Monitor*, July 16, 1943, 3; "American Civil

Liberties Union, For Release, "War-Time Prosecutions for Speech and Publications," September 1, 1943, 1, American Civil Liberties Union Cases, 1943, Sedition, Correspondence, vol. 2507, American Civil Liberties Union Papers, Mudd Library, Princeton University, Princeton, NJ; and James West Davidson, Brian DeLay, Christine Leigh Heyrman, Mark Lytle, and Michael Stoff, *Experience History: Interpreting America's Past* (New York: McGraw Hill, 2019), 667.

2. Richard W. Steele, *Free Speech in the Good War* (New York: St. Martin's Press, 1999), 1.

3. Steele, *Free Speech in the Good War*, 11.

4. Steele, *Free Speech in the Good War*, 232; and Laura Weinrib, *The Taming of Free Speech: America's Civil Liberties Compromise* (Cambridge, MA: Harvard University Press, 2016), 265.

5. Francis Biddle, *In Brief Authority* (1962; repr., Westport, CT: Greenwood Press, 1976), 238; David M. Kennedy, *Over Here: The First World War and American Society* (New York: Oxford University Press, 1980), 77–78; and Steele, *Free Speech in the Good War*, 231.

6. Richard W. Steele, "Fear of the Mob and Faith in Government in Free Speech Discourse, 1919–1941," *American Journal of Legal History* 38, no. 1 (January 1994): 74; and John T. Flynn, "Other People's Money," *New Republic* 102, no. 11, March 11, 1940, 345.

7. Catherine M. Tarrant, "To 'Insure Domestic Tranquility': Congress and the Law of Seditious Conspiracy, 1859–1861," *American Journal of Legal History* 15, no. 2 (1971): 118–23; Geoffrey R. Stone, "Free Speech in World War II: 'When Are You Going to Indict the Seditionists,'" *International Journal of Constitutional Law*, 2, no. 2 (2004): 336–37; Roger Greene, "Sixteen 'Conspirators'—They Sing a Song of Innocence and March off to Their Cells," *Atlanta Constitution*, January 16, 1940, 5; "G-Man Hoover's Nazi Plot," *New Republic* 110, no. 12, March 18, 1940, 365; "'Front' Case Data Prepared for Jury," *New York Times*, January 20, 1940, 3; and United States of America v. John T. Prout, Jr. et al., United States District Court, Eastern District of New York, Indictment, February 7, 1940, National Archives at New York City.

8. Steele, *Free Speech in the Good War*, 38, 43, 45.

9. Charles R. Gallagher, *Nazis of Copley Square: The Forgotten Story of the Christian Front* (Cambridge, MA: Harvard University Press, 2021), 58–64, 69–70.

10. "G-Man Hoover's Nazi Plot," *New Republic* 110, no. 12, March 18, 1940, 365; and Gallagher, *Nazis of Copley Square*, 66–69.

11. "Stone "Free Speech in World War II," 337; Gallagher, *Nazis of Copley Square*, 63; and "Nine Acquitted of Sedition Plot; Mistrial Is Declared in Four Cases," *New York Times*, June 25, 1940, 1.

12. C. P. Trussell, "Senators Strike at Fifth Column," *Baltimore Sun*, May 26, 1940, 1, 7; Belknap, The Smith Act, 23; Dorothy Thompson, "A Nation of Suckers," *Atlanta Constitution*, May 28, 1940, 7; and Steele, *Free Speech in the Good War*, 81.

13. Maximilian St.-George and Lawrence Dennis, *A Trial on Trial: The Great Sedition Trial of 1944*, National Civil Rights Committee, 1946), 84–85; and Belknap, *Smith Act*, 26.

14. St.-George and Dennis, *Trial on Trial*, 84–85; and Bruce J. Dierenfield, *Keeper of the Rules: Congressman Howard W. Smith of Virginia* (Charlottesville, VA: University Press of Virginia, 1987), 79–80.

15. Steele, *Free Speech in the Good War*, 130–33.

16. American Civil Liberties Union, For Immediate Release, "ACLU and Attorney General Debate Issues in Minneapolis Indictment of Trotskyites," November 12, 1941, vol. 2438, Correspondence–Censorship, Post Office Censorship, 1943, Vol. 2438, American Civil Liberties Union Papers, Mudd Library, Princeton University, Princeton, NJ; and Louis Stark, "President Attacks Inter-Union Raids," *New York Times*, June 14, 1941, 1; and Steele, *Free Speech in the Good War*, 131–32.

17. Belknap, *Smith Act*, 39; "Workers' Party Leaders Facing Sedition Trial," *Atlanta Constitution*, June 28, 1941, 8; "Civil Liberties in Minneapolis," *New Republic* 105, no. 4, July 28, 1941, 103; and "29 Indicted in Roundup of 'Conspirators,'" *Atlanta Constitution*, July 16, 1941, 20.

18. James A. Wechsler, "First Peace-Time Trial in 150 Years Opens," *PM*, October 20, 1941, 13; Daniel Eastman, "The Minneapolis 'Sedition' Trial," *New Republic* 105, no. 16, October 20, 1941, 503; and I. F. Stone, "The G-String Conspiracy," *Nation* 153, no. 4, July 26, 1941, 66, 68.

19. Carl Winter, "Minneapolis Trial Shows Labor Wary of Trotzkyites," *Daily Worker*, December 19, 1941, 5; Percival Roberts Bailey, "Progressive Lawyers: A History of the National Lawyers Guild, 1936–1958" (PhD diss., Rutgers University, 1979), 296; and "How Odd It Is," *Chicago Daily Tribune*, July 18, 1941, 10.

20. Stone, "Free Speech in World War II," 338–39; Francis Biddle, *In Brief Authority*, 151–52; and Steele, *Free Speech in the Good War*, 140–42.

21. "18 Convicted in Socialist Workers' Trial," *Washington Post*, December 2, 1941, 1; Belknap, *Smith Act*, 39; Biddle, *In Brief Authority*, 152; and Steele, *Free Speech in the Good War*, 140–41.

22. Anthony Gregory, *American Surveillance: Intelligence, Privacy, and the Fourth Amendment* (Madison: University of Wisconsin Press, 2016), 40; and "Jackson Asks Care in Liberties Cases," *New York Times*, April 2, 1940, 9; and "Quit Sleuthing, State Defense Groups Told," *Atlanta Constitution*, August 11, 1940, 2A.

23. "WW Is Nazis' Choice, Wallace Tells ALP Rally … Lewis Hit," *PM*, November 1, 1940, 11; and John W. Jeffries, *A Third Term for FDR: The Election of 1940* (Lawrence, KS: University Press of Kansas, 2007), 144.

24. Ralph G. Martin, *Cissy: The Extraordinary Life of Eleanor Medill Patterson* (New York: Simon & Schuster, 1979), 398, 415–16; Paul F. Healy, *Cissy: A Biography of Eleanor M. "Cissy" Patterson* (New York: Doubleday and Company, 1966), 275, 283; Amanda Smith, *Newspaper Titan: The Infamous Life and Monumental Times of Cissy Patterson* (New York: Alfred A. Knopf, 2011), 380; Joseph Gies, *The Colonel of Chicago* (New York: E. P. Dutton, 1979), 163; and Frank C. Waldrop, *McCormick of Chicago: An Unconventional Portrait of a Controversial Figure* (Englewood Cliffs, NJ: Prentice-Hall, 1966), 233.

25. William V. Nessly, "Chief Justice Hughes Retires July 1; Jackson Most Likely Successor," *Washington Post*, June 3, 1941, 1; Joseph Shaplen, "Biddle Warns U.S. of War Discipline," *New York Times*, June 3, 1941, 11.

26. Patrick S. Washburn, *A Question of Sedition: The Federal Government's Investigation of the Black Press During World War II* (New York: Oxford University Press, 1986), 50; Glen Jeansonne, *Women of the Far Right: The Mothers' Movement and World War II* (Chicago: University of Chicago Press, 1996), 152–53; Steele, *Free Speech in the Good War*, 120–23; and Biddle, *In Brief Authority*, 238.

27. Roosevelt to Biddle, November 17, 1941, PSF, Justice Department, 1940–1944, Franklin D. Roosevelt Presidential Library and Museum, Hyde Park, NY; Stone, "Free Speech in World War II," 338; and Cabell Phillips, "'No Witch Hunts,'" *New York Times*, September 21, 1941, SM8.

28. Roger N. Baldwin, "Liberty in War Time," *Nation* 14, no. 6, February 7, 1942, 175; and Washburn, *Question of Sedition*, 51.

29. Ralph G. Martin, *Cissy*, 418–20; and Waldrop, *McCormick of Chicago*, 234.

30. Roosevelt to Hoover, January 21, 1942, PSF Justice Department, 1940–1944, Franklin D. Roosevelt Presidential Library and Museum, Hyde Park, NY; J. Edgar Hoover, Continued, Box 57, Franklin D. Roosevelt Presidential Library and Museum, Hyde Park, NY; Stephen T. Early to Roosevelt, March 20, 1942, PSF, Justice Department, 1940–1944, Franklin D. Roosevelt Presidential Library and Museum, Hyde Park, NY; and Biddle, *In Brief Authority*, 237–38.

31. Steele, *Free Speech in the Good War*, 71; Reinhold Niebuhr, "The Limits of Liberty," *Nation* 154, no. 4, January 24, 1942, 88; and Stephen Mark Gens, "Paranoia Bordering on Resignation: Norman Thomas and the American Socialist Party, 1939–48" (PhD diss., University of Oklahoma, 1982), 38–39.

32. Freda Kirchwey, "Curb the Fascist Press!" *Nation* 154, no. 13, March 28, 1942, 357; Freda Kirchwey, "Biddle and Bridges," *Nation* 154, no. 23, June 6, 1942, 646; Union for Democratic Action, General Principles, 1944, Folder: Committee for Constitutional Government and CIO Political Action Committee, Box 357, Clinton P. Anderson Papers, Manuscript Division, Library of Congress, Washington, DC; and Steele, *Free Speech in the Good War*, 156.

33. Michael Straight, "Hitler's Guerrillas Over Here," *New Republic* 106, no. 15, April 13, 1942, 481–83; and Union for Democratic Action, General Principles, 1944, Folder: Committee for Constitutional Government and CIO Political Action Committee, Box 357, Clinton P. Anderson Papers, Manuscript Division, Library of Congress, Washington, DC.

34. William L. Shirer, "The Poison Pen," *Atlantic Monthly* 169, no. 5, May 1942, 548–52; Gies, *Colonel of Chicago*, 198; 77 Cong. Rec., H3453–54 (daily ed., April 13, 1942); and William L. Shirer, Diary, March 28, 1942, Series 4 Diaries-Loose pages-1924-197, folder 1941-1944, William L. Shirer Papers, George T. Henry College Archives, Stewart Memorial Library, Coe College, Cedar Rapids, IA.

35. "Voices of Defeat," *Life* 12, no. 1, April 13, 1942, 88–95, 100; and *Directory of Newspapers and Periodicals* (Philadelphia: N. W. Ayer and Sons, 1942), 222, 409, 668–69.

36. Roger N. Baldwin, "Liberty in War Time," *Nation* 14, no. 6, February 7, 1942, 175; and Roger N. Baldwin, "Repression v. Propaganda," *Nation*, April 11, 1942, 444.

37. Roger N. Baldwin, "Free Speech for Native Fascists," *New Republic* 106, no. 17, April 27, 1942, 574.

38. Washburn, *Question of Sedition*, 69–70, 120; and Press Conference #814, Executive Office of the President, March 24, 1942, 231–32, Press Conferences of Franklin D. Roosevelt, 1933–1945, Franklin D. Roosevelt Presidential Library and Museum, Hyde Park, NY, accessed January 20, 2020, http://www.fdrlibrary.marist.edu/_resources/images/pc/pc0133.pdf.

39. Michael S. Sweeney, *Secrets of Victory: The Office of Censorship in the American Press and Radio in World War II* (Chapel Hill: University of North Carolina Press, 2001), 76–77; Steele, *Free Speech in the Good War*, 154–55; and Biddle, *In Brief Authority*, 245.

40. Biddle to Frank C. Walker, April 14, 1942, American Civil Liberties Cases, 1943, Sedition, Correspondence, 3, vol. 2498, American Civil Liberties Union Papers, Mudd Library, Princeton University, Princeton, NJ; David M. Kennedy, *Over Here: The First World War and American Society* (New York: Oxford University Press, 1980), 76; and Washburn, *Question of Sedition*, 13–14.

41. Biddle to Walker, April 14, 1942, American Civil Liberties Cases, 1943, Sedition, Correspondence, 3, vol. 2498, American Civil Liberties Union Papers, Mudd Library, Princeton University, Princeton, NJ.

42. "Clearing the Mails," editorial, *Christian Science Monitor*, April 16, 1942, 24; "The Shape of Things," *Nation* 14, no. 20, May 16, 1942, 558; St.-George and Dennis, *Trial on Trial*, 104; and "Milquetoast Gets Muscles," *Time* 39, no. 15, April 13, 1942, 20.

43. "Is Coughlin the Target, or Press Freedom?" *Los Angeles Times*, April 16, 1942, A4; "Coughlinites Prepare for Legal Fray-Gerald Smith to Help," *City Reporter* 4, no. 17, April 23, 1942, 2 American Civil Liberties Cases, 1943, Sedition, Correspondence, 3, vol. 2498, American Civil Liberties Union Papers, Mudd Library, Princeton University, Princeton, NJ; Moley to Hays, April 17, 1942, American Civil Liberties Cases, 1943, Sedition, Correspondence 6., vol. 2501, American Civil Liberties Union Papers, Mudd Library, Princeton University, Princeton, NJ.

44. "New Communist Drive" [from Editor and Publisher], *Chicago Daily Tribune*, May 17, 1942, 16; New York City Chapter, National Lawyers Guild, For Release, May 11, 1942, American Civil Liberties Cases, 1943, Sedition, Correspondence, 3, vol. 2498, American Civil Liberties Papers, Mudd Library, Princeton University, Princeton, NJ; "Support You 100% in Prosecution of Defeatists, Marcantonio Tells Biddle," *Daily Worker*, May 2, 1942, 3; and "What About Them Mr. Biddle? The Enemies Within," *New Masses*, April 26, 1942, 14.

45. Sweeney, *Secrets of Victory*, 76; "Text of MacLeish's Address Warning Against Nazi 'Peace' Drive," *New York Times*, April 21, 1942, I5; and "MacLeish Urges Press to Accept Responsibility of Guiding Opinion in Talk Before Editors," *Washington Post*, April 18, 1942, 15.

46. Moley to Hays, April 17, 1942, American Civil Liberties Cases, 1943, Sedition, Correspondence 6, vol. 2501, American Civil Liberties Union Papers, Mudd Library, Princeton University, Princeton, NJ; and Chesly Manly, "Senators Warn of Drive to 'Gag' Critical Press," *Chicago Daily Tribune*, May 7, 1942, 2.

47. Arthur Garfield Hays and Roger N. Baldwin to Frank C. Walker, April 15, 1942, American Civil Liberties Cases, 1943, Sedition, Correspondence, 3, vol. 2498, American Civil Liberties Union Papers, Mudd Library, Princeton University, Princeton, NJ; Shawn Michael Lynch, "'In Defense of True Americanism': The Civil Liberties Union of Massachusetts and Radical Free Speech, 1915–1945" (PhD diss., Boston College, 2006), 27–30, 243–244; and Steele, *Free Speech in the Good War*, 72.

48. Henry S. Canby [*Saturday Review*], April 22, 1942, American Civil Liberties Cases, 1943, Sedition, Correspondence, 3, vol. 2498, American Civil Liberties Union Papers, Mudd Library, Princeton University, Princeton, NJ; and Leo P. Ribuffo, "United States v.

McWilliams: The Roosevelt Administration and the Far Right," in *American Political Trials,* ed. Michael R. Belknap (Westport, CT: Greenwood Press, 199), 183–84.

49. Ernst to Roosevelt, April 8, 1942, May 23, 1942, June 10, 1942, Ernst to Roosevelt, September 25, 1942, Ernst to Roosevelt, June 10, 1942, PSF 132 / Folder: Ernst, Morris L., 1940–1942, Box 132, Franklin D. Roosevelt Presidential Library and Museum, Hyde Park, NY; and Ribuffo, "United States v. McWilliams," 185.

50. "The American Way," *The Progressive,* April 25, 1942, 12; and John E. Miller, "Fighting for the Cause: The Rhetoric of Symbolism of the Wisconsin Progressive Movement," *Wisconsin Magazine of History* 87, no. 4 (Summer 2004), 24–25.

51. Biddle, *In Brief Authority,* 247; Ribuffo, "United States v. McWilliams," 185; and Steele, *Free Speech in the Good War,* 164–66.

52. Steele, *Free Speech in the Good War,* 167; and Washburn, *Question of Sedition,* 80.

53. Attorney General VI, Seditionists (2), 680. Notebooks, Francis Biddle Papers, Franklin D. Roosevelt Presidential Library, Hyde Park, NY; and Washburn, *Question of Sedition,* 79.

54. Amanda Smith, *Newspaper Titan,* 412; and Sweeney, *Secrets of Victory,* 3, 79–81.

55. Smith, *Newspaper Titan,* 412; and Sweeney, *Secrets of Victory,* 3, 79–81.

56. "On the 'News' and the War," *PM,* July 26, 1942, 9; "Still Spraying Our Side with Disunity Gas!" cartoon, *PM,* August 10, 1942, 22; and Paul Milkman, *PM: A New Deal in Journalism, 1940–1948* (Denver, CO: Outskirts Press, 2016), 143.

57. Milkman, *PM,* xiii, 58, 60, 90, 108–10, 143, 385; N.W. Ayer and Sons, *Directory of Newspapers and Periodicals* (Philadelphia, PA: N.W. Ayer and Sons, 1942), 669; and Ralph G. Martin, *Cissy,* 413.

58. American Civil Liberties Union, Wartime Prosecutions for Speech and Publications, May 1943, 15, American Civil Liberties Cases 1943, Sedition, Correspondence, 12, vol. 2507, American Civil Liberties Union Papers, Mudd Library, Princeton University, Princeton, NJ; Steele, *Free Speech in the Good War,* 170; and O. A. Hilton, "Freedom of the Press in Wartime, 1917–1919,"*Southwestern Social Science Quarterly* 28, March 1948: 353.

59. Steele, *Free Speech in the Good War,* 168.

60. "'Sedition,' and 'Heresy' Laws Are Instruments of 'Totalitarianism,'" editorial, *Boise Valley Herald* (Middleton, ID), September 24, 1942, 2.

61. Dorothy Kenyon to Lucille B. Milner, September 24, 1942, Norman Thomas to Baldwin, September 10, 1942, American Civil Liberties Cases, September 10, 1942, Correspondence–Cases By State: Georgia, Idaho, 1940–1942, vol. 2408, American Civil Liberties Union Papers, Mudd Library, Princeton University, Princeton, NJ; "'The Fifth Column' Complex as It Works," editorial, *Boise Valley Herald* (Middleton, ID), March 5, 1942; "Nazism Again Shows Its Head in Idaho," editorial, *Boise Valley Herald* (Middleton, ID), April 23, 1942, 2; Bayard Rustin, "Non-Violence Vs Jim Crow" [originally in *Fellowship*], *Boise Valley Herald* (Middleton, ID), July 25, 1942, 4; "The Deadly Parallel: When a Black Man Kills a White, When a White Man Kills a Black," *Boise Valley Herald* (Middleton, ID), June 11, 1942, 1; "The Election's Over, The 'Gesture Making' Period Is Passed," editorial, *Boise Valley Herald* (Middleton, ID), November 14, 1940, 2; "Things That Kellogg Column Overlooks," *Boise Valley Herald* (Middleton, ID), November 21, 1940, 2; and Brent Cornell (grandson of Adelbert Cornell, publisher editor of the *Boise Valley Herald*), interview by author, February 22, 2020.

62. George H. Curtis [secretary of state] to Lucille B. Milner, September 14, 1942, American Civil Liberties Cases, 1940–1942, Correspondence–Cases By State: Georgia, Idaho, vol. 2408, American Civil Liberties Union Papers, Mudd Library, Princeton University, Princeton, NJ; "Three Landslides in a Row But—Righteousness Exalteth a Nation," editorial, *Boise Valley Herald* (Middleton, ID), November 14, 1940, 2; "Air Letter to Civil Liberties Union," *Boise Valley Herald* (Middleton, ID), September 10, 1942, 2; "A Christian Nation 'Violently' Attacked," *Boise Valley Herald* (Middleton, ID), December 11, 1941, 2; and Brent Cornell (grandson of Adelbert Cornell, publisher-editor of the *Boise Valley Herald*), interview by author, February 22, 2020.

63. Curtis to Milner; and "Conscience Faces Certainty of Punishment," *Boise Valley Herald* (Middleton, ID), January 6, 1941, 2.

64. Post Office Department, Information Service, For Release in the Morning Papers, September 4, 1942, Correspondence–Censorship, Post Office Censorship, 1943, vol. 2438, American Civil Liberties Union Papers, Mudd Library, Princeton University, Princeton, NJ.

65. "The 'Fifth Column' Complex, As It Works," editorial, *Boise Valley Herald* (Middleton, ID), March 5, 1942, 2.

66. Cornell, interview; and Post Office Department, Information Service, For Release in the Morning Papers, September 4, 1942, Correspondence–Censorship, Post Office Censorship, 1943, vol. 2408, American Civil Liberties Union Papers, Mudd Library, Princeton University, Princeton, NJ.

67. "Young Japanese Do Honor to Citizenship," editorial, *Boise Valley Herald* (Middleton, ID), March 12, 1942, 2.

68. "Circular Letter to Fellow Americans," editorial, *Boise Valley Herald* (Middleton, ID), October 1, 1942, 2; Adelbert Cornell to Civil Liberties Union, September 19, 1942, October 12, 1942, Correspondence–Cases By State: Georgia, Idaho, 1940–1942, vol. 2408, American Civil Liberties Union Papers, Mudd Library, Princeton University, Princeton, NJ; "Rogues Gallery–Revised to Aug. 20," *Boise Valley Herald* (Middleton, ID), September 10, 1942, 1; and "We Are Permitted to Send Stamped Mail," *Boise Valley Herald* (Middleton, ID), December 17, 1942, 2.

69. Paul D. Holtzman, "Village Weekly Demands Jury Trial Before Paper Is Banned," *Socialist Call*, December 25, 1942, 7; "Too Small to Sprout," *Idaho Statesman* (Boise), September 5, 1942, 4; and "The Cornell Case Again" [reprinted from the *Idaho Free Press*, (Nampa, ID), October 19, 1942], *Boise Valley Herald* (Middleton, ID), October 22, 1942, 4.

70. Forster to Sol M. Alpher, September 18, 1942, Correspondence-Cases By State: Georgia, Idaho, 1940–1942, vol. 2408, American Civil Liberties Union Papers, Mudd Library, Princeton University, Princeton, NJ; and "P.O. Restores Rights to Idaho Weekly," *Denver Labor Advocate*, January 6, 1944, Correspondence–Cases by State. Idaho, vol. 2523, 1942–1944, the American Civil Liberties Union Papers, Mudd Library, Princeton University, Princeton, NJ.

71. "We Are Permitted to Send Stamped Mail," *Boise Valley Herald* (Middleton, ID), December 17, 1942, 2; Vincent M. Miles to Arthur Garfield Hays, December 7, 1942, Baldwin to Cornell, October 22, 1942, Cornell to the American Civil Liberties Union, September 9, 1942, Correspondence–Cases By State: Georgia, Idaho, 1940–1942, vol.

2408, American Civil Liberties Union Papers, Mudd Library, Princeton University, Princeton, NJ.

72. Brent Cornell, interview; "Peace Without Victory," editorial, *Boise Valley Herald* (Middleton, ID), June 11, 1942, 2.

73. Dillard Stokes, "U.S. Suspends N.Y. Weekly for Sedition," *Washington Post*, March 8, 1943, 3.

74. American Civil Liberties Union, Memorandum on the Revocation of the Second-Class Mailing Privileges of "The Militant," organ of the Socialist Workers Party, with Headquarters at New York," 1–3, April 5, 1942, March 3, 1943, Correspondence–Censorship: Post Office Censorship, 1943, vol. 2438, American Civil Liberties Union Papers, Mudd Library, Princeton University, Princeton, NJ; The Militant, City Editor, For Immediate Release, Post Office Department Moves to Revoke Second-class Mailing Privileges of Trotskyist Paper, January 6, 1942, The Militant, Excerpts, Exhibit A; and Frank C. Walker, Postmaster, General Order No. 20260, March 3, 1943, Correspondence–Censorship: Post Office Censorship, 1943, vol. 2438, American Civil Liberties Union Papers, Mudd Library, Princeton University, Princeton, NJ.

75. Minutes of the Sedition Committee in the office of Arthur Garfield Hays, February 17, 1943, American Civil Liberties Union, Correspondence–General: Sedition-Organizational Matters-Sedition Committee, vol. 2605, American Civil Liberties Union Papers, Mudd Library, Princeton University, Princeton, NJ; American Civil Liberties Union, Minutes, Board of Directors, January 11, 1943; American Civil Liberties Union, For Immediate Release, American Civil Liberties Union and Attorney General Debate Issues; United States Post Office Department v. The Militant, Brief of American Civil Liberties Union, n.d., 7, Hays and Baldwin to L. M. C Smith, Chief War Policies Unit, January 13, 1943, American Civil Liberties Union, Monthly Bulletin #11, and Hays and Baldwin to L. M. C. Smith, Chief War Policies Unit, January 13, 1943, American Civil Liberties Union, 1943, Censorship, Correspondence, 5, vol. 2438, American Civil Liberties Union Papers, Mudd Library, Princeton University, Princeton, NJ.

76. "The Shape of Things," *Nation* 15, no. 24, December 12, 1942, 635; Editorial Comment of Post Office Proceeding Against the "Militant," Correspondence–Censorship, Post Office Censorship, 1943, vol. 2438, American Civil Liberties Union Papers, Mudd Library, Princeton University, Princeton, NJ; "Mr. Browder Gets His Trotskyites," editorial, *Chicago Daily Tribune*, January 26, 1943, 8.

77. American Civil Liberties Union, Memorandum on the Revocation of the Second-Class Mailing Privileges of "The Militant," organ of the Socialist Workers Party, with Headquarters at New York, 1–3, April 5, 1942, Correspondence–Censorship, Post Office Censorship, 1943, Vol. 2438, American Civil Liberties Union Papers, Mudd Library, Princeton University, Princeton, NJ.

78. "The 'Militant' Case," *New York Times*, April 28, 1943, 22.

79. Steele, *Free Speech in the Good War*, 164–65.

80. Washburn, *Question of Sedition*, 8, 99–100.

81. Washburn, *Question of Sedition*, 52–53, 80–81, 107.

82. Washburn, *Question of Sedition*, 89–94.

83. Washburn, *Question of Sedition*, 131–32, 139.

84. Washburn, *Question of Sedition*, 135.

85. Washburn, *Question of Sedition*, 82–84, 130.

86. Washburn, *Question of Sedition*, 163–64.

87. Washburn, *Question of Sedition*, 130.

88. Washburn, *Question of Sedition*, 140.

89. Steele, *Free Speech in the Good War*, 4.

90. Steele, *Free Speech in the Good War*, 41, 79.

Chapter 9: The Forgotten Sedition-Trial Fiasco

1. Leo P. Ribuffo, "United States v. McWilliams: The Roosevelt Administration and the Far Right," in *American Political Trials*, ed. Michael R. Belknap (Westport, CT: Greenwood Press, 1994), 182.

2. Ribuffo, "United States v. McWilliams," 183; and "Indictments and New Spy Hunt Point to Subversion Crackdown," *Newsweek* 20, no. 5, August 3, 1942, 26.

3. "Mrs. Dilling, 27 Others Hit by U.S. Grand Jury," *Chicago Daily Tribune*, July 23, 1942, 1, 11; and Lewis Wood, "28 Are Indicted on Sedition Charge," *New York Times*, July 24, 1942, 1, 8.

4. Virgil W. Dean, "Another Wichita Seditionist? Elmer J. Garner and the Radical Right's Opposition to World War II," *Kansas History* 17, no. 1 (Spring 1994): 52–53, 55, 61–62.

5. Department of Justice, For Immediate Release, July 23, 1942, 4–6, American Civil Liberties Cases, 1943, Sedition, Correspondence 6, vol. 2501, American Civil Liberties Union Papers, Mudd Library, Princeton University, Princeton, NJ.

6. James Barron, "The Enquirer Is Returning to Where It All Started," *New York Times*, May 7, 2014, A22; "Griffin Offers Letter as Link with Roosevelt," *Washington Post*, November 6, 1942, B10; "Griffin Receives Scroll," *New York Times*, June 10, 1937, 27; and "Griffin Presents 'Loyalty' Evidence," *Christian Science Monitor*, November 13, 1942, 7.

7. "War Foes Plan Meeting," *New York Times*, October 8, 1939, 46; "Griffin Presents 'Loyalty' Evidence," *Christian Science Monitor*, November 13, 1942, 7; "Mrs. Dilling, 27 Others Hit by U.S. Grand Jury," *Chicago Daily Tribune*, July 23, 1942, 1, 11; "Griffin Denies Memory of Viereck Pay," *Washington Post*, June 13, 1942, 19; and "Griffin Defends Trip to Germany," *New York Times*, November 5, 1942, 27.

8. "Seeks Churchill Assets," *New York Times*, October 11, 1939, 2; and "Churchill Is Winner in Griffin Libel Suit," *New York Times*, October 22, 1942, 13; and Richard M. Langworth, *Winston Churchill, Myth and Reality: What He Actually Did and Said* (Jefferson, NC: McFarland and Company, 2017), 1–77; and Michael McMenamin, "Griffin and Churchill: Another View," *Finest Hour* 152 (Autumn 2011), accessed December 19, 2022, https://winstonchurchill.org/publications/finest-hour/finest-hour-152/griffin-and-churchill-another-view/.

9. "Indictments and New Spy Hunt Point to Subversion Crackdown," *Newsweek* 20, no. 5, August 3, 1942, 26; Ribuffo, "United States v. McWilliams," 183; and Department of Justice, For Immediate Release, July 23, 1942, 3–6, American Civil Liberties Cases, 1943, Sedition, Correspondence 6, vol. 2501, American Civil Liberties Union Papers, Mudd Library, Princeton University, Princeton, NJ.

10. Glen Jeansonne, *Women of the Far Right: The Mothers Movement and World War II* (Chicago: University of Chicago Press, 1996, 20–21, 152–56; "Guilt Is Denied by Mrs. Dilling; Freed on Bond," July 24, 1942, 2; and "Trial Hardships Told in Appeal by Mrs. Dilling," *Chicago Daily Tribune*, August 5, 1942, 10.

11. "Small-Shot Conspiracy," *New Republic* 107, no. 5, August 3, 1942, 135.

12. John Haynes Holmes, "Position of the ACLU" [Letter to the Editor], *Nation* 154, no. 21, May 23, 1942, 611; American Civil Liberties Union, "The Federal Espionage Act Prosecutions" (Summary of Report of Special Committee), adopted by Board, July 6, 1942, vol. 2501, American Civil Liberties Cases, 1943, Sedition, Correspondence 6; Mudd Library, Princeton University, Princeton, NJ; Memorandum by Roger N. Baldwin, Director of the Union to the members of the Corporation, January 19, 1943, American Civil Liberties Cases 1943, Sedition, Correspondence, 12, vol. 2507, American Civil Liberties Union Papers, Mudd Library, Princeton University, Princeton, NJ; "Baldwin to George Dession, December 15, 1942, American Civil Liberties Cases, 1943, Race Discrimination 2–Sedition 1, American Civil Liberties Union, Minutes of the Board of Directors, January 18, 1943, American Civil Liberties Cases, 1943, Outside Organizations, Religious Freedom–Negroes, Correspondence, vol. 2488, American Civil Liberties Union Papers, Mudd Library, Princeton University, Princeton, NJ.

13. Baldwin to the Board of Directors, August 13, 1942, Baldwin to the Board of Directors, August 13, 1942, American Civil Liberties Cases, 1943, Sedition, Correspondence 6, vol. 2501, American Civil Liberties Union Papers, Mudd Library, Princeton University, Princeton, NJ; Carey McWilliams to Baldwin, August 3, 1942, American Civil Liberties Cases, 1943, Sedition, Correspondence 2, vol. 2497, American Civil Liberties Union Papers, Mudd Library, Princeton University, Princeton, NJ; Draft of letter [to the attorney general] to be considered at the meeting of the Board on January 4, 1943, American Civil Liberties Cases 1943, Sedition, Correspondence, 12, vol. 2507, American Civil Liberties Union Papers, Mudd Library, Princeton University, Princeton, NJ; and Statement to Accompany Appeal Taken by Osmond K. Fraenkel and Others, January 28, 1943, American Civil Liberties Cases, 1943, Sedition 13–War Correspondence, vol. 2508, American Civil Liberties Union Papers, Mudd Library, Princeton University, Princeton, NJ; and American Civil Liberties, Minutes of the Board of Directors, January 4, 1943, American Civil Liberties Cases, 1943, Outside Organizations, Religious Freedom–Negroes 1, Correspondence, vol. 2488, American Civil Liberties Union Papers, Mudd Library, Princeton University, Princeton, NJ.

14. "Attorney John F. Finerty Dies; Figured in Civil Rights Cases," *Washington Post*, June 7, 1967, B5; "Dorothy Dunbar Bromley, 89, A Writer on Women's Issues," *New York Times*, January 6, 1986, B7; "Civil Rights Lawyer Osmond Fraenkel," *Chicago Daily Tribune*, May 18, 1983, A4; "Rev. Allan Chalmers, 74, Dies; Led the Broadway Tabernacle," *New York Times*, January 24, 1972, 34; Charles Marsh, *God's Long Summer: Stories of Faith and Civil Rights* (Princeton, NJ: Princeton University Press, 1997), 121–22; Arthur Garfield Hays, *Baltimore Sun*, December 15, 1954, 18; "Dr. John Holmes Dies; Helped Found NAACP," *New Journal and Guide* (Norfolk, VA), April 18, 1964, 3; Robert McG. Thomas Jr., "Alfred Bingham, 93, Dies, Once Radical Intellectual," *New York Times*, November 5, 1998, D4; "Raymond L. Wise, 91, Dies: Former Director of ACLU," *New York Times*, July 8, 1986, B5; Fraenkel to American Civil Liberties Union, January 12, 1943, American Civil

Liberties Cases 1943, Sedition, Correspondence, 12, vol. 2507, American Civil Liberties Union Papers, Mudd Library, Princeton University, Princeton, NJ; and Statement to Accompany Appeal Taken by Osmond K. Fraenkel and Others, January 29, 1942, American Civil Liberties Cases, 1943, Sedition 13-War, Correspondence, vol. 2508, American Civil Liberties Union Papers, Mudd Library, Princeton University, Princeton, NJ.

15. (Signed) Whitney North Seymour, for the Board of Directors, American Civil Liberties Union, Statement on Behalf of the Majority of the Board in Opposition to the Appeal Taken by Osmond K. Fraenkel and Others, 1–3, January 28, 1943, American Civil Liberties Cases, 1945, Sedition 2, Correspondence, vol. 2686, American Civil Liberties Union Papers, Mudd Library, Princeton University, Princeton, NJ; and American Civil Liberties Union, Minutes of the Board of Directors, March 1, 1943, American Civil Liberties Cases, 1945, American Civil Liberties Union, Correspondence–General: Sedition-Organizational Matters-Sedition Committee, vol. 2605, American Civil Liberties Union Papers, Mudd Library, Princeton University, Princeton, NJ.

16. Sarah H. Ludington, "The Dogs That Did Not Bark: The Silence of the Legal Academy During World War II," *Journal of Legal Education* 60, no. 3 (February 2011): 428; Nancy Peterson Hill, *A Very Private Public Citizen: The Life of Grenville Clark* (Columbia, MO: University of Missouri Press, 2044), 148, 242; Laura Weinrib, *The Taming of Free Speech: America's Civil Liberties Compromise* (Cambridge, MA: Harvard University Press, 2016), 317–8; Richard Lee Strout, "The War and Civil Liberties," *New Republic* 106, no. 11, March 16, 1942, 357; and (Signed) Whitney North Seymour, for the Board of Directors, American Civil Liberties Union, Statement on Behalf of the Majority of the Board in Opposition to the Appeal Taken by Osmond K. Fraenkel and Others, 1–3, January 28, 1943, American Civil Liberties Cases, 1945, Sedition 2, Correspondence, vol. 2686, American Civil Liberties Union Papers, Mudd Library, Princeton University, Princeton, NJ.

17. Dr. Alexander Meikeljohn and Roger N. Baldwin representing the Union, Confidential Memorandum of Conversations with Officials at Washington on August 20, 1942, American Civil Liberties Cases, 1943, Sedition, Correspondence 6, vol. 2501, American Civil Liberties Union Papers, Mudd Library, Princeton University, Princeton, NJ; and Confidential Memorandum, Seditious Conspiracy Cases, by Roger N. Baldwin, August 21, 1942, American Civil Liberties Cases, 1943, Outside Organizations, Religious Freedom Negroes 1, Correspondence, vol. 2488, American Civil Liberties Union Papers, Mudd Library, Princeton University, Princeton, NJ.

18. Ribuffo, "United States vs. McWilliams," 183–84; and Weinrib, *Taming of Free Speech,* 265, 313.

19. Ribuffo, "United States vs. McWilliams," 198–99; Ernst to Roosevelt, October 3, 1942, October 15, 1942, Roosevelt to Ernst, October 6, 1942, President's Secretary File 132 / Folder: Ernst, Morris L., 1940–1942, Box 132, Franklin D. Roosevelt Presidential Library; "Roosevelt Sends Reporter Iron Cross," *New York Times*, December 19, 1942, 23; and Frank Hughes, "N.Y. Post Churns Muck in Bottom of Smear Sewer," *Chicago Daily Tribune*, March 1, 1944, 7.

20. Paul F. Healy, *Cissy: A Biography of Eleanor M. "Cissy" Patterson* (New York: Doubleday and Company, 1966), 292–93.

21. Francis MacDonnell, *Insidious Foes: The Axis Fifth Column and the American Home Front* (New York: Oxford University Press, 1995), 95–96; and "League Head Attacks 'America First,'" *Anti-Nazi Bulletin* 7, no. 3 (September 1941): 1.

22. Richard Rollins, "Richard Rollins Writes 'I Find Treason,'" *Anti-Nazi Bulletin* 6 (May 1940): 14; and U.S. Congress, House Select Committee to Investigate the Federal Communications Commission, *Hearings*, 78th Cong., 1st Sess. (Washington, DC: United States Government Printing Office, 1943), 748.

23. Rex Stout, *The Illustrious Dunderheads* (New York: Alfred A. Knopf, 1942); MacDonnell, *Insidious Foes*, 96; and Amanda Smith, *Newspaper Titan*, 460.

24. L. M. Birkhead and Roy G. Tozier to Baldwin, January 21, 1941, American Civil Liberties Cases, 1941, Outside Organizations, Correspondence, 1, vol. 2294, American Civil Liberties Union Papers, Mudd Library, Princeton University, Princeton, NJ; and Baldwin to James H. Sheldon, December 24, 1943, American Civil Liberties Cases, 1943, Outside Organizations, 3, Religious Freedom–Negroes, Correspondence, vol. 2488, American Civil Liberties Union Papers, Mudd Library, Princeton University, Princeton, NJ.

25. "Griffin Offers Letter as Link with Roosevelt," *Washington Post*, November 6, 1942, B10.

26. Chesly Manly, "Taft Doubts Plot Between Many of the 28 Indicted," Washington *Times-Herald* (Washington, DC), November 21, 1942; Purge and Washington Indictments, 1942, Box 769, Robert A. Taft Papers, Library of Congress, Washington, DC; Wheeler to Biddle, December 16, 1942, Folder: Civil Liberties and Criminal Indictments from the District of Columbia, Jan. 1, 1942–Dec. 31, 1944, Zechariah Chafee Jr. Papers, Harvard Law School, Library, Historical and Special Collections, Harvard University, Cambridge, MA.

27. Dillard Stokes, "Wheeler Defends Sedition Suspects, Although a Nazi Used Him as a Front," *Washington Post*, December 20, 1942, 1, 10; "The Shape of Things," *Nation* 156, no. 1, January 2, 1943, 3; Chafee to Wheeler, January 12, 1943, Folder: Civil Liberties and Criminal Indictments from the District of Columbia, Zechariah Chafee Jr. Papers, Harvard Law School Library, Historical and Special Collections, Harvard University, Cambridge, MA; and "Harvard Legal Expert Decries U.S. Actions in Sedition Case," *Chicago Daily Tribune*, February 4, 1943, 4.

28. Milton Mayer, "How Liberalism Disappears," *The Progressive* 7, no. 3, January 18, 1943, 5; and Morris H. Rubin [editor], "The Last Column," *The Progressive* 7, no. 11, March 15, 1943, 12.

29. Ribuffo, "United States v. McWilliams," 183–84; James Rowe Jr. to Biddle, February 25, 1943, President's Secretary File, Justice Dept.: Biddle, Francis, 1941–1943 (Continued), Box 56, Franklin D. Roosevelt Presidential Library and Museum, Hyde Park, NY; and Viereck v. United States, 130 F.2d 945 (D.C. Cir. 1942, decided September 21, 1942), accessed August 22, 2022, https://law.justia.com/cases/federal/appellate-courts/F2/130/945/1474108/.

30. Amanda Smith, *Newspaper Titan*, 445–46; "Chatter Checked," *Newsweek* 21, no. 8, February 22, 1943, 92–94; "Controversial Broadcast Not Scandalous, Says Knox," *Washington Post*, February 10, 1943, 7; Friends of Democracy, Memorandum–Correspon-

dents' Group, February 12, 1943, February 26, 1943, American Civil Liberties Cases, 1943, Outside Organizations, Correspondence, 1, vol. 2486, American Civil Liberties Union Papers, Mudd Library, Princeton University, Princeton, NJ.

31. Ribuffo, "United States v. McWilliams," 184; Francis Biddle, *In Brief Authority* (1962; repr., Westport, CT: Greenwood Press, 1976), 239–40; James Rowe Jr. to Biddle, February 25, 1943, President's Secretary File, Justice Dept.: Biddle, Francis, 1941–1943 (Continued), Box 56, Franklin D. Roosevelt Presidential Library and Museum, Hyde Park, NY; and "Appeasement Is Folly," editorial, *Washington Post*, February 8, 1943, 8.

32. Jeansonne, *Women of the Far Right,* 154; Ribuffo, "United States v. McWilliams," 184; and "Rogge Is Named U.S. Prosecutor in Sedition Case," *Chicago Daily Tribune*, February 7, 1943, 12.

33. James Rowe Jr. to Biddle, February 25, 1943, President's Secretary File, Justice Dept.: Biddle, Francis, 1941–1943 (Part 2), Box 56, Franklin D. Roosevelt Presidential Library, Hyde Park, NY; and *Viereck v. United States*, 318 U.S. 236 (1943), accessed August 29, 2022, https://supreme.justia.com/cases/federal/us/318/236/.

34. Steele, *Free Speech in the Good War*, 219.

35. Washburn, *Question of Sedition,* 144–45; "Wheeler Hits War Security Bill in the Senate, *Omaha World-Herald* (Nebraska), February 19, 1943, 13; "War Security Bill Approved," *The Oregonian* (Portland, OR), March 5, 1943, 4; "Constructive Treason," *Chicago Daily Tribune*, April 26, 1943, 12; and "House Passes Spy-Death Bill—with Press Provision," *Chicago Sun*, April 3, 1943, 3.

36. "New Deal Propaganda Perils Free Press: Knox," *Chicago Daily News,* June 23, 1938, 7.

37. Amanda Smith, *Newspaper Titan,* 409; Frank C. Waldrop, *McCormick of Chicago: An Unconventional Portrait of a Controversial Figure* (Englewood Cliffs, NJ: Prentice-Hall, 1966), 260; and Walter Trohan, *Political Animals: Memoirs of a Sentimental Critic* (Garden City, NY: Doubleday and Company, 1975), 171.

38. Ernst to Roosevelt, October 16, 1941, September 2, 1942, September 25, 1942, Folder: Ernst, Morris L., 1940–1942, Box 132, Franklin D. Roosevelt Presidential Library; Biddle to Roosevelt, June 22, 1943, Roosevelt to Biddle, September 27, 1943, Biddle to Roosevelt, September 28, 1943, President's Secretary File, Justice Dept.: Biddle, Francis, 1941–1943 (Part 2), Box 56, Franklin D. Roosevelt Presidential Library; and "Do It by Subpoena," *New Republic* 102, no. 7, February 12, 1940, 197.

39. Maximilian St.-George and Lawrence Dennis, *A Trial on Trial: The Great Sedition Trial of 1944* [place of publication not identified]: National Civil Rights Committee, 1946), 91; Baldwin to Julia R. Stull, June 3, 1944, American Civil Liberties Union, Correspondence–General: Sedition-Organizational Matters-Sedition Committee, vol. 2605, American Civil Liberties Union Papers, Mudd Library, Princeton University, Princeton, NJ; Wheeler to Baldwin, April 14, 1943, Baldwin to Wheeler, April 19, 1943, American Civil Liberties Cases, 1943, Outside Organizations, Religious Freedom–Negroes 1., Correspondence, vol. 2488, American Civil Liberties Union Papers, Mudd Library, Princeton University, Princeton, NJ; and Ribuffo, "United States v. McWilliams," 183.

40. "Carlson's Backer and Endorser 'Purchases Discharge from the Navy,'" *National Republic* 31, no. 6, October 1943, 29; Peter Edson, "The Situation in Washington," *Riverside*

Daily Press (Riverside, CA), October 23, 1943, 12; Sydney J. Harris, "Some Letdown! No Soviet Gold Aids 'Evil' East," *Chicago Daily News*, November 2, 1943, 11; and "Democratic Dynamite," *Anti-Nazi Bulletin* 8, no. 5 (October 1943): 2.

41. John Roy Carlson, *Under Cover: My Four Years in the Nazi Underworld of America —The Amazing Revelation of How Axis Agents and Our Enemies Within Are Now Plotting to Destroy the United States* (New York: E. P. Dutton and Company, 1943), title page, 302–8, 474–76, 485–87; and "The Nation's Morale and World Peace," August 23, 1943, Freedom House, WEVD, Radio Transcript, Folder: Broadcast Radio Reports, Box 116, John T. Flynn Papers, Special Collections and University Archives, University of Oregon Libraries, Eugene, OR.

42. John T. Flynn to Burton K. Wheeler, January 3, 1944, Folder: Carlson-Wheeler, John T. Flynn Papers, Special Collections and University Archives, University of Oregon Libraries, Eugene, OR.

43. Ribuffo, "United States v. McWilliams," 184; and St.-George and Dennis, *Trial on Trial,* 115.

44. St.-George and Dennis, *Trial on Trial,* 121; and Ribuffo, "United States v. McWilliams," 188.

45. "House Leaders Back Griffin for Debt Post," *Washington Post,* May 7, 1939, 2; "Urged Griffin for Mayor," *New York Times,* July 24, 1942, 8; "The Enemy Within Our Gates," *National Republic* 31, no. 10, February 1944, 24; "Publisher Fights Removal Order," *Christian Science Monitor,* November 17, 1942, 8; "Griffin Arrested in Hospital Here," *New York Times,* July 25, 1942, 1; "Griffin Defends Trip to Germany," *New York Times,* November 5, 1942, 27; and Bureau of Propaganda Investigation, Overall Report of Pending Federal Trial Situation, January 23, 1943, 6, Folder 24-26, Box 274; Non-Sectarian Anti-Nazi League to Champion Human Rights, Records, Rare Book and Manuscript Library, Columbia University.

46. Ribuffo, "United States v. McWilliams," 185–87; Dennis to Chafee, December 21, 1943, Civil Liberties and Criminal Indictments from the District of Columbia, Folder: 001776-027-0390, Jan. 1, 1942–Dec. 31, 1944, Zechariah Chafee Jr. Papers, Harvard Law School Library, Historical and Special Collections, Harvard University, Cambridge, MA; Carlson, *Under Cover,* 71; and Ronald Radosh, *Prophets on the Right: Profiles of Conservative Critics of American Globalism* (New York: Simon & Schuster, 1975), 278–88.

47. "Liberal Wheelhorse," *Time* 32, no. 24, December 12, 1938, 61; Ribuffo, "United States v. McWilliams," 186; and St.-George and Dennis, *Trial on Trial,* 338.

48. Of twelve unsigned editorials available on Genealogy Bank, and ProQuest Historical Newspapers, eight were supportive, one opposed (the *Chicago Daily Tribune*), and three expressed no opinion. James A. Wechsler, "Press Axis Screams 'Frame Up' at Sedition Trial," *PM,* April 17, 1944, 7; James A. Wechsler, "Chicago-Washington Press Axis Is Mouthpiece—In Headlines—for 30 Accused Seditionists," *PM,* April 30, 1944, 3; "Bring Them to Book," *New Masses* 51, no. 3, April 18, 1944, 9; "The Treason Trial," *Daily Worker,* April 20, 1944, 6; "An 'Innocent' Question," *Daily Worker,* April 22, 1944, 6; and Percival Roberts Bailey, "Progressive Lawyers: A History of the National Lawyers Guild, 1936–1958" (PhD, Rutgers University, 1979), 299; and "The Issue in the Conspiracy Trial," editorial, *Chicago Sun,* April 20, 1944, 12.

49. St.-George and Dennis, *Trial on Trial,* 104, 339; Drew Pearson, "Washington Merry-Go-Round," *Dallas Morning News,* May 9, 1944, 2; and "Walter Winchell on Broadway," *Richmond Times-Dispatch* (Virginia), April 25, 1944, 20.

50. Baldwin to Kate Crane Gartz, February 8, 1944, Baldwin to Wheeler, March 27, 1944, American Civil Liberties Union, Correspondence–General: Sedition-Organizational Matters-Sedition Committee, vol. 2605, American Civil Liberties Union Papers, Mudd Library, Princeton University, Princeton, NJ; Oswald Garrison Villard, "Smothering Criticism," *The Progressive* 8, no. 6, February 7, 1944, 2; and Milton Mayer, "The Sedition Trial," *The Progressive* 8, no. 20, May 15, 1944, 5.

51. George S. Schuyler, "Views and Reviews," *Pittsburgh Courier* (Pittsburgh, PA), March 18, 1944, 7.

52. Sam O'Neal, "Mrs. Dilling and 23 Deny Sedition Guilt," *Chicago Sun,* April 18, 1944, 4.

53. Sam O'Neal, "Sedition Defense Assails Plot Charge as 'Farcical,'" *Chicago Sun,* May 19, 1944, 1, 8; "Sedition Trial Jury Sworn After 4 Weeks," *Chicago Sun,* May 17, 1944, 4; and "Sedition Case Figure Dies," *Chicago Sun,* May 5, 1944, 1.

54. "Bedlam Touched Off by Charge That Fuehrer Was Picked," *Chicago Sun,* May 18, 1944, 1; St.-George and Dennis, 212; and Sam O'Neal, "U.S. Bares New Evidence in Sedition Trial Test," *Chicago Sun,* June 20, 1944, 4.

55. St.-George and Dennis, *Trial on Trial,* 176, 289.

56. Jeansonne, *Women of the Far Right,* 158; Ribuffo, "United States v. McWilliams," 191; and Kenesaw M. Landis to Chafee, April 23, 1944, Civil Liberties and Criminal Indictments from the District of Columbia, Folder: 001776-027-0390, Jan. 1, 1942–Dec. 31, 1944, Zechariah Chafee Jr. Papers, Harvard Law School Library. Historical and Special Collections, Harvard University, Cambridge, MA.

57. "The Shape of Things," *Nation* 158, no. 25, June 3, 1944, 639; George W. Norris, "A Letter from George W. Norris," *Temple University Law Quarterly* 18 (1944): 474–5; Ribuffo, "United States v. McWilliams," 191–92; and [Abraham] Ajay, "The Scuttles," *Chicago Sun,* August 5, 1944, 6.

58. Jeansonne, *Women of the Far Right,* 161; Ribuffo, "United States v. McWilliams," 186, 194; and St.-George and Dennis, *Trial on Trial,* 23.

59. Jeansonne, *Women of the Far Right,* 163; Ribuffo, "United States v. McWilliams," 191; *Hartzel v. United States,* 322 U.S. 680 (1944); and "Mass Trial," editorial, *Washington Post,* July 1, 1944, B4.

60. Attorney General V, Seditionists, Notebooks, 632, Francis Biddle Papers, Franklin D. Roosevelt Presidential Library and Museum, Hyde Park, NY; Ribuffo, "United States v. McWilliams," 193–94; "Mr. Meyer's Crow Supper," editorial, *Chicago Daily Tribune,* August 5, 1944, 6; "Mass Trial," *Washington Post,* July 16, 1944, and "Inside Washington," *Christian Science Monitor,* August 4, 1944, 8.

61. St.-George and Dennis, *Trial on Trial,* 268; and Ribuffo, "United States v. McWilliams," 194–95.

62. Baldwin to Charles Horsky, October 23, 1944, American Civil Liberties Cases, 1945, Sedition 2, Correspondence, vol. 2686, American Civil Liberties Union Papers; and Baldwin to Villard, November 21, 1944, American Civil Liberties Union, Correspondence–General:

Sedition-Organizational Matters-Sedition Committee, vol. 2605, American Civil Liberties Union Papers, Mudd Library, Princeton University, Princeton, NJ.

63. Attorney General V, Seditionists, Notebooks, 636, Francis Biddle Papers, Franklin D. Roosevelt Presidential Library and Museum, Hyde Park, NY; Sam O'Neal, "Death of Justice Eicher Ends Mass Sedition Trial," *Chicago Sun,* December 1, 1944, 12; and 79 Cong. Rec., S157 (daily ed., January 1, 1945).

64. K. M. Landis II, "Tragedy Puts an End to a Thorny Problem," *Chicago Sun,* December 4, 1944, 10.

65. John P. Lewis, "The Seditionist Case," *PM,* December 8, 1944, 27; Walter Winchell, "A Report to the Nation," *Arkansas Gazette* (Little Rock, AR), July 2, 1945, 4; Baldwin, Memorandum on Sedition Trial, December 28, 1944, Biddle to Phillip Murray of the CIO, June 15, 1945, reprinted in Department of Justice, Immediate Release, June 15, 1945, American Civil Liberties Cases, 1945, Sedition 2, Correspondence, 2686, American Civil Liberties Union Papers, Mudd Library, Princeton University, Princeton, NJ; and "The Shape of Things, *Nation* 159, no. 24, December 9, 1944, 702.

66. James A. Wechsler, "Sedition Prosecutor Warns of Pro-Fascist Revival," *PM,* January 31, 1946, 5; Jeansonne, *Women of the Far Right,* 164; "The Shape of Things," *Nation* 263, no. 4, July 27, 1946, 87; "Why I Was Fired from the Justice Department: An Exclusive Interview With O. John Rogge," *In Fact* 14, no. 18, February 3, 1947, 1; and "Justice Department Fires Rogge: Dismissed for Sedition Case 'Nazi' Speech," *Chicago Daily Tribune,* October 26, 1946, 1.

67. Jeansonne, *Women of the Far Right,* 164; and Ribuffo, "United States v. McWilliams," 197.

68. George S. Schuyler, "Views and Reviews," *Pittsburgh Courier* (Pittsburgh, PA), December 14, 1946, 7; and Walter Winchell, "On Broadway," *Star-Ledger* (Newark, NJ), January 1, 1947, 9.

69. Michael R. Belknap, *The Smith Act, the Communist Party, and American Civil Liberties* (Westport, CT: Greenwood Press, 1977), 45; Ribuffo, "United States v. McWilliams," 199; "Blueprint for American Fascism, Another Exclusive Interview with O. John Rogge," *In Fact* 14, no. 19, February 10, 1947, 3; "The Sedition Case," editorial, *Chicago Daily Tribune,* July 2, 1947, 16; and Phillip Deery, "'A Divided Soul?' The Cold War Odyssey of O. John Rogge," *Cold War History* 6, no. 2 (2006): 3.

70. Ribuffo, "United States v. McWilliams," 198; "Mass Sedition Trial Victims Seek G.O.P. Aid," *Chicago Daily Tribune,* May 8, 1948, A7; and "Dr. Beard Calls Sedition Trial a Sad Travesty," *Chicago Daily Tribune,* June 15, 1948, 3.

Conclusion

1. Samuel B. Pettengill, "Smoke Screen," *Record Argus* (Greenville, PA), October 31, 1940, 3; Committee for Constitutional Government, *Needed Now—Capacity for Leadership, Courage to Lead* (New York: Committee for Constitutional Government, 1944), 19, 43; Richard Polenberg, "The National Committee for Constitutional Government, 1937–1941," *Journal of American History* 56, no. 3 (December 1965): 596–97; and Committee for Constitutional Government, September 5, 1944, Box 357, Folder: Committee for

Constitutional Government and CIO Political Action Committee, Clinton P. Anderson
Papers, Manuscript Division, Library of Congress, Washington, DC.

2. Joanne Dunnebecke, "The Crusade for Individual Liberty: The Committee for
Constitutional Government, 1937–1958" (master's thesis, University of Wyoming, 1987),
103–4; John D. Morris, "Movement to Put Ceiling on Federal Tax Hikes Grows," *Corpus
Christi Times* (Corpus Christi, TX), January 3, 1952, 6; and Isaac William Martin, *Rich
People's Movements: Grassroots Campaigns to Untax the One Percent* (New York: Oxford
University Press, 2013), 94–100.

3. "Report on Rumely Groups, Installment I," *Democracy's Battle* 8, no. 3 and 4
(February 1950): 1; "Opposition Piles Up Against Gannett Tax-Cut Bill, *PM*, March 22,
1945, 11; Dunnebecke, "Crusade for Individual Liberty," 104–5, 160; Martin, *Rich People's
Movements,* 99–100; and Nancy Beck Young, *Wright Patman: Populism, Liberalism and the
American Dream* (Dallas: Southern Methodist University Press, 2000), 134–36.

4. "Inquiry Centers on Coercion in $1 Contributions to P.A.C.," *Christian Science
Monitor,* July 13, 1944, 10; Dunnebecke, "Crusade for Individual Liberty," 107; "Speech
by Gene Cox of Georgia," 2–7, Communism, Buchanan Committee on Lobbying,
1951–1953; Undated, James Westbrook Pegler Papers, Research Room, Manuscript Collections, Herbert Hoover Presidential Library and Museum, West Branch, IA; "The Real
Subversives," *Nation* 159, no. 16, October 14, 1944, 424; and Norman Vincent Peale to all
editors, September 21, 1944, Box 859, Folder: Committee for Constitutional Government,
Clinton P. Anderson Papers, Manuscript Division, Liberty of Congress, Washington, DC.

5. Steve Fraser, *Labor Will Rule: Sidney Hillman and the Rise of American Labor* (New
York: The Free Press, 1991), 515–16, 526–31.

6. U.S. Congress, House of Representatives, Committee to Investigate Campaign
Expenditures, *Investigation of Campaign Expenditures*, September 7, 1944, Part 7, 78th
Cong., 2nd Sess. (Washington, DC: United States Government Printing Office, 1944), 408,
417, 435.

7. U.S. Congress, House of Representatives, Committee to Investigate Campaign
Expenditures, *Investigation of Campaign Expenditures,* September 25, 1944, Part 7, 78th
Cong., 2nd Sess. (Washington, DC: United States Government Printing Office, 1944), 448,
454, 461–62.

8. Lawrence Burd, "Contempt Writ Voted Against Fund Collector," *Chicago Daily
Tribune,* September 27, 1944, 23; "Rumely Indicted for Holding Data," *New York Times,*
October 3, 1944, 13; "Gannett Vows Fight to End for Rumely," *Chicago Daily Tribune,*
September 28, 1944, 7; and "The Real Subversives," *Nation* 159, no. 16, October 14, 1944,
424.

9. "Rumely Denies Contempt Charge," *Christian Science Monitor,* October 20, 1944,
12; and "Foe of Gannett Has New Tactic," *Gazette and Daily* (York, PA), March 15, 1945,
2.

10. Dunnebecke, "Crusade for Individual Liberty," 110.

11. Sumner Gerard to Pegler, December 29, 1950, Folder: Communism—Opponents
of Committee for Constitutional Government, 1941–1950, James Westbrook Pegler
Papers, Herbert Hoover Presidential Library and Museum, West Branch, IA; Sallie M.
Connolly, Copy of Notarized Affidavit, October 17, 1944, Folder: Communism—Opponents of Committee for Constitutional Government, 1941–1950, James Westbrook Pegler

Papers, Herbert Hoover Presidential Library and Museum, West Branch, IA; and Gerard to Rumely, October 18, 1944, Folder: Committee for Constitutional Government, Clinton P. Anderson Papers, Manuscript Division, Library of Congress, Washington, DC.

12. Anderson to Rumely, December 28, 1944, Gerard to Anderson, December 29, 1944; James H. Sheldon to Anderson, January 5, 1945, Anderson to Rumely, January 2, 1945, Box 859, Folder: Committee for Constitutional Government, Clinton P. Anderson Papers, Manuscript Division, Library of Congress, Washington, DC; Anderson to Gerard, December 28, 1944, Folder: Communism—Opponents of Committee for Constitutional Government, 1941–1950, James Westbrook Pegler Papers, Herbert Hoover Presidential Library and Museum, West Branch, IA; and "Probe of Committee for Constitutional Government Asked," *Tipton Daily Tribune* (Tipton, IN), December 30, 1944, 6.

13. Gerard to Anderson, December 29, 1944, Committee for Constitutional Inc. to Anderson, January 1, 1945, Anderson to Rumely, January 2, 1945, Box 859, Folder: Committee for Constitutional Government, Clinton P. Anderson Papers, Manuscript Division, Library of Congress, Washington, DC; and "Committee for Constitutional Government, Inc. Charges 'Misinterpretation' of Case," *Lubbock Morning Avalanche* (Lubbock, TX), January 5, 1945, 2.

14. Joseph N. Pew, Jr. Brands 'Anti-Semitic Postcard' Charge as "Scurrilous Falsehood,'" For Release, November 22, 1944, Anderson to Pew, November 24, 1944, Anderson to Franklyn Waltman, December 4, 1944, Folder: Campaign Investigations Committee, Box 859, Clinton P. Anderson Papers, Manuscript Division, Library of Congress, Washington, DC.

15. "The Swag for Big Business and Bag for the Little Fellow," *Capital Times* (Madison, WI), June 7, 1945, 2; Lowell Mellett, "On the Other Hand," *Evening Star* (Washington, DC), June 26, 1945, A9; and Dunnebecke, "Crusade for Individual Liberty," 121–23, 132.

16. "Treasury Plugs Gannett Fund Tax Loophole," *PM*, March 14, 1945, 10; Anderson to Joseph D. Nunan Jr., Commissioner, Bureau of Internal Revenue, February 12, 1945, and Anderson to Wendell Berge, February 21, 1945, Box 859, Folder: Committee for Constitutional Government, Clinton P. Anderson Papers, Manuscript Division, Library of Congress, Washington, DC; and John Roy Carlson, *Under Cover: My Four Years in the Nazi Underworld of America—The Amazing Revelation of How Axis Agents and Our Enemies Within Are Now Plotting to Destroy the United States* (New York: E.P. Dutton Company, 1943), 473–77.

17. Anderson to Patman, February 20, 1945, Anderson to George Seldes, March 20, 1945, Box 859, Folder: Committee for Constitutional Government, Clinton P. Anderson Papers, Manuscript Division, Library of Congress, Washington, DC.

18. "Jury Disagrees in Rumely Trial," *New York Times*, October 14, 1945, 4; "Rumely Wins Acquittal in Contempt Case," *Washington Post*, April 19, 1946, 16; and Drew Pearson, "Merry-Go-Round," *Bakersfield Californian*, June 12, 1948, 32.

19. Gerard to Pegler, December 29, 1950, Folder: Communism—Opponents of Committee for Constitutional Government, 1941–1950, James Westbrook Pegler Papers, Herbert Hoover Presidential Library and Museum, West Branch, IA; Anderson to Joseph P. Kamp, March 4, 1947, Box 858, Folder: Joseph Kamp, Clinton P. Anderson Papers, Manuscript Division, Library of Congress, Washington, DC; and Brian Douglas Reese, "A Mutual Charge: The Shared Mission of Herbert Hoover and Harry S. Truman to Allevi-

ate Global Hunger in a Postwar World," PhD diss., Portland State University, Portland, Oregon, 2018, 11, 43, 48.

20. Peter Edson, "Pressure Boys Aim Guns at Special Session," *Cumberland Evening News* (Cumberland, MD), November 6, 1947, 4.

21. "Damn the Torpedoes!" *New Republic* 119, no. 20, November 15, 1948, 1, 6; Drew Pearson, "Washington Merry-Go-Round," *Wilkes-Barre Record* (Wilkes-Barre, PA), March 24, 1949, 16; Joseph D. Keenan, "Round 2 for L.L.P.E," *American Federationist* 57, no. 1 (January 1950): 20–21; Walter Winchell, "In New York, Broadway Heartbeat," *Washington Post*, May 31, 1950, B11; and Harry S. Truman, Informal Remarks in New York, October 29, 1948, The American Presidency, accessed April 20, 2020, https://www.presidency.ucsb.edu/documents/informal-remarks-new-york.

22. "Truman Supports Lobbying Inquiry," *New York Times*, December 1, 1948, 20.

23. "House Will Investigate All Lobbies 'On Its Own,'" *New York Times*, October 9, 1949, E7; Karl Schriftgiesser, *The Lobbyists: The Art and Business of Influencing Lawmakers* (Boston: Little, Brown and Company, 1951), 115–17; and "Ask Action to Save Taft Housing Bill," *New York Times*, May 2, 1948, 20.

24. Dunnebecke, "Crusade for Individual Liberty," 121–23; John T. Flynn, *The Road Ahead: America's Creeping Revolution* (New York: Devin-Adair, 1949); "The Rumely Case," editorial, *Editor and Publisher* 84, no. 21 (May 19, 1950): 34; and Schriftgiesser, *Lobbyists,* 194–95, 202–5.

25. Schriftgiesser, *Lobbyists,* 202–05; and "A Report on the Rumely Enterprises, Installment I. 1950," *Democracy's Battle* 8, nos. 3–4 (February 1950), 3.

26. "Another Constitutional Error," editorial, *Hutchinson News* (Hutchinson, KS), June 28, 1951, 4; John O'Donnell, "Three Major Money Proposals Slated," *Knoxville Journal* (Knoxville, TN), December 24, 1952, 4; and Dunnebecke, "Crusade for Individual Liberty," 173.

27. 81 Cong. Rec. H8339 (daily ed., June 8, 1950).

28. 81 Cong. Rec. H9031 (daily ed., June 21, 1950); "Fair Deal Intimidation," editorial, *Plain Dealer* (Cleveland, OH), June 16, 1950, 10; and "Lobby Probers Near Pay Dirt; Papers Suppress Names of 166 Corporations Backing Reaction," *In Fact* 21, no. 13 (June 26, 1950): 2.

29. Schriftgiesser, *Lobbyists,* 148–49; and C.P. Trussell, "Real Estate Lobby Put Under Inquiry," *New York Times*, April 20, 1950, 19.

30. 81 Cong. Rec. A6246 (daily ed., June 8, 1950); and Edward A. Rumely to Flynn, July 7, 1950, Folder: Committee for Constitutional Government, Box 17, John T. Flynn Papers, Special Collections and University Archives, University of Oregon Libraries, Eugene, OR.

31. "Inland Steel Head Defies Buchanan," *New York Times*, June 14, 1950, 23; William C. Mullendore to Frank Buchanan, June 5, 1950, Folder: Committee for Constitutional Government, Box 17, John T. Flynn Papers, Special Collections and University Archives, University of Oregon Libraries, Eugene, OR; Rumely to Frank Gannett, May 26, 1950, Folder: Committee for Constitutional Government, Box 17, John T. Flynn Papers; and US House of Representatives. Select Committee on Lobbying Activities. *Lobbying, Direct and Indirect*, Part 4 of hearings, 81st Cong., 2nd sess., June 6, 20, 21, and 28, 1950 (Washington, DC: United States Government Printing Office, 1950), 26–29.

32. U.S. House of Representatives, Select Committee on Lobbying Activities, *Lobbying, Direct and Indirect*, Part 4 of hearings, 81st Congress., 2nd sess., June 6, 20, 21, and 28, 1950 (Washington, DC: Government Printing Office, 1950), 7–10, 14–17; and Mullendore to Leonard Read, July 5, 1950, Foundation for Economic Education Papers, Foundation for Economic Education, Atlanta, GA.

33. Read to Mullendore, July 5, 1950, Foundation for Economic Education Papers, Atlanta, GA; and US House of Representatives, Select Committee on Lobbying Activities, *Lobbying, Direct and Indirect*, Part 8 of hearings, 81st Cong., 2nd sess., July 18, 1950 (Washington, DC: United States Government Printing Office, 1950), 110.

34. "Fair Deal Intimidation," editorial, *Plain Dealer* (Cleveland, OH), June 16, 1950, 10; "Pernicious Probe," editorial, *Nashville Banner* (Nashville, TN), June 15, 1950, 14; "Mr. Buchanan Can Jump," editorial, *Richmond News Leader* (Richmond, VA), June 15, 1950; "Buchanan off the Track," editorial, *Pittsburgh Post-Gazette* (Pittsburgh, PA), June 14, 1950, clippings, Folder: Committee for Constitutional Government Box 17, John T. Flynn Papers, Special Collections and University Archives, University of Oregon Libraries, Eugene, OR; and "Another Black Committee," editorial, *Chicago Daily Tribune*, June 12, 1950, 12.

35. "Editorial," *Editor and Publisher*, June 16, 1950, clipping, Folder: Committee for Constitutional Government, John T. Flynn Papers, Special Collections and University Archives, University of Oregon Libraries, Eugene, OR; Marquis Childs, "Lobby Investigation: Possible Contempt on the Right," *Washington Post*, June 14, 1950, 11; "Walter Winchell on Broadway," *Brownsville Herald* (Brownsville, TX), June 15, 1950, 8; Gervase N. Love, "Lobbyists Unite to Try Impoverishing Uncle Sam," *CIO News* 13, no. 13 (March 27, 1950): 6, 9; and "Raise the Spotlight a Little Higher," *CIO News* 13, no. 29 (July 17, 1950), 5.

36. Schriftgiesser, *Lobbyists,* 133.

37. 81 Cong. Rec. H8680 (daily ed., June 15, 1950).

38. "House Group Sets Up Frameup for CRC Head," *Daily Worker*, August 4, 1950, 9; "Biddle Defends Lobby Group in House Probe," *Chicago Daily Tribune*, July 12, 1950, 16; and "Lobby Investigation," *Congressional Quarterly Almanac*, 81st Cong., 2nd Sess., 1950, vol. 6 (Washington, DC: Congressional Quarterly, 1951), 762–64.

39. U.S. House, Select Committee on Lobbying Activities, *Lobbying, Direct and Indirect,* Part 9 of hearings, 81st Cong., 2nd sess., August 3 and 4 (Washington, DC: United States Government Printing Office, 1950), 31, 44, 51.

40. "Congress Set to Investigate Civil Rights Organization," *New Journal and Guide* (Norfolk, VA), September 9, 1950, B4; 81 Cong. Rec. H12388–89 (daily ed., August 11, 1950); Michelle Brattain, *The Politics of Whiteness: Race, Workers, and Culture in the Modern South* (Princeton, NJ: Princeton University Press, 2001), 154–55; and Henderson Lanham to R. E. Busey, August 7, 1950, Box 31, Folder 1, Henderson Lanham Papers, Richard B. Russell Library for Political Research and Studies, University of Georgia Libraries, Athens, GA.

41. Aubrey Grossman to Members of Congress, August 28, 1950, A, Lobbying Activities (1949–1950), George H. Wilson Collection, Box 11, Folder 11, Carl Albert Center, Congressional Archives; David D. Lloyd, Memorandum for the Files, Subject: Continu-

ation of the Buchanan Committee, August 2, 1950, Files of David D. Lloyd, Harry S. Truman Papers.

42. Dunnebecke, "Crusade for Individual Liberty," 174; John T. Flynn: Radio broadcast, March 23, 1953, Folder 159-224, Box 15, John T. Flynn Papers, Special Collections and University Archives, University of Oregon Libraries, Eugene, OR; 81 Cong. Rec. H8692 (daily ed., June 15, 1950); and John McDowell to Westbrook Pegler, December 19, 1951, Folder: Communism—Opponents of Committee for Constitutional Government, 1949–1950, John Westbrook Pegler Papers, Herbert Hoover Presidential Library and Museum, West Branch, IA.

43. "Lobby Group Cites Three in Contempt," *New York Times*, August 27, 1950, 47; 81 Cong. Rec. H13892 (daily ed., August 30, 1950); 81 Cong. Rec. H13787 (daily ed., August 29, 1950); and Frank Buchanan, "What Is There to Hide?" *American Federationist* 57, no. 9 (September 1950): 17.

44. 81 Cong. Rec. H13900–13901 (daily ed., August 30, 1950); 78 Cong. Rec. H728–29 (daily ed., February 8, 1943); 81 Cong. Rec. H13900–13893 (daily ed., August 30, 1950); and "Vote to Cite Rumely, Patterson, Kamp for Contempt of House Lobbying Committee," n.d., Files of David D. Lloyd, Harry S. Truman Papers, Harry S. Truman Presidential Library, Independence, MO.

45. Rob F. Hall, "House Cites Wm. Patterson, CRC Head, for Contempt," *Daily Worker*, August 31, 1950, 2.

46. Lanham to Henry DeLand Strack, August 16, 1950, Series II, Box 31, Folder 7, Henderson Lanham Papers, Richard B. Russell Library for Political Research and Studies, University of Georgia Libraries, Athens, GA; and 81 Cong. Rec. H13902–3 (daily ed., August 30, 1950).

47. "Buchanan Committee Dangers," editorial, *Wall Street Journal*, September 1, 1950, 4; and Willard Shelton, "Billion-Dollar Lobbying," *Nation* 171, no. 14 (September 30, 1950), 281–82.

48. Westbrook Pegler, "As It Looks to Pegler," *Galveston Daily News* (Galveston, TX), October 20, 1950, 4, November 10, 1950, 4; "Probe One Sided," *Post-Standard* (Syracuse, NY), July 7, 1950, 13; and Westbrook Pegler, "British Tried and Convicted Distributor of Truthful Book: 'The Road Ahead,'" *Dixon Evening Telegraph* (Dixon, IL), November 13, 1951, 4.

49. L. M. Birkhead to J. Howard McGrath, August 11, 1950, Folder: Communism, Friends of Democracy, 1941–1966, James Westbrook Pegler Papers, Herbert Hoover Presidential Library, West Branch, IA.

50. "Rumely Sentenced to Suspended Jail Term for Contempt," *Christian Science Monitor*, May 19, 1951, 7; "Rumely Pleads Press Freedom in Defense," *Washington Post*, April 18, 1951, 6; Walter Winchell, "In New York," April 24, 1951, B13; and "Contempt of Congress," editorial, *Washington Post*, April 21, 1951, 8.

51. "Frank Buchanan Congressman, Dies," *New York Times,* April 28, 1951, 10; 81 Cong. Rec. H4558 (daily ed., April 30, 1951; and Pegler, "Fair Enough," *Detroit Times*, November 13, 1951, 22.

52. Rumely to Member of Congress and Fellow American, April 20, 1953, Committee for Constitutional Government, 1953, Box 5, Folder 51, Frank E. Gannett Papers, Division of Rare and Manuscript Collections, Carl L. Kroch Library, Cornell University, Ithaca,

NY; Lloyd, Memorandum for the Files, August 2, 1950; Files of David D. Lloyd, Harry S. Truman Presidential Library, Independence, MO; and Harry S. Truman, "Address at the Armory in Manchester, New Hampshire, October 16, 1952, The American Presidency Project, accessed August 29, 2022, https://www.presidency.ucsb.edu/documents/address-the-armory-manchester-new-hampshire.

53. Rumely v. United States, 197 F. 2d, 166. [1952]; United States v. Rumely, 345 U.S. 41 [1953]; and Dunnebecke, "Crusade for Individual Liberty," 146–47.

54. United States v. Rumely at 57; and Rumely to Isabel Rumely, March 9, 1953, Folder 21, Box 2, Edward E. Rumely Papers, Special Collections and University Archives Repository, University of Oregon Libraries, Eugene, OR.

55. August Raymond Ogden, *The Dies Committee: A Study of the Special House Committee for the Investigation of Un-American Activities, 1938–1944* (Washington, DC: Catholic University of America Press, 1945), 194–201; Carl Beck, *Contempt of Congress: A Study of the Prosecutions Initiated by the Committee on Un-American Activities, 1945–1957* (New Orleans, LA: Hauser Press, 1959), 214–28; Martha M. Driver, "Constitutional Limitations on the Power of Congress to Punish Contempts of Its Investigating Committees: Part II," *Virginia Law Review* 38, no. 8 (December 1952): 1013–14; and Robert K. Carr, "The Un-American Activities Committee and the Courts," *Louisiana Law Review* 11, no. 3 (March 1951): 311–13.

56. Marquis Childs, "Lobby Investigation," *Washington Post*, June 14, 1950, 11; Corliss Lamont, "Challenge to McCarthy," *Nation* 177, no. 24, December 12, 1953, 511; "Lattimore Renews Indictment Attack," *New York Times*, March 31, 1953, 8; "Probe of Author by Senate Draws Challenge," *Christian Science Monitor*, September 24, 1953, 3; "Committee Jurisdiction," editorial, *Washington Post and Times Herald*, August 23, 1954, 6; and Laurent B. Frantz, "The Bankrupt Inquisition," *Nation* 185, no. 2, July 20, 1957, 26.

57. Frank Chodorov, "Is Lobbying Honest?" *Freeman* 3, no. 21 (July 13, 1954): 732, 741–43; and Chodorov, *The Income Tax: Root of All Evil* (New York: Devin-Adair, 1953), 51.

58. Arthur J. Sabin, *In Calmer Times: The Supreme Court and Red Monday* (Philadelphia: University of Pennsylvania Press, 2011), 153–60; Beck, *Contempt of Congress*, 156–62; and Watkins v. United States, 354 U.S. 179 (1957).

59. NAACP v. ex rel. Alabama (357 U.S. 449 [1958]).

Selected Bibliography

Abt, John J. *Advocate and Activist: Memoirs of an American Communist Lawyer.* Urbana: University of Illinois Press, 1993.

Agur, Colin. "Negotiated Order: The Fourth Amendment, Telephone Surveillance, and Social Interaction, 1878–1968." *Information and Culture* 48, no. 4 (2013).

American Bar Association. "Report of the Standing Committee on Communications to the American Bar Association." *Annual Report of the American Bar Association* 61 (1936).

American Bar Association. "Report of the Standing Committee on Radio Law." *Annual Report of the American Bar Association* 52 (1929): 404–506.

American Civil Liberties Union (ACLU). Papers. Mudd Library, Princeton University, Princeton, NJ.

American Economic Association. *Report of the Organization of the American Economic Association* 1, no. 1 (March 1886). Baltimore: Publications of the American Economic Association, 1886.

Anderson, Clinton P. Papers. Manuscript Division, James Madison Memorial Library, Library of Congress, Washington, DC.

Anderson, William. *The Wild Man from Sugar Creek: The Political Career of Eugene Talmadge.* Baton Rouge: Louisiana University Press, 1975.

Arbuckle, Mark Roger. "Herbert Hoover's National Radio Conferences and the Origin of Public Interest Content Regulation of United States Broadcasting: 1922–1925." PhD diss., Southern Illinois University at Carbondale, 2001.

Baek, Misook. "Public Interest and Technological Rationality Social Determinants of American Broadcasting, 1920." PhD diss., University of Iowa, 2003.

Bailey, Percival Roberts. "Progressive Lawyers: A History of the National Lawyers Guild, 1936–1958." PhD diss., Rutgers University, 1979.

Baker, Leonard. *Black to Back: The Duel Between FDR and the Supreme Court.* New York: MacMillan, 1967.

Bannai, Lorraine K. *Enduring Conviction: Fred Korematsu and His Quest for Justice.* Seattle: University of Washington Press, 2015.

Barbas, Samantha. *The Rise and Fall of Morris Ernst, Free Speech Renegade.* Chicago: University of Chicago Press, 2021.

Barnett, Claude A. Papers. Chicago History Museum, Research Center, Chicago, IL.

Barnouw, Erik. *The Golden Web: A History of Broadcasting in the United States, 1933–1953.* New York: Oxford University Press, 1968.

———. *A Tower in Babel: A History of Broadcasting in the United States,* vol. 1 (to 1933). New York: Oxford University Press, 1966.

Baughman, James L. *Same Time, Same Station: Creating American Television, 1948–1961.* Baltimore: Johns Hopkins University Press, 2007.

Bean, Jonathan, ed. *Race and Liberty in America: The Essential Reader.* Lexington: University Press of Kentucky, 2009.

Beck, Carl. *Contempt of Congress: A Study of the Prosecutions Initiated by the Committee on Un-American Activities, 1945–1957.* New Orleans, LA: The Hauser Press, 1959.

Belknap, Michael R. *The Smith Act, the Communist Party and American Civil Liberties.* Westport, CT: Greenwood Press, 1977.

Benjamin, Louise Margaret. "Radio Regulation in the 1920s: Free Speech Issues on the Department of Radio and the Radio Act of 1927." PhD diss., University of Iowa, 1985.

Benson Ford Research Center. Fair Lane. Papers. Henry Ford Museum of American Innovation, Dearborn, MI.

———. "Ford Sunday Evening Hour (1934–43)." Henry Ford Museum of American Innovation, Dearborn, MI.

Berkin, Carol, Christopher Miller, Robert Cherny, and James Gormly. *Making America: A History of the United States.* Belmont, CA: Wadsworth, 2014.

Berman, Geoffrey D. "A New Deal for Free Speech: Free Speech and the Labor Movement in the 1930s." *Virginia Law Review* 80, no. 1 (February 1994).

Bernstein, David E. *Only One Place of Redress: African Americans, Labor Regulations, and the Courts from Reconstruction to the New Deal.* Durham, NC: Duke University Press, 2001.

Best, Gary Dean. *The Critical Press and the New Deal: The Press Versus Presidential Power, 1933–1938.* Westport, CT: Praeger, 1993.

Biddle, Francis. *In Brief Authority.* 1962. Reprint, Westport, CT: Greenwood Press, 1976.

———. Papers. Franklin D. Roosevelt Presidential Library and Museum, Hyde Park, NY.

Biles, Roger. "Robert Church Jr. of Memphis: Black Republican Leader in the Age of Democratic Ascendancy, 1928–1940." *Tennessee Historical Quarterly* 42, no. 4 (Winter 1983).

Black, Hugo L. Papers. Manuscript Division, James Madison Memorial Library, Library of Congress, Washington, DC.

Brattain, Michelle. *The Politics of Whiteness: Race, Workers, and Culture in the Modern South*. Princeton, NJ: Princeton University Press, 2001.

Brindze, Ruth. *Not to Be Broadcast: The Truth About Radio*. New York: Vanguard Press, 1937.

Brinkley, Alan. *Voices of Protest: Huey Long, Father Coughlin, and the Great Depression*. New York: Vintage Books, 1983.

Brinkley, Alan, Andrew Huebner, and John Giggie. *The Unfinished Nation: A Concise History of the American People*. Boston: McGraw Hill, 2016.

Brown, Robert J. *Manipulating the Ether: The Power of Broadcast Radio in Thirties America*. Jefferson, NC: McFarland and Company, 1998.

Buchanan, Frank. "What Is There to Hide?" *American Federationist* 57, no. 9 (September 1950).

Bunche, Ralph J. *The Political Status of the Negro in the Age of FDR*. Chicago: University of Chicago Press, 1973.

Burk, Robert F. *The Corporate State and the Broker State: The Du Ponts and American National Politics, 1925–1940*. Cambridge, MA: Harvard University Press, 1990.

Burns, James MacGregor. *Roosevelt: The Lion and the Fox*. 1956. Reprint, San Diego, CA: Harcourt Brace Jovanovich, 1984.

Caldwell, Louis G. "Censorship of Radio Programs." *Journal of Radio Law* 1, no. 3 (October 1931).

———. "Freedom of Speech and Radio Broadcasting." *Annals of the American Academy of Political and Social Science* 177 (January 1935).

———. "Principles Governing the Licensing of Broadcasting Stations." *University of Pennsylvania Law Review and American Law Register* 79, no. 2 (December 1930).

Carey, James C. "The Farmers' Independence Council of America, 1935–1938." *Agricultural History Society* 35, no. 2 (April 1961).

Carr, Robert K. "The Un-American Activities Committee and the Courts." *Louisiana Law Review* 11, no. 3 (March 1951).

"Censorship of Radio," *Broadcasting* 1, no. 4 (December 1, 1931).

Chafee, Zechariah, Jr. Papers. Harvard Law School Library, Historical and Special Collections, Harvard University, Cambridge, MA.

Choate, Jean. *Disputed Ground: Farm Groups That Opposed the New Deal Agricultural Program*. Jefferson, NC: McFarland and Company, 2002.

Chodorov, Frank. "Is Lobbying Honest?" *Freeman* 3, no. 21 (July 13, 1954).

Church, Robert R. Church Family Papers. Special Collections, McWherter Library, University of Memphis, Memphis, TN.

Clark, David Gillis. "The Dean of Commentators: A Biography of H. V. Kaltenborn." PhD diss., University of Wisconsin, 1965.

Clark, Grenville. "The Prospects for Civil Liberty." *American Bar Association Journal* 24 (1938).

Clark, Thomas G. Correspondence. Department of Justice, Criminal Division. National Archives, Washington, DC.

Committee for Constitutional Government. *Needed Now—Capacity for Leadership, Courage to Lead.* New York: Committee for Constitutional Government, 1944.

Corcoran, David H. "Sherman Minton: New Deal Senator." PhD diss., University of Kentucky, 1977.

Corcoran, Thomas. Papers. Manuscript Division, James Madison Memorial Library, Library of Congress, Washington, DC.

Cottrell, Robert C. *Roger Nash Baldwin and the American Civil Liberties Union.* New York: Columbia University Press, 2000.

Coyle, Gene A. "John Franklin Carter: Journalist, FDR's Secret Investigator, Soviet Agent?" *International Journal of Intelligence* 24 (2011).

Croly, Herbert. *The Promise of American Life.* 1909. Reprint, Boston: Northeastern University Press, 1989.

Crump, E. H. Papers. Memphis and Shelby County Public Library, Memphis, TN.

Culbert, David. "'Croak' Carter: Radio's 'Voice of Doom.'" *Pennsylvania Magazine of History and Biography* 97, no. 3 (July 1973).

Czaplicki, Michael Stephen. "The Corruption of Hope: Political Scandal, Congressional Investigations, and New Deal Moral Authority, 1932–1952." PhD diss., University of Chicago, 2010.

Daniels, Roger. *Prisoners without Trial: Japanese Americans and World War II.* 1993. Reprint, New York: Hill and Wang, 2004.

Daniels, Roger, ed. *American Concentration Camps,* vol. 2 (January 1, 1942–February 19, 1942) and vol. 3 (February 20, 1942–March 31, 1942). New York: Garland Publishing, 1989.

Davidson, James West, Brian DeLay, Christine Leigh Heyrman, Mark H. Lytle, and Michael B. Stoff. *Experience History: Interpreting America's Past.* New York: McGraw Hill, 2011.

Davis, Kenneth S. *FDR: The Beckoning of Destiny, 1882–1928: A History.* New York: G. P. Putnam's Sons, 1972.

Davis, W. Jefferson. "The Radio Act of 1927," *Virginia Law Review* 12, no. 8 (June 1927).

Dean, Virgil W. "Another Wichita Seditionist? Elmer J. Garner and the Radical Right's Opposition to World War II." *Kansas History* 17, no. 1 (Spring 1994).

DeCosta-Willis, Miriam. *Notable Black Memphians.* Amherst, NY: Cambria Press, 2008.

Deery, Phillip. "'A Divided Soul?' The Cold War Odyssey of O. John Rogge." *Cold War History* 6, no. 2 (2006).

Dierenfield, Bruce J. *Keeper of the Rules: Congressman Howard J. Smith of Virginia.* Charlottesville: University Press of Virginia, 1987.

Divine, Robert A., H. W. Brands, T. H. Breen, Hal Williams, and Ariela J. Gross. *America: Past and Present,* combined edition. London: Pearson, 2013.

Doerksen, Clifford J. *American Babel: Rogue Radio Broadcasters of the Jazz Age.* Philadelphia: University of Pennsylvania Press, 2005.

Dorsett, Lyle W. *Franklin D. Roosevelt and the City Bosses.* Port Washington, NY: Kennikat Press, 1977.

Drinnon, Richard. *Keeper of the Concentration Camps: Dillon S. Myer and American Racism.* Berkeley: University of California Press, 1987.

Driver, Martha M. "Constitutional Limitations on the Power of Congress to Punish Contempts of Its Investigating Committees: Part II." *Virginia Law Review* 38, no. 8 (December 1952).

Dubie, Sven Hutchins. "Forging the Sword: The Formative Years of the Civil Rights Division, 1939–1961." PhD diss., University of Delaware, 2004.

Dunnebecke, Joanne. "The Crusade for Individual Liberty: The Committee for Constitutional Government, 1937–1958." Master's thesis, University of Wyoming, 1987.

Dunwoody, Charles G. Interview with Charles G. Dunwoody. By Amelia P. Fry, November 26, 1966. Oral History Center, Bancroft Library, University of California, Berkeley, CA.

Duram, James C. "Norman Thomas as Presidential Conscience." *Presidential Studies Quarterly* 20, no. 3 (Summer 1990).

Early, Stephen. Papers. Franklin D. Roosevelt Presidential Library and Museum, Hyde Park, NY.

Easton, Eric B. "The Colonel's Finest Campaign: Robert R. McCormick and Near v. Minnesota." *Federal Communications Law Journal* 60, no. 2 (March 2008).

Euken, Jamie C. "Evil, Greed, Treachery, Deception, and Fraud: The World of Lobbying According to Senator Hugo Black." *Federal History,* no. 6 (January 2014).

Everett-Phillips, Max. "The Pre-War Fear of Japanese Espionage: Its Impact and Legacy." *Journal of Contemporary History* 42 (2007).

Farabaugh, Patrick. "Carl McIntire and His Crusade against the Fairness Doctrine." PhD diss., Pennsylvania State University, 2010.

Faragher, John Mack, Mari Jo Buhle, Daniel H. Czitrom, and Susah H. Armitage. *Out of Many: A History of the American People,* combined volume. Boston: Pearson, 2020.

Farley, James A. Papers. Manuscript Division, James Madison Memorial Library, Library of Congress, Washington, DC.

Fine, Sidney. *Laissez-Faire and the General Welfare State*. Ann Arbor: University of Michigan Press, 1956.

Fischer, Nick. *Spider Web: The Birth of American Anti-Communism*. Urbana: University of Illinois Press, 2016.

Flynn, John T. Papers. Special Collections and University Archives, University of Oregon Libraries, Eugene, OR.

_____. *The Road Ahead: America's Creeping Revolution*. New York: Devin-Adair, 1949.

Folsom, Burton W., Jr. *New Deal or Raw Deal? How FDR's Economic Legacy Has Damaged America*. New York: Simon & Schuster, 2008.

Folsom, Burton W., Jr., and Anita Folsom. *FDR Goes to War: How Expanded Executive Power, Spiraling National Debt, and Restricted Civil Liberties Shaped Wartime America*. New York: Simon & Schuster, 2011.

Foner, Eric. *Give Me Liberty: An American History*, vol. 2. New York: W. W. Norton, 2014.

Fones-Wolfe, Elizabeth. "Creating a Favorable Business Climate: Corporations and Radio Broadcasting, 1934 to 1954." *Business History Review* 73 (Summer 1999).

Foundation for Economic Education (FEE). Papers. Foundation for Economic Education, Atlanta, GA.

Fraser, Steve. *Labor Will Rule: Sidney Hillman and the Rise of American Labor*. New York: The Free Press, 1991.

Freidel, Frank. *Franklin D. Roosevelt: The Apprenticeship*. Boston: Little Brown and Company, 1952.

Freyer, Tony A. *Hugo L. Black and the Dilemma of American Liberalism*. New York: Pearson Longman, 2008.

Gallagher, Charles R. *Nazis of Copley Square: The Forgotten Story of the Christian Front*. Cambridge, MA: Harvard University Press, 2021.

Gamble, Richard M. *The War for Righteousness: Progressive Christianity, the Great War, and the Rise of the Messianic Nation*. Wilmington, DE: ISI Books, 2003.

Gannett, Frank E. Papers. Division of Rare and Manuscript Collections, Carl L. Krotch Library, Cornell University, Ithaca, NY.

Gellman, Irwin W. *Secret Affairs: FDR, Cordell Hull, and Sumner Welles*. New York: Enigma Books, 1995.

Gens, Stephen Mark. "Paranoia Bordering on Resignation: Norman Thomas and the American Socialist Party." PhD diss., University of Oklahoma, 1982.

Gentry, Curt. *J. Edgar Hoover: The Man and His Secrets*. New York: W. W. Norton, 1991.

Gies, Joseph. *The Colonel of Chicago*. New York: E. P. Dutton, 1979.

Girdner, Audrie, and Anne Loftis. *The Great Betrayal: The Evacuation of the Japanese-Americans during World War II*. London: MacMillan, 1969.

Goluboff, Risa L. *The Lost Promise of Civil Rights.* Cambridge, MA: Harvard University Press, 2007.

Goodman, David. *Radio's Civic Ambition: American Broadcasting and Democracy in the 1930s.* New York: Oxford University Press, 2011.

Gordon, Lynn D. "Why Dorothy Thompson Lost Her Job: Political Columnists and the Press Wars of the 1930s and 1940s." *History of Education Quarterly* 34, no. 3 (Fall 1994).

Green, Theodore F. Papers. Manuscript Division, James Madison Memorial Building, Library of Congress, Washington, DC.

Greenberg, Cheryl. "Black and Jewish Responses to Japanese Internment." *Journal of American Ethnic History* 14, no. 2 (Winter 1995).

Gregory, Anthony. *American Surveillance: Intelligence, Privacy, and the Fourth Amendment.* Madison: University of Wisconsin Press, 2016.

Gregory, William A., and Rennard Strickland. "Hugo Black's Congressional Investigation of Lobbying and the Public Utility Holding Company Act: A Historical View of the Power Trust, New Deal Politics, and Regulatory Propaganda." *Oklahoma Law Review* 29, no. 3 (1976): 569.

Gritter, Elizabeth. "Black Politics in the Age of Jim Crow, Memphis, Tennessee, 1865–1954." PhD diss., University of North Carolina at Chapel Hill, 2010.

———. *River of Hope: Black Politics and the Memphis Freedom Movement, 1865–1954.* Lexington: University Press of Kentucky, 2014.

Grossman, Aubrey. George H. Wilson Collection, Carl Albert Center. Congressional Archives, Washington, DC.

Gugin, Linda C., and James E. St. Clair. *Sherman Minton: New Deal Senator, Cold War Justice.* Indianapolis: Indiana Historical Society, 1987.

Gunter, Matthew C. *The Capra Touch: A Study of the Director's Hollywood Classics and War Documentaries, 1934–45.* Jefferson, NC: McFarland, 2012.

Halsey, Edwin A. *Factual Campaign Information.* Washington, DC: United States Government Printing Office, 1939.

Hatley, Aaron Robertson. "Tin Lizzie Dreams: Henry Ford and Antimodern American Culture, 1919–1942." PhD diss., Harvard University, 2015.

Hayashi, Brian Masaru. "Kilsoo Haan, American Intelligence, and the Anticipated Japanese Invasion of California, 1931–1943." *Pacific Historical Review* 83, no. 2 (May 2014).

Hays, Arthur Garfield. "Civic Discussion over the Air." *Annals of the American Academy of Social and Political Science* 213 (January 1, 1941).

Hazlett, Thomas W. "Oak Leaves and the Origins of the 1927 Radio Act: Comment." *Public Choice* 95, nos. 3–4 (June 1998).

————. *The Political Spectrum: The Tumultuous Liberation of Wireless Technology—from Herbert Hoover to the Smartphone*. New Haven, CT: Yale University Press, 2017.

Healy, Paul F. *Cissy: A Biography of Eleanor M. "Cissy" Patterson*. New York: Doubleday and Company, 1966.

Henretta, James A., Rebecca Edwards, Eric Hinderaker, Robert O. Self, and James A. Henretta. *America's History, Since 1865*, vol. 2. Boston: Bedford/St. Martin's, 2018.

Hill, Nancy Peterson. *A Very Private Public Citizen: The Life of Grenville Clark*. Columbia: University of Missouri Press, 2014.

Hilton, O. A. "Freedom of the Press in Wartime: 1917–1919." *Southwestern Social Science Quarterly* 28 (1948).

Hochfelder, David. "Constructing an Industrial Divide: Western Union, AT&T, and the Federal Government, 1876–1971. *Business History Review* 76, no. 4 (Winter 2000): 705–32.

Holli, Melvin G. *The Wizard of Washington: Emil Hurja, Franklin Roosevelt, and the Birth of Public Opinion Polling*. New York: Palgrave, 2002.

Hoover, Herbert C. *The Memoirs of Herbert Hoover: The Cabinet and the Presidency, 1920–1933*. New York: Macmillan, 1952.

Hoover, J. Edgar. Correspondence. Franklin D. Roosevelt Presidential Library, Hyde Park, NY.

Hull, Elizabeth Anne. "Sherman Minton and the Cold War Court." PhD diss., New School for Social Research, 1976.

Ickes, Harold. *The Secret Diary of Harold Ickes: The First Thousand Days, 1933–1936*. New York: Simon & Schuster, 1953.

"Injunctions—Protection of Broadcasting Status from Interference." *Georgetown Law Journal* 15, no. 469 (1927): 476.

"Interim Report on Radio Legislation." *American Bar Association Journal* 12, no. 12 (December 1926).

Irons, Peter. *Justice at War: The Story of the Japanese American Internment Cases*. New York: Oxford University Press, 1983.

Jeansonne, Glen. *Women of the Far Right: The Mothers Movement and World War II*. Chicago: University of Chicago Press, 1996.

Jeffries, John W. *A Third Term for FDR: The Election of 1940*. Lawrence: University Press of Kansas, 2017.

Johnson, Marc C. *Political Hell-Raiser: The Life and Times of Senator Burton K. Wheeler of Montana*. Norman: University of Oklahoma Press, 2019.

Johnson, Nelson. *Battleground New Jersey: Vanderbilt, Hague, and Their Fight for Justice*. New Brunswick, NJ: Rutgers University Press, 2014.

Jome, Hiram L. "Property in the Air as Affected by the Airplane and the Radio." *Journal of Land and Public Utility Economics* 4, no. 3 (August 1928).

Jordan, Jason. "'We'll Have No Race Trouble Here': Racial Politics and Memphis's Reign of Terror." In *An Unseen Light: Black Struggles for Freedom in Memphis, Tennessee*, edited by Aram Goudsouzian and Charles W. McKinney Jr., 130–49. Lexington: University Press of Kentucky, 2018.

Kassner, Minna F. "Radio Censorship." *Air Law Review* 8, no. 97 (April 1937).

Katznelson, Ira. *Fear Itself: The New Deal and the Origins of Our Time.* New York: W. W. Norton, 2013.

Keiler, Allan. *Marian Anderson: A Singer's Journey.* Urbana: University of Illinois Press, 2002.

Kenneally, James J. "Black Republicans during the New Deal: The Role of Joseph W. Martin, Jr." *Review of Politics* 55, no. 1 (Winter 1993).

Kennedy, David M. *Over Here: The First World War and American Society.* New York: Oxford University Press, 1980.

Kennedy, David M., and Lizabeth Cohen. *American Pageant: A History of the American People.* Boston: Wadsworth, 2013.

Kerr, Albert Samuel. "The Roosevelt Haters: A Study in Economic Motivation." PhD diss., University of Southern California, 1956.

Kersh, Ken I. *Conservatives and the Constitution: Imagining Constitutional Restoration in the Heyday of American Liberalism.* New York: Cambridge University Press, 2019.

Kessler, Jeremy K. "The Early Years of First Amendment Lochnerism." *Columbia Law Review* 118, no. 8 (December 2016).

Kirkpatrick, Bill. "Localism in American Media, 1920–1934." PhD diss., University of Wisconsin, 2006.

Lambeth, Edmund B. "The Lost Career of Paul Y. Anderson." *Journalism Quarterly* 60, no. 3. September 1, 1983: 401–06.

Lane, Frederick S. *American Privacy: The 400-Year History of Our Most Contested Right.* Boston: Beacon Hill, 2009.

Lanham, Henderson. Papers. Richard B. Russell Library for Political Research and Studies. University of Georgia Libraries, Athens, GA.

"League Head Attacks 'America First.'" *Anti-Nazi Bulletin* 7, no. 3 (September 1941).

Lee, David D. "Senator Black's Investigation of the Airmail, 1933–1934." *Historian* 53, no. 3 (Spring 1991).

Leonard, Thomas C. *Illiberal Reformers: Race, Eugenics and American Economics in the Progressive Era.* Princeton, NJ: Princeton University Press, 2016.

Leuchtenburg, William E. "A Klansman Joins the Court: The Appointment of Hugo L. Black." *University of Chicago Law Review* 41, no. 1 (Fall 1973).

_____. *The FDR Years: On Roosevelt and His Legacy.* New York: Columbia University Press, 1995.

Lichtman, Alan J. *White Protestant Nation: The Rise of the American Conservative Movement.* New York: Atlantic Monthly Press, 2008.

Littell, Norman M. *My Roosevelt Years.* Seattle: University of Washington Press, 1987.

Longworth, Richard W. *Winston Churchill, Myth and Reality: What He Actually Said and Did.* Jefferson, NC: McFarland and Company, 2017.

Lotchin, Roger W. *Japanese American Relocation in World War II: A Reconsideration.* Cambridge: Cambridge University Press, 2018.

Love, Gervase N. "Lobbyists Unite to Try Impoverishing Uncle Sam." *CIO News* 13, no. 13 (March 27, 1950).

Ludington, Sarah H. "The Dogs That Did Not Bark: The Silence of the Legal Academy during World War II." *Journal of Legal Education* 60, no. 3 (February 2011).

Lunde, Paul David. "The Broadcast Editorial." Master's thesis, Northwestern University, 1958.

Lynch, Shawn Michael. "In Defense of True Americanism: The Civil Liberties Union of Massachusetts and Radical Free Speech, 1915–1945. PhD diss., Boston College, 2006.

MacDonnell, Francis. *Insidious Foes: The Axis Fifth Column and the American Home Front.* New York: Oxford University Press, 1995.

Mackey, David R. "The National Association of Broadcasters—The First Twenty Years." PhD diss., Northwestern University, 1956.

Malkin, Michelle. *In Defense of Internment: The Case for 'Racial Profiling' in World War II and the War on Terror.* Washington, DC: Regnery Publishing, 2004.

Marcus, Sheldon. *Father Coughlin: The Tumultuous Life of the Priest of the Little Flower.* Boston: Little, Brown and Company, 1973.

Markoe, Arnold M. "The Black Committee: A Study of the Senate Investigation of the Public Utility Holding Company Lobby." PhD diss., New York University, 1972.

Marsh, Charles. *God's Long Summer: Stories of Faith and Civil Rights.* Princeton, NJ: Princeton University Press, 1997.

Martin, Isaac William. *Rich People's Movements: Grassroots Campaigns to Untax the One Percent.* New York: Oxford University Press, 2013.

Martin, Ralph G. *Cissy.* New York: Simon & Schuster, 1979.

Mass, Bonnie. "Puerto Rico: A Case Study of Population Control." *Latin American Perspectives* 4, no. 4 (Autumn 1977).

McBride, Joseph. *Frank Capra: The Catastrophe of Success.* New York: Simon & Schuster, 1992.

McChesney, Robert W. *Telecommunications, Mass Media, and Democracy: The Battle for the Control of U.S. Broadcasting, 1928–1935.* New York: Oxford University Press, 1993.

McCormick, Robert R. Papers. Colonel Robert R. McCormick Research Center, First Division Museum at Cantigny Park, Wheaton, IL.

McKean, Dayton David. *The Boss: The Hague Machine in Action.* Boston: Houghton Mifflin, 1940.

McMenamin, Michael. "Griffin and Churchill: Another View." *Finest Hour* 152 (Autumn 2011).

Milkman, Paul. *PM: A New Deal in Journalism, 1940–1948.* Denver, CO: Outskirts Press, 2016.

Minear, Richard H. *Dr. Seuss Goes to War: The World War II Editorial Cartoons of Theodor Seuss Geisel.* New York: W. W. Norton, 1999.

Modras, Ronald. "Father Coughlin and Anti-Semitism: Fifty Years Later." *Journal of Church and State* 31, no. 2 (Spring 1989).

Moley, Raymond. *After Seven Years.* New York: Harper & Brothers, 1939.

Morgan, Ted. *FDR: A Biography.* New York: Simon & Schuster, 1985.

Morgenthau, Henry, Jr. *Diaries of Henry Morgenthau Jr.* Franklin D. Roosevelt Presidential Library and Museum, Hyde Park, NY.

National Association for the Advancement of Colored People (NAACP). Papers. Manuscript Division, James Madison Memorial Library, Library of Congress, Washington, DC.

Neal, Steve. *Dark Horse: A Biography of Wendell Willkie.* Garden City, NY: Doubleday, 1984.

Newman, Kathy M. *Radio Active: Advertising and Consumer Activism, 1935–1947.* Berkeley: University of California Press, 2004.

Newman, Roger K. *Hugo Black: A Biography.* New York: Fordham University Press, 1994.

Nicolaides, Becky M. "Radio Electioneering in the American Presidential Campaigns of 1932 and 1936." *Historical Journal of Film, Radio and Television* 8, no. 2 (1988).

Non-Sectarian Anti-Nazi League. Papers. Rare Book and Manuscript Library, Columbia University, New York, NY.

Ogden, August Raymond. *The Dies Committee: A Study of the Special House Committee for the Investigation of Un-American Activities, 1938–1944.* Washington, DC: Catholic University of America Press, 1945.

O'Reilly, Kenneth. "The Roosevelt Administration and Black America: Federal Surveillance Policy and Civil Rights during the New Deal and World War II Years." *Phylon* 48, no. 1 (First Quarter, 1987).

Overton, Watkins. Papers. Mississippi Valley Collection, Brister Library, Memphis State University, Memphis, TN.

Patterson, James T. *Congressional Conservatism and the New Deal: The Growth of the Conservative Coalition in Congress, 1933–1939.* Lexington: University of Kentucky Press, 1967.

Pedersen, Vernon L. "Jerry O'Connell, Montana's Communist Congressman." *Montana: The Magazine of Western History* 62, no. 1 (Spring 2012).

Pegler, James Westbrook. Papers. Herbert Hoover Presidential Library and Museum, West Branch, IA.

Perino, Michael. *The Hellhound of Wall Street: How Ferdinand Pecora's Investigation of the Great Crash Forever Changed American Finance.* New York: Penguin Press, 2010.

Phipps, Steven. "'Order Out of Chaos': A Reexamination of the Historical Basis for the Scarcity of Channels Concept." *Journal of Broadcasting and Electronic Media* 45, no. 1 (2001).

Pinchot, Amos. Papers. Manuscript Division, James Madison Memorial Library, Library of Congress, Washington, DC.

Platt, Janice Lyn. "Taxation Proposals for the Funding of American Broadcasting, 1922–1926." PhD diss., University of Missouri, 1981.

Polenberg, Richard. "The National Committee to Uphold Constitutional Government, 1937–1941." *The Journal of American History* 52, no. 3 (December 1965).

———. *Reorganizing Roosevelt's Government: The Controversy over Executive Reorganization.* Cambridge, MA: Harvard University Press, 1966.

Powe, Lucas, Jr. *American Broadcasting and the First Amendment.* Berkeley: University of California Press, 1987.

Procter, Ben. *William Randolph Hearst: The Later Years, 1911–1951.* New York: Oxford University Press, 2007.

Rabban, David M. *Free Speech in Its Forgotten Years.* Cambridge, UK: Cambridge University Press, 1997.

"Radio Censorship and the Federal Communications Commission." *Columbia Law Review* 39, no. 3 (March 1939).

Radosh, Ronald. *Prophets on the Right: Profiles of Conservative Critics of American Globalism.* New York: Simon & Schuster, 1975.

Ragland, James. "Merchandisers of the First Amendment: Freedom and Responsibility of the Press in the Age of Roosevelt, 1933–1940." *Georgia Review* 16 (Winter 1962).

"Raise the Spotlight a Little Higher." *CIO News* 13, no. 29 (July 17, 1950).

Reeves, Richard. *Infamy: The Shocking Story of the Japanese Internment in World War II.* New York: Henry Holt, 2015.

Reitzig, Stephanie. "'By the Code of Humanity': Ralph Carr Takes a Stand for Japanese-American Rights in World War II." *History Teacher* 51, no. 1 (November 2017).

"Report on Rumely Groups, Installment III." *Democracy's Battle* 8, nos. 7–8 (April 1950).

Ribuffo, Leo P. "United States v. McWilliams: The Roosevelt Administration and the Far Right." In *American Political Trials,* edited by Michael R. Belknap. Westport, CT: Greenwood Press, 1994.

Ritchie, Donald A. "What Makes a Successful Congressional Investigation?" *OAH Magazine of History* 12, no. 4 (Summer 1998).

Roark, James L., Michael P. Johnson, Francois Furstenberg, Patricia Cline Cohen, Sarah Stage, Susan M. Hartmann, and Sarah E. Igo. *The American Promise: A History of the United States, From 1865,* vol. 2. Boston: Bedford/St. Martin's, 2020.

Robinson, Greg. *By Order of the President: FDR and the Internment of Japanese Americans.* Cambridge, MA: Harvard University Press, 2001.

Rodgers, Daniel T. *Atlantic Crossings: Social Politics in a Progressive Age.* Cambridge, MA: The Belknap Press of Harvard University, 1998.

Rollins, Richard. "Richard Rollins Writes 'I Find Treason.'" *Anti-Nazi Bulletin* 6 (January 1940).

Roosevelt, Eleanor. Papers. Eleanor Roosevelt Collection, Franklin D. Roosevelt Presidential Library and Museum, Hyde Park, NY.

Roosevelt, Franklin D. Papers. Franklin D. Roosevelt Presidential Library and Museum, Hyde Park, NY.

Roosevelt, Theodore. *The Autobiography of Theodore Roosevelt.* Overland Park, KS: DigiReads.com, 2019.

Rothstein, Richard. *The Color of Law: A Forgotten History of How Our Government Segregated America.* New York: W. W. Norton, 2017.

Rowley, Frank S. "Problems in the Law of Radio Communication." *University of Cincinnati Law Review* 1, no. 1 (January 1927).

Rumely, Edward E. Papers. Special Collections and University Archives Repository, University of Oregon Libraries, Eugene, OR.

Schiller, Reuel E. "Free Speech and Expertise: Administrative Censorship and the Birth of the Modern First Amendment." *Virginia Law Review* 86, no. 1 (2000).

Schlesinger, Arthur M., Jr. *The Politics of Upheaval: 1935–1936, The Age of Roosevelt.* Boston: Houghton Mifflin, 1960.

Scholnick, Myron I. *The New Deal and Anti-Semitism in America.* New York: Garland Publishing, 1990.

Schrager, Adam. *The Principled Politician: Governor Ralph Carr and the Fight against Japanese American Internment.* Golden, CO: Fulcrum, 2009.

Schrecker, Ellen. *Many Are the Crimes: McCarthyism in America.* Princeton, NJ: Princeton University Press, 1998.

Schriftgiesser, Karl. *The Lobbyists: The Art and Business of Influencing Lawmakers.* Boston: Little, Brown and Company, 1951.

Schweinhaut, Henry A. "The Civil Liberties Section of the Department of Justice." *Bill of Rights Review* 1, no. 3 (Spring 1941).

Seldes, George. *Lords of the Press.* New York: Julian Messner, 1938.

Shesol, Jeff. *Supreme Power: Franklin Roosevelt v. the Supreme Court.* New York: W. W. Norton, 2010.

Shi, David Emory. *America: A Narrative History*, vol. 2. New York: W. W. Norton, 2019.

Shirer, William L. Papers. George T. Henry College Archives, Stewart Memorial Library, Coe College, Cedar Rapids, IA.

Shlaes, Amity. *The Forgotten Man: A New History of the Great Depression.* New York: HarperCollins, 2007.

Shuler, Robert. *"Fighting Bob" Shuler of Los Angeles.* Indianapolis, IN: Dog Ear Publishing, 2012.

Siegel, Seymour N. "Censorship in Radio." *Air Law Review* 7, no. 1 (January 1936).

"Silas Hardy Strawn, 1866–1946." *American Bar Association Journal* 32, no. 3 (March 1946).

Smith, Amanda. *Newspaper Titan: The Infamous Life and Monumental Times of Cissy Patterson.* New York: Alfred A. Knopf, 2011.

Smith, Jason Scott. "New Deal Public Works at War: The WPA and Japanese American Internment." *Pacific Historical Review* 72, no. 1 (February 2003).

Smith, Page. *Democracy on Trial: The Japanese American Evacuation and Relocation in World War II.* New York: Simon & Schuster, 1995.

Steel, Ronald. *Walter Lippmann and the American Century.* Boston: Little, Brown and Company, 1980.

Steele, Richard W. "Fear of the Mob and Faith in Government in Free Speech Discourse, 1919–1941." *American Journal of Legal History* 38, no. 1 (January 1994).

————. *Free Speech in the Good War.* New York: St. Martin's Press, 1999.

————. *Propaganda in an Open Society: The Roosevelt Administration and the Media, 1933–1941.* Westport, CT: Greenwood Press, 1985.

Stein, Leon Seymour. "A Developmental Analysis of the Problem of Federal Regulation of Editorializing by Broadcast Licenses." PhD diss., New York University, 1965.

St.-George, Maximilian, and Lawrence Dennis. *A Trial on Trial: The Great Sedition Trial of 1944.* National Civil Rights Committee, 1946.

Still, Mark Sumner. "'Fighting Bob' Shuler: Fundamentalist and Reformer." PhD diss., The Claremont Graduate School, 1988.

Stone, Geoffrey R. "Free Speech in World War II: 'When Are You Going to Indict the Seditionists?'" *International Journal of Constitutional Law*, 2, no. 2 (2004).

Streeter, Thomas. *Selling the Air: A Critique of the Policy of Commercial Broadcasting in the United States.* Chicago: University of Chicago Press, 1996.

Swanberg, W. A. *Norman Thomas: The Last Idealist.* New York: Charles Scribner's Sons, 1976.

Sweeney. Michael S. *Secrets of Victory: The Office of Censorship in the American Press and Radio in World War II.* Chapel Hill: University of North Carolina Press, 2001.

Taft, Robert A. Papers. Manuscript Division, James Madison Memorial Library, Library of Congress, Washington, DC.

Tarrant, Catherine M. "To 'Insure Domestic Tranquility': Congress and the Law of Seditious Conspiracy, 1859–1861." *American Journal of Legal History* 15, no. 2 (1971).

Taugher, James Patrick. "The Law of Radio Communication with Particular Reference to a Property Right in a Radio Wave Length." *Marquette Law Review* 12 (1928): 316.

Theoharis, Athan G. *The FBI and American Democracy: A Brief Critical History.* Lawrence: University Press of Kansas, 2004.

———. *Spying on Americans: Political Surveillance from Hoover to the Huston Plan.* Philadelphia: Temple University Press, 1978.

Trohan, Walter. *Political Animals: Memoirs of a Sentimental Critic.* Garden City, NY: Doubleday and Company, 1975.

Truman, Harry S. Papers. Harry S. Truman Presidential Library, Independence, MO.

Tucker, David M. *Lieutenant Lee of Beale Street.* Nashville, TN: Vanderbilt University Press, 1971.

Twight, Charlotte. "What Congressmen Knew and When They Knew It: Further Evidence on the Origins of U.S. Broadcasting Regulation." *Public Choice* 95 (1998).

U.S. Bureau of Internal Revenue. *Treasury Decisions Under Internal-Review Laws,* vol. 34. Washington, DC: United States Government Printing Office, 1939.

U.S. Department of Justice, Criminal Division, Class 144 (Civil Rights Litigation Case Files and Enclosures, 1936–1997), National Archives, Washington, DC.

U.S. Federal Communications Commission. General Records. National Archives, Washington, DC.

U.S. Federal Radio Commission. *Second Annual Report* (1928). Washington, DC: United States Government Printing Office, 1928.

U.S. Federal Radio Commission. *Third Annual Report* (1929). Washington, DC: United States Government Printing Office, 1930.

U.S. House of Representatives. Committee on the Merchant Marine and Fisheries. *Hearings before the Committee on the Merchant Marine and Fisheries on H.R. 7357.* Washington, DC: United States Government Printing Office, 1924.

U.S. House of Representatives. Committee to Investigate Campaign Expenditures (House of Representatives). *Investigation of Campaign Expenditures,* September 7, 1944, Part 7. Washington, DC: United States Government Printing Office, 1944.

U.S. House of Representatives. Select Committee to Investigate the Federal Communications Commission (House of Representatives). *Hearings*, Part 2. Washington, DC: United States Government Printing Office, 1944.

U.S. Senate. Select Committee on Lobbying Activities (House of Representatives). *Lobbying, Direct and Indirect*, Part 4 of hearings, 81st Cong., 2nd sess., June 6, 20, 21, and 28, 1950. Washington, DC: United States Government Printing Office, 1950.

U.S. Senate. Special Committee on Lobbying (U.S. Senate), Records, 74th and 75th Congress, 1935–1938. National Archives, Washington, DC.

U.S. Senate. Special Committee to Investigate Lobby Activities. *Hearings before a Special Committee to Investigate Lobby Activities*. Washington, DC: United States Government Printing Office, 1938.

U.S. Western Defense Command and Fourth Army United States. *Final Report, Japanese Evacuation of the West Coast, 1942*. Washington, DC: United States Government Printing Office, 1943.

"Validity of Subpoena Issued by Senate Committee for All Telegraphic Correspondence over Named Period." *Columbia Law Review* 36, no. 5 (May 1936).

Vickers, Kenneth W. "John Ranking: Democrat and Demagogue." Master's thesis, Mississippi State University, 1993.

Waldrop, Frank C. *McCormick of Chicago: An Unconventional Portrait of a Controversial Figure*. Englewood Cliffs, NJ: Prentice-Hall, 1966.

Washburn, Patrick S. *A Question of Sedition: The Federal Government's Investigation of the Black Press During World War II*. New York: Oxford University Press, 1986.

Webb, Arthur L. Collection. Memphis and Shelby County Public Library, Memphis, TN.

Webber, Michael J. *New Deal Fat Cats: Business, Labor, and Campaign Finance in the 1936 Presidential Election*. New York: Fordham University Press, 2000.

Weinrib, Laura. *The Taming of Free Speech: America's Civil Liberties Compromise*. Cambridge, MA: Harvard University Press, 2016.

Wells, Alan. *Mass Media and Society*. Bethesda, MD: National Press Books, 1972.

Western Union Telegraph Company. Records. Archives Center, National Museum of American History, Washington, DC.

Westin, Alan F. *Privacy and Freedom*. New York: Atheneum, 1967.

White, Graham J. *FDR and the Press*. Chicago: University of Chicago Press, 1979.

White, Wallace, Jr. "Whys and Wherefores of Radio Legislation," *Broadcasting* 1, no. 2 (November 1, 1931).

Winfield, Betty Houchin. *FDR and the News Media*. Urbana: University of Illinois Press, 1993.

Wolfskill, George. *The Revolt of the Conservatives: A History of the American Liberty League, 1934–1940.* Boston: Houghton Mifflin, 1962.

Wollenberg, Charles. *Rebel Lawyer: Wayne Collins and the Defense of Japanese American Rights.* Berkeley, CA: Heyday, 2018.

Young, Darius Jamal. "The Gentleman from Memphis: Robert R. Church Jr. and the Politics of the Early Civil Rights Movement." PhD diss., University of Memphis, 2011.

Young, Nancy Beck. *Wright Patman: Populism, Liberalism and the American Dream.* Dallas: Southern Methodist University Press, 2000.

Zane, Sherry. "'I Did It for the Uplift of Humanity and the Navy': Same-Sex Acts and the Origins of the National Security State, 1919–1921," *New England Quarterly* 91, no. 2 (June 2018).

Zollman, Carl. "Recent Federal Legislation, Radio Act of 1927," *Marquette Law Review* 2, no. 3 (April 1927).

Index

About the Author

DAVID T. BEITO is a Research Fellow at the Independent Institute and Professor Emeritus at the University of Alabama. He received his PhD in history at the University of Wisconsin and is the author of *T.R.M. Howard: Doctor, Entrepreneur, and Civil Rights Pioneer* (with Linda Royster Beito) and *From Mutual Aid to the Welfare State: Fraternal Societies and Social Services, 1890-1967*. He is also co-editor of *The Voluntary City: Choice, Community and Civil Society* and the forthcoming *Rose Lane Says: Thoughts on Liberty and Equality, 1942-1945*.

His honors include awards for best biography from the Independent Book Publishers Association (the largest organization of its kind) and for best film screenplay by the Alabama Writers' Conclave. The College Board and Advanced Placement Program has rated his US history course as one of the top twenty examples of "best practices" for a single year.

In addition, he has served as chair of the Alabama State Advisory Committee of the United States Commission on Civil Rights and as president of the Alabama Scholars Association.

Professor Beito has been published in the *Journal of Southern History*, the *Journal of Policy History*, the *Journal of Interdisciplinary History*, *Journal of Urban History*, *Nevada Historical Society Quarterly*, the *Journal of Firearms and Public Policy*, and *The Independent Review*.

His popular articles have appeared in the *Wall Street Journal*, *The Hill*, the *Los Angeles Times*, the *Atlanta-Journal Constitution*, the *Washington Examiner*, *Perspectives*, the History News Network, *National Review*, *Reason*, and elsewhere.

He lives in Northport, Alabama, with his wife, Linda, and his children, Quale and Keith.

Independent Institute Studies in Political Economy

Independent Institute Studies in Political Economy

MAKING POOR NATIONS RICH |
edited by Benjamin Powell

MARKET FAILURE OR SUCCESS |
edited by Tyler Cowen & Eric Crampton

THE MIDAS PARADOX | *by Scott Sumner*

MONEY AND THE NATION STATE |
edited by Kevin Dowd & Richard H. Timberlake, Jr.

NATURE UNBOUND |
by Randy T Simmons, Ryan M. Yonk, and Kenneth J. Sim

NEITHER LIBERTY NOR SAFETY | *by Robert Higgs*

THE NEW HOLY WARS | *by Robert H. Nelson*

NEW WAY TO CARE | *by John C. Goodman*

NO WAR FOR OIL | *by Ivan Eland*

OPPOSING THE CRUSADER STATE |
edited by Robert Higgs & Carl P. Close

OUT OF WORK |
by Richard K. Vedder & Lowell E. Gallaway

PARTITIONING FOR PEACE | *by Ivan Eland*

PATENT TROLLS | *by William J. Watkins, Jr.*

PLOWSHARES AND PORK BARRELS |
by E. C. Pasour, Jr. & Randal R. Rucker

POPE FRANCIS AND THE CARING SOCIETY |
edited by Robert M. Whaples

A POVERTY OF REASON | *by Wilfred Beckerman*

THE POWER OF HABEAS CORPUS IN AMERICA |
by Anthony Gregory

PRICELESS | *by John C. Goodman*

PROPERTY RIGHTS | *edited by Bruce L. Benson*

THE PURSUIT OF JUSTICE | *edited by Edward J. López*

RACE & LIBERTY IN AMERICA |
edited by Jonathan Bean

REALLY GOOD SCHOOLS | *by James Tooley*

RECARVING RUSHMORE | *by Ivan Eland*

RECLAIMING THE AMERICAN REVOLUTION |
by William J. Watkins, Jr.

REGULATION AND THE REAGAN ERA |
edited by Roger E. Meiners & Bruce Yandle

RESTORING FREE SPEECH AND LIBERTY ON
CAMPUS | *by Donald A. Downs*

RESTORING THE PROMISE | *by Richard K. Vedder*

RESURGENCE OF THE WARFARE STATE |
by Robert Higgs

RE-THINKING GREEN | *edited by Robert Higgs
& Carl P. Close*

THE RIGHT TO BEAR ARMS | *by Stephen P. Halbrook*

RISKY BUSINESS | *edited by Lawrence S. Powell*

SECURING CIVIL RIGHTS | *by Stephen P. Halbrook*

STRANGE BREW | *by Douglas Glen Whitman*

STREET SMART | *edited by Gabriel Roth*

TAKING A STAND | *by Robert Higgs*

TAXING CHOICE | *edited by William F. Shughart II*

THE TERRIBLE 10 | *by Burton A. Abrams*

THAT EVERY MAN BE ARMED |
by Stephen P. Halbrook

TO SERVE AND PROTECT | *by Bruce L. Benson*

T.R.M. HOWARD |
by David T. Beito and Linda Royster Beito

VIETNAM RISING | *by William Ratliff*

THE VOLUNTARY CITY | *edited by David T. Beito,
Peter Gordon & Alexander Tabarrok*

WAR AND THE ROGUE PRESIDENCY |
by Ivan Eland

WINNERS, LOSERS & MICROSOFT |
by Stan J. Liebowitz & Stephen E. Margolis

WRITING OFF IDEAS | *by Randall G. Holcombe*

INDEPENDENT
I N S T I T U T E
100 SWAN WAY, OAKLAND, CA 94621-1428

For further information:
510-632-1366 • orders@independent.org • http://www.independent.org/publications/books/